STATE AND POLITICS
IN THE USSR

DAVID LANE

State and Politics
in the USSR

NEW YORK UNIVERSITY PRESS
WASHINGTON SQUARE, NEW YORK

First published in 1985 in the USA by
New York University Press,
Washington Square, New York, N.Y. 10003

Library of Congress Cataloging in Publication Data

Lane, David Stuart.
    State and politics in the USSR.
    Includes bibliographies.
    Includes index.
    1. Soviet Union—Politics and government—1917—
    2. Communism—Soviet Union.
    I. Title.
    JN6511.L27   1984   947.085   84–16713
    ISBN 0-8147-5013-3
    ISBN 0-8147-5014-1 (pbk.)
    p 10 9 8 7 6 5 4 3 2
    c 10 9 8 7 6 5 4 3 2

Printed in the United States of America

CONTENTS

LIST OF TABLES

LIST OF DIAGRAMS

LIST OF MAPS

PREFACE

It is fourteen years since I published *Politics and Society in the USSR*. Two books have grown out of it. The present one deals principally with Soviet politics – including the recent history of Russia and the fundamental ideas of Marxist-Leninist thought. It is self-contained and is particularly suitable for students reading politics, political sociology, history and Soviet studies. The second book, *Soviet Economy and Society*, greatly expands my earlier work on such topics as class, social stratification, the family, nationalities, religion, education, and economic planning and performance. It is intended for students of sociology, economics, social studies and Soviet society. Both volumes are written in a style which should be accessible to non-specialist readers who wish to be acquainted with modern Soviet society, its history and contemporary structure. It is hoped that the book will enhance a more comparative approach to the study of society: not only to bring home to Soviet 'area specialists' the fact that Soviet society is in many ways like other industrial societies, but also to awaken the interests of sociologists and others to the problems of 'directed' social change and to the structure of a command or state socialist society.

Among the most crucial problems of writing a book about the USSR are those of selection and emphasis. Here the Soviet Union is depicted as a modernizing industrial society, and those past events and policies have been selected which elucidate the present and, hopefully, point to the future. I have concentrated more on structures but have also sketched in details of the leading personalities; as political history is well covered in other books, I have minimized my coverage of it in favour of economic and social history. Considerable attention is paid to political groupings and the process of politics. As the USSR sees itself as a competitor to the political systems and social order of the West, much writing about it is infused with political prejudice. I have tried to describe Soviet society in its own, as it were 'official', terms while also taking into account the major criticisms made by non-Soviet commentators. To write a book on the Soviet Union involves the discussion of Western views on the Soviet Union. The present coverage, it is hoped, will serve to introduce students to some of the major problems of analysis of modern societies. In addition to the Western concepts of totalitarianism, more recent notions of 'socialist pluralism' and 'corporatism' are added.

The book has the following plan. In Part I are summarized the social and economic changes which occurred from the emancipation of the serfs in 1861 to the October Revolution of 1917, and I bring out the attitude of the Bolsheviks to social and political change. There is a full discussion of Marxism and its contemporary critique. In this section are described not only the events of 1917 but also the main reasons for the successful seizure of power by the Bolsheviks. In Chapter 3, the historical development of Soviet Russia is outlined. First, I consider the major policy decisions which were taken between 1917 and the beginning of the Second World War, then go on to evaluate their chief effects (industrialization, centralization of political power and collectivization of agriculture), not only in European Russia but also in Soviet Central Asia. This is followed by a summary of the USSR's changing role in the international arena. Here again both the perspective of the ruling Bolsheviks and the views of some of their critics are noted. Finally, political developments following the Second World War, under the changing leadership of Stalin, Khrushchev, Brezhnev, Andropov and Chernenko, are outlined. This chapter is not intended to be a full-blooded history but is designed to give the reader an understanding of the development of the Soviet Union and to pose some of the dilemmas which her leaders have had to face. The concluding section on political leaders is intended to act as a bridge between historical development and contemporary politics.

In the next part we turn from historical narrative to the political dimensions of contemporary Soviet society. In Chapters 5 and 6 are outlined the Soviet conception of building socialism and the main political institutions – the Communist Party of the Soviet Union, the Soviets (or parliaments) and the executive arm of government are described. By way of contrast, the major Western interpretation of Soviet society, totalitarianism, is noted. In Chapters 7 and 8 the political process in the party, the role of pressure groups and of the citizen in politics are considered. The notion of developed socialism is contrasted with the Western concepts of 'socialist pluralism' and 'corporatism'. In Chapter 9, political counter-cultures are considered and concepts of civil rights and various types of dissent are discussed, and finally in Chapter 10 possible scenarios of political change are outlined. The Soviet Constitution and the Party Rules are appended.

Whenever possible, I have referred to English language editions so that the widest range of readers may use them. The bibliographies at the end of each part are intended to systematize references given in the text and may be used for more detailed study. I am indebted to many people for helping me to complete this book: some are mentioned in footnotes to specific chapters; my thanks also to D. Taylor, J. Brough and D. Davies who did most of the typing.

Birmingham   David Lane

THE UNION OF SOVIET SOCIALIST REPUBLICS

Legend:

1 Lithuania S.S.R.
2 Latvia S.S.R.
3 Estonia S.S.R.
4 Moldavia S.S.R.
5 Mordovina A.S.S.R.
6 Chuvash A.S.S.R.
7 Mari A.S.S.R.
8 Tatar A.S.S.R.
9 Udmurt A.S.S.R.
10 Bashkir A.S.S.R.
11 Abkhaz A.S.S.R.
12 Adzhar A.S.S.R.
13 Kabardin A.S.S.R.
14 North Osetia A.S.S.R.
15 Georgia S.S.R.
16 Dagestan A.S.S.R.
17 Armenia S.S.R.
18 Nakhicheva A.S.S.R.
19 Azerbaidzhan S.S.R.
20 Kalmyt A.S.S.R.

Scale: 0 — 500 Miles

ICELAND
SCOTLAND
ARCTIC OCEAN
WRANGEL I.
NEW SIBERIAN IS.
SEVERNAYA ZEMLYA
NOVAYA ZEMLYA
Kamchatka Peninsula
SAKHALIN
JAPAN
SEA OF JAPAN
CHINA
MONGOLIA
TUVIN A.S.S.R.
BURYAT A.S.S.R.
Y A K U T S K A. S. S. R.
R.   S.   F.   S.   R.
KOMI A.S.S.R.
KARELIA A.S.S.R.
FINLAND
POLAND
BYELORUSSIA S.S.R.
UKRAINE S.S.R.
ROMANIA
TURKEY
PERSIA
AFGHANISTAN
KAZAKHSTAN S.S.R.
UZBEKISTAN S.S.R.
TURKMENISTAN S.S.R.
TADZHIK S.S.R.
KHIRGIZ S.S.R.
ARAL SEA
CASPIAN SEA
BLACK SEA
Lake Balkhash
Lake Baikal
Lake Ladoga
Lake Onega
White Sea

Cities:
Vladivostok
Khabarovsk
Okhotsk
Verkhoyansk
Yakutsk
Vilyuisk
Igarka
Ulan Ude
Irkutsk
Krasnoyarsk
Novosibirsk
Tomsk
Omsk
Karaganda
Alma Ata
Tashkent
Ashkabad
Baku
Tbilisi
Astrakhan
Guryev
Karsakpai
Salekhard
Tobolsk
Sverdlovsk
Perm
Syktyvkar
Archangel
Leningrad
MOSCOW
Gorky
Kazan
Ufa
Kuibyshev
Volgograd
Rostov
Kharkov
Odessa
Kiev
Minsk
Riga

Part I
HISTORY

1

RUSSIA BEFORE SOVIET POWER

The Soviet Union is a country which, at least ostensibly, is devoted to the achievement of a singular goal – the building of a communist society. In practice, the understanding of communism is shaped by the ideology which the political leaders and the masses inherit. Also, the way forward is conditioned by various influences from the past, by the traditions of Russian culture, by the level of productive forces which the leaders have at their disposal and by the intellectual resources of the people. The future grows out of the present and the present is structured by the past. In the first two chapters of this book we shall consider the past and how Russian and Soviet history and ideology have shaped the present.

Marx and his generation of followers saw socialism arising out of advanced capitalist society, from the interplay of class forces between bourgeoisie and proletariat. Russia, however, was different. Unlike the countries of western Europe where the bourgeoisie had already abolished feudalism, in late nineteenth-century Russia wealth and power were controlled by an agrarian aristocratic ruling class. Before 1861, the conditions for rapid economic growth in Russia were not as favourable as in western Europe: there was an archaic agricultural framework, there was no influential elite either materially or ideally interested in economic change and there was no value system favouring entrepreneurial activity. The industrial revolution of the late eighteenth century had had little economic influence on Russia. Geographically, she was relatively isolated, cut off by her land mass and poor communications. But, even before the emancipation of the serfs in 1861, Russia was stirring. Her population was growing rapidly, while the market and money relations were replacing barter. Following her defeat in the Crimean War, modern communications and armaments were seen to be necessary for security, thus providing a stimulus for industrialization.

The Economy

A convenient point at which to begin our analysis is the emancipation of the serfs in 1861. Until the emancipation, Russian peasants had been bound to the land. As it was owned by the Tsar, Church or lord, this meant that a peasant was largely dependent on the landowner. Politically, peasants were deprived of rights; socially, they were regarded as inferior; economically, they were restricted to working the land: they could change neither their occupation nor place of residence. The peasant was required to work on the landowner's land (or in some cases pay money instead) for about half his working time, after which he could farm his own allotment.

The main provisions of the emancipation were to allow the peasants to use the lands they had previously farmed; they were no longer bound to their masters and were able, subject to the permission of the village assembly or commune, to move to the towns. The details and implementation of the settlement varied from one region to another. Generally, the landlord kept the land he had farmed; to the serfs went their cottages and garden patches. The communal fields previously worked by the serfs were made over to the village commune for peasant use. In fact, the peasants often received less land than they had before the reform, and Lyashchenko has shown that in the regions with black earth average land holdings declined, though in other poorer areas they increased.[1]

The peasants did not own the 'emancipated' land as private property. Its control was vested in the village assembly which was responsible for paying, over a period of 49 years, an indemnity to the government as compensation to the previous landowners. After 1861, the peasant became dependent on the commune. He could not leave his place of residence without its permission and was 'tied' to the commune in a similar way as before he was 'tied' to the feudal lord, though in practice many peasants left to work in the towns. The commune periodically redistributed the land, which was held in unconsolidated strips, according to the size of the peasant household.

The effects of the emancipation of the serfs were five-fold. First, dues in kind were abolished, furthering the growth of a money economy. Second, labour mobility between occupations and between town and country was improved, though many restrictions remained. Third, the subsequent sale by the aristocracy of parts of the land enabled differentiation to take place among the peasantry. Fourth, though there were some exceptions, the technologically backward open field and strip farming was perpetuated. Fifth, the functions of the village commune, elected by the heads of families, were extended. It collected taxes, distributed land, issued passports and resolved disputes.

The process of differentiation among the peasantry was speeded up by the establishment of a Peasants' Bank in 1882 and by the Stolypin reform of 1906. The former assisted groups of peasants to buy land from large estate owners – or garden plots from inefficient peasants. The Stolypin reform pinned its hopes on the creation of a group of property-owning farmers which would act as a political prop to the regime. Peasants were allowed to 'enclose' or to consolidate commune land into private holdings. The process of peasant differentiation was, however, slow. In 1877, the peasantry owned only 6.3 per cent of the land, and by 1900 the share under their private ownership was still only 15.4 per cent.[2] Between 1907 and 1915 only two million peasant land holdings came onto the market, and some of these had been given up by migrants to Siberia.

On the eve of the First World War, the 'peasant problem' had not been solved. Adequate land *ownership* was still largely the prerogative of relatively few large-scale estate owners. The majority of the peasantry either subsisted on small private plots or utilized commune land. As these latter units were inefficient, they absorbed much of their own agricultural produce. The large estates, located in southern Russia* and to the east of the lower Volga, catered for the market.

To satisfy the peasants' demand for land, the large estates would have had to be redivided among some fifteen million peasant households. Such a redivision would have met the peasants' political demands, but would have been disastrous for the urban population – for the supply of marketable grain would rapidly have fallen. The effects would also have harmed Russia's balance of payments, for she was chiefly an agricultural exporter and an industrial-goods importer: at the beginning of the twentieth century, a third of world wheat imports originated from Russia. The destruction of the large estates, therefore, would seriously have threatened the town population and would have prevented Russia paying for industrial imports. From the 1890s, American grain coming onto the world market caused world prices to fall. Russia increased her grain exports by squeezing the peasants, for example by forcing them to pay taxes soon after the harvest when grain prices were low.[3]

The agrarian changes discussed above were only one aspect of the developments taking place in nineteenth-century Russia. In addition, the total population of the Russian Empire was growing rapidly: from an estimated 42.5 million in 1815 to 125.6 million in 1897.[4] In the early

---

*The term Russia is used to refer to *Rossiya,* or the whole Russian Empire as shown on map 1. The territory inhabited by the Russians (*russkie*) is much smaller area, including the area shown on the map from St. Petersburg (now Leningrad) to the Volga and extending to the Urals in the east and beyond to Siberia.

nineteenth century, the issue of money increased as did production for the market; for example, trade in the Nizhenovgorod market increased four to five-fold between 1817 and 1861.[5] After the ignominious defeat of the Russians in the Crimean War (1853–56), Tsar Alexander II encouraged industrial development. 'The tariff was lowered, foreign capital and know-how invited. As Russians hurried again to Western Europe, Western books, ideas, experts and standards of doing things flowed into Russia'.[6] A modern system of communications was built. The railways had only some thousand miles of line in 1860, but this increased to forty-eight thousand miles by 1914: a network linking Warsaw to the Pacific coast and St Petersburg to the Volga and Tashkent. Improved rail communications were paralleled by the growth of a network of telegraph and telephone lines.

At the time of the emancipation of the serfs, Russia's industrial capacity rested on a traditional iron industry founded on the ore of the Urals, a craftsman kind of textile industry in the area to the north-east of Moscow, and handicraft industries in the western territories, the Caucasus and Volga areas. During the latter half of the nineteenth century, however, large-scale investment and factory production of a more advanced type based on the western European model were introduced. The Donbass quickly outstripped the Urals areas in output of metal, and large textile enterprises were set up in Poland, Ivanovo-Voznesensk and St Petersburg. For example, coal output in the Donbass increased from 15.6 million *puds*[7] in 1870 to 671.1 million in 1900; iron smelting rose from 2 million *puds* in 1885 to 50.6 million in 1900, when it accounted for over half of Russian iron smelting.[8]

The late nineteenth-century industrialization was carried out with the aid of West European skill and capital. British, French, German and Belgian money was invested in Russia, and western engineers supervised the erection and operation of the new industrial plants. To take the example of Donbass, only one of the nine blast furnaces was wholly Russian-owned[9] and more than half the mines were under Franco-Belgian ownership. British interests were well represented in textiles and oil. Even oil production had increased so rapidly that in 1901 Russian production surpassed the total American output. The newer industrial areas were characterized by western capital and modern capital-intensive production, while in the older traditional regions, in the Urals particularly, and to some degree around Moscow, almost pre-industrial methods continued, and ownership and control were largely in Russian hands.

The activity of the government was one of the most important factors in encouraging this economic growth. Protective tariffs supported the new industry: foreign investors were often guaranteed a fixed rate of return on

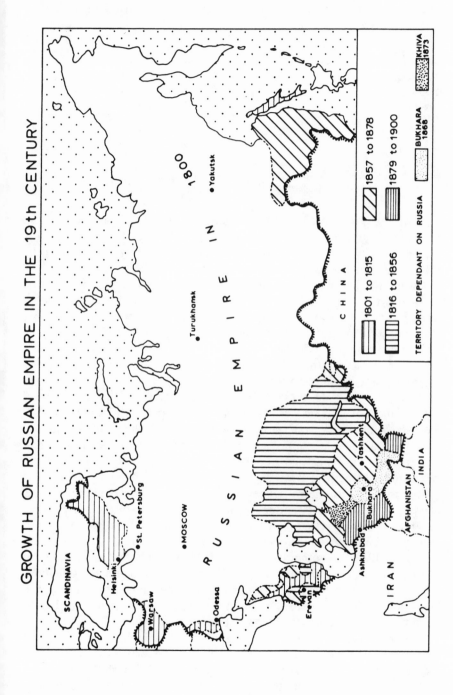

TABLE 1.1: AVERAGE ANNUAL RATES OF GROWTH OF INDUSTRIAL OUTPUT
(PER CENT), 1885–1913[10]

Period	Russia	USA	UK	Germany
1870–1884	—	4.65	1.98	4.22
1885–1889	6.10	8.75	4.56	5.15
1890–1899	8.03	5.47	1.80	5.44
1907–1913	6.25	3.52	2.72	3.90
1885–1913	5.83	5.26	2.11	4.49

Source: A. Gerschenkron, 'The Rate of Industrial Growth in Russia since 1885', *The Journal of Economic History*, 1947 vol. 7 (Supplement), p. 156.

capital, the government was a large purchaser of Russian industrial produce. The government itself directly owned and managed many factories, particularly in brewing and armaments, and by 1900 most of the railway system had been nationalized.

During the late nineteenth century and particularly between 1890 and 1899 and between 1907 and 1913, Russia experienced a rapid rate of growth. The Russian growth rates are shown in the second column of table 1.1. Industrial production increased five-fold between 1885 and 1913, an annual growth rate of 5.72 per cent from 1861 to 1913. The table shows growth rates larger than those in the USA, the United Kingdom and Germany in similar periods.

Of course, despite these large strides forward in the direction of industrialization, Russia was very backward compared with the industrialized states of the West. A Soviet estimate is that the value of Russian industrial large-scale output was only 6.9 per cent of American gross industrial output, and Russian *per capita* production in 1913 was only 4.8 per cent of American.[11]

A corollary to this industrial development was the growth of the working class. Its exact size is a matter of some dispute. One of the most widely accepted estimates is that of A.G. Rashin who has said that the number of factory and mining workers increased from 800,000 in 1861–70 to some 2.5 million in 1913.[12] Another estimate by Shkaratan which includes those in industry, as well as in mining and quarrying, puts the figure at 3.6 million. When one adds to this total non-manual workers and those employed in transport, building, services and agriculture, the number in paid labour would approximate to 20 million.[13]

The introduction of modern industry led to a high concentration of workers in Russian industry. In 1910, the proportion of workers in factories with over five hundred employed was 53.5 per cent compared with only 33 per cent in the USA.[14] While this fact may have been important from a social and political point of view, from an economic one it is misleading, for Russian industry was more labour-intensive and less efficient than American at this time. In terms of horsepower per industrial worker in large scale industry, the Russian figures were much lower; three-fifths of the English figure and only a third of the American.[15] More striking figures illustrating Russia's industrial backwardness are the horsepower used in production as a proportion of the population: in the early twentieth century Russia had only 1.6 (per hundred of the population), the USA 25, Germany 13 and England 24.[16]

The Russian economy, then, under the Tsars at the beginning of the twentieth century had the following salient features. Under the impetus of government control and encouragement, the economy was growing swiftly; a network of communications had been established, as had a base for heavy industry, textiles, chemicals and oil. But compared to Western European states, Russia was economically backward. Her industrial development had features which were quite different from the western states. A modern economic system was largely 'imported' by the government, it did not grow out of an indigenous capitalist class – and that class was under the tutelage of the state.

The political formations did not conform to a classical Marxist situation. The government, not the bourgeoisie, played the dominant role in the industrial development of capitalism which in its turn promoted the growth of the proletariat. On the basis of this, it would hardly be fair to reject the Marxist prognosis of history (see below, pp 27–9). The fact that the *Russian* bourgeoisie played a small part in economic development does not refute the hypothesis that the bourgeoisie *as a whole* had a major role in the transformation of Russia after 1861. Russia, Marxists would argue, was part and parcel of the world capitalist economic system and cannot be understood independently of it. The underlying need for security, the finance and organization of Russian industry, the technological innovation all stemmed from the western bourgeoisie. To be viable and realistic, analysis has to take into account the effects, on the internal political and social structure of a country, of economic development largely performed by a foreign bourgeoisie. Whereas in the West, industrial development could take place in a stable, more or less parliamentary, political structure, in Russia both bourgeois and proletarian groups found themselves constrained by an autocratic strait jacket.

Social Groups

The Russian social structure in the late nineteenth and early twentieth century was under stress from the changes that were taking place in the economy. These changes in social structure in turn affected the political and economic order. Here we shall consider the demographic data on Russia before the revolution and some of the more important social and national divisions of the population.

The official social classification of Russia's population was based on estate: the gentry (or nobility), townsman and peasant. One's estate gave certain legal rights and it also had social significance. The system of 'estates' signified a stratified but mutually interdependent and harmonious social order. Theoretically, membership of an estate was fixed at birth, though in Russia social movement was possible.

The Russian *nobility* (*dvoryanstvo*) or gentry included the hereditary owners of large estates, senior government officials and officers of state. The nobility was stratified into 14 different ranks ranging from Chancellor (or Field-Marshall in the army) to a College Registrar: some intermediary ranks, for instance, were of an army Colonel in sixth position, and a Second-Lieutenant in the twelfth (there were corresponding civilian categories too). The first of the three main divisions of the nobility was the *potomstvennoe* (hereditary) whose members until 1861 had enjoyed the privilege of owning serfs; secondly, the *lichnoe* (personal), who held their title for life only; and thirdly, the *kupechestvo* (merchants), who held office in the two highest guilds (members needed a certain minimum capital and had to pay fees). The *townsman's* estate (*meshchanstvo*) was composed of men living in the town who had certain property or professional qualifications. The *peasantry* (*krest' yanstvo*) consisted of people who were 'bound to' the soil and came under the jurisdiction of a village court. In addition to these three main strata there was the clergy who held office in the Orthodox Church. These then were the formal legal divisions of the population.

The estates in Russia were not rigid in structure. The nobility strata were relatively open to new members irrespective of birth. In addition to honours conferred by the Tsar, the attainment of positions in state service automatically brought ennoblement. One could, by having sufficient wealth, join one of the merchant guilds which gave *dvoryanin* status. A university degree was also a sufficient condition to give entry to the nobility. The relative ease of entry to the Russian nobility compared with that of western Europe is sometimes recognized by giving it the wider social term, 'gentry'.

After 1861, the legal and actual position of the estates was undermined. The emancipation denied the right to the hereditary nobility to own serfs, and from 1874 all estates had to perform military service. Internal passports were issued by the police and not the estate offices. The growth of industry resulted in the appearance of managerial and commercial occupations. The development of education and health services increased the numbers of professional groups which could not be easily assimilated into the estate structure. Factory workers, recruited from all estates, albeit disproportionately from the peasantry, appeared on the social scene. The 'peasantry' was heterogeneous: some were substantial landowners – 'rich peasants' or *'kulaks'* – others were agricultural labourers, or factory workers. The only thing 'the peasants' had in common was their common subjection to the village *mir* (or community) to which they had to apply for passports and which had civil jurisdiction over them. In short, the 'estate' of an individual indicated social origin which should not be ignored, but did not connote any collective norms. Moreover, one of the main reasons for the break-up of the old social structure was explosive population growth, already briefly mentioned above in discussing the economy.

Population

The population of Russia was growing well before the nineteenth century. Between 1722 and 1796 the Russian ethnic population had increased from 14 to 36 million.[17] In the nineteenth century the population rose even more rapidly reaching a total of 94 million in 1897.[18] The growth was due to changes in the birth and death rate: the former rising from 43.7 (per thousand of the total population) in the years 1801 to 1810 to 52.4 between 1851 and 1860. The birth rate in other countries from 1851 to 1860 was: France 26, Prussia 38, England 34, Sweden 36. In 1801 to 1810[19] the death rate in Russia was 27.1 – higher than in other European countries – and between 1891 and 1900 it rose to 32.8: in England in the latter period it was 18.2, in France 21.5, Germany 22.2 and Sweden 16.4 (per thousand of the population).[20] The enormous growth is illustrated by the fact that the population trebled between 1815 and 1900. The national increase was 1.66 per cent in 1801–1810 and 1.3 per cent between 1851 and 1860.

The 1897 census for the whole Russian Empire showed the main divisions as follows:

Nobility (all ranks and including chinovniki*)*	*2,193,000*
Clergy	*588,900*
Merchants	*281,100*
Townsmen	*13,386,300*
Peasants	*96,896,500*
Cossacks	*2,928,700*

(*Pervaya vseobshchaya perepis' naseleniya* (*Obshchi svod*), vol. 1 (1905), pp. 160–1).

* State officials not having noble status

Obviously, the figures are only a very rough guide to the actual configuration of social groups. Notable, as one would expect, is the large number of peasants (97 million) and townsmen (13 million); many of the latter were Jews. The official classification ignores those engaged in industry and commerce. Industrial workers, therefore, would be in all the above groups, though most were in the peasant bracket. Khromov says that 21.7 million (including members of families) were engaged in industry and trade.[21] More detailed figures have been worked out by Eason. Of a total population of 139 million in 1913, he estimates that 16.7 per cent (or 23 million) were wage and salary earners, excluding another 7.2 per cent who were handicraftsmen (cobblers, watch-makers and so on).[22]

As I have mentioned above, by the beginning of the twentieth century the industrial working class was still small in size. It had grown from about 0.4 per cent of the population in 1815 to 1.41 per cent in 1913. Lorimer's estimates are shown in table 1.2. The comparable figure in the United States in 1910 was 11.6 per cent.

TABLE 1.2: THE NUMBER AND PROPORTION OF INDUSTRIAL WORKERS IN RUSSIA, 1815–1913 (SELECTED YEARS)

Year	Estimated Total Population (000s)	Industrial Workers (000s)	Industrial Workers as Per Cent of Total Population
1815	42,510	173	0.4
1835	60,185	288	0.48
1860	74,120	565	0.76
1900	131,710	1,692	1.28
1913	161,723	2,282	1.41

Source: Frank Lorimer, The Population of the Soviet Union (Geneva, 1946).

According to Rashin, of the some 2.5 million industrial workers in 1913, under half (918,000) were employed in textiles, just over a third of a million were in the (385,000) metal industries and 215,000 in mining.[23] The industrial working class was concentrated in certain areas of the Empire, particularly in Moscow and Vladimir provinces (over half a million 1913) and St Petersburg (218,000). The southern metal and mining area, though it had sustained a very high growth rate, encompassed only about ten per cent of all industrial workers in the same year. In Siberia and Central Asia, industrialization had made hardly any headway. In Siberia there were about 37,000 industrial workers in 1908 – only 0.4 per cent of the total population. In Central Asia and the Asiatic Steppe there were some 21,000 workers of whom about a third were employed in cotton-ginning and another fifth in the petroleum and silk industries. The Caucasus was little touched by industrial activity, except in the oilfields of Baku where about 55,000 workers were employed.[24]

The growth in population and the changes in production methods led to a shift in balance between town and country. In 1850 the urban population has been estimated at 5.5 per cent or only some 3 million.[25] By 1870 the figure had risen to 12.3 per cent and on the eve of the First World War it was 14.6 per cent, when the total population living in towns was over 20 million. The degree of urbanization varied considerably between different areas of the Russian Empire: in 1897, whereas in Poland 23 per cent of the population was urban, in the rest of European Russia it was half this figure (12.9 per cent), while in Siberia it was only 9 per cent.[26] By way of comparison, it is worth pointing out that in Great Britain 50 per cent of the population was urban in 1800, and 77 per cent in 1897.

In the recruitment of labour, Russian industrialization followed a similar process to that in other countries developing today. Surplus population moved from the village to the town. In a survey of 31 provinces of European Russia before 1917, 31.3 per cent of the factory workers (or their families) had land; and 20.9 per cent, with the aid of their families, continued to work on it.[27] Land-working varied between regions and kinds of industries. The textile workers in the central and northern provinces had relatively stronger links with the countryside than the metal workers; in the Ukraine only 5.7 per cent of the latter had any land (figures for 1914–17). A survey of 5,723 factory workers in Shuya (situated to the northeast of Moscow) in 1899 showed that over half were of the farming peasantry.[28]

The attitudes of the migrants to town life and the degree to which they considered themselves as 'workers' rather than peasants are extremely complex and difficult questions. Some, in areas with close links between town and country, were no doubt 'anxious to find a way to return to the peasant villages whence they had recently come';[29] others, however, quickly adapted to town life. The following quotation from the memoirs of a worker in the northern textile industry is probably typical of many such uprooted men. 'At first ... all seemed better than in the village. Although there was no cow's milk on holidays there was white bread and despite the tiring factory work, urban life seemed more interesting and attractive.'[30] In this area of Russia, the Soviet writers Varentsova and Bagaev have argued that village life had little attraction because of the small amount and poor quality of land available.[31] The notion that the new urban workers idealized a peasant world of staunch yeoman values been much exaggerated.

The large rural population was mainly peasant and Russia was one of the first societies which had experienced the impact of foreign investment and industrialization on the Western model. Some writers have pointed to the 'dual' nature of Russia before (and after) 1917. Herzen described this social dualism as follows: 'On the one hand there was governmental, imperial, aristocratic Russia, rich in money, armed not only with bayonets but with all the bureaucratic and police techniques taken from Germany. On the other was the Russia of the dark people, poor, agricultural, communal, democratic, helpless, taken by surprise, conquered, as it were, without battle.'[32]

The peasant society for commentators such as Chayanov remained relatively 'closed'[33] and isolated from the changes occurring in the towns. The peasants remained in many ways a separate estate perpetuating traditional values and beliefs which would be an obstacle to the many new revolutionary incumbents of political power. But the development of industry and commerce, the growth of a labour market, migration, educational reform, population increase and military service all played a role in breaking down the traditional household and communal form of living.

The break-up of the old social structure and the development of classes on the pattern of industrial society was a feature of Russia at the turn of the century. The categories of estate and class divided the population horizontally. In addition, however, the various national, religious and linguistic groups united vertically the various occupational, estate and class divisions.

Several groupings may be distinguished. The largest was a 'Great Russian' area in which some two-thirds of the population spoke Russian and were Orthodox by religion. This is the traditional Russian land mass before 1800 (see map 1). This area centred on Moscow and was bounded by the Urals in the East, St. Petersburg in the North and the Don area in the South. In the Polish parts the Catholics predominated. In the southern and western areas the main languages spoken were Ukrainian and Byelo-russian, though in some provinces in the south-west (Minsk, Kherson, Vilna and Grodno, for example) more than ten per cent of the population were Jews. The Baltic provinces and Finland were again ethnically and linguistically apart. Central Asia and Siberia had been penetrated by Russian settlers, but were mainly populated by diverse and small indigenous Asiatic groups. The Caucasus had mixed racial, linguistic, and religious stock, ranging from the Christian Georgians to the small groups of Muslims making up the population of Azerbaidzhan.

Here we may conclude that social divisions in the pre-revolutionary Russian Empire were great. The population was extremely heterogeneous with regard to occupation, religious belief, language, national and racial background. Many of the problems which later faced the Bolshevik government were concerned with welding together into a communal state these disparate groups.

The Polity

Before 1905, complete political authority was vested in the Tsar. Article 1 of the Fundamental Laws (1892) decreed: 'The all-Russian Emperor is an autocrat and unlimited monarch – God himself commands his supreme power be obeyed out of conscience as well as fear.' In fact, given the complexity of government, the Tsar was advised by a number of committees and individuals. While we cannot study here the complex structure of the Tsarist administration, it is important to note that the main holders of political influence were the ministers (especially of Finance, the Interior and the Army) and the governors of each province. Nicholas II, who reigned from 1894 to 1917, when faced with the difficult problems of ruling the Russian Empire vacillated between the advice offered him by his many advisers, among whom figured the mystic Rasputin, and remained a weak and ineffectual ruler. It should not be thought, however, that the dynasty eventually fell simply because of a weak ruler. A decisive change was required to bring into correspondence the social, economic and political structure.

The Tsarist system as it was in the early twentieth century may illustrate the difficulties which are inherent in an autocratic system failing to represent the interests which an industrial order creates and which, to a greater or lesser extent, are ensured by parliamentary representation. The possible reaction of important social groups could not be well gauged by the government. Furthermore, a social harmony of interests – landowners, peasants, workers, bourgeoisie, national groups – could not be reached within the framework of the autocratic Tsarist political system.

While, until 1905, no representation prevailed at the national all-Russian level, this was not the case in local government. The *Zemstva* were first set up in 1864 and were concerned with the administration of the post office, education, public health, works and sanitation; they provided services for agriculture and collected statistics. In addition to providing accommodation for police and other officials, in some areas the *Zemstva* were required to pay the salaries of local priests.[34] Their social composition, however, was hopelessly unrepresentative. Of deputies elected to the *Zemstva* between 1865 and 1867, 74.2 per cent were of the gentry, 10.9 per cent from the merchant strata, and 10.6 per cent peasants (4.3 per cent were unclassified).[35]

In the sphere of political liberty Russia lagged behind the advanced countries of western Europe. White has shown that, compared to western democracies, such as the United Kingdom and the United States, in the period 1815 to 1914, Russia had no selection of the government executive by election, no parliamentary responsibility and no 'legislative effectiveness'. Even by 1910, Russia had the highest parliamentary representation of the nobility (51 per cent) and the lowest of the middle class (24.2 per cent).[36] Until 1905, political parties and trade unions were illegal – for they sought to 'represent' particular interests and were, therefore, inimical to autocratic Tsarist rule. There were, however, associations of industrialists who met to discuss their common industrial interests, and friendly and benevolent societies, such as the Red Cross. Among the working class, mutual aid associations flourished to provide for sickness, unemployment and funerals. There were no trade unions comparable to western European ones. In an attempt to keep the workers' organizations under control, the police had organized workers' unions which sometimes discussed problems with the factory administration. It is not true to say that there were no organized groups in Russia before 1905. But as the groups were illegal, the political system was under no compulsion to come to terms with them, hence they functioned weakly as influences on the political system. Political parties, whose *raison d'être* is to influence the government, only existed in the underground. In 1905, they came into the open and contested elections. These groups had a complex history going back into the nineteenth century. Here we may consider only the general background.

Before 1861, the emancipation of the peasant dominated Russian politics. Alexander Herzen, in the 1850s, had postulated a new social order based on a self-sufficient and self-governing village commune. Influenced by these ideas, *Populist* (or *Narodnik*) groups in the 1880s conducted revolutionary activity with the aim of establishing a form of peasant socialism. Most of these groups opposed the centralized autocratic state and advocated populism or a form of decentralized agrarian socialism with small-scale handicraft industry – but not the capitalist industrial order of Germany and Great Britain. Particularly noteworthy are the groups following Tkachev and Nechaev, which advocated a revolutionary seizure of power, developed terrorism as a means of change and set up a secret centralized organization to accomplish the revolution. But these groups, which idealized the peasant and saw salvation in a socialist but mainly agrarian social order, failed and were superseded by the Marxists. Probably the most important reason for failure was that the Narodniks did not penetrate the peasantry, and remained essentially a movement of intellectuals.[37]

From the middle of the 1880, *Marxism* began to make an impact in Russia, and numerous circles were organized. In these it was argued by the Marxists that large-scale industrialization was not only inevitable in the unfolding of history, but was also desirable, for capitalism brought with it progress – a higher level of economic and social development. We cannot study these groups here, but they were the forerunners of the political parties which came into the open in 1905. A description of the latter will give a good idea of the political alternatives suggested for Russia's future development.

Political Parties

The main peasants' party was formed by the *Socialist Revolutionaries* (SRs), the heir to the populist tradition. Their main characteristics were as follows. The party was revolutionary: many activists supported terrorist tactics (assassination and bomb-throwing) and the seizure of the land by the peasants (some wanted to compensate the landlords, but others did not). It advocated a decentralized economy with small-scale industrial manufacture. While many Utopian Socialist Revolutionaries wanted a form of cooperative socialist agriculture based on the old Russian commune (the *obshchina*), many others, probably the majority, wanted an independent yeomanry with small holdings. The numerous national minorities were to be given the right of self-determination. Though the leaders of the Socialist Revolutionaries were intellectuals, their popular support lay with the peasantry.

The *Constitutional Democratic Party (Cadets)*, or the Russian liberal party, was supported by the professional classes – the leading academic, legal and journalistic groups. Its policy was the adoption of parliamentary democracy based on the Duma (an advisory body to the Tsar). It wanted the peasants' land area to be increased, but the landlords were to be indemnified. It advocated labour legislation for the protection of child and female labour and wanted to set up a sort of labour relations board to resolve industrial conflicts. It was, in other words, a 'progressive' liberal party. Though persuasion and peaceful change were preferred to abolish the autocracy, the party conceded that revolution might be necessary to achieve a democratic republic.

The *Octobrist Party* was a centre party. It supported civil liberties and representative government, but firmly believed in a constitutional monarchy rather than the republic wanted by the liberal groups. The party believed that labour legislation should protect workers from exploitation and that they should also have the right to strike and form unions. Based on the promise of a constitutional regime in the October Manifesto, from which the party took its name, it was strongly anti-revolutionary and advocated change by peaceful means. (This was a manifesto put out by the Tsar in October 1905, promising a constitutional form of government. See below p. 21).

The *Union of the Russian People* was an extreme right wing party. Its policy was based on 'Orthodoxy, Autocracy and Nationalism'. 'Orthodoxy'

represented the values and the religious outlook of the Russian Orthodox
Church. 'Autocracy' was support for the ruling Tsar. The nationalism of the
party was grounded on the Great Russian nation. It is sometimes said that
the ideas of the Union were one of the earliest manifestations of Fascist
ideology: belief in a personal figurehead (the Tsar), Great Russian folk
supremacy (they were particularly hostile to Jews), and opposition to
parliamentary institutions and socialist ideas.

The chief Marxist party was the *Russian Social Democratic Labour Party*
(RSDLP). As this was the forerunner of the Communist Party of the Soviet
Union we shall study it more closely than its rivals. It was formed in 1903.
At its formation, however, the party split into two parts: the Bolsheviks,
led by Lenin, and Mensheviks, headed by Martov and others. (The term
Bolshevik and Menshevik are derived from the Russian words for majority
and minority). As Marxists, the social democrats of both factions believed
that capitalism had to develop in Russia. It was impossible to build a form
of socialism on the basis of the peasant commune, as advocated by the
socialist-revolutionaries.

Both factions of the party, Bolsheviks and Mensheviks, agreed that the
next stage in the evolution of Russia was the bourgeois-democratic. But
they disagreed on the role that the social democrats should play during and
after the bourgeois-democratic revolution. Though we shall dwell on this
later, it might be pointed out here that the Mensheviks felt that the
bourgeoisie could and should complete the revolution. The Bolsheviks,
however, argued that the social democratic party had a leading part to
play. Another difference between the factions was on the question of the
form of party organization relevant to Russian conditions. Lenin and the
Bolsheviks at that time wanted a centralized party of Marxist revolutionaries (see discussion below, pp. 40–3), whereas the Mensheviks advocated
a more widely based party with a strong trade union wing, rather like the
German Social Democratic Party (and the British Labour Party today). If
one bears in mind that the Mensheviks anticipated a liberal-democratic
society after the abolition of the autocracy, their party organizational
theory follows quite logically from this assumption.

The social democrats of both factions were mainly led by intellectuals.
The Mensheviks tended to be supported by the more highly skilled workers
and the Bolsheviks drew more support from the unskilled. Another
difference was that the Bolsheviks were largely Great Russian, whereas the
Mensheviks were composed of the non-Russian national groups (particularly Georgians and Jews),[38] though they too had some support among the
Great Russians.

The Russian political scene in 1905 had a different set of leading actors
compared to America one hundred years earlier. The 'bourgeois' interests

founded on manufacturing were very weak. The largest party, the socialist-revolutionaries, had no English counterpart, based as it was on the agrarian demands of the peasantry. The well organized urban social democrats had no analogous grouping in America during its revolution, when a large industrial working class had yet to be formed and the Marxist conception of class struggle remained to be formulated. Yet Russia was a divided nation in terms of both class and nationality. Among the Poles, Ukrainians and Georgians, let alone the nascent ethnic groups of Asia, some opposition existed to the politically dominant Russians.

Political Activity: The 1905 Revolution

We have seen that at the beginning of the twentieth century, the Tsar was under pressure: from the growing entrepreneurial, managerial and professional groups for liberal conditions as in western Europe, from the working classes for better living conditions and higher pay, from the peasantry to reduce their land repayments and taxes. The general discontent erupted in a series of revolts known as the 1905 Revolution, which Lenin later regarded as a 'dress rehearsal' for October 1917. It will be instructive to study the events of 1905 before turning to the more decisive happenings of 1917.

Strikes and disturbances were not new phenomena to the Russian scene. But nothing quite like the demonstration of 9 January 1905 had taken place before. On that day, Father Gapon, a celebrated Orthodox priest, organized a petition to the Tsar calling upon him to help the people. The petitioners, some thousands strong, with banners proclaiming their needs, converged on the Royal Palace. These were loyal subjects who regarded the Tsar as a protector; their message was one of despair, not revolt, and their ikons held high showed their patriotic fervour and religious zeal. The demonstrators, however, were forcibly dispersed and reports claimed that several hundreds were killed or wounded. The event has become known as the 'Bloody Sunday' massacre.

Gapon was later murdered by a socialist-revolutionary. He had been a police agent 'planted' among the workers both to inform on them and to lead them along a peaceful, non-revolutionary, path of change, though he was probably sincere and had a genuine concern for the workers. It is significant too, that the workers in the Gapon demonstrations revered the Tsar and looked to him, over the heads of the officials and industrial leaders, to ameliorate their position. The firing on the crowd severely weakened this belief and had the effect of strengthening support for the revolutionary elements. In the spring and summer, strikes and uprisings continued to be directed against factory administrations, landlords and the

Tsar. The government, worried by the continuing outbreaks, made concessions: a limited consultative assembly was promised. (The Bulygin Duma envisaged was a consultative assembly formed mainly from landowners.) Self-government was also granted to the universities, an act which later in the year gave the revolutionaries a sanctuary. These actions did not assuage the rebellious clamour and by the end of October the country was locked in general strike, which included students and even ballerinas, showing the width of feeling against the Tsarist order.

In the course of the strikes, meetings took place between the leaders, who had formed quite spontaneously Councils (or Soviets) of Workers' Deputies. The first was formed in the textile town of Ivanovo-Voznesensk in May and was followed by others, the best known of which were in Moscow and St. Petersburg. The Soviets were composed of workers' representatives and frequently led by social democrats of both factions (Bolsheviks and Mensheviks). They agitated for improvements in working conditions (especially for the eight hour day) and democratic rights. In December the police dissolved the St Petersburg Soviet, led by Trotsky, and its leaders were arrested and put on trial. No armed resistance was offered in the capital. In other areas, armed uprisings took place. In Moscow, the insurgents led by the Soviet erected barricades and controlled parts of the town. At the end of December, troops put down the revolt at the cost of some thousand casualties. In Moscow, as in other places where armed conflict took place, Bolshevik organizations and, to a lesser extent, socialist revolutionaries were at the head of popular revolts. The Mensheviks supported and participated in the revolutionary activities.

In the armed forces some insubordination occurred. Russia had been engaged in the Russo-Japanese War (1904–5). She had refused to withdraw from Manchuria and sought further concessions in Korea. While few land forces had been involved in the war, the Russian fleet was annihilated in May 1905, at the battle of Tsushima. The peace treaty of September gave the Japanese further territories in the east. This war had only minimal internal impact. The famous Battleship Potemkin had mutinied in the spring. In the winter, a few troops fraternized with strikers, and those returning from the Far East through Siberia were particularly militant. But, on the whole, the armed forces remained disciplined and loyal to their commanders. With the crushing of the Moscow uprising, the revolution was over.

What was the significance of the revolution? It must be said that it did not achieve a rapid and decisive change in the social, political or economic order. But the constitutional position of the Tsar was undermined and after October he was in a much weaker position. On 17 October 1905, the October Manifesto was published. This was not a constitution, but a promise by the Tsar of civil freedoms: inviolability of the person, freedom of conscience, speech, assembly and association; an elected Duma, with legislative powers and participation in the supervision of officers of state. It was promised to admit all classes to participate in the affairs of the Duma. Consequently, in 1906, the First Duma was elected. It was part of a two-chamber legislature, the upper house appointed by the Tsar having equal power with the lower which was indirectly elected through electoral colleges based on social class. It was thought by the government that the peasantry was pro-Tsarist: it chose the largest proportion of deputies, 43.4 per cent (the landlords chose 31.8 per cent, the townsmen 22.4 per cent and the workers 2.4 per cent).[39]

Because of the biased representation, the left-wing parties did not fully participate in the election. Despite this, the radicals, many of whom were elected by the peasantry, emerged with a majority. The Cadets (Constitutional Democrats) were the largest party with 177 members out of 524. But political power was firmly left in the hands of the Tsar. He appointed ministers who were responsible to him and not to the Duma, which could show its displeasure but could not remove a minister. The control of the budget was ineffective and military expenditure was outside the Duma's competence. The Tsar could veto acts passed by both chambers. In practice the Tsar by-passed the Duma. Legislation was carried out by decree which was quite legal when the Duma was not in session. After 1906, the Duma was made even less representative by an increase in the proportion of deputies with landowning qualifications.

The chief effects of the 1905 Revolution were that some concessions were made to liberal and democratic forces. In the Duma, freedom of speech was ensured and public criticism was made of the government. But a wider degree of civil liberty was not attained: people were still liable to arbitrary arrest, correspondence was examined by the police, censorship continued and political parties and trade unions remained underground, though the representatives of the political parties participated in the Duma. Perhaps the greatest change was that the legitimacy of the autocracy had been undermined. The Tsar had admitted the rights of society to participate in the government of the country. Thereafter, his legitimacy had been compromised: he was no longer 'the supreme power to be obeyed out of conscience'.

The events of 1905–1907 resulted in the failure of the revolutionaries to seize power. The October Manifesto, with its promise of a liberal constitution, was a turning point: following its publication, many elements of the bourgeoisie called off the revolutionary struggle. The Mensheviks' view of the revolution proved erroneous: the bourgeoisie did not seize power. The Bolsheviks were premature: the uprisings of workers and others were crushed (see below pp. 39–40). In fact, the Tsar still remained supreme ruler and a liberal-democratic regime was not set up.

After 1907, revolutionary activity declined. The membership and morale of the social democrats was at a low ebb. Many left the party. Economic growth, which received a set-back in 1905–7, picked up and averaged 6.25 per cent between 1907 and 1913. It seemed that the autocracy, having come through the storm of 1905, might be able to continue indefinitely. The hindsight of history tells us that this was an incorrect view.

From 1905 to 1914 the main social problems still remained unsolved. The Duma became less representative and had little effective control over the government. The social strata seeking a liberal-democratic regime were not politically satisfied and could not be expected to support the autocracy. An alternative was the development of a yeoman peasantry, a free small-holder class of moderately prosperous landowning farmers, who would politically uphold the Tsarist order in the same way that the old nobility had done. Stolypin encouraged the peasants to leave the commune and to buy land through the Pesants' Land Bank and he gave assistance to them to settle in Siberia and central Asia. But by the beginning of the First World War his policy had not succeeded in breaking down the communal pattern of ownership. The Russian countryside was still farmed mainly in the traditional manner: three-field rotation based on strip farming. Plots were uneconomic and too small, ranging from a half to two-and-a-half acres in size. By 1915, less than one tenth of peasant holdings had been consolidated into small farms. Unlike the farmers of the West who were individual landowners, or at least tenant farmers, the Russian peasants remained largely members of a community (the village commune). In the towns, the workers' demands for better conditions had not been satisfied. The liberal bourgeoisie was excluded from the apex of political power. The Tsar had admitted the right of the people to participate in government, but had not subsequently acted on it. Russia had fared badly in the international arena: she had suffered an ignominious defeat in the war with Japan to whom she had ceded some of her eastern territories. Public confidence in the Tsar was low. These factors, which precipitated political and social change, were aggravated by the First World War, which Russia had entered on the side of the allies.

During the war fifteen and a half million men had been drafted into the armed forces. They were poorly armed and incompetently led; in the war six to eight million Russians were killed, wounded or captured. The mobilization withdrew approximately a third of the male labour force from industry and agriculture. Agricultural and industrial production declined between 1915 and 1917. By the end of 1916, the amount of grain marketed dropped by at least a third and the amount transported by rail dwindled by as much as sixty per cent.[40] In 1917, the value of money fell; by the summer bread prices had increased three times, and meat prices seven times, peasants refused to market grain and supplies were requisitioned by the government. In 1915 and 1916 the Russian army was badly defeated; morale was low, and in 1916 some million and a half men deserted. The Tsarist court had no consistent policy, ministers were dismissed and replaced, but no improvement occurred. The Tsar fell largely under the influence of the Tsarina and the mystic Rasputin. Such a system could not endure. By the beginning of 1917 all social groups – military, intelligentsia, entrepreneurs, civil service, peasantry and working class – were ready for a radical change. In February and October 1917 two sudden changes in government were to take place: in the first, the autocracy collapsed and the Provisional Government was formed; in the second, the Bolsheviks came to power. These two events have come to be regarded as the Russian Revolution of 1917; though to be precise there were two revolutions: the February and the October.

NOTES

1 P.I. Lyashchenko, *History of the National Economy of Russia* (1949), p. 382.
2 P.A. Khromov, *Ekonomicheskoe razvitie Rossii v XIX-XX vekakh* (1950),
   pp. 156–7.
3 Theodore H. Von Laue, *Sergei Witte and the Industrialisation of Russia* (1963),
   pp. 26, 30–31.
4 See below, p. 11 *et seq.*
5 P.A. Khromov, *Ekonomicheskoe razvitie Rossii v XIX-XX vekakh* (1950),
   p. 91. See this book for a discussion of the growth of an internal market in Russia.
6 Von Laue, *Sergei Witte...*, p. 6.
7 A Russian *pud* equals 36.1 British pounds.
8 S.I. Potolov, *Rabochie Donbassa v XIX veke* (1963), pp. 80–81.
9 Potolov, ibid., pp. 88–89.
10 Alexander Gerschenkron, 'The Rate of Industrial Growth in Russia since 1805',
   The Journal of Economic History, 1947 vol. 7 (Supplement), pp. 146, 155.
11 Cited by Gerschenkron, p. 155.
12 A.G. Rashin, *Formirovanie rabochego klassa Rossii* (1958), p. 192.
13 O.I. Shkaratan, *Problemy sotsial'noy struktury rabochego klassa SSSR* (1970),
   p. 127.
14 P.I. Lyashchenko, *History of the National Economy...*, pp. 669–70.
15 Figures for Russia in 1908, USA 1910, England 1907: Lyashchenko, p. 673.
16 Lyashchenko, ibid.
17 P.A. Khromov, *Ekonomicheskoe razvitie Rossii* (1950), p. 79.
18 Here we refer to the *Russian* (*russki*) ethnic population; the total population of
   the Russian Empire in 1897 was 125.6 million. See F. Lorimer, *The Population
   of the Soviet Union* (1946), p. 10.
19 Figures cited in Khromov, *Ekonomicheskoe razvitie Rossii...*, p. 81.
20 Khromov, ibid., pp. 240–41.
21 Khromov, ibid., pp. 228–9.
22 Warren W. Eason, 'Population Changes', in Cyril E. Black, *The Transformation of Russian Society* (1960), p. 88. The figures include dependents.
23 A.G. Rashin, *Formirovanie rabochego klassa Rossii* (1958), p. 48.
24 Lorimer, *The Population of the Soviet Union*, p. 23.
25 Eason, 'Population Changes' p. 83.
26 *Pervaya vseobschaya perepis' naseleniya* (Obshchi svod), vol. 1 (1905), p. 6.
27 Rashin, *Formirovanie*, p. 575.
28 A.V. Shipulina, 'Ivanovo-voznesenskie rabochie nakanune pervoy russkoy
   revolyutsii', *Doklady i soobshcheniya instituta istorii*, No. 8 (1955), p. 48.
29 R.A. Feldmesser, 'Social Classes and Political Structure', in Black *The
   Transformation...*, p. 244.
30 F.N. Samoylov, *Vospominaniya ob Ivanovo-Voznesenskom rabochem dvizhenii*,
   part I (1922), p. 9.
31 O.A. Varentsova and M.A. Bagaev *Za 10 let* (1930), p. 18.

32 A.I. Herzon, cited by R.C. Tucker, 'The Image of Dual Russia', in Black *The Transformation...*, (1960), p. 590.
33 T. Shanin, *The Awkward Class* (1972), p. 25.
34 Alexander Vucinich, 'The State and the Local Community', in Black, *The Transformation...*, (1960), p. 199.
35 'Zemskaya reforma 1864', *Bol'shaya Sovetskaya entsiklopediya,* vol. 17 (1952), p. 37.
36 S. White, *Political Culture and Soviet Politics* (1979), pp. 28–9.
37 See Franco Venturi, *The Roots of Revolution* (1960), M. Perrie, *The Agrarian Policy of the Russian Socialist Revolutionary Party* (1977).
38 For a detailed analysis of the social composition of both factions see: David Lane, *The Roots of Russian Communism* (1975).
39 F. Dan, 'Vtoraya Duma', in Yu. O. Martov, P. Maslov, and A. Potresov, *Obshchestvennoe dvizhenie v Rossii v nachale XX-go veka* (1909–14), vol. 4, part ii.
40 M. Dobb, *Soviet Economic Development Since 1917* (1966), p. 71.

2

MARXISM IN RUSSIA

It was against this background that Marxism developed in Russia. It is important to study the roots of what has become an ideology. On it the contemporary Soviet *Weltanschauung* (world-view) is based. Official ideology is often of a simplified and dogmatic type but it shapes and legitimates policy. It provides a unifying and more or less integrating set of values for the explanation of the past, for the description of the present and for the prescription of the future. It provides a vocabulary in which Soviet politics are discussed. Our task here is to describe briefly the ideology of Soviet Marxism–Leninism as it has been adapted from the original ideas of Marx.

Marxism as social and political theory seeks to explain the course of human history and the structure of past, present, and future societies: it postulates a model of society and an explanation of the nature of social change. There are many interpretations of Marxism as a doctrine or theory of society. In this book we are primarily interested in the Soviet version, the authoritative statement of which may be studied in *Fundamentals of Marxism–Leninism*.[1] But Soviet and non-Soviet Marxists alike share certain common views about the nature of societies and the process of social change. These basic tenets of Soviet Marxism may be explained under three main headings: the materialist conception of history, the political economy of capitalism, the nature of socialism and communism. The question of whether the USSR fulfils sufficient conditions to qualify as a 'socialist' society is the cause of much disagreement between Soviet and non-Soviet Marxists. (The discussion of socialism is taken up further in chapter 5).

26

The Materialist Conception of History

Marxists hold that the 'primary component' of the life of a society is labour, which provides the material means to control nature, and which makes tools and creates cultural life.

We must begin by stating the first presupposition of all human existence, and therefore of all history, namely, that men must be in a position to live in order to be able to 'make history'. But life involves before everything else eating and drinking, a habitation, clothing, and many other things. The first historical act is, therefore, production of material life itself. This is indeed a historical act, a fundamental condition of all history, which today, as thousands of years ago, must be accomplished every day and every hour merely in order to sustain human life.[2]

The 'productive forces' of a society are, on the one hand, the instruments of production (tools) and, on the other, labour. Production is social and derived from interdependent human activity, based on the division of labour. Except in very simple societies, the ownership of the productive forces is separated from those who use them. This phenomenon, the ownership of the means of production separated from labour, gives rise to social classes. At the capitalist stage of society, the two main classes determined by the ownership of capital goods (the ruling class), or non-ownership (the exploited class) are the bourgeoisie and the proletariat. Social class in Marxist usage is not concerned with gradations of status or honour as it is sometimes used in non-Marxist literature: it is a general concept bringing together into one category those who are 'employed' (wage labour) and into another those who own and live off property (the proletariat, the bourgeoisie). Such a bare definition does not do justice to the complexity of class relationships. To the owners of the means of production are added those who act as their agents in replicating capitalist relations – the leading managerial, police, military, judicial, intellectual and political personnel.

The course of human history is explained by Marx in terms of such class relationships: 'The history of all hitherto existing society is the history of class struggles.'[3] The causes of social change are not to be found in ideas, but in material processes: 'The ultimate causes of all social changes and political revolutions are to be sought, not in the minds of men, in their increasing insight into eternal truth and justice but in changes in the mode of production and exchange. They are not to be sought in the philosophy but in the economics of the epoch concerned.'[4] The ruling classes and, therefore, the forms of economic and social relations, are not identical in all societies, which are classified into five 'ideal types':* primitive-

---

*By 'ideal type' we mean an idealization of a pure form. In practice, societies are much more fluid and may contain elements of many of these types.

communal, slave, feudal, capitalist and communist.[5] These are what Marxists call 'modes of production'.[6]

In primitive-communal society there were no social classes. Classes were first formed because some individuals had control over weapons, stocks of materials and other human beings – slaves. This form of 'slave society', however, could not continue indefinitely. Within it another class developed based on ownership of land and knowledge of agricultural techniques. By a revolutionary process the landowners defeated the slave-owning classes and created feudal society. Feudal society again developed productive forces in the form of manufacture, and the groups of traders, merchants and industrialists who needed to meet demands for trade and commerce generated by feudal society formed the basis of a new capitalist class, which in turn overthrew feudalism and set up the capitalist form of society in its place. Capitalism in turn is to dig its own grave, the working class fulfilling its class interest by the abolition of capitalism and the establishment of communist society.

Each class, therefore, goes through three functional stages in its relationship to society. First, it is a revolutionary class struggling to assert its own power. Second, it is dominant, being necessary for and promoting economic development. Third, it is in decline, being a parasitical social group no longer essential for the further growth of society.

The theoretical underpinning of Marxism – Leninism is the dialectic which explains the relationships between all forms of matter and all processes of change. Matter (or unity) is divided into opposing elements which interact one with another.

A developing thing has within it the embryo of something else. It contains within itself its own antithesis, a 'negating' element which prevents it from remaining inert and immutable. It contains an objective contradiction; opposite tendencies operate within it and a mutual counteraction or 'struggle' of opposite forces or sides takes place, leading eventually to the resolution of the contradiction in a radical qualitative change of the thing.[7]

In other words, matter may be divided into 'thesis' and 'antithesis'. The two elements react on each other to form a new state, 'synthesis'. An example from history was given above when it was pointed out that medieval society was composed of two elements: the landowning gentry (thesis) and the bourgeoisie (antithesis). Through the struggle of these two social groups, the contradiction is resolved in the synthesis of capitalism. Capitalism itself is subject to the same laws, and within it the embryo of socialism is to be found. This interacts with the thesis of capitalism to form a new synthesis, communism. The dialectic is concerned with the processes or logic of change, with the ways in which in nature one thing is transformed into another. It does not provide us with a knowledge of the structure of nature. The anatomy of human society is described by Marxists in terms of basis and superstructure. We may explain these concepts by considering the Marxist interpretation of capitalism.

The Marxist Interpretation of Capitalism

Capitalism is a mode of production. A definition of a *mode of production* is a *distinct ensemble of forces of production, relations of production and superstructural arrangements with congruent relationships between basis and superstructure.* A mode of production has to be conceived in terms of an economic, political and social entity: economy, polity and social institutions (family, education, religion) are interdependent and 'knit together'. Except for communist society, modes of production contain contradictions (irreconcilable interests between classes), the resolution of which lead to a new and different mode of production, culminating in communist society. For Marxists, capitalism is important not only because it is the form of society in contemporary Britain and the United States, but because it is the last class society.

The economics of society, or the nature of its productive forces, form the basis, which is made up of two elements: the forces of production (the tools, or technology, or the stock of capital goods) and the relations to the means of production – the property relationships. The kind of technology or tools (the power-press or automated production line), together with the ruling class (owners of the means of production and those who control the apparatus of the state), shape the remaining special institutions of the society, which are called the superstructure. There is a basis and superstructure in all forms of society. Here examples are given from the capitalist stage. 'The sum total of these relations of production constitutes the economic structure of society – the real foundation, on which rise legal and political superstructures and to which correspond definite forms of social consciousness.'[8] In capitalist society, the superstructure includes, for example, such institutions as the government, political parties, religious bodies, voluntary associations, the educational system, the press and mass media. The superstructure is made up of human associations of these groups and the ideas and processes which are part of them. The 'dominant institutions' (such as the government, judiciary and mass media) promote the interests and share the values of the ruling class.

The relationship between basis and superstructure is often regarded as a weak link in Marxist theory. It is often seen as a monistic interpretation of society, changes in the superstructure being determined by the basis. But Engels in one passage recognized that the superstructure could influence the basis:

Because we denied that the different ideological spheres, which play a part in history, have an independent historical development, we were supposed therewith to have denied that they have an *historical efficacy* ... a historical factor, once it has been brought into the world by another – ultimately economic factor – is able to re-act upon its surroundings and even affect its own causes.[9]

The superstructure also includes the institutions of the exploited – in capitalist societies, the working class has its own values expressed in political organizations, such as trade unions and socialist parties. Such groups cannot live in harmony with the capitalist class: conflict is inherent in the exploiting relationship, and when capitalist society has reached its zenith, a revolutionary transformation takes place, bringing to power the working class. In terms of dialectics, the thesis is the capitalist class, its opposite (or antithesis) the working class, the revolutionary transformation creates the synthesis, in this case communist society.

At the root of the anarchy of capitalism is competition between firms ('capitals') in their search for profit ('surplus'). Production takes place on the basis of exchange through a market. The capitalist is driven by inexorable economic laws to make profit. He is forced through competition to greater production and to expansion of his business: he is possessed by what Marx called the 'fetishism of commodity production', the urge to amass capital and profits. Competition forces him to keep his costs as low as possible. Increases in productivity are limited and therefore reductions in the total wage bill must be made. Technological advance giving economies of scale to large firms forces the small ones out of production through price competition. Prices fall, however, not only because of changes in supply conditions, but also because of insufficiency of demand. Demand falls because wages of the employed are forced down by firms seeking to reduce prices, because technological innovation results in redundancy, and because a part of the 'surplus' received from labour (in the form of profits) remains unspent. These economic forces provide the objective conditions for the irreconcilable class conflict between labour and capital.

Such class conflict is derived from exploitation of the worker. What this means may be understood from a consideration of the theory of value. By value, Marx means the amount of labour which is expended on the production of good. This is unlike modern economic theory, where value and price are identical. The worker does not receive the full reward for his labour: a part is alienated from him and goes to the capitalist: this is 'surplus value'. This is the essence of exploitation and the cause of irreconcilable class conflict. The extent to which the worker is exploited is measured by the ratio of surplus value to the value embodied in a commodity. As labour is purchased by the capitalist, he is able to pay the worker an amount less than his labour value. This is because the bargaining process is weighted against the worker: there are many workers chasing few jobs and there is a tendency for real wages to fall.

The theory has important social and political implications. The profit of the capitalist is not a reward: capital is not a scarce factor of production which justifies recompense, but profit represents a political relationship in which the capitalist is able to extract from the worker part of his labour. This economic relationship forms the antagonistic character of class relations. At the same time it provides the legitimacy for the expropriation of the capitalist: his private property is theft; only the working class has a right to the produce of property, for the working class alone is the producing class. Under capitalism there is a lack of correspondence between the real needs of the worker and what is thrust on him by the capitalist system. The worker is 'alienated': his life is fragmented, he lacks a unity within himself, with other people and with nature.

The ideology of capitalism, argues Marx, seeks to deceive the worker, to persuade him that profit is justified as a payment for risk or the consumption forgone by the investor, that capitalist and worker have a common, not a conflicting interest. To accept such views is to show one's 'false consciousness': that is, to be unaware of one's real class interest. Marx believed that the proletariat would become class-conscious. The education necessary to operate a highly developed economy, together with the growing intensity of the class struggle, of the increasing 'immiseration of the proletariat', would transform it from a class 'in itself' to a class 'for itself'. (A class 'in itself' may be identified simply by the fact of class position (workers, capitalists); a class 'for itself' is one highly aware of its political aims and the antagonistic nature of its class opponent – it is dynamic, seeking to change the *status quo*.) In this way the subjective psychological and political condition of the proletariat coincides with the objective forces just described.

> Along with the constantly diminishing number of the magnates of capital, who usurp and monopolise all advantages of this process of transformation, grows the mass of misery, oppression, slavery, degradation, exploitation; but with this too grows the revolt of the working-class, a class always increasing in numbers, and disciplined, united and organised by the very mechanism of the process of capitalist production itself. The monopoly of capital becomes a fetter upon the mode of production, which has sprung up and flourished with, and under it. Centralisation of the means of production and socialisation of labour at last reach a point where they become incompatible with their capitalist integument. This integument is burst asunder. The knell of capitalist private property sounds. The expropriators are expropriated.[10]

Revolution would usher in socialism, the first stage of communist society. (On the analysis of communism, see below chapter 5).

To summarize, we may define *capitalism*, in a Marxist sense, *as an antagonistic mode of production having commodity production with goods exchanged on a market for profit (surplus); ownership of the means of production and sale of labour power give rise to two antagonistic social classes – bourgeoisie and proletariat.* Some of the essential features of capitalism are shown in Table 2.1. In Marx's analysis of capitalism, the salient points may be stated as follows. First, production takes place for the sale of products to realize profit (or surplus) for the capitalist. Second, this process entails the extraction of profit from the working class: this is class exploitation. Third, the relationship between the capitalist class (or bourgeoisie) and the proletariat, being based on exploitation, is antagonistic. Fourth, the state apparatus and other social institutions, such as schools, function to replicate the capitalist system. They are not politically neutral bodies, but are 'in correspondence' with the interests of the dominant capitalist class.[11] Fifth, competitive production, and class antagonism, entail an irrational economic system and a polarized political one. The resolution of such conflicts may be achieved only by revolution which is ensured by the class consciousness and political awareness of the working class. Sixth, the working class, from being a class 'in itself', becomes a revolutionary class 'for itself'.

In a nutshell, modern industrial society is not characterized by political consensus, social harmony and economic equilibrium but by class conflict, instability (slumps and unemployment) and war.

TABLE 2.1: CAPITALISM AS MODE OF PRODUCTION

Economy:	Capital – intensive production
	Private ownership
	Competition of capitals: anarchy of market
	Production for exchange
	Extraction of surplus value (profit)
	Wage labour: division of labour
	Commodity fetishism
Polity:	Ruling class: bourgeoisie
	State as political instrument of bourgeoisie: coercive and ideological institutions
	Exploited class: proletariat
	Political process: conflict between classes
Social:	Family reproducing capitalist relations
	Distribution (goods, services) by class position – privileges of bourgeoisie
	Alienation of workers
	Capitalists alienated through 'fetishism' of commodity production

Criticisms of Marxism

During the past hundred years a major concern of Western scholarship has been to debate, and to refute, Marx's theory of capitalism and to deny the possibility of socialism. The nature of Soviet society has been a component in this debate and we shall take up, at other places in this book, some of the major issues. Here, however, we may attempt to encapsulate some of the principal arguments advanced in opposition to the views outlined above. Many of these arguments are a general critique of Marxism, in addition to being a delegitimation of the policy of the Bolsheviks and the structure and process of contemporary socialist states.[12]

The Marxist conception of capitalism may be analysed at different levels: (a) as a theory of history, (b) as a description of the major features of modern Western society and (c) as a prescription for the evolution of socialism. The essence of the non-Marxist position is that modern industrial systems are characterized by rationality, consensus and inter-dependence. By rationality it is asserted that social actions and the outcomes of collective decisions (through government) are the results of the calculated pursuit of individual, group and social interests. Rather than there being an anarchy of production and government, the recent history of mankind has been toward greater rational decision, to the fulfilment of human need. Modern Western societies are based on consensus, on a common set of values which are shared by almost all strata of the population. Such values are those of freedom of the individual, the right to own property, to individual advancement and striving, to compromise over disagreements. There is a widely held view that the distribution of resources (wealth, money, power) is legitimate, and that reallocations may be achieved through parliamentary-type politics. There is an interdependence of various parts of the social system. No one institution (say the economic system) plays a predetermining role. The political, social and economic areas of life intersect and influence each other. There is a constant web of interactions, of mutual adjustment, of complementarity and trust. In this view of modern society, conflict and antagonism are not absent: rather, they are reconciled and regulated through a constant process of mutual adjustment, compromise and accommodation. This orientation in outlook might be termed one of mutual exchange.

Such lines of reasoning, it will be appreciated, have not been articulated by any one writer, but represent, in my own view, an alternative conception of an 'industrial society' which is explicitly, but more often implicitly, used as a rejection of the Marxist position. I would single out four main components in this approach.

First, specialization and the division of labour have enabled capital – intensive industrialization to take place. This has greatly expanded the levels of production, but it has not given rise to class conflict on the basis of property relations. Social stratification, with a hierarchy of occupational and educational groups, is a more relevant criterion of social position than class position. A further implication of this argument is that, if economic (property) classes are not a fundamental determinant of social relations, then the abolition of such classes will not lead to a really 'classless' society. Some, it is argued, will always be taking decisions and others, the majority, will be subject to them. This is a consequence of the division of labour, not of ownership relations. The obvious Marxist retort to this is that under communism there will be no division of labour. Some Marxists, however, have taken this point, and conceded that, though the abolition of classes is a fundamental objective of Marxism, the division of labour in some form will prevail, even under communism.[13]

Second, non-Marxists might concede that Marx in the *early* days of capitalism may have pointed to a significant opposition between bourgeoisie and proletariat. This is not so in the later twentieth century. Ralph Dahrendorf has denied that 'capitalism' in its nineteenth-century form still exists. The 'typical capitalist', he says, is concurrently: 'legal owner of his factory, practical manager of production and supreme commander of his workers'.[14] Modern industrial society, however, is distinguished by a division of ownership from control. The individual factory owner has been superseded by the mass shareholders of the modern corporation: ownership has been widely distributed through pension schemes and the like. The entrepreneur as 'supreme commander of his workers' has been replaced by a bureaucratic system of organization with salaried officials. They are not part of a 'class struggle' but represent responsible management. They seek more than the extraction of surplus value and profit maximization. Non-Marxists hold that they have a responsibility to the workforce and to society at large.[15]

Third, the Marxist idea of politics being the expression of class struggle has been falsified by the historical experience of the twentieth century. Socialist revolutions have occurred in relatively backward peasant countries like Russia with a dominant feudal class and where the bourgeoisie has been insignificant and the proletariat small. In advanced industrial countries the working class has lacked revolutionary consciousness. Marx's view of industrial relations has been falsified. It is claimed that workers have been able to improve their position *vis-à-vis* capitalists through the stronger bargaining power afforded by trade unions. Therefore, proletarian immiseration and degradation and polarized class relations have not occurred. The modern state is an institution which has mitigated many of the ills foreseen by Marx: it acts to redistribute wealth, to prevent structural unemployment and to provide social welfare. Social relations too may be determined by racial, ethnic, national or status factors; and these may outweigh purely class considerations.

There is no single focus of politics in modern industrial societies. Non-Marxists would point to a moving constellation of pressure group interests and political parties. The complexity of modern society leads to bureaucracy and professionalism. Bureaucrats in administering (and making) the rules and professionals claiming specialized knowledge and expertise become entrenched opponents of democracy. Soviet-type societies, furthermore, become bureaucracies par excellence. A Western socialist perspective stemming from this position opposes Soviet communism on the grounds that organization and centralization are by definition anti-democratic. Such writers stress the spontaneity of the masses, and advocate grass roots democracy based on workers' control. This is an anarchist criticism of Marxism and Leninism: it sees government, hierarchy, authority and bureaucracy as the opponents of freedom and democracy. Marxist–Leninists would retort that property is more important than authority and that in practice both 'spontaneity' and workers' control are irrelevant and even harmful to the revolutionary struggle under capitalism. Successful revolutionary activity in the twentieth century, they would add, has been based on Lenin's world view, and both social democracy and anarcho-syndicalism have failed to counter capitalism with a mass-based revolutionary movement. But this argument in turn, it may be pointed out, concedes a fault in Marx's own analysis – the working class in advanced capitalist countries has not developed its own revolutionary consciousness; it has participated in 'bourgeois' rather than 'proletarian' politics.

Fourth, all the points noted above lead non-Marxists to reject the tenets of historical and dialectical materialism. They argue that the historical process is a continuous stream of events and processes which are not reducible to thesis, antithesis and synthesis. The Marxist view of social change, of progressive leaps from one stage to another, does not adequately explain decay or stagnation. The relationship between the basis and superstructure is often ambiguous. If one admits that the superstructure can play a determinant role in social change, then the power of economic factors is reduced. Critics of Marxism have pointed out that the role of 'great men' as agents of social change is belittled and that the theory ignores chance. The notion of a 'communist' society meeting human needs is Utopian. It is claimed that 'abundance' in the Marxist sense is a pipe-dream, for abundance is only relative; there will always be shortages of some goods relative to others. Social hierarchy, it is claimed, will always persist, because some men and women are inherently superior to others – by intelligence or physical dexterity – while some men and women will have occupational roles which give them status – the scientist, the politician, the doctor, the creative writer. At the root of all objections to the notion of a communist society is a pessimistic view of human nature: that man seeks power and desires inequality, that conflict is endemic, that police will always be necessary to maintain order and control. There is no authority to which one may appeal to resolve this disagreement; it is a matter of belief about the potential of the human race.

In criticizing rather dogmatic interpretations of Marx, it is easy to become dogmatic oneself; to see Marx's writings as a doctrine or as a prophecy which can be either true or false. Marx has been badly served by many of his followers: Marx himself once retorted to over-simplified versions of his views that he was 'not a Marxist'. It is also important to point out that many contemporary interpreters of Marx would concede some of the points of criticism made above and would argue that all scientific theories (of which Marxism is one) call for constant renewal and reinterpretation in the light of historical experience.

Marx has been superseded by history, by events, by the writings of others. Victor Kiernan in a (Marxist) appraisal of Marx's theory of history has granted that capitalists as such may not have 'willed modern capitalism'; some upheavals are 'semi-accidental'. He also comments that individuals and elite groups must be taken into account in explaining social change.[16] Ernest Mandel has pointed out that the tendencies or trends identified by Marx have become criss-crossed with contradictory ones, and a long-term perspective is needed to distinguish the dynamics of development.[17] Contemporary Marxists emphasize the world capitalist system rather than individual capitalist countries. Tom Bottomore has recognized that Marxism is undeveloped in its understanding of the modern state and the phenomenon of nationalism.[18] Marx's writings provide certain insights which need to be revised in the light of practice. His work is a contribution to the study of society in which no one person can have the last word. Contemporary Marxists, however, would contend that the development of capitalism, when seen in long-term perspective, has led to the concentration of capital, to the decline in the numbers of self-employed and to the growing homogeneity of the employed work-force. Competition leads to economic crises, under-consumption, unemployment and the instability of capitalism as a world system.[19]

The experience and status of socialist countries, like the Soviet Union, is also a bone of contention in the debate on the accuracy of Marx's claims. First, it is contended that Soviet philosophers and politicians use Marxism as an ideological tool – to justify the structure and process of their own society and to make illegitimate that of their political opponents: Soviet Marxism–Leninism becomes a kind of ethic of the development of productive forces. Second, it is questioned whether the character of the Russian Revolution may be explained in Marxist terms. Such writers bring into question the 'socialist' character of the Soviet Union and its legitimacy as a Marxist system.

A Socialist Revolution in Russia?

In western Europe, at the turn of the nineteenth century, Marxists agreed that social change was the result of a dialectic process; that capitalist society developed out of feudalism, from the class conflict between the land-owning nobility and the ascendant industrial and commercial bourgeoisie. Communist society is the synthesis arising from the clash of the dominant social forces of bourgeoisie and proletariat. How was this notion related to Russia at the beginning of the twentieth century? How did Russian Marxists perceive the course of change?

Russia did not fit very easily into either of the ideal types of feudal or bourgeois society. Political power was held by the autocracy and based, in the Marxist analysis, on land ownership. The ruling class was the landed gentry whose values and interests were defended by the Tsar. We have seen that its power was on the wane: the serfs had been emancipated, the landowners' estates were being sold, capitalist enterprises were being set up. At first sight, it would seem that the classical antithesis between aristocracy and bourgeoisie was taking place. But we have seen that much of the entrepreneurial activity was carried out at the behest of the Tsar and ownership of the new industry was largely foreign. Russia lacked a strong indigenous bourgeoisie. At the same time we have seen that the factory proletariat had grown rapidly and was highly concentrated in large factories. In terms of their own theory, Marxists had to account for a trinity, rather than a duality, of social interests: nobility, bourgeoisie and proletariat. We should note here that the peasantry was *not* regarded as a social class: it was divided roughly into poor landless peasants (the 'rural proletariat') and the richer land-owning peasantry (the rural petty bourgeoisie). What role should the proletariat play in a country where a feudal rather than a capitalist ruling class existed? All Marxists agreed that they could not live in harmony. All three had antagonistic class interests. But what combination of interests could promote the advance of the proletariat?

Martov and the Mensheviks adopted a traditional Marxist position. In the struggle with nobility, the social democrats should not play a decisive or even a leading role, for this was the responsibility of the bourgeoisie which would bring about a revolution. The revolution would legalize trade unions and political parties and create conditions for a social democratic party on the model of German social democracy. The party, recommended Martov, was to prepare for the time when it would be in opposition to (or the antithesis of) the bourgeoisie. In practical terms this meant the widening of the base of the party and grafting on to it where possible the emerging trade unions. After the successful bourgeois revolution, the party should not participate in the provisional government as this would entail identification with the actions of the bourgeoisie.

Trotsky (with Parvus) differed by suggesting the thesis of 'permanent revolution' or the 'law of combined development'. They argued that in Russia the bourgeoisie was too weak to carry through the bourgeois-democratic revolution. In support of their argument were used some of the facts already known to us: the Russian state had played a leading role in industrialization, foreign capital predominated, a politically weak indigenous bourgeoisie relied on the Tsarist government for support. Under these conditions the bourgeoisie would not play a role as a revolutionary vanguard. The Russian proletariat, on the other hand, was a more potent revolutionary force. Russian industry had borrowed the most advanced techniques of production from the West. The Russian proletariat had assimilated socialist (Marxist) doctrine and was highly class conscious. The proletariat, therefore, argued Trotsky, could play a dominant role in a revolutionary upheaval. The impending Russian revolution would not stop at the bourgeois stage but would pass on into the proletarian. 'Once the revolution is victorious, political power necessarily passes over into the hands of the class that has played the leading role in the struggle, the working class.'[20] It 'necessarily passes over' to the working class because the bourgeoisie would resist the workers' demands (say, for the eight-hour day). Trotsky and Parvus argued further that a proletarian dictatorship, under the leadership of the social democrats, would be supported by the poor peasantry. While the poor peasantry's political interest was similar to the proletariat's, it did not have the political organization or the political consciousness to lead a revolution. Trotsky saw no active role for the peasantry either independently or in alliance with the urban proletariat.[21] For Trotsky and Parvus, in 1905, the role of the social democratic party should be to lead an insurrection which would pass into a socialist revolution.

Lenin and the Bolsheviks

It fell to Vladimir Ilich Ulyanov, known as Lenin, to formulate a theory of revolution which was to have a lasting impact on the world. Lenin was a Russian. He was born in the provinces, in Simbirsk on the Volga on 22 April 1870. (He died on 21 January 1924.) It is one of the touching ironies of history that his first name was derived from the Russian word *vlast'*, meaning rule, and *mir*, the world. He came from a fairly well-to-do family. His father had had a university education at Kazan and had become a teacher, then a school inspector; he was a devout Orthodox Christian, loyal to the Tsar and was awarded a place as a State Councillor in the lower ranks of the nobility in 1874. Lenin's mother was also from the professional classes. Lenin's early education was received at home, where he was taught by private tutors. He entered the local grammar school and then Kazan University. Here he began his revolutionary activity following the execution of his brother, Alexander, for conspiring to assassinate the Tsar. Lenin was first attracted to the Populists (*Narodnaya Volya*); he became a Marxist in 1892 and thenceforth became involved in social democratic revolutionary activities.

In his first major work, *The Development of Capitalism in Russia* (1899), Lenin analysed the impact of capitalism as it had spread from western Europe. By 1905 he formulated a theory of political action based on the ideas of uneven development. He agreed with Trotsky that the bourgeoisie alone would not carry out the bourgeois-democratic revolution. The bourgeois class was too weakly formed in Russia, and part of it, while opposing the autocracy, would shrink from revolution which, if carried out, would put it at the mercy of the proletariat. Lenin argued that as the revolution would not be carried out by the bourgeoisie, then the party should not prepare itself for a period of opposition in a liberal-democratic republic, the view held by the Mensheviks.

But Lenin in 1905 agreed that the country was not sufficiently mature to support a socialist revolution: social democracy representing the proletariat could not introduce the 'dictatorship of the proletariat' (i.e. the state embodying, through its coercive and ideological apparatuses, the interests of the working class). Lenin objected to Parvus's view that the 'revolutionary provisional government of Russia will be a government of labour democracy... will be an integral government with a Social-Democratic majority.' This could not be so,

> because only a revolutionary dictatorship relying on the overwhelming majority of the people can be at all durable... The proletariat, however, at present constitutes a minority of the population in Russia... It would be harmful to it if any illusions were entertained on this score... The objective logic of historical development confronts [the masses] at the present time, not with the task of making a socialist revolution, but with the task of making a democratic revolution.[22]

Lenin's recommendations for action were based on his analysis of the political stratification of Russia. He saw the bourgeoisie as divided into two parts: the large-scale urban capitalist magnates and the petty bourgeoisie. The large-scale capitalist elements were closely linked to, and dependent on, the Tsarist government. The small-scale capitalists or petty bourgeoisie, comprising the middle and richer peasants and some elements of the urban professional classes, were truly revolutionary; they would be prepared to consummate the revolution. The social democrats (composed of both rural and urban proletariat), therefore, should join an alliance with the petty bourgeoisie to destroy the autocracy and set up a revolutionary provisional government. Lenin felt that a greater role could be played by the petty bourgeois peasantry than did Trotsky. The Bolsheviks should play the leading role in the seizure of power; for the class consciousness of the proletariat and the organization of the Bolsheviks were superior to those of the petty bourgeoisie. The proletariat would have to partner the petty bourgeoisie in the provisional revolutionary government. This was necessary for three reasons: first, to ensure that the revolution went its full course; second, to prevent counter-revolution from the deposed ruling groups; and third, to secure the minimum programme of Russian social-democracy – the eight-hour day, freedom of the press, trade unions and political parties. But the revolution would *not* make a socialist society. Its class character would be bourgeois.

Marxists are absolutely convinced of the bourgeois character of the Russian revolution. What does this mean? It means that the democratic changes in the political regime and the social and economic changes which have become necessary for Russia do not in themselves imply the undermining of capitalism, the undermining of bourgeois domination; on the contrary, they will, for the first time, properly clear the ground for a wide and rapid European, and not Asiatic, development of capitalism, they will, for the first time, make it possible for the bourgeoisie to rule as a class.[23]

The socialist revolution would only be achieved after the increased development of productive forces and the growth of the proletariat. This was Lenin's position in 1905. By 1917 we shall see that his views had changed and he had moved closer to the position of Parvus and Trotsky in some ways. The Bolshevik faction of the Russian Social Democratic Labour Party sought to provide the leadership of the working class under the conditions of a Tsarist autocracy. In its organization it differed considerably from social democratic parties in Western Europe at that time.

Lenin's Theory of Party Organization

We have already seen in our discussion of Marxism that the dominance of the bourgeoisie would be subverted by the proletariat. Lenin devised tactics for the Russian working class to achieve and maintain political power. Leninism, after Marxism, provides a second major ingredient of Soviet political ideology. Lenin may be regarded as adding the dimension of political *action* to Marxism. Marx formulated laws of the development of history, whereas Lenin devoted his attention to political activity. Lenin's work may be considered as the praxis of socialist revolution. There are three elements to Lenin's outlook which must be considered in combination: a theory of decision-making and political party organization; the idea of the uneven development of capitalism; a theory of imperialism.[24]

According to Lenin, under Russian conditions in the early twentieth century, the Russian working class would not spontaneously develop into a revolutionary body. Many workers, not seeing their long-term interests, would concentrate on short-term trade-union 'economistic' activity confined to marginal improvements in wages and conditions. Those convinced of the need for revolutionary action should be organized in a revolutionary party, with disciplined and dedicated leaders and members, to lead the working class.[25]

The need for firm leadership and the desirability of democratic participation were to be reconciled in the doctrine of 'democratic centralism'. Resolute action against the proletariat's class enemies called for a party based on 'absolute centralism' and the 'strictest discipline'. To provide decisive political leadership the party had to be monolithic: that is, unified and centralized in its organization structure, its members bound by strict discipline, its pronouncements being definitive and representing the unanimous voice of the party.

Marxism ... teaches that only the political party of the working class, i.e. the Communist Party, is capable of uniting, training and organising a vanguard of the proletariat and of the whole mass of the working people, a vanguard that alone will be capable of withstanding the inevitable petty bourgeois vacillations of this mass and the inevitable traditions and relapses of narrow craft unionism or craft prejudices among the proletariat, and of guiding all the united activities of the whole proletariat, i.e. of leading it politically, and through it, the whole mass of the working people.[26]

The other side of the equation is the 'democratic' nature of the party. By this Lenin saw the party congress as being sovereign over policy. Delegates representing party members help formulate policy. The executive of the party, its central committee, decides the implementation of policy by majority vote. The leading officers of the Party are also elected by its members. In this way Lenin sought to combine democratic participation by a Marxist membership with the need for centralized authority and control.

Originally, the main reasons for firm leadership and strict discipline and a limited party membership were the conditions in which the social democrats had to operate in pre-revolutionary Russia. As political parties and trade unions were illegal, 'open' forms of workers' organizations, as found in western Europe, led to their penetration by the police and their subsequent downfall. Lenin's form of party organization, therefore, was specifically devised to promote the interests of the working class under autocratic conditions. As Lenin put it: 'Only an incorrigible utopian would have a *broad* organisation of workers, with elections, reports, universal suffrage, etc. under the autocracy.'[27] Though central control of day-to-day policy and strict discipline were important, democratic participation was also an ingredient in the party's organizational form. All party members were to have an equal voice over general policy and the party leadership was to be elected and answerable to the party congress. (The organizational forms of the modern party are described below, chapter 5).

Western writing on Lenin's theory of party organization often stresses its centralism, and the directing role of the centre. It must be emphasized that a narrow monolithic party organization was only seen by Lenin to be necessary at a particular moment in Russian history. In 1907 he said that 'the basic mistake made by those who now criticise *What is to be Done?* is to treat the pamphlet apart from its connection with the concrete historical situation of a definite and now long past period of the development of our Party.'[28]

Lenin's justification for the hegemony of one party leading the working class was based on his interpretation of Marx's theory of class. The working class, being unified socially and having a homogeneous political interest in the abolition of capitalism, needed a single united party devoted to the promotion of the revolution. A politically fragmented working class organized in separate trade unions and numerous socialist parties (often based on nationalist sentiment) could only weaken and might even thwart its revolutionary potential. Therefore, one party composed of workers from all trades and nationalities was essential, though membership had to be restricted, at the time of writing *What is to be Done?* (1903), to political activists.

Lenin distinguished between the social composition of a party and its political goals. The fact that a party is composed of, and led by, workers does not ensure its Marxist nature. On the contrary: 'The history of all countries shows that the working class, solely by its own forces, is able to work out merely trade-union consciousness i.e. the conviction of the need for combining in unions, for fighting against the employers and for trying to prevail upon the government to pass laws necessary for the workers and so on.' The theory of Marxism and revolutionary tactics developed by some of the revolutionary bourgeois intelligentsia had to be transmitted to the workers. It was necessary that the awareness of the 'irreconcilable contradiction of their interests with the whole modern political and social system ... be brought to them from the outside.'[29] This was the task of the revolutionary intelligentsia and, of course, revolutionary working men organized in a revolutionary Marxist party. Here Lenin was opposing the more orthodox social democratic parties of western Europe, based on wide trade-union organizations. Neil Harding has pointed out that many of Lenin's views were shared with other prominent Russian socialists, such as Akselrod and Plekhanov; his views in party organization were 'the orthodoxy of Russian Marxism'.[30]

Lenin argued that such Balkanized trade union movements would weaken the proletariat as a class; they would define its social interest in specific 'trade-union' terms, be more concerned with short-term gains, which would be ephemeral, at the expense of workers' power. One group of workers (say the skilled) would be turned against another (the unskilled) and the capitalists having a divided enemy would remain supreme. Lenin considered Marxism to be a doctrine which emphasized the historic role of the proletariat as a progenitor of socialist society; his own contribution was to devise, as it were, the organizational weapon – the party – as the means to bring about a proletarian revolution.

The main additions to Marxism made by Lenin's theory of party organization may be summarized as follows: first, that ideas had to be brought to the proletariat by the revolutionary Marxist intelligentsia; second, that a political party should be formed to lead the proletariat in its revolutionary struggle; third, that the party should be based on an organizational pattern of 'democratic centralism'. These ideas of Lenin, it should be borne in mind, were developed before 1917.

Critics of Lenin's Theory of the Party

Marxist critics of such views have argued that, if the workers by themselves would not develop a revolutionary class consciousness, then Marx's analysis of class (particularly the realization by the proletariat of its own class interest) is undermined, and that Lenin's theory of the party, therefore, contradicts Marx's theory of class. Marx, obviously, was concerned with the more economically advanced countries of the West having a relatively large proletariat and a more open liberal-democratic political life. More orthodox Marxists opposed Lenin's ideas on party organization and advocated trade-union activity to ameliorate the pressing problems of the workers; they believed that workers would, by virtue of the class struggle, develop spontaneously class consciousness. This argument, even if relevant to western Europe, had little support in Russia, where unions and other forms of workers' associations were illegal. Under the Russian autocracy political organization was more important. Leninism is compatible with Marxism in that it stresses the revolutionary role of the proletariat and the revolutionary nature of social and political change. It should be conceded, however, that Marx had much more faith in the spontaneous growth of the proletariat's class consciousness. Lenin's emphasis on the role of the intelligentsia bringing ideas to the proletariat and helping to create a revolutionary consciousness is alien to Marx. This has led to the charge that the intelligentsia takes on a directing role *over* the proletariat.

Whether Lenin's theory of the party contradicts Marx's theory of class very much depends on the way that one interprets the role of basis and superstructure in social change. Most Marxists of Lenin's generation tended to stress the determinism of the former; i.e., the economic basis 'conditions' politics and class consciousness. Lenin, however, by emphasizing the role of ideas and organization, regarded Marxism as a more voluntaristic and flexible doctrine. When Lenin spoke of the 'unity' of the working class, he referred to what the working class would be if it were imbued with Marxist ideas and aware of its objective class position. He assumed that there was such a thing as an 'objective' class consciousness, which only the party could properly articulate. Lenin fully realized that, in fact, the subjective feelings of the workers did not coincide with their objective class position and led to non-Marxist political leanings which his form of organization sought to combat. Lenin, probably sincerely, believed that the working class as a whole would, with time and education, readily accept party leadership. Lenin, however, left himself open to the criticism of self-interest. The centralization of decision-making in the party, and the absence of adequate democratic controls over the leadership, left effective power with the executive of the party and particularly with the leader. In practice, the 'democratic' elements of democratic centralism were outweighed by centralism: the Party Congress met only infrequently, and initiative, information and day-to-day activity were in the hands of the centre. Lenin, it is argued by his adversaries, was concerned with maximizing his own personal power, and therefore he was ruthless and 'centralist' to suit his own desires for political power. Rosa Luxembourg raised this point just after *What is to be Done?* was published. She wrote: 'The ultra-centralism asked by Lenin is full of the sterile spirit of the overseer. It is not a positive and creative spirit. *Lenin's concern is not so much to make the activity of the party more fruitful as to control the party – to narrow the movement rather than to develop it, to bind rather than to unify it.*'[31]

While it is true that Lenin – like all political leaders – was motivated by a desire for power, this view overlooks the purposes for which Lenin wanted power and the socio-political goals of the Bolsheviks. Furthermore, it is unfair only to single out Lenin for adverse comment in this respect. The advantages of central direction by the Party was a position shared by many other Russian Marxists, as we noted above. Lenin emphasized that the role of the Party was to provide the *leadership* of the working class: the Party could not substitute itself for that class.

This was the background to developments in Russian social democracy before the momentous year of 1917. In that year two revolutions were to take place (in February and in October) and Lenin's strategy was to change.[32]

THE RUSSIAN REVOLUTION

From February to October 1917

In February 1917 strikes and riots took place in the capital. The government's conduct of the First World War and of internal policy was under strong criticism in the Duma (Parliament). On 28 February, the Petrograd garrison mutinied. It became impossible for loyal Tsarist officers to find troops to maintain public order. Soldiers and workers were in revolt against the government, which became powerless. On 1 March, the Duma Committee reluctantly assumed responsibility for maintaining public order. The Tsar abdicated. Rule by autocracy was ended. But what form of government was to replace it?

The Duma, the 'official' forum of public criticism of the autocracy, was not the only alternative organ of government. The Soviets, which had sprung up in 1905, began to assert their authority. In the revolution of 1905 members of the St Petersburg Soviet had been arrested and it did not become a very effective force, though in Moscow it organized a seizure of power. In 1917, Soviets were to a much greater extent composed of soldiers and took more radical and concerted action.

Between February and October 1917, political power was divided between the Provisional Government and the Soviets. The Tsar having abdicated in March 1917, the Duma Committee was the legal government. Formally, the Provisional Government replaced the Duma after the abdication of the Tsar; it was headed by Prince Lvov and then Kerensky. Effective power, however, lay with the Soviets, which had control over the army, communications and the streets. The Soviets independently issued directives: in March the eight-hour day was proclaimed. Soviet Order No. 1 decreed that:

1. all units were to elect men to the Soviets,
2. all military units were to obey the Soviety,
3. all units were to execute orders of the military commission of the Duma unless they conflicted with the Soviet,

4. company committees were to control arms, which were not to be given to officers,
5. soldiers were to have the same political rights as other citizens.[33]

From the time it assumed power, the Provisional Government's authority crumbled. As we have seen, it was in no way representative of the nation as a whole: it had weak links with the peasantry and working class. The activity of the government ensured its downfall. Its policy was to continue the war with the allies and to postpone economic and social change until the end of hostilities with the Germans. This policy only aggravated a situation which had dislodged the autocracy in the first place. The armed forces would not continue the struggle against the Germans and therefore became hostile to the new government. Both the peasantry's demand for land and the working classes' demands for better conditions went unfulfilled. With the abdication of the Tsar, claims for autonomy were asserted by groups among the non-Russian peoples.

As for the organized political parties, only the Bolsheviks, some Left Socialist Revolutionaries (SRs) and the anarchists completely rejected the Provisional Government's policy. The Mensheviks and SRs supported the government with reservations. Russia had to continue the war of self-defence against the Germans. The international working class, however, was called on by the Mensheviks to renounce all imperialistic aims. Fundamental social change had to wait until the end of the war. The leaders of the Cadets, Socialist Revolutionaries (SRs) and Mensheviks all identified themselves with the Provisional Government's policies. The Bolsheviks and Left SRs campaigned against the war and advocated the immediate confiscation of the large estates.

It would be wrong, however, to represent the political parties and groups as having a clear and consistent policy. Many leaders were abroad and confusion was paramount. The Bolsheviks in Russia were inclined to compromise with other groups and until the summer of 1917 had no intention of seizing power. In April 1917, Lenin arrived in Russia from exile. He had a clear analysis of the situation and now advocated a socialist revolution. On arrival he said, 'The robbers' imperialistic war is the beginning of civil war in Europe ... Any day may come the crash of European imperialism. The Russian Revolution, which you have carried out, has laid the foundation for it and opened a new epoch. Long live the world-wide socialist revolution!' Lenin's views in the summer of 1917 were more radical than his analysis of 1905. By 1917, Lenin saw in Russia a possibility for moving from the bourgeois to the socialist revolution: 'The country is passing from the first stage of the revolution to its second stage, which must place power in the hands of the proletariat and the poorest sections of the peasants.'[34]

The crucial difference in Lenin's thinking in 1917 compared to 1905 was his analysis of capitalism on a global scale, summarized in his work on *Imperialism: The Highest Stage of Capitalism* (1916).

Imperialism

Imperialism set in place the final piece of Lenin's conception of socialist revolution in Russia. There were now stronger preconditions for a socialist revolution. Important in Lenin's thinking was the role of the proletariat abroad. If the proletariat in the advanced European states could overthrow the bourgeoisie, then help would be forthcoming for the Russian proletariat. 'We stand on the threshold of a world-wide proletarian revolution ... If we come out now, we shall have on our side all proletarian Europe.'[35] As Russia was part of the world capitalist system and the 'weakest link' in its chain, it was necessary for the Russian proletariat to take the initiative, to overthrow the bourgeois Provisional Government and thereby set off a chain reaction in western Europe. The first task was to seize power, beaking capitalism at its weakest link.

Imperialism, in its Leninist sense, emphasizes the international character of capitalism and the domination of small relatively undeveloped countries by international monopolies, politically linked to the leading state powers. Imperialism, 'the monopoly stage' of capitalism, has five main characteristics:

1 the concentration of production and capital, developed to such a high stage that it has created monopolies which play a decisive role in economic life;
2 the merging of bank capital with industrial capital and the creation, on the basis of this 'finance-capital', of a financial oligarchy;
3 the export of capital, which has become extremely important, as distinguished from the export of commodities;
4 the formation of international capitalist monopolies which share the world among themselves;
5 the territorial division of the whole world among the greatest capitalist powers.[36].

The theory has many interesting implications and is regarded by many Marxists as an adaptation of Marxism to conditions of the twentieth century. What innovations then did Lenin bring to Marxist thought?

First, the contradictions of the capitalist order are 'exported' to backward nations where class conflict becomes most intense. Exploitation of native labour takes place to provide cheap materials for the homeland. In colonial lands, the ruling class is not only a capitalist class but a foreign class carrying out its role through intermediaries and backed up by the presence of foreign armies. Undeveloped nations, therefore, become the centre of the class struggle and national liberation movements play a most important role in the international class struggle.[37]

Second, in the advanced capitalist states, the proletarian revolution is temporarily staved off. This is for two reasons: the working class is able to get concessions from the bourgeoisie, albeit at the expense of the people of underdeveloped societies abroad; and monopoly capitalism, by encouraging state regulation of the economy, reduces the internal stresses of capitalism in the advanced states. It is interesting to note that Lenin cites Engels's thesis of the *bourgeoisification* of the English working class:

The English proletariat is becoming more and more bourgeois, so that this most bourgeois of all nations is apparently aiming ultimately at the possession of a bourgeois aristocracy, and a bourgeois proletariat as well as a *bourgeoisie*. For a nation which exploits the whole world this is, of course, to a certain extent justifiable.

Lenin described this tendency as follows:

Imperialism ... creates the economic possibility of corrupting the upper strata of the proletariat, and thereby fosters, gives form to, and strengthens opportunism.[38]

Here then we have a link with the theory of the party (described above), for 'trade union' activity tended to segment and bind together the more privileged union members to secure their short-term interests. On a world scale the improvement of workers' standards in the advanced capitalist nations is at the expense of the impoverished in the underdeveloped countries.

Third, monopolies protected by state powers compete with each other. Such competition takes on a national form, resulting in international conflicts which are resolved by war. The class struggle, therefore, assumes a global pattern: the class contradictions of classical Marxism are resolved in the international arena and are linked to conflict between nations. Lenin, in emphasizing the role of relatively underdeveloped countries, also justified the Russian October Revolution as a first step on the way to a communist world.

The original Marxist prognosis of history, therefore, underwent an important change. For Lenin, the advanced Western capitalist states were no longer the main scene in which the proletariat would play out the class struggle with the bourgeoisie. Though capitalism was in 'crisis', it was a crisis on a world scale. Its centre of gravity had moved from the industralized West to the industrializing East.

The Bolsheviks in 1917

Lenin's changed world outlook coloured his policy in 1917, which was set out in his 'April Theses'. It called for a boycott of the Provisional Government and the installation of a 'Republic of Workers', Agricultural Labourers' and Peasants' Deputies'. Lenin now saw imperialist monopoly capitalism resulting in a horrendous capitalist war in Europe (World War I) which had brought the European working class to the brink of revolution. Lenin in effect was advocating a similar revolutionary course to that of Parvus and Trotsky in 1905 – uninterrupted revolution. But a major component in Lenin's theory was the role which would be carried out by the European working class – they would follow the lead of the Bolsheviks. Lenin gave a greater role to the peasantry than did Trotsky, and he saw that an important foundation of Bolshevik power was the poor peasants. He advocated the confiscation of all landlords' estates, the establishment of a single national bank and the elimination of the army, police and official class. He said that the Bolsheviks should adopt the name of Communist Party. This would symbolize the Party's revolutionary aims and separate it from the reformist social democrats. Finally, he called for the nationalization of the land and the control of production by a government made up of the Soviets of Workers' Deputies.

From April, the Bolsheviks began to mobilize support for revolution. The Party's slogans were 'Bread, Peace and Land', and later 'All Power to the Soviets'. Bolshevik strength was growing, particularly among the workers in Petrograd and Moscow, among the soldiers of the garrison and among the sailors of the Baltic Fleet. At the end of May, three-quarters of the delegates to the Conference of Petrograd Factory Committees were Bolshevik. But Lenin did not yet control the Soviets. Of some eight hundred delegates to the First Congress of Soviets early in June, only one-eighth were Bolsheviks.

The reaction of the Provisional Government was to ban the Bolshevik party, to destroy its press and to imprison many of its leaders (Kamenev and Lunacharsky). Others (Lenin and Zinoviev) went into hiding. The Bolsheviks of course were not unused to organizing illegally, and party organization remained intact and membership even grew. In August, at the Sixth Congress, a total membership of 200,000 was claimed.

At the end of August 1917, General Kornilov, commander-in-chief of the armed forces, sought to destroy the Soviets and reorganize the Provisional Government. He marched troops on Petrograd. His venture failed dismally. Resistance was put up by the Soviets and the General was unable to find troops loyal to his command. Trains were sabotaged and agitators persuaded his men not to fight against the government. The failure of Kornilov showed the weakness of the Right and of the army officers to organize an alternative government. After the Kornilov offensive, the tide turned for the Bolsheviks: on 31 August and 5 September they gained majorities in the Petrograd and Moscow Soviets respectively. Of the delegates to the First All-Russian Conference of

Factory Committees, the Bolsheviks had 62 per cent of the delegates, the Socialist-Revolutionaries 16 per cent and the Mensheviks 6 per cent.

In September, Lenin felt that the time was ripe for insurrection. He coined the slogan: 'All Power to the Soviets'. This meant 'radically reshaping the entire old state apparatus, that bureaucratic apparatus which hampers everything democratic. It means removing this apparatus and substituting for it a new popular one ... i.e. the organised and armed majority of the people – the workers, soldiers, and peasants.'[39] The Central Committee of the party, however, was not in full agreement. Kamenev and Zinoviev, for example, believed that a *coup* might succeed in Moscow and Petrograd, but a social revolution could not yet be carried through. They maintained that the majority of the Russian population and the international proletariat were not with the Bolsheviks. On 9 October, by 10 votes to 2 (Kamenev and Zinoviev opposing), the Central Committee decided to prepare for an armed insurrection. Armed detachments were mobilized.

On 25 October the Bolsheviks seized the Winter Palace. The Provisional Government was overthrown. Kerensky fled. The Military Revolutionary Committee proclaimed:

All railway stations and the telephone, post and telegraph offices are occupied. The telephones of the Winter Palace and the Staff Headquarters are disconnected. The State Bank is in our hands. The Winter Palace and the Staff have surrendered ... The Provisional Government is deposed. Power is in the hands of the Revolutionary Committee of the Petrograd Soviet of Workers' and Soldiers' Deputies. Long live the Revolution![40]

On 26 October, the Government of People's Commissars was established. The first decree nationalized the land. Peace was offered to the Germans. The Bolsheviks had taken power.

Causes of the Revolution

A 'revolution' has been defined by Louis Gottschalk as a 'popular movement whereby a significant change in the structure of a nation or society is effected. Usually an overthrow of the existing government and the substitution by another comes early in such a movement and significant social and economic changes follow.'[41] A similar approach is taken by Theda Skocpol who defines social revolutions as 'rapid, basic transformations of a society's state and class structures; and they are accompanied and in part carried through by class-based revolts from below.'[42] In terms of Gottschalk's definition, the February 'Revolution' was only partial, involving a change of government but not carrying out 'significant social and economic changes'. The October Revolution continued the process of upheaval and led immediately and in subsequent years to significant changes in economy, polity and society.

Why were the Bolsheviks successful in seizing political power? What were the causes of the Revolution? In discussing the revolutionary process, Lawrence Stone has distinguished between the long-run causes (the preconditions) and the immediate factors (the precipitants).[43] It is useful to study the revolution in these terms. The long-run causes have already been discussed: the forces of population growth and industrialization created social classes which could not be absorbed into the autocratic system of government. The state lacked the support of any major social class: peasants, workers, intellectuals were alienated from it; the landlord class lacked strength. The Tsars were unable to adapt the political system to the new demands put on it. The precipitants were the war and its ensuing chaos. Russia's allies, who might have injected sufficient economic aid to save the government, were locked in the grave struggle with the Germans. The legal government, instead of being insulated from direct stresses by political parties and groups which articulated and modified interests, was directly exposed to mass activity, and organs of direct rule, the Soviets, were organized.

As Skocpol has pointed out, there are important structural causes of revolution. Regimes collapse. Revolutions are not started by revolutionary activists – the leaders of the Bolshevik faction were abroad, in hiding, or in prison in the late summer of 1917. Barrington Moore points to three reasons for revolutionary transformation: (i) the hostility of the peasants to existing property relationships, (ii) the 'alienation and dismay ... of nearly all influential sectors of the population' and (iii) the 'disintegration ... of the main instruments of repression, the army, the police forces. This disintegration was decisive. It was not the power of the revolutionary explosion that brought down the Tsarist edifice. It was the collapse of its defenders.'[44] There was a conjunction of government collapse, economic crisis and lack of international support. Skocpol's 'structural' analysis focuses on the ways that parts of the social system (economy, polity, society) are unable to cohere; the lack of integration between the various parts leads to collapse. This structuralist explanation minimizes the role of political-change actors. Like Moore she argues that revolutions are not the result of human agency but of system disintegration.

While the Tsarist order collapsed in February, it was not replaced by new institutions until October. The importance of the vanguard party of the Bolsheviks must be emphasized here. It organized the revolutionary urban workers and armed forces which (unlike in the February Revolution) provided a basis of support. One should not ignore the social character of the October Revolution. Writers such as Kornhauser and Barrington Moore[45] tend to dismiss the urban working class because of its smallness. Moore and Skocpol bring out the role of the peasantry and peasant protest and attribute the revolutionary impetus to the peasantry in Russia.[46]

This emphasis on the peasantry as a revolutionary force is misplaced. Even though the peasant was not an individual landowner, but dependent on the commune, and opposed to the forms of land property relations legitimated by the Tsars and the Provisional Government, this does not necessarily involve a high degree of 'peasant' consciousness, for the commune contained a highly differentiated peasantry. It is also extremely difficult to isolate 'peasant' behaviour from the influence of the towns and to speak of peasant 'mass support' for a revolution as does Moore.[47] The peasantry was differentiated not only between poor and rich, but also in terms of its access to and connexion with the town. The movement of peasants to urban areas and their subsequent transfer of money to the village community is well known. This had the effect of undermining the structure of the traditional village community. As Moore scorns quantitative approaches, he provides no evidence for his assertion that 'the peasantry' was a prime factor behind the Revolution. The fact that a revolution takes place in a mainly peasant society is again not evidence that the peasantry plays an active role in the revolution. The peasantry certainly acquiesced to the Bolshevik seizure of power and were no longer a mainstay to the Romanovs (prior to February 1917) or to the Provisional Government. It is germane to point out that much of the action for change in 1917 came not from the peasant village, but from the army, where the peasant was exposed to urban values and ideas and where he had suffered deprivation. It is also true that in purely economic terms the real income of the peasant family rose during the First World War.[48] The leadership of the revolution (as Moore concedes) was non-peasant. The peasants, if they did share social norms as a collective group (a debatable proposition), had insufficient *political* consciousness to act collectively. Their outbursts were largely spontaneous, uncoordinated, local insurrections or riots. They were incapable of leading a revolution. Trotsky has correctly pointed out: 'as all modern history attests – especially the Russian experience of the last twenty-five years – an insurmountable obstacle on the road to the creation of a peasants' party is the petty bourgeoisie's lack of economic and political independence and its deep internal differentiation.'[49] To determine the social character of the Revolution one must turn to the social support of the Bolsheviks.

The Bolsheviks had their strength in the urban areas of the Russian-speaking parts of the Empire, where their support lay among the proletarian strata. Even ten years before the October Revolution, the Bolsheviks were entrenched in the older industrial areas of Moscow, St. Petersburg and the Urals. It is true that they had only nine million or 25 per cent of the votes in the election to the Constituent Assembly in November 1917. A careful examination of the voting statistics, however, shows that in the industrial centres of Petrograd and Moscow they also had over half the votes (an average of 53 per cent), and in Vladimir province 56 per cent. In the armed forces in the key northern and western fronts they had over half the votes. But more than half of the peasants' party's votes (the Socialist-Revolutionaries (SRs)) were from non-Russian nationalities.[50] The national complexion of the Bolsheviks is important: they were drawn from relatively homogeneous areas socially, which were Russian and Orthodox.[51] Their location was important strategically: it gave them control of Petrograd and Moscow.

Finally, to return to Stone's 'precipitants' of revolution, no explanation can exclude Lenin's leadership of the Bolshevik faction. The Revolution did not 'just happen'. It was led by the Bolsheviks, particularly Lenin. This is where structural explanations like that of Skocpol break down. The ideological and organizational resources of the Bolsheviks had existed for a decade before 1917. A conscious decision was made by Lenin to bring about a *Bolshevik* revolution. His charisma over his Bolshevik followers, his analysis of the situation, the timing of the *coup* – all contributed to the victory of the Bolshevik Party. The slogans of 'Bread, Peace and Land' and 'All Power to the Soviets' caught and galvanized the public mood. In the summer of 1917 economic conditions in Petrograd worsened. The expectations of an early peace dwindled.[52] These factors, given the decline in political allegiance to the incumbent political elites and the severe political and economic disjunctions exacerbated by war, enabled the seizure of power by a socialist party to take place in a backward agrarian country. Within structural limits it is people who make their own history.

The 'dictatorship of the proletariat', paradoxically for Marxists, took place in the country where the working class was in a minority. The Constituent Assembly, which met in the winter of 1917, had a majority of Socialist Revolutionaries (410 delegates) compared to the Bolshevik 175 (the nationalist minority parties had 86, the Cadets 17 and the Mensheviks 16). These figures do not coincide with voting strength: the Bolsheviks had some 25 per cent of the votes compared to the Socialist Revolutionaries' 38 per cent; the Mensheviks had only 3 per cent.

Whatever interpretation one may put on the Bolshevik strategy of revolution in October 1917, there can be no doubt that Russia had not reached the peak of bourgeois social and economic development. Despite considerable industrial growth before the revolution, the country was still backward. As we have seen, economic take-off had occurred, but the country had a low industrial capacity, a small working class, and the greatest part of the peasantry was illiterate. Can it be said that the Bolshevik Revolution proves Marxism to be a false doctrine? Some contemporary writers argue that it does. First they argue that, rather than the revolutionary proletariat destroying capitalism, in fact the 'bourgeois revolution' was about to be carried out by a movement hostile to the traditional aims of the middle class. Second, it is said that the Marxian interpretation of history has been falsified by the historical process itself: feudalism does not lead to socialism via capitalism. 'One conclusion at least must be drawn from the Soviet experiment and this is that history can bypass the phase of capitalism. The main task of the Soviet regime has been the growth of the economy, the building of heavy industry, which were the tasks which Marx allocated to capitalism.'[53] This interpretation of Marxist doctrine is formal; it assumes that Marxism is a 'doctrine'. Rather like Stalin's conception of the USSR as a 'socialist' society (see below pp. 141–2), it is mechanical and scholastic in approach. Marxism is a method of analysing society, and as a method it may be modified and amended in the light of experience; otherwise it is a dogma. Marxism, both as a theory of revolution and as a predictor of the course of development of societies, is itself open to amendment in the light of historical development and experience. All scientific advancements lead to new problems and new dilemmas which require creative thought. The question of whether a revolution fulfils Marxist prophecy is a pointless one, because Marx was not a prophet. The Bolshevik Revolution was not an inevitable event in history for there are no inevitable events. The social and economic changes once started in the nineteenth century continued under their own momentum and undermined the autocracy. The administrative machinery could not cope. The war aggravated the economic and political problems. The lack of leadership by the Provisional Government perpetuated the stresses in the social system. The Bolshevik Party capitalized on this situation. It provided intellectual and organizational resources to carry out a revolution. Its leaders were the only ones who were capable of seizing power and keeping it. Any adequate analysis of the revolutionary process must take into account both long-run and precipitating elements: they include chance and economic, military, ideological, and individual factors. Structural and voluntarist factors have to be combined to explain revolution.

NOTES

1 Foreign Languages Publishing House (1961). See also H. Fleischer, *Short Handbook of Communist Ideology* (1965).
2 'The German Ideology', cited by T.B. Bottomore and M. Rubel, *Karl Marx, Selected Writings in Sociology and Social Philosophy* (1963), p. 75.
3 'The Manifesto of the Communist Party', in K. Marx and F. Engels, *Selected Works* (1958), vol. 1, p. 34.
4 F. Engels, *Anti-Dühring* (1954), p. 369.
5 *Fundamentals of Marxism–Leninism* (1961), p. 154. An alternative formulation is Asiatic, ancient, feudal, bourgeois, and communist. K. Marx, 'Preface to the Critique of Political Economy', in *Selected Works* (1958), vol. 1, p. 363.
6 For a modern critique, see V. Kiernan, 'History', in David McLellan, *Marx: The First Hundred Years* (1983).
7 *Fundamentals of Marxism–Leninism* (1961), pp. 94–5.
8 K. Marx, 'Preface to the Critique of Political Economy', *Selected Works* (1958), vol. 1, p. 363.
9 F. Engels, 'Letter to Mehring', 14 July 1893, cited by S. Hook, *Towards the Understanding of Karl Marx* (1933), pp. 282–3.
10 *Capital*, vol. 1 (1958), p. 763.
11 This line of reasoning is stressed by G.A. Cohen, *Karl Marx's Theory of History: A Defence* (1978).
12 For further accounts and criticism see: C.W. Mills, *The Marxists* (1962); R.N. Carew Hunt, *The Theory and Practice of Communism* (1963); K.R. Popper, *The Open Society and its Enemies* (1945); R.C. Tucker, *Philosophy and Myth in Karl Marx* (1961); R. Dahrendorf, *Class and Class Conflict in an Industrial Society* (1959); L. Kolakowski, *Main Currents of Marxism*, 3 vols (1978); D. Lane, *Leninism: A Sociological Interpretation* (1981); D. McLellan, *Marxism After Marx* (1980); D. McLellan (ed.) *Marx: The First Hundred Years* (1983); E. Mandel, *Revolutionary Marxism Today* (1979).
13 See A. Rattansi, *Marx and the Division of Labour* (1982).
14 R. Dahrendorf, *Class and Class Conflict in an Industrial Society* (1959), p. 40.
15 See particularly, J.K. Galbraith, *The New Industrial State* (1967).
16 V. Kiernan, 'History', in McLellan, *Marx: The First Hundred Years* (1983), pp. 94–5.
17 E. Mandel, 'Economics', in McLellan, p. 202.
18 T. Bottomore, 'Sociology', in McLellan, p. 140.
19 E. Mandel, 'Economics', in McLellan, ibid.

20 L. Trotsky, *The Permanent Revolution*; see also, B. Knei-Paz, *The Social and Political Thought of Leon Trotsky* (1978).

21 See Knei-Paz, ibid., pp. 41–7.

22 V.I. Lenin, 'The Two Tactics of Social Democracy in the Democratic Revolution', *Selected Works* (1936), vol. 3, pp. 35–6. See also David Lane, *Leninism: A Sociological Interpretation* (1981), Chapter 2.

23 V.I. Lenin, 'The Two Tactics of Social-Democracy in the Democratic Revolution', *Selected Works*, vol. 3 (1936), p. 73.

24 For a more detailed account of Lenin's method and theory of revolution see: D. Lane, *Leninism* (1981), Chapters 1 and 2.

25 The classic statement of Lenin's views is to be found in 'Organisations of Workers and Organisations of Revolutionaries', 'What is to be Done?', *Collected Works*, vol. 5 (1961).

26 V.I. Lenin, 'Tenth Congress of the RCP(B)', *Collected Works*, vol. 32 (1965), p. 246.

27 'What is to be Done?', *Collected Works*, vol. 5 (1961), p. 459.

28 Preface to the collection, 'Twelve Years', *Collected Works*, vol. 13, p. 101. Cited by N. Harding, *Lenin's Political Thought*, vol. 1 (1977), p. 161.

29 V.I. Lenin, 'What is to be Done'? *Collected Works*, vol. 5 (1961), p. 459.

30 Harding, *Lenin's Political Thought*, vol. 1. p. 187.

31 R. Luxembourg, *Leninism or Marxism?* (1961), p. 94. Italics in original.

32 For an introductory overview see: S. Fitzpatrick, *The Russian Revolution* (1982). For more detailed accounts: J.L.H. Keep, *The Russian Revolution: A Study in Mass Mobilisation* (1976), A. Rabinowitch, *The Bolsheviks Come to Power. The Revolution of 1917 in Petrograd* (1976).

33 *Izvestiya*, 2 March 1917. Translation in *Soviet Studies*, vol. 19 (1968).

34 V.I. Lenin, 'The Tasks of the Proletariat in the Present Revolution', *Selected Works*, vol. 2 (1977) p. 30. His reference to the 'Russian Revolution' was to the February events – for Lenin, the beginning of the revolution.

35 V.I. Lenin, cited by E.H. Carr, *The Bolshevik Revolution, 1917–1923*, (1950), vol. 1, pp. 94–5.

36 V.I. Lenin, *Imperialism, the Highest State of Capitalism* (1948), p. 108.

37 See A. Meyer, *Leninism* (1957), Part IV.

38 Engels to Marx, Oct. 1858, cited by V.I. Lenin, *Imperialism* ..., pp. 129, 126. See also N. Harding, *Lenin's Political Thought*, vol. 2 (1981).

39 Lenin, 'On Compromises', cited by A. Rabinowitch, *The Bolsheviks Come to Power.* (1976), p. 171. Rabinowitch provides a detailed and readable account of the eventful year of 1917.

40 Cited in James Bunyan and H.H. Fisher, *The Bolshevik Revolution, 1917–18* (1934), p. 100.

41 Louis Gottschalk, 'Causes of Revolution', *American Journal of Sociology* (1944), vol. 50, no. 1, p. 4.

42 Theda Skocpol, *States and Social Revolutions* (1979), p. 4.

43 Lawrence Stone, 'Theories of Revolution', *World Politics* (1966), vol. 18, no. 2, p. 164.

44 Barrington Moore, *Injustice: The Social Bases of Obedience and Revolt* (1978), p. 358.
45 W. Kornhauser, *The Politics of Mass Society* (1960). B. Moore, *Social Origins of Dictatorship and Democracy* (1967), p. 427, and in *Injustice:* ..., p. 357.
46 On the agrarian disorders, see J.L.H. Keep, *The Russian Revolution* (1976), especially part III.
47 *Social Origins*, p. 427.
48 M.T. Florinsky estimates that it rose by 18 per cent. *The End of the Russian Empire* (1961), p. 190.
49 L. Trotsky, *The Permanent Revolution* (1931), republished 1962, p. 154.
50 V.I. Lenin, 'The Constituent Assembly Elections and the Dictatorship of the Proletariat', *Collected Works*, vol. 30 (1965), pp. 253–74.
51 See D. Lane, *The Roots of Russian Communism* (1975), pp. 45–6.
52 See Rabinowitch, *The Bolsheviks Come to Power*..., pp. 310–11.
53 Raymond Aron, *Democracy and Totalitarianism* (1968), p. 206. For a novel Marxist interpretation see: U. Melotti, *Marx and the Third World* (1977). The implications of the October revolution for Marxist theory are further discussed below, in chapters 3 and 5.

3

BUILDING SOCIALISM IN ONE COUNTRY

After the Revolution, Soviet Russia's leaders were faced with the problems of reconstruction. As Marxists, they believed in the establishment of a new form of society previously unknown to history. But what form should this society take? On the ruins of capitalism would rise communism: the polity was to be democratic, the economy was to be governed by the principle of production for use, not for profit, and social relations were to be harmonious, not exploitative. The needs of the people were to be fulfilled by a rational plan and not the whims of the market. In the Communist Manifesto, Marx had said: 'When in the course of development class distinctions have disappeared and all production has been concentrated in the hands of a vast association of the whole nation, the public power will lose its political character.'[1]

Marx and Engels, however, had formulated no plans for the actual organization of a socialist society. The immediate post-revolutionary period was regarded by the Bolshevik government as a transitional one. The 'dictatorship of the proletariat' rather than democracy would be necessary to prevent the revival of counter-revolutionary groups. It was expected that socialist revolutions would occur in the advanced industrial countries of the West. The 'building of socialism' would not be Russia's task alone: as Lenin pointed out in the summer of 1918:

We do not close our eyes to the fact that we cannot achieve a socialist revolution in one country alone, even if that country were less backward than Russia and even if we lived under easier conditions than those created by four years of hard, distressing war ... We are deeply convinced that in the near future historical events will bring the West European proletariat to supreme power, and in this respect we shall not be alone in the world arena as we are now. Through this, the road to Socialism and its embodiment in life will be made easier.[2]

58

The Bolsheviks' Immediate Policy

The period from October 1917 to the summer of 1918 did not see 'the introduction of socialism' in Russia. Politically, the Bolsheviks consolidated their power: from July 1918 other opposing 'bourgeois' parties were banned; a one-party state was set up. The freedom of the press was curtailed. The enemies of the regime were harassed. Trotsky, who was Commissar for War between 1918 and 1925, declared, 'You protest against the mild terror which we are directing against our class enemies. But you should know that not later than a month from now the terror will assume very violent forms after the example of the great French revolutionaries. The guillotine will be ready for our enemies and not merely the jail.'[3] The Bolshevik secret police organization, the Cheka, was soon formed. In 1918, the Red Terror took place against the enemies of the regime. The Tsar and his family were murdered, though this was not condoned by the Bolshevik leaders. Some other virulent opponents of the new order were shot. The Cheka was the instrument of class justice. 'The Cheka is the defence of the Revolution as the Red Army is. And just as in the civil war the Red Army cannot stop to ask whether or not it may harm individuals ... the Cheka is obliged to defend the Revolution and conquer the enemy, even if its sword does by chance sometimes fall upon the heads of the innocent.'[4] An estimated 50,000 were shot by the Cheka during the Civil War.[5]

On 3 March 1918, a peace treaty with Germany was signed at Brest-Litovsk. The most important terms of the treaty entailed that Russia lost considerable territories, including much of Poland, the Baltic Provinces and some of the Ukraine. The imperialist war was not turned into a civil war. Lenin sued for peace when he realized that the army was exhausted.

During the first six months of Soviet rule, spontaneous seizures of power took place, workers introduced 'workers' control'. Some left-wing socialists, rather naively, held that such elemental activity was the introduction of proletarian democracy and many workers' committees regarded their factories as 'their own'.

The main objective for the Bolshevik leadership was to secure the 'commanding heights' of the economy. The first steps of the new government were to nationalize the land and to take measures to give the proletariat 'control' over capitalist industry. It was not until June 1918 that a decree was published nationalizing the key industries of the economy: coal, oil, iron and steel, chemicals and textiles. In December 1920, nationalization extended to all enterprises employing more than five workers using any kind of mechanical power or more than ten workers

without mechanical power. Nationalization went further than the Bolsheviks had intended in October 1917 for two main reasons: first, the workers,
like the peasants, had carried out a *de facto* seizure of property; second,
legal nationalization, it was thought, would thwart intervention by foreign
governments to protect their nationals' property. In Industrial organization, ideas current immediately before October were not implemented.
The 'April Theses' (The Tasks of the Proletariat in The Present
Revolution) declared the Soviets sovereign, but special organs of central
and local administration were set up.

One-man control of factories and industrial discipline were introduced.
Syndicalism and workers' control were repudiated.[6] It is important to point
out, however, that a cardinal tenet of Bolshevism is party control. The
activities of the Soviets and workers' control were always regarded by
Lenin as taking place within the context of the leading role of the party.
Lenin was never a Utopian, 'we do not "dream" of dispensing *at once* with
all administrations, with all subordination ... We want socialist revolution
with people as they are now, with people who cannot dispense with
subordination, control and "foreman and accountants".'[7]

The role of the state was clearly defined in Marxist thought and Lenin in
August/September 1917 had attempted to apply Marxist doctrine to what
he believed was the impending revolution in Russia. In *The State and
Revolution* he argued that under capitalism the state was the instrument of
the bankers and industrialists for the exploitation of the oppressed class.
The bourgeois state machine had to be smashed. The police, the standing
army and the bureaucracy had to be 'abolished'. The salaries of all officials,
who were to be elected and be subject to recall at any time, were 'not to
exceed the average wage of a competent worker'.[8]

With the abolition of the capitalist state, it would be necessary, argued
Lenin, to replace it with government institutions controlled by the
proletariat. In the short run, the state would not begin to 'wither away', but
the *dictatorship of the proletariat* or the proletariat organized as the ruling
class would be appropriate. This was necessary to 'abolish completely all
exploitation', to defend the proletariat against a possible counter-
revolution and to organize a socialist economy. The dictatorship of the
proletariat was essential during the transitional period from capitalism to
communism. 'Revolution consists not in the new class commanding,
governing with the aid of the *old* state machine, but in this class *smashing* this machine and commanding, governing with the aid of a *new*
machine' (*State and Revolution*). Lenin pointed out that only under
communism, when no exploiting class would exist, would no 'special
apparatus of suppression' be necessary. Only with the development of
society from capitalism to communism, would the state begin to 'wither

away'. Under the conditions of communist society Lenin looked to '... the *mass* of the population ... taking an *independent* part not only in voting and elections, *but also in the everyday administration of the state*'.[9] This was an ideal, and far from the reality of Soviet Russia.

War Communism

From 1918 to 1921 the country was enveloped in the chaos of civil war and foreign intervention: it was a period known as 'War Communism'. For much of the time the Bolsheviks ruled only one-seventh of Russian territory, mainly the Great Russian areas of the country, the remainder being occupied by other governments. The White Armies opposing the Bolsheviks had the support of foreign powers whose troops symbolically fought at their side.[10] The decisive factor in this struggle was the allegiance of the peasantry. While the Red Army confiscated the farms' produce, they defended the rights of the peasants to the land they possessed. Although it is not true to say that the peasantry 'supported' the Bolsheviks, they were even more opposed to the White Armies who it was believed did not recognize their rights to the land which had been seized. The fundamental social factory probably gave victory to the Red Army.

In the sphere of industry, the Soviet government in these early years tried to set up a centralized system of production and exchange. This was facilitated by the role the state had played in the past and by the extra war-time controls over the private sector which had been imposed by the Tsarist government. During War Communism an attempt was made to organize supply and output in a centralized manner though, due to the general chaos, this was not particularly effective. The central powers had insufficient information to plan properly and, in short, could not enforce their decisions. In fact, only war industries and some other large industrial units were amenable to control; the majority of enterprises produced what they could barter best locally.

In the countryside, the 'friendly alliance' between worker and peasant was disrupted. To meet the needs of the Red Army and the town population, the Bolsheviks sent armed detachments to the countryside to confiscate agricultural produce, which led to the claim that 'little short of war had been declared by the town on the country'.[11] Lenin's April Theses had recommended the creation of large farms on confiscated estates. These were set up only where technical organization of production was required, such as in sugarbeet and flax. The elemental land seizure and division of the larger units resulted in an equalization in the size of land holdings. Whereas in 1917, 58 per cent of arable land was farmed in units of under four *desyatinas*[12] in size, by 1920 the proportion was 86 per cent.[13] Lenin's pre-revolutionary policy was not implemented: large-scale socialist collective production was not introduced; private small holdings proliferated and flourished.

The economic and administrative chaos cannot simply be attributed to the Bolsheviks' intention of destroying the bourgeois state, though this added to the confusion. The breakdown was caused by the after-effects of the First World War, by the seizure of the land and by the stress of the civil war. Money lost its value and exchange was conducted through barter. Rationing of necessities was introduced: in 1918 there were four rationing categories depending on the recipient's contribution to the economy; by 1920 these had increased to thirty; finally the number was reduced to five. By 1921, money payment of rations, fuel, lodgings, newspapers, medical supplies and post and telegraph services was abolished. Under War Communism, output fell considerably. By 1920 total industrial output was only twenty per cent of the 1913 figures.[14] The decline of output, the inflation and the almost complete paralysis of trade did not bode well for the government.

The worsening economic conditions led to unrest and dissent among the working class. Demonstrations were held against the government in Petrograd and Moscow and in March 1921, the garrison in Kronstadt mutinied.[15] These protests called not only for economic reforms but also for political ones – for freedom of speech and of the press for the anarchists and left socialist groups. The immediate response of the Bolshevik government was to put down the insurgents by the use of force. The first days of Soviet power were ones of turmoil; the Bolsheviks were not only confronted by the systemic social and economic problems which had brought down the Tsar, but also by disruption and collapse which ensued from Civil War. A more significant political response was the introduction of the New Economic Policy (NEP) which involved a return to some forms of private enterprise.

The New Economic Policy

In the West, the abolition of War Communism was regarded by many as proving the failure of planning and communism in general. This view was based on the assumption that War Communism was an attempt to introduce a communist system. Of course, it was nothing of the kind. 'War Communism' signified the complete breakdown of market production and exchange; it was an expeditious attempt by the Soviet government to shore up the economy. The 'abolition' of money was no more the introduction of communism than was the use of cigarettes for currency in Germany after the Second World War. Other proposals, such as those for 'free love', were also a reflection of the breakdown of social norms rather than of the introduction of 'communism'. In Lenin's words: 'War Communism was thrust upon us by war and ruin. It was not, nor could be, a policy that corresponded to the economy tasks of the proletariat. It was a temporary measure.'[16]

The New Economic Policy (NEP) was introduced primarily to get the economy back on its feet. To the control of the commanding heights of the economy (through the nationalization of banking and large scale enterprise) was grafted a market mechanism similar to that in capitalist societies. Soviet Russia moved from *de jure* administrative control to a mixed economy, in which large industrial units were nationalized, but small industrial units and almost the whole of agriculture were privately owned. Prices were determined by the market through the operation of supply and demand. Other policies moved away from the immediate post-revolutionary administrative system. Gradually wage differentials were increased and higher payments to 'specialists' were justified. In this respect Lenin before the revolution had overestimated both the degree to which a modern economy could be run without wage differentials and incentives and the ability of the proletariat to perform the functions of bourgeois technical staff. NEP added financial stimuli to promote production.

The economic aims of the government were to restore the value of money, to induce the peasants to give up grain to feed the towns, and to bring up industrial production to the pre-war level. The arbitrary requistioning of peasants' produce was stopped. In its place, the peasant had to hand over to the state by way of a 'tax in kind', a certain proportion of his produce, the remainder of which he could trade on the market. While large industrial enterprises and banks continued under government ownership, other enterprises were de-nationalized. With the exception of war industries, municipal enterprises, locomotive works and factories concerned with major government projects, state institutions were allowed to trade with each other in the same way that free trade took place between town and country. In order to encourage efficiency, 'profit and loss' criteria were introduced and all undertakings were to be managed on a commercial basis.

By 1926 industrial production was roughly back to pre-war (1913) level. By 1927 the gross value output of large-scale industry was 123.6 compared with a base of 100 in 1913, while by 1928 the index had risen to 154.2.[17] The immediate economic objectives of the NEP had been realized. In the political and social spheres the Bolsheviks were now established as a government and were no longer an illegal political party. But the powers of tradition, of day-to-day administration, were beginning to assert themselves over the more revolutionary aspects of Bolshevik policy.[18] The position of the new government was insecure, many of the policies adopted were determined by expediency and long-term policies had still to be worked out.

On the political side, the greater freedom afforded to the peasantry was intended to assuage the farmers and to secure the gains of the revolution until, as Lenin still hoped, revolution would spread to the West. A consequence of the existence of private agriculture and trade, however, was the flourishing of groups with political interests opposed to Soviet power. As we have seen, Russia's Bolshevik rulers believed that economic class determined political behaviour. As social classes could not live harmoniously, Russia's political structure of the late 1920s could not endure. The Bolshevik leaders had always lived in the hope that revolution would occur in the West and that the victorious European proletariat would come to their aid. As the years passed, this hope faded. The Soviet Union was the first socialist and was situated in a hostile world environment. A greater rate of increase in industrial development was essential. Such an increase would enlarge the proletariat, strengthen the Communist Party's hold internally and provide the means for greater military security from the capitalist state. The questions arose, therefore, of how such industrialization could take place and at what pace it should proceed.

Socialism in One Country

We have seen that one of the justifications for the Bolshevik seizure of power in 1917 was the belief that help would come from the proletariat of advanced European states. In the absence of a proletarian revolution abroad and the apparent 'stabilization of the capitalist world', the problem of the course of development for the USSR was sharply posed. At the crux of the matter was the interpretation of historical materialism. Earlier, we saw that Russia under the Tsars was regarded by Marxists as being in the feudal stage of development and that the Mensheviks regarded the creation of a capitalist bourgeois society to be the next principal development. Trotsky, on the other hand, it will be recalled, argued for passing straight through the capitalist to the socialist stage. This argument was taken up again during the period of the New Economic Policy and afterwards. In this post-revolutionary situation, the argument shifted from the problem of carrying out a socialist revolution to that of building a socialist society after the revolution had been achieved. The chief antagonists were now Trotsky and Stalin.

Both men had had a long history in the Communist Party going back to the days before the revolution. In 1879, in Gori, Georgia, Iosif Vissarionovich Djugasvili (universally known as Stalin) was born. (He died on 5 March 1953.) His parents had been serfs: his father became a cobbler, his mother was a washerwoman. Uniquely among the Bolshevik leaders of the 1917 insurrection, Stalin was from the working class. He was educated in a church school, then a theological seminary in Tbilisi, Georgia. He is said to have been expelled from the seminary at the age of twenty, when he became a Marxist. His first job was that of clerk, then he became a professional revolutionary. In 1902 he was arrested and exiled to Siberia, where he later made several other enforced visits. He was coopted, at Lenin's request, to the Central Committee of the party in 1912: he had attended the party congresses, as a Bolshevik, in 1906 and 1907. He wrote *Anarchism or Socialism?* in 1906 and later *Marxism and the National Question* (1912–13). He was a loyal supporter of Lenin's seizure of power in 1917. He became People's Commissar for Affairs of Nationalities. He was a tough, able and dedicated organizer, and he became a secretary of the Central Committee in 1922.

Lev Davidovich Bronstein (pseudonym Trotsky) lived from 26 October 1879 to 20 August 1940. Born in Yanovka, in the Ukraine, of Jewish parents, Trotsky was brought up on a 250 acre farm which his father owned (in addition he rented another 400 acres). He attended a school in Odessa which had been founded by Germans and later finished his education in a secondary school in Nikolaev. In 1897, the eighteen-year-old Trotsky became a Marxist. In 1898 he was arrested and sent to Siberia till 1902, when he escaped and fled the country. In 1903 he attended the Second Congress of the party. Here he sided against Lenin. He opposed his ideas on party organization and favoured more those of the Mensheviks. In 1905 he was chairman of the St. Petersburg Soviet of Workers' Deputies. After its demise, he again involuntarily journeyed to Siberia. Trotsky' views on 'permanent revolution' have been described above. Though he was more militant in his policy than the Mensheviks, he did not join the Bolsheviks until 1917–until that time he remained 'outside the factions'. After travels to France and the USA, Trotsky arrived in Petrograd in May 1917. He became a firm supporter of Lenin's position and helped organize the revolution in October. Subsequently he became People's Commissar for Foreign Affairs and then Commissar for Military and Naval Affairs. This was the background of the two men who sought to control Russia's destiny after the death of Lenin in 1924.[19]

The core of Trotsky's argument was that a socialist social system could not be completed by the proletariat in one country alone. Capitalism was seen as international in character and could only be destroyed by an international revolution. Trotsky pointed out that Lenin in the earliest days of the infant Soviet republic made it a 'fundamental task' to establish a 'socialist organisation of society and the victory of socialism in all countries'.[20] The building of socialism, argued Trotsky, was dependent on the victory of the proletariat abroad: 'The real rise of a socialist economy in Russia will become possible only after the victory of the proletariat in the most important countries of Europe.'[21] He therefore emphasized the international character of socialism and the international role the USSR should play in supporting workers' revolutions abroad.

Stalin, writing in *Foundations of Leninism* (April 1924), had taken a similar theoretical position to Trotsky:[22]

... overthrowing the power of the bourgeoisie and establishing the power of the proletariat in a single country does not yet guarantee the complete victory of socialism. After entrenching itself in power and leading the peasantry after it, the proletariat of the victorious country can and must build up socialist society. But does that mean that in this way the proletariat will secure a complete and final victory for socialism, i.e. does it mean that with the forces of a single country it can finally consolidate socialism and fully guarantee that country against intervention, which means against restoration? Certainly not. That requires the victory for the revolution in several countries.[23]

Stalin's views, however, changed between April 1924 and January 1926, when, in *Problems of Leninism,* he wrote that the above-quoted formulation was 'inadequate' and 'inaccurate'.[24] In the same article Stalin says that the victory of socialism 'means the possibility of the proletariat seizing power and using that power for the construction of a complete socialist society in our country, with the sympathy and support of the workers of other countries, but without the preliminary victory of the proletarian revolution in other countries ... To deny such a possibility is to display lack of faith in the task of building socialism, is to abandon Leninism.'[25] Stalin too found references in the works of Lenin to support his view that socialism could be built in one country: '... the victory of socialism is possible in the first instance in a few capitalist countries or even in one single capitalist country.'[26]

It is somewhat fruitless to pursue the question of who had the right Marxist pedigree. Stalin was in command and his analysis became enshrined as official doctrine. The credo that socialism could be achieved by the efforts of Soviet Russia alone became a system of belief which acted as a stimulus for the population to carry out the later rapid industrialization. It harnessed traditional national and patriotic values and it directed them to definite economic tasks. Politically, it was a positive policy involving independent social action by the Soviet Republic. 'Stalinism' as an ideology contained many of the values specific to Russia's peasant past; it reified the official ideology of the Tsars: *samoderzhavie* (autocracy) became embodied in Stalin the leader, *pravoslavie* (orthodoxy) became the rigidified dogma of the Communist Party, *narodnost'* (national community) became the peculiar Soviet concept of socialism. The doctrine of 'socialism in one country' joined popular sentiment to the Bolsheviks' cause. As E.H. Carr has put it, just as the English worker believed that 'there is nothing better than England', so the ordinary people of Russia became impregnated with the idea 'that Soviet society is the best society in the world, that nothing at all in the capitalist states can compare with it'.[27] On the other hand, as Trotskyists have argued, Stalin lay himself open to charges of neglecting the world proletariat. In terms of Marxist theory, Trotsky had the better case. 'Contradictions' would continue to exist in the USSR as long as there was a state apparatus which would be necessary to defend the USSR from the capitalist world. The level of productive forces was still woefully low compared to the capitalist West. The political consciousness of the masses was still embedded in traditional Russian values rather than socialist ones. In terms of practical policy, there was much to be said from a Soviet point of view for Stalin's policy: from the Kremlin of the late 1920s the forces of world capitalism looked formidably strong and those of socialism extremely weak.

The doctrine of 'socialism in one country' was the basis of Soviet policy and it entailed the postponement of the final victory of world communism. The communist parties subscribing to the Communist International were pledged to give priority to the development of socialism in the USSR. Stalinism was an ideology which adapted Marxism to Soviet conditions of the late-1920s. In a nutshell it provided both a political and spiritual framework for industrialization. It was a Soviet atheistic version of the Protestant Ethic.

To build socialism in Soviet Russia, Stalin embarked on three interrelated courses: rapid industrialization, collectivization and centralized political control,[28] each of which we shall consider in turn.

Industrialization and Economy Change

What were the possible courses for industrialization open to the Soviet leaders? There were four main economic alternatives. The first was one of the policies adopted by the Tsarist government: investment in agriculture to promote the export of grain which could be used to import industrial capital goods. As Russia had a greater comparative advantage in agriculture than in industry, it followed from the theory of international trade that she could gain by exchanging agricultural produce for industrial goods. This course was rejected by the Soviet government, mainly on political grounds. Internally, it would have entailed (at least at the time the scheme was put forward) the growth of an independent, free, farming community which might have politically undermined the Bolshevik regime. It would also have left the Soviet Union dependent on a 'hostile capitalist world' for strategic imports.

A second possible course was to invite foreign investment and loans, or to give concessions to foreign firms to build factories in the USSR (in a similar fashion to the later agreement with the Fiat motor company in 1966–7). The difficulties here were two-fold: such agreements would again have made the USSR dependent on capitalist states and foreign firms, and governments for their part were highly suspicious of the new Bolshevik order which had renounced the debts of the Tsarist government. Thus loans and help from this direction were not a practical proposition.

If industrialization could not be financed with outside capital, either earned with exports or borrowed from foreigners, then capital had to be found internally. Trotsky and his followers, the 'left-wing opposition', argued that this 'saving' should be achieved by squeezing the peasantry. This was the third alternative. In this way 'primitive socialist accummulation' could take place. Very simply, this meant that the peasantry would give more in value to the industrial sector than it would receive back, at least in the short run, and the difference could be used for investment. When this plan was put forward, it was rejected principally because it was felt that political stability depended on the *smychka* (or alliance) between the proletariat and the peasantry.

The fourth alternative was to make real savings in industry itself. If production could rise and real wages were kept constant then a surplus would be available for investment. Obviously, if some of this surplus could also be used for raising the standard of living, then the population would be better off and also the rate of growth could increase. The net investment of the NEP period came mainly from this source. The chief drawback here was that the margin for such saving was small and a substantial growth-rate for very long could not be expected from this source.

The political climate altered in the USSR between the death of Lenin in 1924 and the rise to power of Stalin by 1928. The First-Year Plan, discussed below, was launched on 1 October of the latter year: it profoundly altered the socio-economic structure. A very high growth rate was set and was based largely on the adoption of the third of the above proposals (squeezing the peasants).

The main feature of Soviet planning from the end of the 1920s was that it aimed to sustain a high industrial growth rate. The First Five-Year Plan (1928–1933) envisaged an annual industrial growth rate of from twenty-two to twenty-five per cent. The bulk of this increase was to go into the capital sector. At the same time, a soical infrastructure was to be built up: considerable investment had to be made in health and education.

Rather than increasing production within the parameters of the existing structure of enterprises, the Soviet government attempted to develop new industrial complexes which in the short run might give lower returns than the expansion of existing units. Spurning conventional economic wisdom which recommended adding more labour inputs (labour of course was abundant and capital scarce) to cheaper, less technologically advanced machinery bought 'second-hand', the new industrial enterprises were made capital-intensive. The policy was intended to bring the USSR up to the industrial standards of the advanced capitalist powers. A similar policy was advocated for industrial location. While greater short-run returns could be achieved by extending the existing industrial structure in the European parts of Russia, in the long run output would be cheaper if based on the minerals located to the east of the Urals. Another and perhaps overriding factor in this last respect was the importance of the development of central Asia and Siberia for defence purposes.

The essence of Stalin's policy was to strengthen the country politically and economically by the creation of an industrial base and the formation of an urban working class. It was not the prime objective of the government to promote the short-term interest of the Russian workers in terms of general standards of living.[29] 'Consumer sovereignty', the touchstone of contemporary capitalism, had no place in the centralized planning advocated by the Soviet government.

Having discussed the principal objective of Soviet economic planning, let us now turn to consider the levels of economic growth for the years 1928–1955.[30] This is a matter of some controversy. Here I shall rely mainly on Western estimates of Soviet achievement. Gerschenkron has estimated on the basis of Soviet figures that Soviet average annual growth between 1928 and 1932 was 20.35 per cent for all industry and between 1928 and 1940 it averaged an annual 17.5 per cent.[31] The relationship between these increases and the growth of Western economies may be seen by expressing Soviet output as a ratio of the American. This is shown in table 3.1.

TABLE 3.1: INDUSTRIAL OUTPUT IN RUSSIA AS PERCENTAGE OF INDUSTRIAL OUTPUT IN THE USA, 1913–1938

Year	Ratio
1913	6.9
1928	6.9
1932	27.3
1938	45.1

Source: Gerschenkron, 'The Rate of Industrial growth in Russia since 1805', p. 166.

Gerschenkron points out that the Soviet figures cited are too big. He suggests that Soviet large-scale industry increased at an annual rate of between 15 and 17 per cent between 1928 and 1938 rather than the claimed 19 per cent, and that the all-industry increase is more likely to be nearer 14 or 16 per cent than the claimed 18 per cent.[32] But these reservations do not change the general picture.

Other indexes have been calculated by Abram Bergson, who has also compared the Soviet and American performance. His contrast is made first on the basis of relatively similar stages of development: the USSR in 1928–1940, the USA 1869–1908, and second, at approximately identical year by year comparisons (see table 3.2). These figures are calculated on a *per capita* basis and show higher Soviet figures for nearly all periods compared; this is especially so if one examines Soviet statistics of the 1928–55 period with the American ones for roughly the same time (4.4 per cent against 1.7 per cent). The only other country with a comparable rate of economic growth has been Japan. One comparative study has estimated Japanese growth of real national product per decade at 24.3 per cent 1881–1913, compared to Russia's 14.4 per cent for 1860 to 1913; from 1913 to 1960, Japan's figure rose to 27.9 and Russia's to 27.4.[33]

TABLE 3.2: RATES OF GROWTH OF 'REAL' GROSS NATIONAL PRODUCT PER CAPITA, USSR AND USA, SELECTED PERIODS

Year	USSR Average annual rate of growth (per cent) with output in ruble factor cost of 1937	Year	USA Average annual rate of growth (per cent) with output:	
			In 1929 dols.	In 1954 dols.
(1)	(2)	(3)	(4)	(5)
1928–1937	4.5	1869/78–1879/88	4.1	—
1937–1940	1.0	1879/88–1889/98	1.2	—
1928–1940	3.6	1889/98–1899/1908	2.6	—
		1869/78–1899/1908	2.6	—
1940–1950	2.9	1899/1908–1929	1.7	—
1950–1955	5.8			
1928–1955	3.8	1929–1948	—	1.5
1928–1955*	4.4	1948–1957	—	1.9
		1929–1957	—	1.7

Note: *Excluding war years.
Source: Abram Bergson, *The Real National Income of Soviet Russia Since 1928* (1961), p. 264.

Such industrial growth was concomitant with rapid urbanization. Raymond Aron is probably correct when he says that this rate of growth 'had no parallel in any western country': the non-agricultural workforce increased from 10 to 45 million between 1926 and 1955; in the USA a similar rate of growth (between 1880 and 1930) took twice as long.[34] According to official Soviet figures, the urban population rose from 28.7

million in 1929 to 63.1 million in 1940 or from 19 to 33 per cent of the total population. The social upheaval in Soviet Russia was as great, if not greater than in the USA, for the urban immigrants were nearly all from the countryside, whereas American immigrants coming from Europe often brought urban values and skills with them.

TABLE 3.3: RATES OF GROWTH OF 'REAL' HOUSEHOLD CONSUMPTION PER CAPITA, USSR AND USA, SELECTED PERIODS

Year	USSR Average annual rate of growth (per cent) with output in adjusted market prices of 1937	Year	USA Average annual rate of growth (per cent) with output:	
			In 1929 dols.	In 1954 dols.
(1)	(2)	(3)	(4)	(5)
1928–1937	− 0.3	1869/78–1879/88	4.1	—
1937–1940	− 1.5	1879/88–1889/98	1.2	—
1928–1940	− 0.6	1889/98–1899/1908	2.6	—
		1869/78–1899/1908	2.6	—
1940–1950	1.9	1899/1908–1929	1.7	—
1950–1955	6.7			
1928–1955	1.7	1929–1948	—	1.5
1928–1955*	2.0	1948–1957	—	1.9
		1929–1957	—	1.7

Note: *Excluding war years.
Source: Abram Bergson, The Real National Income of Soviet Russia Since 1928 (1961), p. 284.

Household consumption, on the other hand, shows a different picture. Table 3.3 shows that, whereas Soviet 'real' household consumption (on average) actually *declined* between 1928 and 1940, at a similar period of development in the USA (between 1869 and 1908) consumption increased. It was not until after 1950 that Soviet consumption actually began to rise – and then at a higher rate than the American. Taking the 1928–1955 period as a whole, Soviet household consumption increased by 1.7 per cent, which is identical to the American rise between 1929 and 1957.

There can be no doubt that Soviet economic growth far exceeded and probably doubled that of Russia before the First World War. By the time of the German invasion of Russia in 1941, the USSR had developed an economic base comparable to other more mature states of Western Europe. But Soviet economic advance was not attained without sacrifice. Collectivization of agriculture and political coercion were also part of the process.

Collectivization and Agriculture

We have seen that the land seizure of 1917–18 resulted both in the dissolution of the large estates and the equalization of land holdings: the proportion of land in peasant hands increased between 1914 and 1928 from 70 per cent to 96 per cent, and the number of peasant households increased by more than a third. In 1927, holdings of between 15 and 27 acres accounted for approximately half of all peasant land compared to one-third before 1914. Bolshevik pre-revolution policy of setting-up large model farms was only implemented on a very small scale: in 1927 they accounted only for two per cent of the total grain crop and covered little more than one per cent of the cultivated area.[35] The scale of peasant farming was too small to allow for intensive agricultural production: productivity was low, and methods were primitive; most sowing, a half of the harvesting and a third of the threshing was still done by hand. While the nationalization of the land and its subsequent division in 1917 had satisfied the peasants socially and politically, it resulted in an agricultural structure unconducive to increasing the marketable surplus.

The New Economic Policy, by allowing 'market' relationships to develop in the countryside, increased the differentiation of the peasants. This had important political repercussions. The party saw the peasantry as composed of three main groups: the rich *kulaks* who were the class enemy; the 'middle' peasants, party allies; the 'poor' peasants who were supporters of the government. The rationale of the market meant that the rich would prosper. While *economically* this had advantages – the size of landholdings and the amount of marketable produce would increase – *politically* it entailed the growth of the government's class enemies. To alleviate economic pressures caused by the market, the poor peasants received tax rebates, were given credit facilities and were encouraged to develop agricultural co-operatives.

By 1926, NEP succeeded in restoring total agricultural production to roughly the pre-war level; but grain production for the market during this period had seriously declined.[36] In 1925–6, marketed grain was only half of that of the 1913 amount.[37] There were two main reasons for this; first, the increase in the number of agricultural holdings and the abolition of the large estates reduced productivity: the number of peasant households increased from 16 million to 25–26 million. Second, the inducement to sell declined: the exchange rate of agricultural against manufactured goods was worse than it had been before the war. In 1927–8, as a short-run measure, the government confiscated grain which peasants refused to deliver at fixed prices and hoarders were imprisoned. The government was in a quandary. There were no grain reserves. State purchases of agricultural produce (*zagotovki*) were of great concern. As Lewin puts it: 'the very existence of the regime was at stake during this campaign. Inevitably, the Soviet authorities found that the *zagotovki* dominated all other considerations, and the were obliged to strain every nerve merely in order to survive.'[38] Between October 1927 and October 1928 grain collections declined by 17 per cent.

The winter of 1927–8 witnessed discussions in the party as to what permanent solution should be adopted. There were two clear-cut alternatives. The moderate policy was based on encouraging the middle peasant to produce for the market: the prices of agricultural commodities should be allowed to rise which would allow coercive action to be stopped. If necessary, in the short run, grain could be imported to meet deficiencies. At the same time, the tempo of industrialization would be slowed down. The moderates did not attach a great deal of importance to the possibility of an attack on the USSR and believed that internal stability could be achieved by agreements with the peasantry who were not regarded as being counter-revolutionary.

The more radical policy was to liquidate private farming and to substitute in its place full collectivization. The advocates of this policy believed that the capitalist enemies of the USSR were a real threat and that the time had come to break the *smychka* (union or alliance) with the peasants.

In 1928, official party policy fell between these extremes. Within the framework of private enterprise, the poor and middle peasant were to be aided by greater credits to increase their surplus. The number of state farms were to be increased and more collectivization was to be introduced. In 1927 Stalin at the Fifteenth Party Congress said: 'The way out is to turn the small and dwarf peasant farms gradually and surely, not by pressure but by example and persuasion, into large farms based on common, co-operative cultivation of the soil, with the use of agricultural machines and tractors and scientific methods of intensive agriculture.'[39] Here Stalin's intentions seemed to favour a more gradual and voluntary development of collective farms. The First Five-Year Plan envisaged only about 15 per cent of the cultivated area being collectivized by 1933.

In 1929, however, the party opened an 'offensive against the *kulaks*'. The Soviet leaders believed that the petty bourgeois 'kulak' class were irreconcilable enemies of the government. The forceful expropriation of these households was politically and economically essential for the survival of Soviet power.[40] It was believed that industrialization could not be achieved without a guaranteed supply of agricultural surpluses. These could only be ensured by administrative control of farms. A market relationship would not maintain the domination of the town over the

country. The collectivization drive began. The livestock and machinery of
private farmers were seized for the use of collective farms. It is sometimes
said that around five million peasants who resisted were exterminated or
dispatched to Siberia. The exact numbers are not known. Stalin, when
asked by Churchill about the collective farms and whether collectivization
was as bad as the war, is said to have replied: 'Oh yes, worse ... Most of
them [kulaks] were liquidated by the peasantry who hated them. Ten
millions of them. But we had to do it to mechanize our agriculture. In the
end, production from the land was doubled.'[41] The suffering of the
deported was terrible. The railways were unable to cope. Many fled the
country. Here is how an eye witness described 'dekulakization'.

Trainloads of deported peasants left for the icy North, the forests, the steppes,
the deserts. These were whole populations, denuded of everything; the old folk
starved to death in mid-journey, new born babies were buried on the banks of the
roadside, and each wilderness had its crop of little crosses or boughs of wood.
Other populations dragging all their possessions on wagons, rushed towards the
frontiers of Poland, Rumania, and China, and crossed them – by no means intact to
be sure – in spite of the machine-guns.[42]

For the Soviet leaders, however, the process was not one of cynical
control over the countryside and a mindless attack on the kulaks. They
thought that a radical restructuring of society was taking place. 'Stalin and
his associates evidently decided that this was a time of revolutionary
break-through, in which manifestations of revolutionary elan, however
extreme, should not for the moment be discouraged; and they were
themselves captivated by this mood, and encouraged it, when only their
own positive intervention could have restrained the lower party
organisations.'[43]

The structure of Soviet agriculture was transformed. Whereas in 1929
only 3.9 per cent of homesteads were collectivized, by 1938 the figure had
grown to 93.5 per cent.[44] Collectivization transformed 25 million individual
peasant farms into 250,000 collective units which were headed by a
chairman sympathetic to the communist government. The land was to be
leased in perpetuity by the collective farm. Collective farmers could farm
private plots from one-quarter to one-half hectare[45] in size; they could
also own small livestock. From 1932 surplus kolkhoz produce and that
from individual gardens could be sold on the free market.

While the collectivization process was successful in establishing urban
and communist control over the countryside, in the short run there were
considerable agricultural losses; the agricultural production index of 104.2
in 1930 (1928 = 100) fell to 92.4 in 1931 and to 81.7 in 1932.[46] To prevent

expropriation, the peasants destroyed their livestock: by 1932 the head of cattle had declined by more than a third composed with the 1929 figure, the number of sheep and goats had fallen by half, and horses by a quarter. Even ten years later, in 1939, the numbers of sheep, goats and pigs were still below the 1929 figure. The slaughter both affected the supply of meat and dairy produce to the towns and curtailed the amount of horsepower for the fields. Total agricultural production declined for the period 1930–1938.[47] As a result of this, famine occurred in which many died of starvation. As Peter Nettl has aptly put it: 'the famine of 1932 became a Soviet legend of horror, just as the simultaneous industrial depression in the West is still the cautionary basis of our industrial folklore.'[48]

A more positive result of collectivization for the government was an increase in marketable produce. Comparing marketable production in 1932–3 with 1926–7, grain and potatoes nearly doubled. The only fall was in the amount of meat marketed, which nearly halved.[49] As Ellman has argued, agriculture made a 'significant contribution' to the development of the Soviet economy during the First Five-Year Plan. It succeeded in supplying the industrial sector with an increased supply of basic agricultural goods, it released personnel to the industrial labour force, and it provided substantial exports.[50]

The extent and timing of the collectivization drive may be criticized. As Lewin has pointed out, no administrative machinery had been devised to take the strain of the new system and the massive slaughter of livestock was a cost Russia had to pay for many years.[51] For the peasant industrialization brought him no short-term gain. He was regimented into the collective farm. If there were shortages, he bore the brunt of them. The concession of small allotments, the possession of a few farm animals, and the possibility of trading surplus on the free market went some of the way to appease the peasants politically. Further concessions followed in 1934, when the peasants were allowed to own animals, and by 1938 three-quarters of the cows and some two-thirds of the pigs and sheep were private, not collective, property. Stalinist agricultural policy had adopted Trotsky's view: the peasants were squeezed to allow industrialization to proceed.

From the peasant yeoman's point of view collectivization was a catastrophe. The whole rhythm of work and life was destroyed. He had no control over decisions concerning planting, his produce was no longer his own but the collective's and he was subject to compulsory food deliveries to the government. The statistical achievements of economic growth and the rise in 'procurement' figures were at the same time a tragedy for the dispossessed peasantry. Not only had some been shot, and others dispatched to Siberia, but the expectations of generations had been shattered.

Fear, violence and disruption reigned during collectivization in the countryside. Fainsod describes a report on an area in Smolensk as follows: '... the looting in the villages had induced an atmosphere of panic among the well-to-do peasants ... a wave of suicides was sweeping the richer households; *kulaks* (rich peasants) were killing their wives and children and taking their own lives. In order to prevent complete property confiscation, many *kulaks* and their wives were entering into fictitious divorces, in the hope that at least some property and the lives of women and children would be spared. Sensing their impending doom, *kulaks* in growing numbers were fleeing to the east (Moscow, the Urals, Siberia). They dekulakized themselves by selling out all they owned, or leaving their property with relatives and friends, or simply abandoning their fields and homes.'[52]

Collectivized agriculture also adopted some features to Tsarist Russia: the peasant householders were bound to the collective farm and the land in a way similar to the *krest'yanin* (peasant) before the emancipation of the serfs. As a form of social organization the collective farm was similar in some respects to the old Russian *mir* or village assembly; it was a social and an administrative unit as well as an economic one.

What then were the more important achievements and failures of the Soviet economy during the Stalin era? Its main accomplishment was rapid industrialization between 1928 and 1955: ranging from an estimated twelve-fold rise (Seton) to a six-fold increase (Nutter) in industrial output.[53] For an economy which had almost no economic aid from the outside (though it did have the advantage of being able to copy advanced technology), this is quite an achievement. The command economy system allowed the government to channel a very large proportion of the Gross National Product to the basic producer-goods industries. Centralization facilitated the injection of advanced technology on a large scale into the economic system; it made possible a very high rate of utilization of capital equipment and promoted economies of scale.

I have already mentioned the impact of collectivization in the countryside. This whole process is seen by many commentators as a complete failure. Not only was there a severe social upheaval, but even in economic terms agricultural output fell and the destruction of livestock was a severe blow. The 'rich peasants' were also good farmers and many for political reasons were annihilated. On the other hand, collectivization ensured the collection of grain which enabled the towns to be fed, and the countryside was politically contained. Economic and social disruption in the countryside were some of the costs of political control, which became authoritarian and centralized. The final element in Stalin's policy was control of the political process.

Centralized Political Control

After the death of Lenin, Stalin gradually asserted his control over the party apparatus and government. At the Fourteenth Congress in 1925, he decisively defeated (by 559 votes to 65) the Left Opposition, then led by Kamenev and Zinoviev. By 1926, Trotsky, Kamenev and Zinoviev had all lost their seats in the Politbureau (i.e. the supreme political body, see below chapter 7) and by 1929, Stalin had emerged as undisputed leader of the Soviet Union. Parallelling the economic policy of industrialization and collectivization in the political sphere, the Soviet Party became more centralized, dictatorial and evolved around the General Secretary, Joseph Stalin.

The centralization of party control and the concomitant loss of participation by the rank and file communist must be seen in terms of Bolshevik organizational theory, the political stress affecting the political leaders and the legacy of a political culture dominated by autocracy. We have seen that a one-party state was introduced in Russia under Lenin. It was not Stalin's invention. The doctrine of democratic centralism was one of the tenets of Bolshevik organization theory from the publication of Lenin's *What is to be Done?* It would be incorrect, therefore, to describe the political regime under Stalin as something new and foreign to the preceding state.

Trotsky, in opposing Stalin, advocated the strengthening of democracy in the party. He believed that members should have the right to communicate with each other and to formulate policies criticizing the leadership. The party, argued Trotsky, was 'living, as it were, on two storeys: the upper where things are decided, and the lower storey where all you do is learn of the decisions.'[54] His view that communists should be able to communicate freely outside official party channels was strictly incompatible with the spirit of the party rules as they had developed in a clandestine revolutionary party. Stalin quoted Lenin's demand for the 'complete extermination of all factionalism' and the 'immediate dissolution of all groups, without exception, that had been formed on the basis of this or that pattern' on pain of 'unconditional and immediate expulsion from the party.'[55] Trotsky lost his party membership in 1927, was banished to central Asia in 1928 and was expelled from Russia in 1929. However, in exile he continued to oppose Stalin's rule: he formed an opposition which advocated the overthrow of the regime by force.

It is probably true that Trotsky's organization and support in the Soviet party was small; the 'opposition' was a 'tiny boat overweighted by a huge sail'.[56] But it is possible, as Deutscher has suggested, that Stalin exaggerated the strength of organized opposition to him in the party.

Not for a moment did Stalin slacken, or allow his propagandists and policemen to relax, in the anti-Trotskyist campaign which he carried into every sphere of thought and activity, and which he stepped up from year to year and from month to month. The fear of the Pretender robbed him of his sleep. He was constantly on the look-out for the Pretender's agents, who might be crossing the frontiers stealthily, smuggling the Pretender's messages, inciting, intriguing, and rallying for action. The suspicion that haunted Stalin's mind sought to read the hidden thoughts that the most subservient of his own subjects might have about Trotsky; and he discovered in the most innocuous of their utterances, even in the flatteries of his courtiers, deliberate and sly allusions to the legitimacy of Trotsky's claims.[57]

The point to be made here is that, in periods of massive social change, irrational factors and fantasies often play on the minds of political leaders, who take what outsiders consider to be wild, even self-destructive actions.

Stalin systematically purged the party. In 1930, 116,000 party members were expelled, in 1933–4 followed over a million others.[58] Purge commissions were set up, before which accused communists had to appear. The aim of the party leadership was to root out 'double-dealers', 'violators of the iron discipline of the party,' 'careerists, self-seekers, bureaucratic elements' and 'moral degenerates.'[59] The most infamous events were to follow in the years 1936–8 when the majority of the Central Committee were arrested and accused of treason and sabotage. Death or imprisonment in corrective labour camps followed: between 1935 and 1938 all Lenin's Politbureau still in Russia were sentenced to death.[60] Sixty per cent of the Party's 1933 membership had lost it six years later.[61] There is no doubt that many innocent men met their death at the hands of Stalin's secret police. A letter from the Central Committee to party organizations described the 'terroristic activity' of the 'counter-revolutionary' forces in the following terms:

Now when it has been proved that the Trotskyite-Zinovievite monsters unite in the struggle against the Soviet state all the most hostile and accused enemies of the toilers of our country – the spies, provocateurs, diversionists, White Guardists, kulaks etc. – when all boundary lines have been wiped out between these elements on the one hand, and the Trotskyites and Zinovievites on the other, all Party organisations, all members of the Party, should understand that Communist vigilance is necessary in every sector and in every situation.[62]

The effects of this and similar party instructions were denunciations and repression. Here is how the situation in Leningrad has been described.

The Leningrad Party organisation suffered particularly large losses ... For a period of four years there was an uninterrupted wave of repressions in Leningrad against honest and completely innocent people. Promotion to a responsible post often amounted to a step toward the brink of a precipice. Many people were annihilated without a trial and investigation on the basis of false, hastily fabricated charges. Not only officials themselves, but also their families were subjected to repressions, even absolutely innocent children, whose lives were thus broken from the very beginning... The repressions... were carried either on Stalin's direct instructions or with his knowledge and approval.[63]

Trials of Old Bolsheviks including Zinoviev and Kamenev were notable for the way the accused admitted conspiracy against the regime. Some said they had planned to kill Lenin, and others that they were connected with foreign espionage agencies. The extent to which these communists had been exposed to physical and mental torture is not known. It is superficial to believe that force was the only or even the main factor which accounts for the confessions of guilt. The explanation goes deeper than this. It is related to the ideas individuals have of their relationship to society. In liberal theory, the individual is supreme, even glorified; but in Leninist doctrine, society is paramount. The individual's rights and duties are determined by society: collectivism has the same importance to Leninists as individualism to liberals. If it can be shown, then, that a thought or an action is, or may be, harmful to society, then an individual may believe himself to be guilty. The point to be made here is that in liberal theory a man's conscience is the final arbiter in his conception of guilt; in Leninist theory the collective conscience is the arbiter. The task of the interrogator is to convince the accused that he has acted objectively against the collective interest. If the interrogator can do this, then a confession may be forthcoming and the subsequent trial becomes a formality, the accused readily admitting the ways he sinned against the community.

The motive of Stalin was to decimate any opposition to his rule, real or potential. It is absurd that members of Lenin's Politbureau could be working for British, German or Japanese intelligence agencies. Clearly, Stalin was strengthening his power against his rivals (and possible rivals). He was creating an atmosphere in which opposition or dissent could not flourish. This he did brutally, though, it must be conceded, successfully. Khrushchev's Twentieth Congress 'secret speech' graphically draws attention to the destructive aspects of Stalin's rule:

... The negative characteristics of Stalin, which, in Lenin's time, were only incipient, transformed themselves during the last five years into a grave abuse of power by Stalin, which caused untold harm to our party.

We have to consider seriously and analyse correctly this matter in order that we may preclude any possibility of a repetition in any form whatever of what took place during the life of Stalin, who absolutely did not tolerate collegiality in leadership and in work, and who practised brutal violence, not only towards everything which opposed him, but also toward that which seemed, to his capricious and despotic character, contrary to his concepts.[64]

The extent of the arrests and deportations to labour camps has been the subject of much speculation and enquiry in the West. Robert Conquest, for instance, has argued that about eight million were imprisoned in 1938 alone, a figure which had risen from 30,000 in 1928.[65] Whilst emigré accounts of the camps have brought home the horrors of the colonies and the brutalities performed in them, as a record of the numbers involved they are inaccurate and unreliable. In an exhaustive study of the sources, Wheatcroft estimates that five million was the maximum number of camp labourers in 1939.[66]

The conditions in the camps have caused much indignation. In the early days they were built by the prisoners themselves: ' "Here you are. This is your camp" – An open snow-field with a post in the middle and a notice on it saying: "GULAG 92 Y.N. 90" – that's all there was.'[67] Food and accommodation were inadequate. The work was hard and arduous: construction, mining and agriculture were the chief tasks of the prisoners; others were released to work for enterprises. Many died. Political and criminal prisoners were not separated. As in Tsarist Russia, some of the camps were mixed, though women accounted for only about ten per cent of the prisoners. The treatment of women seems to have been similar in Tsarist and Stalinist Russia: rape was common and they were required to work hard. (Compare, for example, the accounts of women prisoners in Tolstoi's *Resurrection* and Solzhenitsyn's *Cancer Ward*.)

The purges also became a means to supply labour. While forced or slave labour is generally recognized as being inefficient, it is possible that for a limited period and in the short run forced labour can be put to effective economic purposes. Though this aspect should not be exaggerated, the secret police became an important supplier of labour and carried out substantial public works. As there was no direction of labour, it became an important means of overcoming a labour supply bottleneck, especially in those areas where free labour would never have ventured. A fairly reliable estimate is that in 1941 some three-and-a-half million men were working under conditions of forced labour,[68] though Robert Conquest doubles that figure.[69] The arrests, of course, increased the labour shortage generally, but caused some enterprises (e.g. defence) to press the secret police to send them more labour. On a national or macro basis this policy was inefficient because labour was not efficiently deployed; but it acted as a justification for police action.[70] Though the purges were undoubtedly motivated by political factors, once under way they became established and other, though less important, factors (such as labour supply) played a part in perpetuating them.

The deportations to the camps were directed at least initially against 'bourgeois' and 'reactionary' opponents of the regime. In addition, the party itself and the administration were also being purged of communists who were possible opponents of Stalin. But the essence of political centralization and control which appeared from 1928 onwards was a ruthless application and development of ideas which were already largely accepted by the communist political leadership elite. Organized factions in the Bolshevik party had always been excluded by Lenin's concept of a disciplined party. Stalin, in enforcing his will, claimed Lenin's authority: 'Whosoever in the least weakens the iron discipline of the party of the proletariat (especially during its dictatorship) actually aids the bourgeoisie against the proletariat.'[71]

The purges had many detrimental consequences. They dislocated the administration. They deprived the economy of experienced managers. They distorted the distribution of skilled labour. The purging of the armed forces debilitated their leadership, which was forced to suffer the consequences of inexperience during the early Nazi invasion. Human suffering was colossal. While *morally* the purges and terror were reprehensible, they also had important *social* implications. The role of the purges in providing a mechanism for the integration of the society is often largely ignored. The emotional outlet provided by the witch hunt is vividly shown in the following statement: 'I love the Central Committee, I love Comrade Stalin, but I think that up to now the Central Committee and Comrade Stalin have taken a conciliatory attitude towards the Trotskyite-Zinoviev group. Now it is necessary to finish them off – the Trotskyites and Zinovievites – and to finish them off for good. We should give them no mercy.'[72] Rapid and violent social and political upheavals require both the destruction of the values of the *ancient régime* and their replacement with a new value system, otherwise society may disintegrate. The purges and terror isolated and frightened men and women and broke down old values; at the same time, for those who did not wish to be purged or terrorized, they acted as mechanisms through which they could affirm their loyalty to the new order.[73]

Stalinism was not an irrational political dictatorship. As Knei-Paz has critically observed:

In so far as Stalin was determined to carry out a social and economic revolution – and collectivisation in itself constituted such a revolution – total regimentation was a pre-requisite, given the economic conditions, the unreliability of spontaneous support and, in fact, the real and anticipated popular resistance. The role of the trials, the purges and the terror was crucial in this connection – as an affirmation of legitimacy, a discouragement of opposition, and a demonstration of potential and actual power.[74]

The purges had positive effects in the area of social mobility. They removed incumbents of elite positions and thereby encouraged upward movement. The new younger party recruits had rapid promotion prospects and provided a basis of support for Stalin's rule.[75] The renewal of party cadres had important consequences for the social composition of the party. Many of the new recruits were men who had been educated under the new regime. The numbers of 'specialists' (men with higher or middle specialized education) in the party rose 77 times between 1928 and 1940: from 1.2 per cent of party membership to 20.6 per cent.[76] From a social and political point of view these men were as important, if not more so, than the purged, although they receive less attention by Western writers because their presence is less dramatic and their activity less deplorable. As R.W. Davies has pointed out, studies of Stalin have understimated 'the influence in the party and on Stalin of those party members who eagerly supported him'.[77]

Kemp-Welch has also suggested that much policy initiative originated from party officials of lower rank. He suggests that policy was formulated by the initiative of lower rank officials who 'felt bold enough to initiate policy changes on their own, and to push proposals upwards as a conscious act of insubordination to their immediate superiors'. The new 'communist intellectuals' also influenced policy: their methodology was one of 'dogmatic orthodoxy culled from superficial reading of the "classics" ' – of Marx, Engels, Lenin and Stalin. Non-party experts – like Makarenko in education, and Lysenko in genetics – also brought their independent views forward, which were adopted by Stalin.[78]

The bureaucracy and official class which had roots deep in Russian history asserted its values. Pintner and Rowney, after an authoritative study of three hundred and fifty years of 'Russian officialdom' conclude that in Russia a central hierarchy of officials was 'the mechanism through which those holding power attempted to achieve their objectives'. Where other European societies used ' "collegial" forms of organisation (parliament, town meetings) ... Russia used officials subordinate to the sovereign.'[79] The tradition of Russian bureaucracy added its own independent dimension to the process of political consolidation and economic modernization.

It is important to bear in mind that the purges and deportations were not carried out by one man alone. A considerable body of opinion supported these policies: many persons, party and non-party alike, were involved in the process. Not just passively, but actively, they aided and abetted Stalin. It is a one-sided and inaccurate view of Russian history of the 1930s which sees Stalin's rule based merely on coercion and violence:

> ... Thus, he lived on earth and ruled
> Holding the reins in his hard hand.
> Just try and find the man who
> Didn't praise and glorify him,
> Just try and find him!
>
> (Alexander Tvardovsky, *Pravda*, 1 May 1960)

It should be borne in mind that by 1936, the Soviet 'intelligentsia', created largely since the revolution, was some ten million strong. Vera Dunham, on the basis of a study of Soviet fiction, has suggested that much support for the regime came from this lower or 'middle class'.[80]

Though Stalin was in no way an inevitable result of Soviet historical development, conditions of acute social stress, economic scarcity and political conflict often throw up a dictatorial leader to whom authority is given. He personified a goal and a future as well as police activity. The memoirs of Evgeniya Ginzburg describe the attitude of people towards Stalin at the time of the purges.

> ... I looked at him [Stalin] with secret hostility, though this was still unconscious, unmotivated, instinctive.
>
> But you should have seen the other people! The writer, Fyodor Gladkov, by then an old man, looked at Stalin with a sort of religious ecstasy. And a young woman writer from Vologda whispered, as if in a trance: 'I have seen Stalin. I can now die happily.'[81]

The social structure was in a permanent state of change. As Deutscher has pointed out: 'The permanent terror' kept 'the whole of the bureaucracy in a state of flux, renewing permanently its composition, and not allowing it to grow out of a protoplasmic or amoeboid condition, to form a compact and articulate body with a socio-political identity of its own ... The managerial groups would not become a new possessing class even if they wanted to ... they were hovering between their offices and the concentration camps.'[82] The purges allowed policies to be carried out without opposition and criticism which might have undermined the tasks that Stalin and the party had set in motion. The moving force in Soviet history was ideological – the building of socialism in one country. Bolshevism was a theory of development. It sought to transform a backward society into a modern one. But in doing so, traditional processes became wedded to the Bolshevik ethic. Policy was not just a result of Stalin's personal ruthlessness, cruelty and vindictiveness.

In liberal-democratic societies, the norms of political life involve all parties playing the political game, in giving and making concessions. Mutual 'exchange' characterizes the polity and economy. The process of politics and economics is incremental. In the Soviet Union in the

1920s and 1930s, politics was linked to the transformation of the economy. The large scale investment projects, the extraction of surplus from the agricultural producer met with resistance. Coercion was utilized.

SOCIAL POLICY AND CHANGE IN CENTRAL ASIA

Discussion of the Soviet Union, particularly under Stalin, is usually restricted to the western areas of the country. An exception is made for Siberia, but discussion in the West focuses mostly on the camps for detainees and forced labour there. As noted above considerable developments took place to the east of the Urals.[83]

In 1922, of the 140 million Soviet citizens, some 30 million, mainly Turkish peoples, still had a semi-feudal, pastoral, or tribal form of life. Soviet policy towards the Central Asian Republics was justified in terms of Marxist–Leninist theory which provides the all-embracing rationale of action. Here Soviet Marxists make a distinction between the European areas of the USSR and the territories in Asia. (A current map of Soviet Central Asia is reproduced in map 2.) The western parts of USSR were recognized as being at the capitalist stage of development in 1917 (the February Revolution was 'bourgeois'), but the areas of Asia had little industry and were only beginning to feel the penetration of the class structure of European Russia.

In Soviet Marxist–Leninist theory, in the European parts of the country the Russian proletariat was building a socialist society; in the Asian areas, however, this theory could not be directly applied for not only was the indigenous society 'pre-capitalist' but also the social mainstay of the Soviet order, the working class, did not exist. The nomads of Kazakhstan and the indigenous pastoral Uzbeks were considered to be respectively at the tribal and feudal stages of development. Under the Tsars, the penetration of Russians into Asia had created a type of 'frontier situation' in which the dominant Russians encountered an indigenous population at a lower level of technology and culture. The present area of Kazakhstan was populated by Kazakhs and Kirgiz. Approximately a quarter of the population was nomadic and more than half was partly nomadic and lived in the *aul* (a kind of mobile village) The *aul* was typically constituted of some ten families and headed by the eldest member of the largest family. Several auls formed a tribe which in turn formed a khanate headed by rulers who claimed descent from the Genghis Khan. The traditional *bays* (rich cattle owners having as many as 12,000 animals) were not only exploiters in an economic sense but were also the heads of kin groups. Despite considerable seizure of Kazakh pasture under the Tsars and the disruption of nomadic life, the

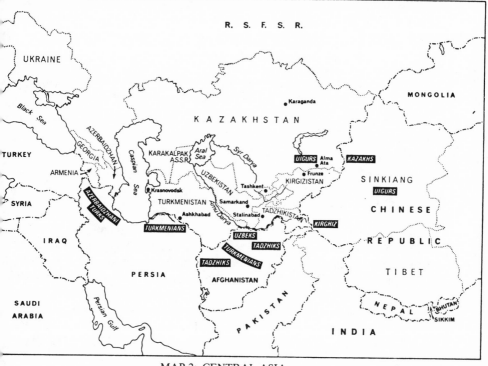

MAP 2: CENTRAL ASIA

Kazakh traditional way of life remained fairly intact into the Soviet period.[84]

Some industrial development had taken place but the exploitation of the considerable mineral resources of the area was hindered by the lack of transport, and the indigenous working class remained very small. The census of 1926 shows clearly the inequality of the national groups. In table 3.4 Kazakhstan is compared with the Ukraine and Uzbekistan. The columns are divided into non-manual and manual groups and sub-divided to indicate the total republican population and that of the native nationalities (i.e. Ukrainians in the Ukraine, Kazakhs and Kirgiz in Kazakhstan). The table shows, as one might expect, that the non-native population (including that of the Ukraine) was over-represented both in non-manual and manual occupations.

The unevenness of development of the various areas and peoples had important implications for policy. The relatively economically advanced areas (particularly the Russian Republic), which, in Leninist theory, had already 'superseded' the capitalist stage, had the obligation to bring about

TABLE 3.4: PROPORTION OF OCCUPIED POPULATION IN MANUAL AND NON-MANUAL OCCUPATIONS (UKRAINE, KAZAKHSTAN, UZBEKISTAN), 1926

Republic	Occupied in non-manual labour: of total republican population (%)	of native nationalities (%)	Occupied in industry and other manual labour, excluding agriculture: of total republican population (%)	of native nationalities (%)
Ukraine	4.4	2.6	11.5	6.6
Kazakh	2.0	0.4	5.7	2.5
Uzbek	3.6	1.3	13.8	10.1

Source: Data cited by Yu. V. Arutyunyan, 'Izmenenie sotsial'noy struktury sovetskikh natsiy', Istoriya SSSR, No. 4, 1972, p. 4.

a major social change in the Soviet areas of Central Asia and Kazakhstan. The crucial agent of change here was the Communist Party which provided the leadership and organized the personnel. Socialism was to be built by the indigenous peoples but with the assistance and guidance of the Russians. Stalin's formulation of the nationalities' policy emphasized the importance of using the native language, of recruiting the local nationalities to positions of power in the administration and, while destroying the pre-industrial class system, of preserving the customs and way of life of the indigenous peoples.

In the short run, Soviet policy involved attacking the leading anti-Soviet classes in the areas, the recruitment of indigenous masses in support of the Soviet cause and the dispatch of leaders from the European Soviet republics to Asia. In the long run, the pattern of internal authority among the native population was to be undermined by changes in property relations and by the political mobilization of the masses through the party and the Soviets. The class structure was changed not only by dispossessing the traditional ruling classes but also by the development of industry and by the systematic creation of a working class. Social institutions, particularly the Soviet school system, were closely geared to the values of the Soviet elites and they sought to change the fundamental values of the indigenous population. Elements of pre-socialist culture were to be retained but only if they could be reconciled with the dominant values of industrialism and Soviet power.

Following 1917 decrees were passed in Asia nationalizing land and water supplies. But in practice land and water remained as private property and were bought and sold freely. In the immediate post-revolutionary period there was 'almost no change in agrarian relations',[85] whereas in the European land areas significant land reforms and seizures of large estates occurred during the revolutionary transformations of 1917 and their immediate aftermath.

The Soviet government tried to restore to the natives land confiscated by the Tsarist government. In Kazakhstan in 1921 some 8,000 *Russian* settlers were displaced as a consequence of a decree providing for the return of land confiscated by the Tsarist colonial administration.[86]

The very small indigenous proletariat was composed mainly of transient labourers and the Communist Party had in practice no organization among the native masses. This was a 'class situation' far removed from any clear dichotomous and overt class conflict on Marxist lines. While class interests undoubtedly were at stake in Soviet Central Asia and Kazakhstan, both the native and European ethnic groups had a sense of ethnic identity. If the All-Russian Communist Party was a 'workers' party', then how could it claim to represent the class needs of the Kazakhs who had no working class? Of course, it did not; for the masses of the indigenous population were bound both economically and ideologically to the pre-industrial ruling classes. From the mid-1920s the Bolsheviks carried out a concerted move against the local rulers. Policy was to try to split the indigenous population on class lines and to win over the poor to the party side. But lacking any firm indigenous support, the brunt of the attack on the local landlord class had to be carried out by party workers of European extraction. Superficially, it may appear that Soviet policy was similar to that of Western European nations in their colonial territories, in that political control was exercised by a new European political elite. A major difference, however, was that the Soviet government attempted to incorporate politically the native population in a much more positive way than had been done in countries such as India or South Africa.

Incorporating the Ethnic Population

Rather than creating a political system exclusive to the European communists, the intention was to incorporate the native population in the major political institutions, both in the party and in the administration. Party policy was to recruit as many of the native population as possible, thereby providing a base which would facilitate further penetration. Two party censuses conducted in 1922 and 1927 provide data on the growth of national cadres. In 1922, for the USSR as a whole, 72 per cent of full party members were Russian by nationality and 4,890 or 1.3 per cent were Kazakh or Kirgiz. By 1927 the share of Russian members and candidates had fallen to 65 per cent: the total (members and candidates) of Kazakhs and Kirgiz rose to 14,731 (1.29 per cent).[87] In 1927 in the Kazakh SSR, per 1,000 of the indigenous population there were 29 communists, in the

Ukraine the index was 40, and the highest index was in Armenia (100). When we compare this index with the total number of communists expressed as a proportion of the total republican population, we see that the European nationalities provided a large number of communist cadres in the Central Asian Republics. In Uzbekistan, for example, non-Uzbek communists exceeded the number of native ones by nearly four thousand; similarly in Kazakhstan, the ratio of non-natives to natives was approximately 2 to 1.

The Communist Party and government apparatus was not founded on an ethnic basis, though the ethnic background influenced the attitudes and behaviour of individuals. Thus the formal organizational structure tried to break down the informal ethnic groupings – unlike racist societies where the formal institutional structure is devised to perpetuate ethnic differences.

In the native auls there was little understanding of the class struggle. Political cleavage was along the lines of kin; often elections were contested on this basis and the party was used instrumentally to further the interests of particular bays. Cases were reported where candidates for executive bodies of the Soviet were selected only from one clan (*roda*).[88]

Class factors were involved in the conflict which had a definite racial or ethnic appearance. Undermining the traditional class structure of the aul involved much more than the confiscation of the cattle of the bays, the power of whom was also based on their role as heads of kin groups around which the whole life of the aul was centred and whose authority was often derived from traditional privilege. Such status and power position were not immediately broken with the destruction of their economic wealth.

The Bolsheviks then inherited a host of social and political problems stemming from the traditional class structure of the indigenous population. One of their solutions was that of collectivization: this created problems of their own making. The collectivization and settling campaign of the 1930s met with considerable resistance from the nomads, resulting in mass slaughter of livestock. One description of the collectivization process is that of Abdykalykov and Pankratova.[89]

Into all auls plenipotentiaries were sent with orders for the Kazakhs to travel immediately to regions assigned to them for pasture and for building of permanent buildings.... After having forcibly communized the cattle and all the property of the nomads [they] ... began to build villages and towns out of the nomads' yurts. In every settlement the yurts ... were set up in straight rows and into each settlement 300–400 households were forced.

There was much resistance against Soviet policy and there were 'anti-Soviet risings' having a 'mass character'.[90]

During the Second Five-Year Plan (1933-7) the resistance was overcome, and by 1936 nearly all the arable land was controlled by state or collective farms. The settling of the nomadic peoples and the destruction of the ruling family groups through collectivization effectively undermined the tribal system and allowed political control to be exercised by the Soviet government in the rural areas of Kazakhstan.

In a Marxist sense, the 'consciousness of the situation' for the dominated ethnic group was defined by the local indigenous ruling classes, and party policy of undermining economically the local ruling strata did have the effect of weakening the traditional allegiance to kin. Evidence of this is again qualitative in the form of reports by party organizers who said that poor peasants came forward to join the party after the bays were deposed.[91] While ethnic forms of identification played an important role in defining the perception of types of conflict it is impossible to understand the political elite's actions independently of class interests. The class interests of the (Russian) working class and Communist Party were opposed to those of the indigenous native ruling class and hence some forms of class and ethnic conflict in fact coincided. In this case the Communist Party sought to undermine the whole fabric of the traditional society. Unlike in capitalist-type colonial situations, the European communists had a definite policy of economic and cultural change and Soviet Marxism – Leninism also provided an ideology of supra-national integration.

Industrial Development and Social Change in Central Asia

A pivotal component in Soviet policy, as we have already seen, was industrial development. Even before 1917, Kazakhstan had begun to exploit her considerable mineral resources.[92] During the early 1930s, Soviet economic plans sought to utilize these resources for the development of the USSR and in Kazakhstan during the First Five-Year Plan 80 per cent of capital investment was devoted to heavy industry: of the total, 45 per cent went to non-ferrous metals, 20 per cent to oil and 15 per cent to coal. Large-scale new industrial centres were created in Karaganda and Balkhash and the average yearly growth of production of industry between 1928 and 1932 was 22 per cent for the USSR, and 30 per cent for Kazakhstan.[93]

The epoch introduced by the Five-Year Plans brought rapid economic growth. Table 3.5 shows the increase in industrial production in the USSR and some of the Republics. Despite the low base, and other possible deficiencies in the statistics (a 1926-7 base results in the overweighting of scarce products in that year), the figures show a remarkable increase in the

TABLE 3.5: OUTPUT OF LARGE-SCALE INDUSTRY IN SELECTED UNION REPUBLICS, 1913–1935 (MILLION RUBLES AT 1926–27 PRICES)

	1913	1935	Growth
USSR	10,251	57,345	5.7 times
RSFSR	7,500	42,904	5.7 times
Georgian SSR	43	640.9	14.9 times
Turkmen SSR	20.9	171.1	8 times
Uzbek SSR	268.8	837.5	3 times
Kazakh SSR	50.9	432.4	8.5 times
Kirghiz SSR	1.2	99.8	83 times

Source: Figures cited in R. Schlesinger, The Nationalities Problem and Soviet Administration (1956).

industrial capacity of the areas. True they were still less industrialized than the Soviet European areas,[94] but were much more so than, say, Britain's African and Indian colonies in the late nineteenth and early twentieth century. The official indexes of industrial production show a twelve-fold increase between 1926 and 1940. The First Five-Year Plan signalled a movement of industry to the east, but the priority for investment remained in traditional European industrial areas. The particular factor endowments of various regions giving comparative advantage to the production of certain products largely determined the kind of investment which took place. By 1940, Central Asia outside Kazakhstan concentrated on the production of agricultural produce and light industry: in Uzbekistan the share of such products in industrial production was 86.7 per cent, in Tadzhikistan it was 70.3 per cent and in Kirgizia 70.1 per cent.[95] By the 1940s and 1950s, the eastern areas of the country began to make a really significant addition to industrial production. Steel smelting for the 'eastern areas' rose from 21 per cent of the total in 1913 to 34 per cent in 1940 and the share of iron ore mined rose from 19.4 per cent in 1913 to 31 per cent in 1938.[96] The Donets basin, which accounted for 87 per cent of coal production in 1913, declined proportionately to 60 per cent in 1938 and to less than half in 1945.[97] Kazakhstan became an important industrial area.

Such changes in Central Asia have to be related and compared to the developments in the Soviet Union as a whole. Such comparisons are illustrated in table 3.6, which shows that the share of workers employed in industry and mining as a proportion of the total population more than doubled between 1897 and 1940, though this increase was not as great as that in the USSR as a whole, which rose from 1.3 per cent to 5.7 per cent between the two dates. In the period between 1940 and 1955, while the numbers engaged in industry and mining in Central Asia again rose, the

TABLE 3.6: ESTIMATES OF OCCUPATIONAL DISTRIBUTION IN CENTRAL ASIA (EXCLUDING KAZAKHSTAN) AND USSR

Country and year	Industry* and mining	Handi-crafts*	Trade	Other non-farm occupa-tions[a]	Agri-culture	Total active	Total popula-tion
Central Asia:			Millions				
1897[b]	0.1	0.2	0.1	0.2	0.9[c]	1.5[c]	5.6
1940	0.2[d]	–	0.2	0.8	3.2	4.4	10.6
1955	0.5[d]	–	0.2	1.3	3.4	5.4	12.1
Soviet Union:							
1897[e]	1.6	3.1	1.5	7.6	17.9[c]	31.7[c]	125.6
1940	11.0[d]	2.8	3.3	19.4	44.5	81	191.7
1955	17.4[d]	1.6	3.8	29.3	36.9	89	197.6
Central Asia:		Percentage of total population					
1897[b]	1.0	3.8	1.3	3.4	17.1[c]	26.6[c]	100
1940	2.1[d]	0.6	1.4	8	30	42	100
1955	3.8[d]	0.4	1.5	11	28	45	100
Soviet Union:							
1897[e]	1.3	2.5	1.2	6.0	14.3[c]	25.2[c]	100
1940	5.7[d]	1.5	1.7	10	23	42	100
1955	8.8[d]	0.8	1.9	15	19	45	100

Notes: * Distribution between industry and handicrafts presents difficulties and generally the figures for industry and handicrafts together are therefore more reliable than those for each of the series separately.
 a Including armed forces
 b Including estimates for Khiva and Bukhara
 c The data considerably understate the numbers engaged in agriculture, as well as the total active population, as in these countries very few women were reported to the census as active in agriculture.
 d "Productive" employment in state enterprises
 e Contemporary territory

Source: 'Regional Economic Policy in the Soviet Union: The Case of Central Asia', Economic Bulletin for Europe, vol. 9, no. 3, Nov. 1957, p. 52.

gap with the USSR as a whole widened. The average annual rate of growth for Central Asia for industrial output between 1940 and 1950 was 6 per cent, the same as for the USSR; between 1950 and 1955 Central Asian industrial output rose on average 11 per cent, while the Soviet Union's increased 13 per cent.[98]

Investment in human capital must be related to changes in the composition of the population stock. In 1913, of the total Central Asian population of some ten-and-a-half million, only about 6 per cent could be classified as of Slavonic stock. As noted above, after the revolution the general tendency was for a movement of population from the European areas to Soviet Central Asia. The urban population rose from 1.3 million in 1913 to 2.4 million in 1939. The non-Asian population rose from 0.4 million to 2.1 million out of a total population of 7.2 million in 1913 and 10.5 million in 1939.[99] It seems a reasonable inference that much of the urban growth was accounted for by immigration and in the inter-war period the urban industries were staffed predominantly by people of European origin.[100]

The Impact of Revolution in Central Asia and Kazakhstan

The impact of the Bolshevik revolution on the character of social relations was uneven. The political structure underwent rapid and significant change, and during the process of collectivization the traditional ruling classes were destroyed. Bolshevik policy was to involve the masses of the native people in politics both in the party and in the administration. In practice, however, the low political and educational level of the indigenous population meant that active involvement was difficult to procure. In the social and economic aspects of life, traditional mores presented a much greater barrier than ownership relations to the Bolshevik policy of forming an advanced industrial society and a working class. The formation of a workforce recruited from the indigenous population succeeded most quickly among the white collar and especially administrative strata. In industrial production the growth of native cadres, both manual and non-manual, was slow.

The different rates of change may best be explained by cultural and institutional factors. Culturally, it was possible through the educational system to create a stratum of white collar personnel who could work principally among the native population. To work in industrial occupations required a movement of the native population from village to town and adjustment to an alien form of labour. In the short run, the training of native manual workers was more costly than importing them from the European areas of the country. The centralization of the industrial ministerial apparatus strengthened the tendency to recruit workers in production from the traditional European working class areas, i.e. it was easier and more efficient to send experienced workers from the west than to train them locally. The growth of clusters of workers of European origin may in turn have made it more difficult for the penetration of native workers in production and have adversely affected the assimilation of the national minorities. One can hardly escape the conclusion that ethnic identity of a cultural and social type still typified the relations between national groups in the inter-war period in Soviet Central Asia. The collectivization movement enabled the dominant class to control politically the indigenous population.

Soviet penetration in Soviet Central Asia involved the decapitation of the indigenous class elites and a cultural revolution directed against traditional values. The hegemony of the Russian communists entailed the destruction of the indigenous ruling groups, the development of the productive forces and the beginnings of a working class from among the indigenous peoples.

The Stalin period in Soviet Central Asia showed similar features to the European areas: political conflict, repression on the one hand, and economic growth, industrialization, 'communist' modernization on the other. In our appraisal of Soviet industrialization of the 1930s, the social, economic and political changes of Soviet Central Asia did much to change the lives of the indigenous inhabitants. The old ruling classes and cultural elites certainly suffered. The traditional cultural way of life was subject to profound change. One's evaluation is not only derived from 'the facts' of Soviet history, but from one's own social position, one's traditions and aspirations. In analysing the era of Stalin's rule one must take into account the political repression, the centralization of decision making, the dispossession of property from hundreds of thousands of people. This caused much misery. But that is not all. The Soviet Union including Central Asia made great strides in the economic, cultural and industrial spheres.

NOTES

1 'The Manifesto of the Communist Party', *Selected Works*, vol. 1 (1958), p. 54.

2 Cited in A. Baykov, *The Development of the Soviet Economic System* (1946), pp. 47–8.

3 Cited by E.H. Carr, *The Bolshevik Revolution, 1917–1923*, vol. 1 (1950), pp. 157–8.

4 Dzerzhinsky, cited by Robert Conquest (ed.), *The Soviet Police System* (1968), p. 15.

5 Ibid.

6 For a definitive account of workers' control, see F.I. Kaplan, *Bolshevik Ideology and the Ethics of Soviet Labor* (1968).

7 V.I. Lenin, 'The State and Revolution', *Selected Works*, vol. 2 (1977), p. 273.

8 'The Tasks of the Proletariat in the Present Revolution', *Collected Works*, vol. 24 (1964).

9 'The State and Revolution', pp. 323–4.

10 John F. Bradley, *Civil War in Russia, 1917–1920* (1975), John F. Bradley, *Allied Intervention in Russia* (1968).

11 A Left S.R., cited by E.H. Carr, *The Bolshevik Revolution* (1963), vol. 2, p. 147.

12 I *desyatina* is equivalent to 2.7 acres (4 *desyatinas* are 10.8 acres).

13 L. Kritsman, *Geroicheski-period velikoy Russkoy revolyutsii* (n.d.), p. 68, cited by E.H. Carr, *The Bolshevik Revolution*, vol. 2, p. 168.

14 Figures cited by A. Baykov, *The Development of the Soviet Economic System*, p. 8.

15 For a detailed account, see P. Avrich, *Kronstadt* (1970).

16 Cited by M. Dobb, *Soviet Economic Development since 1917*, 6th edn, (1966), p. 123.

17 A. Gerschenkron, 'The Rate of Industrial Growth in Russia since 1805', *The Journal of Economic History*, vol. 7 (Supplement), p. 161.

18 For a detailed account see R. Pethybridge, *The Social Prelude to Stalinism* (1974).

19 Further details see: Bertram D. Wolfe, *Three Who Made a Revolution* (1956), This source has extended biographies of Lenin, Stalin and Trotsky.

20 V.I. Lenin, 'The Declaration of the Rights of the Toiling and Exploited People', cited by L. Trotsky, *The Revolution Betrayed* (1957), p. 291.

21 L. Trotsky, cited by E.H. Carr, *Socialism in One Country* (1959), vol. 2, p. 42.

22 Trotsky cites the following passage from the same work: 'For the final victory of socialism, for the organisation of socialist production, the efforts of one country, especially a peasant country like ours, are not enough – for this we must have the efforts of the proletarians of several advanced countries' (*The Revolution Betrayed*, p. 291).

23 *Foundations of Leninism* (Moscow, 1934), p. 36.

24 *Problems of Leninism* (Moscow, 1934), p. 138.
25 Ibid., p. 140.
26 Cited in E.H. Carr, *Socialism in One Country* (Part Two), pp. 40–41. A full discussion of this point is given here.
27 The second quotation is that of Kalinin, E.H. Carr and R.W. Davies, *Foundations of a Planned Economy 1926–29*, vol. 2 (1971), p. 427.
28 For a detailed economic history, see Alec Nove, *An Economic History of the USSR* (1969).
29 See discussion and comparison of Russia and Western industrialization in E.H. Carr, *Foundations of a Planned Economy*, vol. 2, pp. 440 ff.
30 For detailed discussion see E.H. Carr and R.W. Davies, *Foundations of a Planned Economy*, vols 1 and 2 (1969 and 1971). E. Zaleski, *Stalinist Planning for Economic Growth 1933–1952* (1980).
31 A Gerschenkron, 'The Rate of Industrial Growth in Russia', pp. 161–5.
32 Ibid., p. 167.
33 R.E. Easterlin, 'Economy Growth', *International Encyclopaedia of the Social Sciences*, vol. 4, 1968 p. 403.
34 Raymond Aron, *18 Lectures on Industrial Society* (1961), p. 150.
35 Maurice Dobb, *Soviet Economic Development Since 1917* (1966), p. 209. For more detailed discussion, see E.H. Carr and R.W. Davies, *Foundations of a Planned Economy*, vols 1 and 2, (1969 and 1971); M. Lewin, *Russian Peasants and Soviet Power* (1968); R.W. Davies, *The Collectivisation of Soviet Agriculture* (1980); R.W. Davies, *The Soviet Collective Farm 1929–1930* (1980).
36 In the North Caucasus the grain harvest in 1928 was only sixty-two per cent of the pre-war figure. See M. Lewin, *Russian Peasants and Soviet Power* (1968), pp. 172–3.
37 M. Dobb, *Soviet Economic Development*, p. 214.
38 *Russian Peasants and Soviet Power*, p. 177. Italics as in original.
39 Cited by M. Dobb, *Soviet Economic Development* p. 222.
40 See R.W. Davies, *The Soviet Collective Farm, 1929–1930* (1980), especially chapter 1.
41 Lord Moran, *Churchill, The Struggle for Survival* (1966), p. 63.
42 Cited by M. Lewin, *Russian Peasants and Soviet Power* (1968), p. 506.
43 R.W. Davies, *The Soviet Collective Farm*, pp. 172–3.
44 A. Baykov, *The Development of the Soviet Economic System* (1946), p. 327.
45 In certain areas they could farm up to 1 hectare. (A hectare is about 2½ acres.)
46 D.G. Johnson and A. Kahan in Joint Economic Committee, US Congress, *Comparisons of the United States and Soviet Economies* (Washington, 1960), Part I, p. 204.
47 See statistics in R.W. Davies, 'Planning for Rapid Growth in the USSR', *Economics of Planning* (1965), vol. 5, nos. 1–2.
48 *The Soviet Achievement* (1967), p. 121.
49 Full data are cited in A. Baykov, *The Development of the Soviet Economic System* (1946), p. 326.

50 M Ellman, 'Agricultrual Surplus and Investment: USSR 1928–32', *Economic Journal*, No. 85 (December 1975), pp. 858–9. See also: J.R. Millar, 'Mass Collectivisation and the Contribution of Soviet Agriculture to the First Five Year Plan', *Slavic Review*, 1974, vol. 33.

51 M. Lewin, *Russian Peasants and Soviet Power*, p. 515.

52 M. Fainsod, *Smolensk under Soviet Rule* (1958), p. 246.

53 See figures in R.W. Davies, 'Planning for Rapid Growth'.

54 *The New Course* (1923, reprinted 1965), p. 13.

55 *Foundations of Leninism*, (1934) p. 94.

56 Heinrich Brandler, cited by I. Deutscher, *The Prophet Outcast* (1963), p. 33.

57 I. Deutscher, *The Prophet Outcast*, pp. 125–6.

58 L. Schapiro, *The Communist Party of the Soviet Union* (1960), p. 435.

59 M. Fainsod, *Smolensk under Soviet Rule* (1958), p. 221. Further accounts may be found here.

60 For details of the trials between 1936 and 1938, see R. Conquest, *The Soviet Police System* (1968), p. 47. Also R. Conquest, *The Great Terror* (1968). On Stalinism in general, see R.C. Tucker (ed.) *Stalinism: Essays in Historical Interpretation* (1977); D. Lane, *Leninism: A Sociological Intepretation* (1981).

61 A.L. Unger, 'Stalin's Renewal of the Leading Stratum', *Soviet Studies*, vol. 20 (Jan. 1969), p. 321.

62 Cited in M. Fainsod, *Smolensk Under Soviet Rule*, p. 233.

63 I.V. Spiridonov, speech at XXII Congress of CPSU. Cited by Conquest, *The Great Terror*, (1968) p. 236.

64 Khrushchev's speech, reprinted in *The 20th Congress and World Trotskyism* (1957), p. 53.

65 Other figures are: 1930, 600,000; 1931–2, 2 million; 1933–5, 5 million; 1935–7, 6 million. R. Conquest, *The Great Terror*, p. 335. During the collectivization campaign about 3½ million peasants, it is alleged, were despatched to the camps (70 per cent of the total) (ibid.).

66 S.G. Wheatcroft, 'On Assessing the Size of Forced Concentration Camp Labour in the Soviet Union, 1929–56' (1981), p. 286.

67 V. Pasternak, *Doctor Zhivago* (1958), p. 492.

68 N. Jasny, *Journal of Political Economy*, vol. 59 (October 1951).

69 R. Conquest, *The Soviet Police System* (1968), p. 81.

70 This interpretation is discussed at length in S. Swianiewicz, *Forced Labour and Economic Development* (1965), chapter 12.

71 V.I. Lenin, cited by J. Stalin, *Foundations of Leninism* p. 93.

72 Cited in M. Fainsod, *Smolensk . . .*, p. 235.

73 For a development of this view, see Z.K. Brzezinski, *The Permanent Purge* (1956).

74 B. Knei-Paz, *The Social and Political Thought of Leon Trotsky* (1978), p. 436.

75 See Fainsod, *Smolensk . . .*, p. 60.

76 A.L. Unger, 'Stalin's Renewal of the Leading Stratum' (1969), pp. 321, 330.

77 R.W. Davies, 'Ruthless Dictator or Prisoner of Coercion', in *Times Higher Educational Supplement* (21 December 1979).

78 A. Kemp-Welch, 'Stalinism and Intellectual Order' in T.H. Rigby, A. Brown and P. Reddaway (eds.), *Authority, Power and Policy in the USSR* (1980), pp. 125–30.

79 W.M. Pintner and D.K. Rowney, 'Officialdom and Bureaucracy: Conclusion', in W.M. Pintner and D.K. Rowney, *Russian Officialdom: The Bureaucratization of Russian Society from the Seventeenth to the Twentieth Century* (1980), pp. 369, 370.

80 Vera Dunham, *In Stalin's Time* (1976), pp. 44–5.

81 *Krutoy Marshrut* cited in *Times Literary Supplement* (27 April 1967).

82 I. Deutscher, *The Prophet Outcast* (1963), pp. 306–7.

83 Parts of the following are derived from my article, 'Ethnic and Class Stratification in Soviet Kazakhstan, 1917–39', which appeared in *Comparative Studies in Society and History*, vol. 17, no. 2 (April 1975).

84 See Irene Winner, 'Some Problems of Nomadism and Social Organization among the Recently Settled Kazakhs', *Central Asian Review* (1963), no. 11.

85 E. Sel'kina, 'Semey'naya reforma v Sredney Azii', *Revolyutsionny vostok*, 1928, no. 3, p. 151.

86 Irene Winner, 'Some Problems of Nomadism . . .', p. 252.

87 *Sotsial'ny i natsial'ny sostav VKP (b). Itogi vsesoyuznoy partiynoy perepisi* (1928), p. 114.

88 See reports printed in: F.I. Goloshchekin (ed.) *Partiynoe stroitel'stvo v Kazakhstane* (1930), esp. p. 69.

89 M. Abdykalykov and A. Pankratova, (eds.) *Istoriya Kazakhskoy SSR* (1943). Cited by I. Winner, 'Some Problems of Nomadism and Social Organisation among Recently Settled Kazakhs', pp. 535–6.

90 F.I. Goloshchekin (ed.), *Partiynoe stroitel'stvo v Kazakhstane*, p. 308.

91 I. Kuramysov, 'Partorganizatisya Kazakhastana za 5 let', (1930), printed in Gloshchekin (ed.), *Partiynoe . . .* p. 13.

92 In the 1930s it was known that Kazakhstan ecompassed 66 per cent of the USSR's copper deposits, 68 per cent of the lead, and 56 per cent of the zinc. See S.B. Nurmukhamedov *et al., Ocherki istorii sotsialisticheskogo stroitel'stva v Kazakhstane (1933–40 gg.)*, vol. 2 (1966), p. 30.

93 S.B. Nurmukhamedov *et al.,* pp. 33, 36.

94 The percentage of the total employed population in 1939 occupied in industry, building and transport was as follows: USSR (average) 30.1, RSFSR 33.9, Uzbekistan 14.3, Kazakhstan 21.7, Kirgizia 13.9, Armenia 17.8, Tadzhikistan 10.9, Turkmenistan 20.3. Cited in A. Nove and J.A. Newth, *The Soviet Middle East* (1967), p. 41.

95 S.B. Nurmukhamedov *et al., Ocherki istorii . . .*, vol. 2.

96 G. Ch. Chulanov *et al., Ocherki istorii narodnogo khozyaystva Kazakhskoy SSR*, vol. 2, (1962), p. 50.

97 Ibid., p. 50 M. Dobb, *Soviet Economic Development Since 1917* (1966), p. 428.

98 'Regional Economic Policy in the Soviet Union: The Case of Central Asia', *Economic Bulletin for Europe*, vol. 9, no. 3 (Nov. 1957), p. 53. Labour productivity grew relatively more quickly in Central Asia than in the USSR as a whole.

 99 For detailed population comparisons, see 'Regional Economic Policy...',
    p. 53.
100 The United Nations report on Soviet Central Asia records that in 1934 all the
    workers in the Tashkent textile combine were Russians and that in the
    mid-1950's Uzbeks made up only 11 per cent of the staff. Similarly at the later
    date the Tashkent engineering works had in employment only 25 per cent of
    Uzbeks. In silk-spinning and tea-packing the local nationalities accounted for
    70 and 80 per cent of the workers. 'See Regional Economic Policy...', p. 54,
    fn. 12.

4

THE MAKING OF MODERN RUSSIA

Foreign Policy

It would be wrong to portray Lenin's and Stalin's policies as stemming solely from the internal needs of Soviet Russia. Lenin had justified the seizure of power in 1917 by reference to the impending collapse of Western capitalism. But the Russian Revolution failed to ignite the revolutionary gunpowder in Western Europe and the Soviet leaders were faced with the necessity of carrying out foreign policy with hostile capitalist states.

In foreign affairs the first official act of the Soviet government on 8 November 1917 was to issue the Decree on Peace. This proposed 'a just and democratic peace'. The Decree appealed over the heads of governments to the exploited classes: 'The Provisional Workers' and Peasants' government of Russia also appeals especially to the class-conscious workers of the three leading nations of humanity and the largest states which are participating in the war, England, France and Germany.'[1] To the masses went the appeal to free themselves from slavery and exploitation. In 1918, the German government expelled the Soviet diplomatic mission for participation in revolutionary activity, and in 1919, Chicherin recalls, 'we sent fewer notes to governments but more appeals to the toiling masses.'[2] Here one can see the duality of Soviet foreign policy. On the one hand, the immediate need was for peace, for this would ensure Bolshevik power. On the other hand was the aspiration for world socialism and the Marxist claim for proletarian solidarity against the bourgeoisie. Trotsky and his followers had always emphasized the importance of the latter objective. Immediately after the October Revolution, Trotsky called for a revolutionary war. But Lenin's view prevailed and the 'Indecent Peace' was concluded with the Germans in March 1918. By the terms of the Treaty of Brest-Litovsk, Russia gave up large territories: Poland, the Ukraine and the Baltic Provinces.

For reasons we cannot explore here,[3] in 1918 the Allies intervened against the Soviet government on the side of the Whites. Though allied troops never numbered more than 10,000,[4] this was interpreted by the Bolsheviks as sure evidence of the intentions of the capitalists to destroy Soviet power. The significance of the allied intervention was not so much the military[5] but the psychological impact. Later it was used as evidence to justify the Soviet's conception of a hostile capitalist world. But in 1918 and 1919, the Russian communists still envisaged a world proletarian revolution, and in March 1919, the Third International (Comintern) was founded in Moscow. Its declared objective was to spread communism through the united efforts of Marxist revolutionary parties. Even at this time the importance of the colonial areas was recognized: 'Colonial slaves of Africa and Asia: the hour of proletarian dictatorship in Europe will also be the hour of your own liberation.'[6]

As the revolutionary fires were put out in Western Europe, Soviet policy changed. The new Soviet state began to play the diplomatic game with Western governments, the Comintern became a movement identified with the success of the *Soviet* state.[7] The East rather than the West was regarded as the centre of the revolutionary stage. As Trotsky put it:

> The road to India may prove at the given moment to be more readily passable and shorter for us than the road to Soviet Hungary. The sort of army, which, at the moment, can be of no great significance in the European scales can upset the unstable balance of Asian relationships, of colonial dependence, give a direct push to an uprising on the part of the oppressed masses, and assure the triumph of such a rising in Asia.[8]

From 1920, Soviet foreign policy was based on the assumption that the capitalist powers would, sooner or later, invade her. The immediate task was to make this later in order to allow her to consolidate the position at home.

The Comintern attempted to enlist opinion in support of the Soviet state, while she exploited where she could 'the contradictions' between capitalist states. To this end, she now sought, not revolution based on the toiling masses, but recognition by the international community. Though the communists gave moral support (and sometimes arms) to insurrectionists, official policy recognized the international *status quo* and, at least temporarily, sought to strengthen Soviet Russia's position in relation to it.

To strengthen Russia, the Rapallo Treaty was concluded with Germany in 1922. It granted to Soviet Russia full diplomatic recognition and to Germany, among other things, access to substantial military equipment. Two further treaties of friendship were signed with Germany, in 1926 and 1929.[9] These made more difficult a concerted Western move against the USSR's borders. The economic aspects of Soviet–German relations were an important aspect of the pact. In 1931, 37 per cent of the USSR's imports came from Germany, and in 1932, 46 per cent.[10] The Germans were able to circumvent the provisions of Versailles on rearmament, and the Russians had German help both for the rebuilding of their armaments industry and for the training of the Red Army. Soviet policy in Europe, then, was to capitalize on the division of the Western powers and to enter into agreements with them.

With China the Soviet leaders faced a different problem. While in 1924 the Soviet Union signed a treaty with the official government, in fact China was in turmoil, and a policy had to be worked out with regard to the various political groups struggling for power. In a short account it is impossible to describe adequately the complex situation. The Kuomintang was a nationalist movement intent on modernizing China; it might broadly be described as a national liberation movement. But its leaders were not communists, who had their own party. In the early 1920s the Comintern advocated the participation of the Chinese communists in the Kuomintang while keeping their own party identity. Their participation in the Kuomintang would put them in a stronger position to steer its policies in an anti-imperialist (pro-Soviet) direction and, of course, would enable the communists later to secure concessions for the working class.

In 1926, however, Chiang Kai-shek restricted the number of communists in the leading positions of the Kuomintang. While the Chinese communists sought a more independent role, Moscow still backed the alliance with Chiang. The time was not ripe, it was argued, for a communist bid for power and the initiative was seized by Chiang Kai-shek, who in 1927 after capturing Shanghai, turned on his communist supporters and annihilated them.

In the USSR this policy led to a stormy controversy between Trotsky and Stalin. It paralleled their divergence over the doctrine of socialism in one country. Trotsky believed that the time had come for a communist-led uprising based on Soviets; he stressed the international role of the Soviet Communist Party. But Stalin was more concerned with the impact of such a policy at home. In 1927, it was premature to support a communist rising: '...the struggle of Canton...dispersed the forces of imperialism, weakened and overturned imperialism, and thereby facilitated the development of the home of the world revolution, the development of the USSR.'[11]

If revolutionary strategy had moved to the East, the greatest threat to security lay in the West. Here the rise of Hitler was seen as a great danger and Nazi Germany came to be regarded as the chief external threat to the USSR. Soviet policy was one of collective security: the Comintern was pledged to the formation of popular fronts. Soviet activity had succeeded in arranging diplomatic relations with the major Western powers, and she had entered the League of Nations. Even so, the USSR was isolated. She tried unsuccessfully to arrange effective military pacts with the Western powers against Germany but she had no 'allies' in the West. In 1936, Germany and Japan made an 'Anti-Comintern Pact'. German rearmament and the growing strength of fascism in Europe were the background to the trials and purges in Soviet Russia which have been described above.

The building of socialism in one country entailed a strengthening of Soviet power internally and against the capitalist world. While still subscribing to Lenin's 'imperialist' analysis, another concept had been grafted on to it: the notion of the 'capitalist encirclement'. This posited the isolation of Soviet Russia in a world of hostile capitalist states, all intent on destroying her, not only by internal sabotage instigated by the intelligence arms of foreign powers, but also by possible armed intervention.

For Trotsky the USSR had abandoned proletarian internationalism and revolution in favour of the Russian national interest. In the *Revolution Betrayed* he said:

> The degeneration of the governing stratum in the Soviet Union could not but be accompanied by a corresponding change of aims and methods in Soviet diplomacy. The 'theory' of socialism in one country, first announced in the autumn of 1924, already signalised an effort to liberate Soviet foreign policy from the programme of international revolution .... From the theory of socialism in a single country, it is a natural transition to that of revolution in a single country.[12]

Soviet leaders did not of course see their actions in such a light. They argued that a wider proletarian revolution could only take place after the strengthening of socialism in Russia. Here we see an example of the way which Marxist revolutionary theory became an ideology which justified the activity of the Soviet state. It would be wrong, however, to regard Stalin's foreign policy as a *rapprochement* with the capitalist states. It was an unstable peaceful cohabitation rather than, as later under Khrushchev, peaceful coexistence. While Trotskyites have emphasized the absence of revolution in Stalin's policy, other have stressed the 'fundamental, not merely incidental intention to use the Soviet Union as a base for world revolution'.[13] Stalin in *Problems of Leninism* said: '... the very development of world revolution ... will be more rapid and more thorough, the more thoroughly Socialism fortifies itself in the first victorious country, the faster this country is transformed into a base for the further unfolding of world revolution, into a lever for the further disintegration of imperialism.'[14]

In terms of practical policy, Stalin sought alliances with the world powers. He played the diplomatic game. He entered into a treaty of mutual assistance with France in 1935. But it is doubtful whether Stalin regarded her as an effective ally in the event of a German attack on Russia.

Therefore, he kept open the possibility of improving relations with the latter country. This was essentially a short-term policy designed to give the USSR more time to build up her military potential.

In 1938, Hitler took the offensive. He joined with Austria in March. The Russians proposed a conference with the Western powers to deter further German expansion – particularly in Czechoslovakia. But the British and French advised the Czechs to cede the Sudetenland to Germany. Subsequently, the Western powers not only backed down against Hitler's pressure at Munich, but also excluded the Russians from the conference.

We cannot deal here with the details of diplomatic history.[15] From the Soviet point of view, it seemed that if the British and French were not prepared to take a stand over Austria and Czechoslovakia, then there would be little likelihood of them preventing a German attack to the east – against the USSR. It is sometimes suggested that the anti-Nazi powers (Poland, Britain and France) risked eventual defeat by the Nazis through their hatred of communism and their reluctance to form an anti-fascist alliance with the Russians. But the Germans could not attack the USSR without first passing through other states, and the British and French had given guarantees to Poland and Rumania.

In August 1939, Soviet policy took an unexpected turn when the USSR concluded a non-aggression pact with Nazi Germany.[16] This included a secret protocol in which any geographical rearrangement would give the eastern areas of Poland to Russia. Doubting the good intentions of the Western powers and their ability to stand up to Hitler, the Russians believed that the pact would prevent an attack on the Soviet Union, at least in the short run.

Subsequently, Germany attacked Poland, and on 3 September, France and Britain declared war on Germany. The Soviet army moved into Poland on 17 September and claimed the eastern territories; later she incorporated Lithuania, Latvia, Estonia, a small part of Finland and Bessarabia.

The changes in Soviet policy shocked communists in the West. From campaigning against the ideology and activity of National Socialism, they were called to justify and support the Molotov-Ribbentrop pact and to advocate peace between the allies and Germany.

Germany overran France and the Low Countries. Britain remained undefeated but weak. It could only be a matter of time before Hitler attacked the USSR.

World War II and its Aftermath

Hitler unleashed his attack on the Soviet Union on 22 June 1941. Russia was at war. The Red Army was routed. On the first day the Red Air Force was incapacitated. Belorussia (White Russia) and the western Ukraine were quickly overrun with the Germans advancing 300 miles in 18 days. The war was to be a nightmare experience, for the USSR lost 20 million people, three million were disabled and twenty-five million were made homeless. In the occupied areas some two-thirds of the national wealth was destroyed. The Soviet Union's alliances changed: she now had to join with the British and the Americans against the Third Reich. As in 1812 a national war was waged against a formidable opponent.

In the West, the Soviet position was thought to be hopeless. The British Ministry of Information gave the Russians a few weeks or at most a couple of months. But resistance was stubborn. If some Russians regarded communism as bad, the Germans showed that they could expect worse from Hitler's anti-Bolshevik crusade. The Slavs were *Untermenschen* (subhumans); like the Jews they were destined for extermination. As Field-Marshal von Manstein ordered: ' ... *In enemy cities, a large part of the population will have to go hungry. Nothing out of a misguided sense of humanity, may be given to prisoners-of-war or to the population*' unless they are in the service of the German Wehrmacht.[17] The German army reached the suburbs of Moscow, to be met by detachments of workers with rifles or hand-made implements.

The war cemented the loyalty of people, state and party. Party membership trebled from two to six million between 1941 and 1944. It was a war not only between Germans and Russians, but between capitalists and communists: national survival meant communist survival. But violence was not only to be committed against Soviet citizens by the Germans. Nationalities thought to be disloyal were uprooted and dispatched to the east. A million persons were so moved: Volga Germans, Crimean Tartars, Kalmyks and four Caucasian minorities (Chechens, Ingushi, Karachai and Balkars).

After its initial defeats, the Red Army recovered. Stalingrad was successfully defended and Leningrad resisted a three-year siege in which a million died, mainly from hunger.[18] The Reds, after a long and heroic struggle, reached Warsaw by July 1944 and took Berlin in May 1945. The military war was over. The Nazi campaign to rid Europe of Bolshevism was instrumental in bringing the Red Army and Soviet power to the banks of the Elbe. In the West, the impact of the war on the Soviet Union is generally underestimated. For Soviet people it is now symbolic of national unity and strength, of suffering and destruction, of *Soviet power* over the might of German militarism. Soviet museums are full of the *Great Patriotic War*; public cemeteries and memorials to the dead are on a scale unknown in the West, including the defeated Germany.

The USSR emerged from the Second World War as a major world

military power. Though she had been weakened by the war, her aggressive neighbours, Germany and Japan, had been vanquished. She was able, moreover, to make important territorial gains in East Europe and she attempted to secure as large an area of influence as was possible.[19] Soviet policy was to consolidate the gains made in the Second World War. She was now a military power with a physical presence in the heart of Europe.

After the Second World War the international structure had a very different complexion compared with 1939. The British and French Empires were in the throes of death. Demands for independence in the Third World were gaining in momentum. The USA had replaced Britain in the leadership of the capitalist countries. The communist parties of the West emerged strengthened from the war. The communist resistance in France had been armed and well-organized and the party had considerable electoral support both there and in Italy. In Britain a socialist (Labour) government had been swept into power at the expense of Winston Churchill and the Conservatives.

Soviet policy, however, was cautious in exploiting these developments. The USSR was intent on reconstruction at home and on consolidating her gains in Eastern Europe. Her policy was a continuation of promoting world socialism by securing it in the USSR. This involved priority being given to the bloc incorporation of the Eastern European states: Poland, Czechoslovakia, Hungary, Romania, Bulgaria, Yugoslavia and Albania,[20] and the then Soviet Zone of Germany. Such a policy not only safeguarded Russia's western border but ensured that these countries were within the Soviet military/economic orbit.

Crucial to the success of Soviet plans and to the structure of Europe after the war was the attitude of the Allies to Soviet policy. At Yalta in February 1945, the broad objectives of each side were discussed and general agreement was reached. Germany was to be disarmed, demilitarized and divided into four zones. Stalin insisted that Poland was to be 'amicably disposed' towards the USSR, and that Germany should pay reparations for war damage.

Stalin's policy is summed up in the following passage:

... The Germans made their invasion of the USSR through Finland, Poland, Romania, Bulgaria and Hungary. The Germans were able to make their invasion through these countries because, at the time, governments hostile to the Soviet Union existed in these countries. As a result of the German invasion, the Soviet Union has lost irretrievably in the fighting against the Germans, and also through the German occupation and the deportation of Soviet citizens to German servitude, a total of about seven million people .... In other words the Soviet Union's loss of life has been several times greater than that of Britain and the USA put together [subsequently estimated at twenty million] .... And so what can there be surprising about the fact that the Soviet Union, anxious for its future safety, is trying to see to it that governments loyal in their attitude to the Soviet Union should exist in these countries? How can anyone who has not taken leave of his senses, describe these peaceful aspirations of the Soviet Union as expansionist tendencies on the part of our State?[21]

The Soviet Union set about creating a 'sphere of influence' in Eastern Europe. Regimes based on the Soviet model were formed in Poland, Hungary, Rumania, Bulgaria and later in Czechoslovakia. Germany was partitioned and the East, under the communist Socialist Unity Party, was incorporated as a people's democracy.

Western policy became hostile to the USSR.[22] This was justified in the West by reference to Soviet policy in Eastern Europe and also to Bolshevik ideology. George F. Kennan wrote in 1947:

Of the original ideology, nothing has been officially junked. Belief is maintained in the basic badness of capitalism, in the inevitability of its destruction, in the obligation of the proletariat to assist in that destruction and to take the power into its own hands. But stress has come to be laid primarily on those concepts which relate most specifically to the Soviet regime itself: to its position as the sole truly Socialist regime in a dark and misguided world, and to the relationships of power within it.

The first of these concepts is that of the innate antagonism between capitalism and Socialism. We have seen how deeply that concept has become imbedded for Russia's conduct as a member of international society. It means that there can never be on Moscow's side any sincere assumption of aims between the Soviet Union and powers which are regarded as capitalist.[23]

The 'Cold War' was the result of two tendencies. On the Western side, there were fears of Soviet expansion and the domination of Western societies by communism and the consolidation of 'socialism in one country' by Soviet policy in Eastern Europe. The Russians justifiably mistrusted the motives of the Allies. Their aims in defeated Germany, Austria and Italy were not only to restore the capitalist system but to use them as bulwarks against the USSR.[24]

The new international conditions after the Second World War led to a change in the Soviet Union's view of socialist-capitalist relations: the theory of capitalist encirclement was superseded by the concept of 'two camps'. With communist governments installed in Eastern Europe (and China), the socialist states formed a relatively equal balance against the capitalist. The geography of the two blocs is shown in map 3. NATO was formed in 1949 but the *formal* alliance between the Eastern European powers and the formation of the Warsaw Treaty Organization was not made until 1955. During this period the Russians believed that there was a possibility of war being unleashed by the capitalist powers. Soviet policy was to keep the West at bay and to avoid a direct military confrontation,

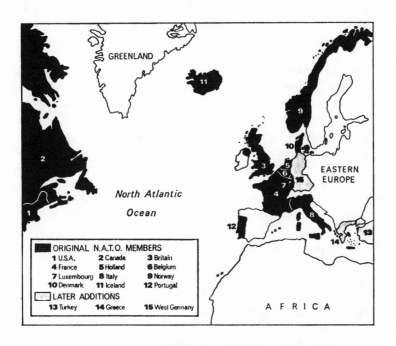

ORIGINAL N.A.T.O. MEMBERS
1 U.S.A.   2 Canada   3 Britain
4 France   5 Holland   6 Belgium
7 Luxembourg 8 Italy   9 Norway
10 Denmark   11 Iceland   12 Portugal
LATER ADDITIONS
13 Turkey   14 Greece   15 West Germany

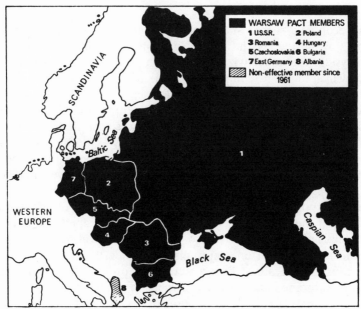

WARSAW PACT MEMBERS
1 U.S.S.R.   2 Poland
3 Romania   4 Hungary
5 Czechoslovakia   6 Bulgaria
7 East Germany   8 Albania
Non-effective member since 1961

MAP 3: NATO AND THE WARSAW PACT COUNTRIES

though differences between the Western powers were exploited (for example, between colonial and non-colonial powers and between European and American countries). During the early cold war, the Soviet bloc was at a nuclear disadvantage, not being in possession of a nuclear strike potential until the mid-fifties when the USSR acquired a nuclear capacity with jet bomber delivery. Soviet policy in Western and Central Europe was cautious, if not conservative: the Russians did not foment revolution in France or Italy, but allowed the communists to be disarmed, nor did they intervene militarily on the side of the communist insurgents in Greece.

In international affairs, then, Stalin had not only consolidated the Soviet state. He had secured international recognition and, as a consequence of World War II, the Soviet Union emerged as a major power. The United States and the USSR were now major world powers. Revolutionary and liberation movements were gaining strength and power in Asia and Africa. In 1945, communist parties in Western Europe had secured sizeable electoral support. The 'spectre of communism' indeed was haunting Europe. In this context, however, military build-up was pursued on both sides. The Cold War became a major impediment to East–West Relations. It might be an appropriate moment to sum up the achievements and inadequacies of the Stalin period.

From Lenin to Stalinism

In an economic sense, Stalin completed the industrialization of Russia which was started by the Tsars. In doing so he brought havoc to the countryside: the collectivization of agriculture was a momentous movement, which might be compared in some respects to the enclosure of the land in England centuries before. In Russia, it ensured the dominance of the city over the country and the political subjugation of the agricultural small-holder. The Stalinist political system was centralized and authoritarian but it would be wrong to regard this simply as a projection of Stalin's personality. It was created by the interaction of many complex factors: the heritage from the Tsarist past, the legacy of administrative and dictatorial rule, of an unsophisticated and backward peasant population, of the absence of popular participation in government; and the organizational structure of the Bolshevik Party which had been shaped during its illegal existence. These facts gave rise to centralized control, to an emphasis on unity in action, to an uncompromising attitude to opponents. It is also erroneous to see Stalinist Russia merely as a projection of Tsarist rule. So much of substance had changed: ownership relations were transformed, private property (with the exception of the peasants' plots) had been abolished, the economic market as a mechanism of resource allocation had been replaced by planning.

Stalinism was a dynamic creed. By the beginning of the Second World

War, the Soviet Union was an industrial power; new industries had been established in the eastern regions. By the end of it, she was a world military force, second only to the United States. Whilst this might have been attained by other means, it seems likely that, in the absence of policies like those laid down by Lenin and Stalin, Russia might have disintegrated. While the purges, the terror and the deportations were destructive of human life, the ideology of Marxism–Leninism, of Soviet nationalism, provided a dynamism to Soviet society. Ideology not only helped to create social cohesiveness, but it provided a value system on which the elites could be judged. Once under way, it constrained the actions of Stalin. He was pledged to the building of socialism in Soviet Russia and in doing so, he was ruthless. Economically, he succeeded. It is a more open question as to whether he built a society which was able to outgrow its dictatorial straitjacket.

Whilst it has been argued above that Stalin succeeded in securing the economic development of the country, the questions must be posed whether *socialism* was being constructed and whether Stalin had fulfilled or betrayed the revolutionary heritage (see also below chapter 5).

In a contemporary Western social democratic circles, socialism is an ideology closely bound up with equality and participation. Socialism is seen as a way of life in which equality characterizes the relationships between people: equal rights to resources – property, income, education – and before the law are crucial components of the socialist ideal. In the Soviet Union, the idea of socialism has different connotations. Whilst these ideals are also subscribed to, socialism is defined on criteria related to the Marxist conception of a mode of production: the forces of production (tools, technology) and relations of production (the property-owning class) (see above pp. 29–30). In practice 'building socialism' has had two major components: (i) industrial and social *development*, building the forces of production, and (ii) political hegemony of the working class expressed through the *political leadership* of the Communist Party. As Russia was at a low level of economic development on the assumption of power by the Bolsheviks, their policies were very much geared to industrial development. As Weber saw puritanism as providing the dynamic of capitalism, Leninism might be regarded as an ideology of socialist development.

Stalin shared with Lenin the view that socialism – in the economic and political sense – could be built in Russia. The government led by the party plays an important part in this process by carrying out capital investment, or the accumulation of capital. To do this, all leading Soviet Bolsheviks (Lenin, Trotsky and Stalin) regarded compulsion by the state to be justifiable; and they all saw the salvation of Russia in copying the advanced forms of industrial organization and scientific techniques. For Trotsky,

'The Soviet system shod with American technique will be socialism.'[25] For Stalin, the practice of Leninism included 'Russian revolutionary sweep and American efficiency'.[26] Hence came the adoption of practices of scientific work study, of Taylorism, which were to be utilized to 'build socialism' in Russia. (Taylorism is the practice of scientific time and motion study as developed in the USA.)

Stalin's world view had an affinity with Lenin's. Both men had a similar approach to Marxism: they recognized the threat of international capitalism to the Soviet state, they justified the necessity for the dictatorship of the proletariat, they placed great stress on the need to build up the material forces of Soviet Russia, they both legitimated the hegemony of the state and the dominant role of the party. Professor Meyer is undoubtedly correct to say that: 'Stalinism can and must be defined as a pattern of thought and action that flows directly from Leninism.'[27]

But to say that there is an 'affinity' does not mean that there is an identity of view and policy between Lenin and Stalin. Lenin, like Trotsky, believed that one country could begin to build socialism: he did not believe that it could be *completed* in one country. In practice, Stalin's vision was limited to the development of the forces of production in Russia and to the strengthening of the Soviet Union's international position. The wider world context of socialism took second place. Democratic centralism, for Lenin, was a method which ensured the participation of party members in decision-making. Under Stalin it became a method of mobilizing people into an industrial society. 'Participation' became a matter of symbolic identity between the masses and the party leadership. The ideals of socialist participation, as envisaged in *State and Revolution*, found no place in Stalin's world view. Lenin justified the state apparatus as necessary in the initial conditions of revolutionary power seized on behalf of the proletariat, but he saw the apparatus as declining through time. Under Stalin the oppressive apparatus of government was strengthened and the party as the collective expression of the working class played no significant role in determining policy. Finally, Stalinism entailed a type of extremism not characteristic of Lenin. As Cohen has put it, 'Stalinism was excess, extraordinary extremism.... It was not ... merely coercive peasant policies, but a virtual civil war against the peasantry; not merely police repression, or even civil war style terror, but a holocaust by terror that victimised tens of millions of people for twenty-five years; not merely a Thermidorian revival of nationalist tradition, but an almost fascist-like chauvinism; not merely a leader cult, but a deification of a despot ... Excesses were the essence of historical Stalinism ...'[28]

Stalin then continued, in an extreme form, the process begun in 1917. Socialism as a way of life, as an ideal society, was not achieved. The revolution furthered by Stalin remained not only incomplete but was characterized by many 'excesses' and 'deviations'. Much owed its origin to the Tsarist and autocratic past. The world situation of the USSR led to its introverted political stance.

We might emphasize the level of social underdevelopment for a socialist revolution. The legacy of history imposed limits on the revolutionary process. As Pethybridge[29] has pointed out, Bolshevik ideology was not only derived from Marxism as interpreted by Lenin, but it also had an important Russian cultural component derived from the pre-revolutionary non-Marxist intelligentsia. The new leaders were also faced by relatively autonomous forces which themselves deflected, or were absorbed into, Bolshevik policy. While it was possible to 'decapitate' the Tsarist administration, the trunk was left untouched and in the post-revolutionary state the officials began to practise their habitual forms of activity. Criticisms of Russian officialdom were made generations earlier than Lenin by Alexander Herzen, Prince Shcherbatov and Karamzin. As Pintner and Rowney have aptly pointed out, Lenin when nominally in charge of the government could not have his way: 'There were always many tasks – always more – to be done and in the Russian tradition the only way to try to get them done was through officials.'[30] To a considerable extent, the new regime was 'situation-determined' and was not willed into being by the Bolshevik leaders. This was particularly the case with the position in international affairs.

Sociologists distinguish between three methods of achieving compliance: coercion, remuneration and normative power. During the Stalin era all three were used. The terror, the deportations, collectivization, the regime of the camps were all based on coercion. The New Economic Policy and later the wider wage differentials of the Five-year Plans introduced an element of utilitarian rewards. But the normative, the ideological, were also important: the manipulation of symbols (Stalin, the hero of socialism), the image of the future ('socialism in one country'), and the propaganda ('the most democratic constitution in the world') all played a role as great, if not greater, than terror, in ensuring the active compliance and mobilization of the population. The belief system has to be viewed not only in terms of Marxism as it arose in Western Europe, but also in the context of Russian traditionalism. The popular ideology and symbolism derived much of their substance from the historical evolution of the Russian state.

The period of Stalin's rule was a transitionary epoch in the history of Russia. In the early years political debate was conducted in the vocabulary of the politics of nineteenth century Marxism: the dictatorship of the proletariat, the building of a socialist society, internal and external class struggle. The conflict between Trotsky and Stalin was fought in the phrases of world revolution. Collectivization and development in the east was legitimated in class terms. The Second World War launched by Hitler against the Soviet Union was explicitly an anti-communist holocaust.

In the post-Stalin period, the vocabulary of politics and the issues in Soviet politics were to change. Now the Soviet Union entered an entirely new era. She was a world power. Internally, the social and political structure was more differentiated. Politics became one of individual and interest group struggle.

The Rise and Fall of Khrushchev

On 5 March 1953, Stalin died. Would the political system collapse or would it continue of its own momentum? Would another 'dictator' take over the reins of power?

The struggle for power was not only between personalities but also between different apparatuses of the political system. There are distinct but overlapping bureaucracies of party, government (executive) and parliamentary (legislative) bodies. The chief committees and councils and their forms of subordination are shown for convenience in table 4.1. (A more detailed discussion of the political institutions follows in chapters 5 and 6.) The main contenders for power had a position (or positions) in the government and/or party apparatus.

After Stalin's death, the first move was made by Malenkov and Beria to form a new government. Malenkov was a party secretary in the Politbureau and a deputy prime minister. Beria was Deputy Prime Minister in charge of state security. Malenkov became the head of the government apparatus (Chairman of the Council of Ministers) and he also remained a secretary of the Politbureau (then called the Bureau of the Presidium of the Central Committee). Malenkov in 1953 was young to be Head of State (he was 51); he had joined the Party during the Civil War and had risen to be a personal assistant to Stalin in the apparatus of the Central Committee. He became a candidate member of the Politbureau in 1941. After the war he occupied a leading place in the government as a Deputy Chairman of the Council of Ministers. He was closely linked to Stalin.

On 14 March, very shortly after Stalin died, Malenkov left his party post: the Central Committee voted 'to grant the request ... of Malenkov to be released from the duties of Secretary of the Party Central Committee'.[31] There was then a division in personnel between the party apparatus and the government one: the former being composed of Khrushchev, Suslov, Pospelov, Shatalin and Ignatiev and the latter of Malenkov, Beria, Molotov, Bulganin and Kaganovich.[32] There followed conflict between

TABLE 4.1: THE THREE MAIN APPARATUSES OF THE SOVIET POLITICAL
SYSTEM

PARTY	GOVERNMENT (or executive)	PARLIAMENT (or legislative)
⌐Politbureau* / General (previously First) \ Secretary	Presidium ↗ Premier / (or Chairman)	Presidium ↗ Chairman \
Central Committee ↑ ↓ Party structure	Council of Ministers ← — — — Ministerial structure	Supreme Soviet ↑ ↓ Parliamentary structure
Branches in factories, the army, and places of work and residence	Including: army, police, economy	Soviets in Republics, towns, villages
	Election — — — — → Decision ───────→	

Note: *Previously called under Stalin, The Presidium.

these leaders for political influence. Unlike Malenkov, who had combined party posts with government ones, Khrushchev uniquely among the political leaders had had a career in the party only. He had been a party official in the Ukraine, and in Moscow he then became a Secretary of the Central Committee from 1949.

In July 1953, Beria was arrested. He was accused of 'trying to set the Ministry of Internal Affairs above the party and the government ....'[33] With his arrest and subsequent execution, the power of the police interests was weakened. The next important turning point was on 7 February 1955, when Malenkov resigned. He was replaced by Bulganin as Chairman of the Council of Ministers. Khrushchev was now in the ascendancy. Khrushchev's opponents (Malenkov, Molotov and Kaganovich) remained leading members of the party. At the Twentieth Party Congress in 1956, Khrushchev turned on them. He delivered his famous 'secret speech' condemning the excesses of Stalin's rule and methods and the association of his opponents with Stalin's policies. Molotov, Kaganovich, Malenkov and Voroshilov objected to Khrushchev's speech. Following the Congress, Molotov was removed from his post as Minister of Foreign Affairs and Kaganovich was demoted. Khrushchev was now supreme leader – though not without opposition. What were the factors underlying these events?

Kremlinologists in their demonic art have emphasized the existence of rivalry and competition for leadership among the members of the elite, and have characterized such conflict as being personal in substance, individual politicians being primarily motivated by their lust for political power, rather than by the desire to implement any policies.[34] As the group structure of Soviet society has been regarded by such writers as exceedingly weak, any possible linking of policy with social groupings was not considered possible.[35] Such writers interpret the outcome of Soviet politics and the rise of Khrushchev as a continuation of the Stalinist system of totalitarian rule. Other writers, favouring a more comparative 'industrial society' approach, regard the leading personalities as representative of, or responsive to, various 'interests'. Struggle for leadership position is a competition between actors who seek different priorities in terms of policies and who have their base in different institutions. Rather than seeing a unitary power bloc, the leadership is regarded as being made up of factions from the government apparatus, which constituted the basis of the 'anti-party' group under Molotov. The 'government apparatus' itself is made up of many different institutions (see below chapter 6); it includes the police, military, heavy and light industry, ministries of foreign trade and foreign affairs. Stalin's effective power came from these groups – particularly the forces of coercion and the heads of heavy industry. The other powerful institutional grouping is the party apparatus. It was here that Khrushchev and his supporters were located.

Khrushchev was able to win the leadership because the party had a legitimacy which the other institutions did not have. Also, the interests in the government apparatus were divided over a number of issues: light versus heavy industry, moderate versus hawkish foreign policy, agriculture versus industry, de-Stalinization versus internal security, consumption versus defence. Khrushchev and his supporters were able to exploit such differences to their advantage.[36] Pethybridge singles out four main policy issues: agriculture, consumer goods versus heavy industry, foreign policy and the reorganization of the economy.[37] Agriculture had been backward under Stalin. Khrushchev advocated material incentives for the farmer and greater party – rather than government – control. He launched (in 1954) a campaign for developing the virgin lands of Kazakhstan for grain production and (in 1958) he wanted to transfer to the ownership of the farms the machinery which had hitherto been under the control of the machine-tractor stations. Malenkov had promised to increase consumer goods production, which he did in 1953. This was opposed by the military and heavy industry interests. In 1955, Malenkov was replaced by Bulganin who had previously been Minister of Defence. In foreign affairs, Khrushchev held that war was no longer inevitable between capitalist and communist states and he also advocated greater toleration for different models of socialism, which could embrace the Jugoslav variety. He thereby indicted Molotov and others who were associated with a 'Stalinist' foreign policy. As Radio Moscow put it: 'He (Molotov) opposed the fundamental proposition worked out by the Party on the possibility of preventing wars in the present conditions, on the possibility of different ways of transition to socialism in different countries, on the necessity of strengthening contacts between the CPSU and progressive parties abroad.'[38] Khrushchev also advocated a decentralization of the administration of industry. He worked to set up economic councils which could control industry in their areas of jurisdiction and this entailed the weakening of the centralized government ministries. Khrushchev's denunciation of Stalin in his famous 'secret speech' at the Twentieth Party Congress in 1956 brought these issues to a head. The 'anti-Party group' of Molotov, Malenkov, Kaganovich and Shepilov had 'tried to bring about changes in the composition of the leading organs of the Party by "anti-Party factional methods".'[39]

The 'anti-party' group opposed Khrushchev and his policies: 'It recruited supporters, held secret meetings behind the Presidium's back, placed cadres with the intention of seizing power.'[40] The issues at dispute were the policies of industrial administration, the virgin lands campaign and foreign policy. Bulganin has recalled: 'In my office the anti-party group (Malenkov, Kaganovich and Molotov) gathered and intrigued about its anti-party factional work. Thus, if at a definite stage I behaved correctly and adhered to party principles, later I in fact shared with them the entire anti-party dirt.'[41] Khrushchev appealed to the Central Committee for support which he received and a new Presidium and Secretariat was elected. Khrushchev's opponents were relegated to obscurity.

Khrushchev then attempted to strengthen party control. By 1957, two-thirds of the Party Presidium (now called the Politbureau) were party men. The power of the police had been curbed. By 1961, only the Chairman of the KGB (Committee for State Security – Secret Police) remained a voting member of the Central Committee. Police representation under Khrushchev continued to decline in the higher organs. A study of the Central Committees of six republican parties found that in 1954 there were eleven chiefs of police having full membership, in 1961 there were five and in 1966 only one.[42]

Under Stalin not only had the party been decimated and the police used as an enforcement agency, but also the ministerial apparatus had been enlarged. It developed a vertically integrated structure. While the party played an important role in enforcement, interest articulation and political recruitment, the state ministries, especially the police, were more important agencies of socio-political change. Under Stalin, the party was weakened. As Conquest has pointed out, 'Stalin's later Politbureaus consisted of figures from the government apparatus. And Stalin himself, in decrees proceeding from both government and party, signed first as representative of the government, allowing his senior subordinate in the Party Secretariat to sign, second, for the Party.'[43] In the succession struggle with Khrushchev, Malenkov based his bid for power on the government executive. As the party journal put it: 'Members of the anti-party group departed from the Leninist understanding of the leading role of the party in the system of the dictatorship of the proletariat ... Some of them ... seeking to substantiate the [alleged] necessity of the primacy of state organs over party, distorted the Leninist doctrine on the role of the party after the victory of the proletarian revolution.'[44] This highlights institutional conflict in Soviet society, and the tension between the party and other elements of the state apparatus.

The 'interest group approach' equally sees Khrushchev's leadership – from 1957 – to be subject to vetoes and constraint from the groups who aided his rise to power. This is illustrated by Carl A. Linden's study of the Soviet leadership between 1957 and 1964. Linden sees

... those around Khrushchev ... not as nonentities or toadies, but men of power who represent real political and organisational interests. At no point do they appear as wholly malleable to the leader's purposes and, while opportunistic and skilled tacticians, they also are ... men who more often than not possessed political identities which placed them to one side or other in the political spectrum of the party. It was through such territory and with such company that Khrushchev made his way and finally stumbled ... The major, but not the exclusive, focus here is the narrow circle of a few dozen figures at the level of the Party Presidium and Secretariat.[45]

Who, then, are the political elites? Michel Tatu, though emphasizing power at the top, defines 'the lobbies' in Soviet politics. (The use of the term 'lobby' is rather misleading, for in the USA it includes persons employed in promoting or defeating bills: no process of the American kind takes place in the USSR.) Tatu's list includes: the military, the police, the 'steel eaters' (supporters of heavy industry), the party *apparatchiki* and economic administrators – the last two being the most important.[46] Khrushchev tried to steer these different groups in a direction which he believed represented the interest of the USSR in the post-Stalin world of the early 1960s. This he did, until unseated by Brezhnev and Kosygin in 1964. In this ousting the support of the military was crucial.

The political role of the military is always important, for the armed forces have the ability to assert their will against other groups by the use of arms. In a modern industrial society, the technology of war is not only expensive, but involves military strategy depending on specialized professional advice, which the armed forces possess or think they possess. The effective waging of war also depends on the morale of the armed forces and their capability to innovate and to show initiative. The military can be expected to play quite an important role in shaping policies in modern industrial societies. There are three areas in which the military exerts influence on Soviet policy-making: '(1) the high-level sphere of party-state policy formulation; (2) the lesser level of military-technical considerations relating to the development and management of the military establishment itself; (3) the area of internal Soviet politics'.[47]

We know that Khrushchev, when pitted against Malenkov, had come to power with much military support.[48] After assuming power, Khrushchev became involved in the policy issue of missiles versus ground forces, and he came down forcibly on the side of the missiles: of 'fire power' rather than the number of 'army great coats'. At the Supreme Soviet in January 1960, Khrushchev argued that large armies, navies and bomber forces were obsolete. The conventional military leaders opposed Khrushchev. Marshall Malinovski said in reply:

The rocket troops are indisputably the main arm of our armed forces. However, we understand that it is not possible to solve all the tasks of war with any one arm of troops. Therefore, proceeding from the thesis that the successful conduct of military operations in modern war is possible only on the basis of the unified use of all means of armed struggle, and combining the efforts of all arms of the armed forces, we are retaining all arms of our armed forces at a definite strength and in relevant sound proportions.[49]

The implications here and elsewhere in the military press were that undue reliance on a rocket defensive arm was inimical to successful defence. Western commentators are agreed that the military had differences with Khrushchev and believed his defence policy to be incorrect. Garthoff comments:

On this issue [the reduction of the armed forces], the political prevailed only in part. As a whole, the military leaders accepted and implemented the decision, but they also fought an effective rear-guard action. They were apparently given the deciding vote in allocating military reductions and in shaping the force structure under the politically imposed manpower ceiling.[50]

In the spring and summer of 1961, with the worsening of international relations (the U-2 incident, the failure of the Paris summit and a new crisis over Berlin), some concessions were made to the military. The manpower cuts were suspended, defence expenditure was increased by one third and the release of servicemen was stopped. In June 1961, Khrushchev recognized that 'the strengthening of the defence of the Soviet Union depends on the perfection of all services of our armed forces – infantry and artillery, engineering corps and signal corps, armoured tank divisions and the navy, the air force, and the missile force.'[51]

While military support, especially that of Zhukov, was an important factor in Khrushchev's rise to power, it seems that it did not play a very active part in his downfall. But this does not diminish the importance of the military as a political interest: the *neutrality* of the military to the anti-Khrushchev coalition helped secure the Brezhnev–Kosygin leadership. As Garthoff has pointed out when commenting on his removal, 'the military were only a part of a coalition involving individual leaders and interest groups.'[52] It cannot be doubted that the military has a voice which it makes heard in the inner councils concerned with policy in the USSR. Military leaders defend their interest against party and other groups. They provide resistance when changes which threaten them are muted. '... While the military's influence on policy is no doubt limited, the extent to which Khrushchev – and with him the entire political leadership – can ignore military opinion also seems to have its limits.'[53]

Another issue on which opinions differed and around which elitist group interest diverged was party control of the economy. While all members of the Council of Ministers and Central Committee are party members, one must distinguish between that group from which Khrushchev sprang, which is wholly dependent on a party career (full-time *party* officials), and a group which runs, through the government apparatus, the industrial ministries. Khrushchev when in power strengthened party control of industry and split up economic administration into regional, rather than ministerial units, which coincided with party administrative boundaries. (We shall examine party control at the factory level below pp. 227–8). This was not simply a move designed to improve administrative efficiency. Khrushchev's motives included: 'the weakening of the influence of his "anti-party" rivals in the central administrative apparatus: and the strengthening of his supporters in the territorial party organisation'.[54] Later Khrushchev divided the party organization into industrial and agricultural hierarchies. By increasing the number of units he in effect reduced the power of many former party First Secretaries who, of course, resented the policy.

Khrushchev then found himself very unpopular with the chief ministerial bureaucrats and with some of the 'old' Party Secretaries. The latter may have played an important role in his downfall, for many of them held positions on the Central Committee, which the secretaries who benefited by the reorganization did not. 'All of the Ukrainian and RSFSR *obkom* secretaries who appeared to be threatened by reorganisation measures were Central Committee members or candidates, while *none* of the "new" secretaries who were beneficiaries of the bifurcation belonged as yet to that body.'[55]

Above, I have identified three interest groups at the top of the Soviet power structure: first, the leaders of the armed forces, who tend to identify Soviet national interests with a strong defence capacity, who actively supported Khrushchev against Molotov in 1957, and whose neutrality to the Brezhnev-Kosygin *coup* ensured Khrushchev's removal in 1964; second, the party secretariat wishing the predominance of the party over the ministries; third, the government bureaucracy which was at logger-heads with Khrushchev over industrial administration during the whole period of his supremacy. It would be superficial to explain elite politics solely in terms of these interest groups. To account adequately for the demise of Khrushchev one must look at other aspects of his policy – on Berlin, Cuba, China, agriculture, education – to gauge how other groups reacted to his leadership.[56]

Here, in summary, we may mention some of the main groups and issues which caused the upheaval in October 1964. It seems improbable to suggest that Khrushchev was ousted over one policy by a single interest group. Rather, a combination of factors was responsible. We have noted some of them already. Khrushchev tried to establish the supremacy of the party over government organs. He succeeded in smashing police power. He weakened, but did not decimate, the bureaucratic government machine. He discredited the secret police by his anti-Stalin campaign which, at least initially, secured him public, and a good deal of party, support. But his policy here backfired. His anti-Stalinism unleashed tremendous political demands. Eastern Europe was in upheaval. Soviet writers, such as Solzhenitsyn, questioned the very basis of party control. He met such stress and demand on the political system by repression – thereby weakening his popularity. While Khrushchev had strengthened the party vis-à-vis the 'anti-party' group, he now became more dependent on the party to maintain his own power. But here he was faced by men of his own ilk, Party Secretaries and officials reared in the Stalin era. While he could not resort to Stalinist methods of terror and coercion – both the social framework, the legitimacy of his own power, and his destruction of the police apparatus prevented this – his attempt at normative controls (the new *Party Programme* – see below, chapter 7) and policy changes created resistance. His crude mannerisms – such as shoe banging at the United Nations General Assembly – were exploited by his enemies. He appeared to be too big for his boots. Khrushchev's last desperate gamble was with the party machine itself. By dividing it, he increased its size: the number of First Secretaries doubled. The new men were younger, probably more progressive, more instrumental than ideological in orienta-tion. But Khrushchev had not politically eliminated his opponents in the party. This was his final undoing. They had a majority in the Central

Committee. With the Presidium by now hostile he could not stay in power. On 14 October 1964 he attended a session of the Central Committee for the last time. His retirement was announced on grounds of failing health and old age. He left in disgrace and was ignored by the Soviet press. He was not buried in the Kremlin.

One of the tasks of party leadership is to promote policies which do not alienate social and political interests. Khruschev fell from grace because he violated this principle of politics. As a Soviet commentator put it:

... in recent years there had been more and more defects in his methods of leadership. The principles of collective leadership were violated. When an idea entered his head he hurried to put it into operation without due thought and without discussion with others. This applied especially to agriculture.

There had been many discussions and disagreements with Khrushchev in the Presidium, which finally felt that his methods had exceeded all possible limits and had become an obstacle.[57]

The Brezhnev Era

The rather ignominious departure of Khrushchev from the political scene quickly led to some significant changes in Soviet politics. In October 1964 the party was reunified. The industrial ministerial system was recentralized. The 'reinstated' Party Secretaries were those who held their posts prior to bifurcation.[58] The most visible change was a more modest style of leadership under the triumvirate of Kosygin, Brezhnev and Podgorny. These three men were to form a 'collective leadership': Brezhnev, the Party's First Secretary*; Kosygin, the head of the administration – Chairman of the Council of Ministers; and Podgorny, the official Head of State, Chairman of the Presidium of the Supreme Soviet. The immediate impression in the West was one of 'greyness' of style: gone were the flamboyant days of Khrushchev's joviality. The Brezhnev period was to be one of consolidation. There was a 'growth of a sense of personal safety among the top elite, the rise of certain informed "constitutional restraints" on the actions of the leader, an increase in the degree of consultation on top policy ... The opening of a large number of policy debates to public participation ... '[59] The triumvirate was to lead the Soviet Union until May 1977, when Podgorny resigned, and he was followed by Kosygin, who also resigned as Premier in October 1980, and died in December of that year. Podgorny's position was taken by Brezhnev himself who had become the leading figure; Kosygin was replaced by Tikhonov.

Podgorny, Brezhnev and Kosygin had all experienced the Civil War in their childhood and had joined the party after 1927 (Brezhnev became a

*He adopted the title of 'General Secretary' (Stalin's designation) in 1966.

member in 1931 and Podgorny in 1930). Brezhnev was born in 1906; he had attended a specialized technical secondary school (*technicum*) and, after work experience in agricultural administration, he graduated from the Dneprodzherzhinsk Metallurgical Institute in 1935. He had a party career: he was a regional Party Secretary in the Ukraine and then First Secretary in Moldavia; in 1952 he was a Secretary to the CPSU Central Committee and a candidate member of the Politbureau. From 1954 he was the Second then First secretary of the Kazakhstan Central Committee and he returned to Moscow in 1956 to become Secretary of the CPSU Central Committee.

Kosygin had had a career as an administrator in the government apparatus. The son of a Petrograd worker, he was born in 1904. He fought for the Red Army during the Civil War. He attended a *technicum* (specialized technical secondary school) and, after some junior managerial posts, he graduated from a Textile Institute in 1935. By 1939 he was People's Commissar for Light Industry and in 1940 Deputy Chairman of the Council of People's Commissars (the Soviet government). In 1946 he became a candidate member of the Politbureau, a position he lost in 1953 and regained in 1957. In 1959 he became Chairman of Gosplan followed by promotion to First Deputy Chairman of the Council of Ministers. Kosygin became Prime Minister in 1964 and remained in this powerful position (though subservient to Brezhnev) until October 1980 when he resigned; he continued as a member of the Politbureau until his death in December 1980.

Podgorny (born 1903) did not join the party until he was 27 years old. He graduated from the Kiev Technological Institute of the Food Industry in 1931. He was Deputy People's Commissar for Food in 1940 and in 1946 he became a member of the USSR Council of Ministers. In 1950, he switched to a party career, becoming First Secretary to the Kharkov Party region. He rose within the Ukrainian Republic, attaining the rank of First Secretary of the Ukraine in 1957 and that of candidate member of the Presidium of the CPSU in 1958. He was elected a candidate member of the Presidium (now Politbureau), becoming a full member in 1960; later, in 1963, he was promoted to Secretary to the Central Committee. He was the least influential of the triumvirate and he fell from grace in 1977. It is believed that he opposed Brezhnev's intention of becoming Head of State by taking over his post as Chairman of the Presidium of the Supreme Soviet.

With the ageing and ill-health of Kosygin, Nikolay Tikhonov gradually took over his responsibilities. In replacing Kosygin, he was the final top leader to serve under Brezhnev. Tikhonov, a Ukrainian, was born in 1905, the son of an engineer. He went to a railway technical secondary school (*technicum*) in Dnepropetrovsk where he completed his studies in 1924. At the age of nineteen he began work as a railway fireman. He then attended the Dnepropetrovsk Metallurgy Institute from which he graduated as an engineer in 1930. He had a career in industry: as a workshop manager, as chief engineer and as factory director. He joined the party in 1940 when he was 35 years old. His administrative experience began in 1950 in the USSR Ministry of Ferrous Metallurgy, of which he became Deputy Minister. In 1957 he was the head of the Dnepropetrovsk *sovnarkhoz* (Regional Economic Council) when he became a member of the Central Committee of the Ukrainian Party. In 1960 he rose to ministerial rank when he was appointed Deputy Chairman of the State Scientific and Economic Council. In the following year he became a candidate member of the Central Committee of the CPSU (he became a full member in 1966). In 1963 he became deputy chairman of Gosplan (the state planning council). In 1965, following Khrushchev's departure, he rose to deputy chairman of the USSR Council of Ministers under Kosygin. After a relatively short period in this post, in September 1976 he became First Deputy Prime Minister. He acquired membership of the Politbureau, as candidate member in November 1978, and in November 1979, at the age of 74, he was elected a full voting member. Tikhonov then has had a working life in industry in government service. He has not had any full-time position as a secretary in the party apparatus. Unlike Kosygin, who had been in textiles and light industry, Tikhonov's roots were in metallurgy and heavy industry. His career overlapped geographically with Brezhnev. In the later 1930s both worked in the Dnepropetrovsk area. He, together with Konstantin Chernenko, Andrey Kirilenko and Vladimir Shcherbitsky, hails from the Ukraine and these men have become known as the 'Brezhnev faction' in the Politbureau. According to some Western commentators, Tikhonov 'has been a reliable ally of the military-industrial complex and has consistently upheld the traditional system of centralized management against attempts to reform or substantially decentralize it'.[60]

Khrushchev's rule was characterized by change, by the denunciation of Stalin, by the assertion of the primacy of the party over the government apparatus, by a policy of 'peaceful coexistence' with the West. Under Brezhnev, Soviet affairs were more tranquil; Gerry Hough has defined politics under Brezhnev as 'The Return to Normalcy'.[61] In addition to reversions in the organization of party and state, mentioned above, Brezhnev played down the discontinuities and oppression of Stalin's time. An attempt was made even to bring out more of the 'positive' features of Stalin's rule. In the Programme of the Communist Party of the Soviet Union, Khrushchev provided a vision of the future (see below chapter 7). By analogy, Brezhnev's ideological innovation was the concept of 'developed socialism'. By this he endorsed the notion of social harmony within the USSR. But he emphasized the role which the 'scientific-technical revolution' would play. It updated Lenin's ideas about the importance of scientific management; it was a managerial policy.

Under Stalin, the 'cult of the individual' was an integrating force. This was revived under Brezhnev, though in a milder form. His portrait, memoirs, and exploits in peace and war became a prominent theme in Soviet propaganda. He became Head of the Armed Forces and also Chief of State – on assuming Podgorny's mantle.

Brezhnev was not an indecisive leader. He conducted the military intervention in Czechoslovakia in August 1968, and in Afghanistan in December 1979. He claimed responsibility for the introduction of the new Soviet Constitution in 1977. He sought to consolidate peaceful coexistence with the West, though he was rebuffed, as was his successor Andropov, by the American administration under Reagan, aided by Thatcher's British government. Brezhnev appears to have played the role of broker, steering a path between different conflicting interests. His course was shaped by a much more complex social and political structure than in the past. Soviet politics were less 'politically determined' than under Stalin and Khrushchev, and were more 'system structured'. The political space in which the leader can manoeuvre is limited not only by internal forces, but also by external ones.

If Stalin presided over the industrialization of the Soviet Union, Brezhnev is identified with the running of an industrial society. In 1959, only 48 per cent of the population was urban, but this had risen to 63 per cent by 1980. The stock of employed people with higher, and specialized educational qualifications had risen from 3.2 million in 1950 to 22.8 million in 1975.[62]

Under Brezhnev there was a general rise in living standards. Between 1960 and 1980 money wages doubled, and between 1964 and 1978 consumption increased at an average yearly rate of 3.4 per cent per person.[63] Production of consumer goods brought the USSR to a level comparable with (though lower than) advanced Western capitalist countries. The Brezhnev era also witnessed an equalization of earnings. Taking the ratio of the highest 10 per cent to the lowest 10 per cent, the index fell from 8:1 in 1956 to 5:1 in 1968 and 4:1 in 1975. The minimum wage rose and the earnings of the collective farm peasants improved.

On 10 November 1982 Brezhnev died. Two days later, at a special meeting of the Central Committee of the CPSU, Uri Vladimirovich Andropov was elected General Secretary of the Communist Party of the Soviet Union.

From Andropov to Chernenko

The first flush of the ascendancy of Andropov did not lead to any major upheaval either in personnel or policy. In the first six months of power, continuity and incremental change were the main characteristics of the new General Secretary. The personnel of the Politbureau changed little: Geidar Aliev became a full member – a promotion from being candidate. Andrey Kirilenko resigned – because of ill-health. Nikolay Ryzhkov was elected to the Party secretariat from the post of first deputy chairman to Gosplan (the State Planning Commission). Andropov did not initially take over Brezhnev's other posts – of Supreme Commander of the Armed Forces, Chairman of the Defence Council and Chairman of the Presidium of the Supreme Soviet. Assumption of these positions was to follow. In May 1983 it was announced that he was Chairman of the USSR Council of Defence and in June 1983 he was elected Chairman of the Presidium of the Supreme Soviet. This probably was the peak of his power. In the late summer (August) he fell ill, and made no further appearances. He died on 9 February 1984.

Uri Andropov, a Russian, grew up under Soviet power. He was born in 1914, the son of a railwayman. At sixteen he began work as a telegraph worker, and concurrently became a member of the Young Communist League (Komsomol) in which he was later to play a prominent role. Then he was employed as a cinema operator's apprentice and he had a spell as a sailor working on the boats of the Volga. At the age of eighteen he enrolled at the Rybinsk Technical School (or *technicum*) of Water Transportation. (It was more of a trade school than an engineering college.) On graduation in 1936, he worked as a secretary in the Komsomol; by 1937 at the age of 24 he was secretary of the Yaroslavl Region Young Communist League Committee.[64]

In this way Andropov, like Brezhnev and Khrushchev before him, was set on a career in politics rather than in industry. During the Second World War he was active in the partisan movement in Karelia and concurrently secretary of the Komsomol. In 1944 he began his party career, as a second secretary in Petrozavodsk and then in Karelia. In 1951, he joined the Party's apparatus in Moscow. He continued his education at Petrozavodsk University and at the Higher Party School in Moscow. Unlike his predecessors as General Secretary, Andropov acquired before his election considerable experience in foreign affairs. In 1953 he became head of one of the departments of the Ministry of Foreign Affairs. Later he served in the Soviet Embassy in Budapest and was Ambassador from July 1954 to March 1957 – during the crucial period of the uprising in 1956. In 1957 he returned to Moscow to a Party post – head of the Department for Liaison with Communist and Workers' Parties of the Socialist Countries. In 1961, he became a full member of the Central Committee and in 1962 he was elected a secretary to it.

In May 1967, Andropov's career changed course. He took over the reins of power of the Chairman of the State Committee for Security (KGB). In the following month he was elected as a candidate member of the Politbureau and he relinquished his secretarial post in the Central Committee. In April 1973, he was elevated to the status of full member of the Politbureau. In May 1982, he relinquished his KGB post and regained his position on the secretariat of the Central Committee.

It is difficult to analyse the behind-the-scenes struggles that took place to ensure Andropov's victory. His chief adversary, later to be his successor, was Konstantin Chernenko, who had acted for some time as Brezhnev's second in command. Konstantin Ustinovich Chernenko (born 24 September, 1911) was the son of a Russian peasant. He began work as a farm hand, joined the Party in 1931 and was educated at a teachers' training college and at the Party's own higher school for party organizers. After serving in the war, he worked as secretary of the Penza District Committee, and in 1948 worked in the Party in the apparatus in Moldavia. In 1956 he moved to Moscow to the propaganda department of the Central Committee; he was a member of the editorial board of *Agitator*. As a Party official, Chernenko was made head of the Central Committee's General Department in 1965, and was promoted by Brezhnev to the post of secretary to the Central Committee in March 1976 and to the Politbureau in 1978. He has travelled abroad on behalf of the Soviet government: he had been a member of the Soviet delegation at the International Conference on Security and Cooperation in Europe (Helsinki 1975) and he had taken part in the Vienna disarmament discussions in 1979.

It is believed that in the last days of Brezhnev, Chernenko had taken a reformist position and had (unsuccessfully) advocated a reduction in the military budget.[65] In the Spring of 1982 he published an article in *Kommunist* calling for greater democratization and implicitly economic reforms. In a review of Chernenko's writings, Marc D. Zlotnik emphasizes the radical proposals that Chernenko put forward: he advocated a more open and democratic Party organization; increased public participation in the Soviets; that greater attention be paid to public opinion; that a larger role be given to trade unions in management; and he wanted more decentralization and opposed distortions associated with the personality cult.[66] In a number of articles he had advocated the enhancement of Party control (see below chapter 7). Chernenko explicitly defended a policy of détente and supported Brezhnev's policy to improve food production – indirectly giving the military a lower priority. Chernenko is also believed to have been criticized because of his lack of experience in managerial posts and in foreign affairs and security.

During Brezhnev's last days, Andropov had taken the lead in exposing corruption at the highest levels of politics. Members of Brezhnev's family were said to have been involved and this may in turn have weakened the stature of his following in the Politbureau.[67] Andropov, it is thought, did not state his policy preferences and thereby did not endanger support from the military. He received the votes of Foriegn Minister, Gromyko, and Defence Minister, Dmitri Ustinov.[68] Vladimir Dolgikh, a Central Committee secretary since 1972, had been appointed candidate member of the Politbureau in May 1982. This had been interpreted as a weakening of Brezhnev's position as has the blockage to the advancement of Ivan Arkhipov to the Politbureau.

The promotion of Romanov who had been a full member of the Politbureau since 1976 to the Central Committee secretariat in June 1983 and the appointment of Sergei Akhromeev and Vitali Shabanov to full membership of the Central Committee has also led some Western commentators to believe that the 'military-industrial' interest had been strengthened under Andropov.[69] Romanov (born 1923) is another Russian with a peasant background; he had been previously head of the Leningrad party organization which he had joined in 1954 and where he had spent his complete political career. In May 1983 he became a secretary of the Central Committee. Geidar Aliev (born 1923) was made a full member of the Politbureau in November 1982. Until 1969, when he became First Secretary of the Azerbaidzhan Party organization, he had been the head of the KGB in that Republic. He is the son of a manual worker and an Azeri by nationality. His advance in the early 1980s is said to indicate a strengthening of police influence at the top of the Soviet power structure. Before Andropov's death some Western commentators saw two loose groupings in the Politbureau. Around Andropov was the 'technical-military-police' coalition. This was said to be composed of Ustinov, Aliev, Romanov, and Gorbachev with further support coming from Dolgikh and Ryzhkov who were candidate members. Vladimir Dolgikh (born 1924) a Russian, is the son of a non-manual worker; he had been a secretary of the CPSU central committee since 1972, and a candidate member of the Politbureau in 1982. Nikolai Ryzhkov (born 1929), a Russian, had a career with Gosplan, the government planning department, until he was promoted to the CPSU's secretariat in November 1982. The 'Party' group around Chernenko was believed to be composed of Tikhonov, the party leaders from Kazakhstan (Kunaev) and Moscow (Grishin), and Gromyko.[70]

With Andropov on his death bed, the Politbureau continued to run the country, though no innovations in policy occurred. Andropov had been widely reported in the West as speaking 'fluent English, (collecting) contemporary American novels and music, (dressing) elegantly and (being) generally Westernised and urbane'.[71] However, he was not associated with effective liberalization in respect of the dissident movement and it is claimed that his concern for economic reform was tempered with greater political and ideological controls.[72] Under him no major changes emanated from the Kremlin on the position of *Solidarity* in Poland or the role of Soviet forces in Afghanistan. He instigated a campaign to improve labour discipline, he rooted out some inefficient administrators and opposed corrupting influences. He sacked many incompetent people holding government posts including the head of the Ministry of Internal Affairs, Nikolay Shchelokov, who was replaced by Vitali Fedorchuk – from the KGB. In the economic field he tried to modernize technology and to increase production. He outlined reforms of the educational system, later pushed through in 1984 by Chernenko.

New appointments were made to the Politbureau. In December 1983, Mikhail Solomentsev and Vitali Vorotnikov were elected to full membership, Viktor Chebrikov to a candidate's place and Egor Ligachev became a new Secretary to the Central Committee. Solomentsev, the Russian son of a peasant, had been made chairman of the Council of Ministers of the RSFSR in 1971, at which time he also became a candidate member of the Politbureau. In June 1983, he headed the Party Control Committee. Vorotnikov, also a Russian, had an early career in the Party apparatus: in 1971, he was elected first secretary of the Voronezh District Party Committee and a full member of the CPSU Central Committee. In 1975, he became a deputy chairman of the RSFSR Council of Ministers. He went as Ambassador to Cuba in 1979, and later returned to a Party First Secretaryship in Krasnodar. In 1983, he took Solomentsev's place as chairman of the RSFSR Council of Minister. Chebrikov, a Russian, on election was the head of the KGB. Until his appointment as deputy-chairman of that organization in 1968, he had followed a Party career. In 1982 he became one of the two first deputy chairman of the KGB, then later in the year its chief. Ligachev, another Russian, has had a party career. In 1959 he worked as a secretary to the Novosibirsk District Committee until 1960, when he moved to the apparatus of the Central Committee in Moscow where he worked until 1965. From that date he worked as first secretary in the Tomsk district; he was elected a candidate member of the Central committee in 1966 and full membership in 1976. In 1983, he became head of the Organization Party Work Department of the Central Committee.

These, then, were the men who were the aides to Andropov during his last days and who nominated Chernenko as his successor. The new younger men (Gorbachev, Vorotnikov, Aliev, Romanov, Dolgikh, and Ryzhkov) represent the new generation of the Soviet leadership, and were supporters and proteges of Andropov. Western commentators writing during the time of Andropov's terminal illness predicted that either Gorbachev or Romanov would succeed him. Jerry Hough wagered on Gorbachev and Vadim Medish argued the odds on Romanov.[73] It is believed in the West that Gorbachev was Andropov's chosen heir.

Neither Romanov nor Gorbachev was nominated General Secretary by the Politbureau and Central Committee. On 13 February 1984, at an extraordinary plenary meeting of the Central Committee, Konstantin Chernenko was elected General Secretary. One cannot but speculate as to why Chernenko was elected the second time around. The personal qualities of the candidates have to be taken into account, in addition to their interests and possible political constituencies. As indicated earlier, Andropov had outmanoeuvred Chernenko. His political position and personal qualities are well known – he has been in the politbureau, as a secretary since 1976, and a member since 1978. It is believed that he had the support of Tikhonov, Gromyko, Ustinov and Grishin. Romanov may be discounted on a number of grounds: his experience was limited to work in the Leningrad party organization and this was not compensated by his position as secretary which he received only six months after Andropov came to power. The young Turk, Gorbachev, joined the secretariat two years after Chernenko and only became a full member of the Politbureau in 1980. Previously an expert in agriculture, under Andropov he took responsibility for the economy. His age and lack of experience were probably against him: at 52 in 1984 he was the youngest full member of the Politbureau. It is possible that the thought of his leadership for at least twenty years may have deterred some of the younger Politbureau members who may have been rivals as well as supporters. The relative newness of some of the younger members would also have made it difficult for them to have formed a consistent bloc. Vorotnikov, Aliev, Romanov, and those on the touchlines, Ligachev, Ryzhkov, Chebrikov would all have a possibility of succeeding Chernenko – not so had Gorbachev been elected.

While Western studies naturally tend to emphasize division and competition between members of the Soviet political leadership, history would suggest that the members of the Politbureau are in agreement on fundamentals, and Soviet policy has a greater consistency and durability than that of Western governments. Stemming from the early days of the Bolshevik Party, Soviet leaders are disciplined and maintain a united front. Chernenko quickly stepped into Andropov's shoes; he became Chairman of the USSR Defence Council and at the first session of the Supreme Soviet in April 1984 was elected President – the official Head of State. For this post he was proposed by Mr Gorbachev, who commented that holding this position was of 'tremendous significance for Soviet foreign policy'.

Chernenko, at 72 years of age, has a somewhat frail appearance. He has continued the Politbureau's policies begun by Andropov: the reform of the educational system was enacted in April 1984; the number of Soviet missiles based in the German Democratic Republic has been increased; he has presided both over a new offensive in Afghanistan and the Soviet withdrawal from the Olympic Games. The top leadership of the USSR should be considered as a collective body. Chernenko, as General Secretary, lacks the personal power of an American President; he is in a position more analogous to that of a British Prime Minister. The latter, however, selects the British Cabinet: the General Secretary of the CPSU is elected by the Politbureau, and the scope of the leader's activity is effectively limited by what that body will support. The influence of the General Secretary lies in his ability to 'steer' the Politbureau. Policy is 'incremental', even conservative. The kinds of demands articulated within the Politbureau and the expectations made on the political leadership will be the subject of the second part of this book.

NOTES

1 Cited by Adam B. Ulam, *Expansion and Coexistence: Soviet Foreign Policy, 1917–1973,* (Second edition 1974) p. 52.
2 Cited by L Kochan, *The Making of Modern Russia* (1962), p. 299.
3 See George F. Kennan, *Russia and the West under Lenin and Stalin* (1961).
4 Ulam, *Expansion and Coexistence.*
5 Ulam, though, argues that intervention prolonged the Civil War: ibid., p. 105.
6 Jane Degras (ed.), *The Communist International, 1919–1943: Documents, I: 1919–1922* (1956), p. 45, cited by Ulam, p. 113.
7 F. Claudin, *The Communist Movement from Comintern to Cominform* (1975).
8 Jan Meijer (ed.), *The Trotsky Papers, 1917–1922,* vol. I (1964), p. 623, cited by Ulam, p. 121.
9 On this topic see, E.H. Carr, *German – Soviet Relations Between the Two World Wars* (1951).
10 Max Beloff, *The Foreign Policy of Soviet Russia, 1929–1941,* vol. 1 (1947), p. 40.
11 J. Stalin in Degras, *Soviet Documents on Foreign Policy,* II, p. 238, cited by Ulam, p. 180.
12 L. Trotsky, *The Revolution Betrayed* (New York, 1945), pp. 186, 203.
13 George Allen Morgan, 'Stalin on Revolution', in Alex Simirenko, *Soviet Sociology* (1967), p. 187.
14 Cited by Morgan, *ibid.*
15 For a good account see Ulam, *Expansion and Coexistence,* and Kennan, *Russia and the West under Lenin and Stalin.*
16 For a detailed account of Soviet relations with Poland, Germany and the West in 1939, see Max Beloff, *The Foreign Policy of Soviet Russia, 1929–1941,* vol. 2 (1949). See also G.I. Weinberg, *Germany and the Soviet Union 1930–41* (1972).
17 Italics in the original. Cited by Alexander Werth, *Russia at War 1941–45* (1964), pp. 637–8. See also Harrison E. Salisbury, *The Siege of Leningrad* (1969); A Clark, *Barbarossa: The Russo-German Conflict 1941–45* (1965); J. Erickson, *The Road to Stalingrad* (1975); D. Clemens, *Yalta* (1970).
18 Harrison E. Salisbury, *The Siege of Leningrad* (1969), p. 516.
19 For a detailed account see Raymond L. Garthoff, *Soviet Military Policy* (1966), chapter 1.
20 For details on each country see Hugh Seton-Watson, *The East European Revolution* (1956). It should be noted here that political activity in Yugoslavia and Albania after the Second World War was from the beginning relatively independent of the USSR.
21 J.V. Stalin, *Post-War International Relations* (1947), p. 5. Cited by L. Churchward, *Contemporary Soviet Government* (1968), pp. 253–4.
22 D. Yergin, *Shattered Peace: The Origins of the Cold War and the National Security State* (1978).

23 George F. Kennan, 'The Sources of Soviet Conduct', *Foreign Affairs*, vol. 25 (July 1947), pp. 571–2.
24 G. Kolko, *The Politics of War* (1972).
25 Cited by B. Knei-Paz, *The Social and Political Thought of Leon Trotsky* (1978), p. 289.
26 J. Stalin, 'Foundations of Leninism' in B. Franklin, *The Essential Stalin*, 1973, p. 184.
27 A.G. Meyer, *Leninism* (1957), p. 282.
28 S.F. Cohen, 'Bolshevism and Stalinism', in R.C. Tucker, *Stalinism* (1977), pp. 12–13.
29 R. Pethybridge, *The Social Prelude to Stalinism* (1974).
30 W.M. Pintner and D.K. Rowney, *Russian Officialdom: The Bureaucratization of Russian Society from the Seventeenth to the Twentieth Century* (1980), p. 373.
31 *Pravda* (21 March 1953). Cited by J. Hough and M. Fainsod, *How the Soviet Union is Governed*, 1979, p. 205.
32 For details see L. Schapiro, *The Communist Party of the Soviet Union*, 1970, pp. 558–9.
33 *Pravda*, (10 July 1953). Cited by Hough and Fainsod, *How the Soviet Union . . .*, p. 206. This source has further details of personnel changes between 1953 and 1956.
34 Probably the best account of the post-Khrushchev period is to be found in M. Tatu, *Power in the Kremlin* (1969). See also Alec Nove, 'The Uses and Abuses of Kremlinology', in *Was Stalin Really Necessary?* (1964).
35 Robert Conquest, *Power and Policy in the USSR* (1961). Robert Conquest rightly said that the Soviet invasion of Czechoslovakia would take place; but his prediction that a 'decisive split at the highest level' in the USSR would develop 'in the fairly near future' did not materialize. R. Conquest, *Russia After Khrushchev* (1965), p. 264.
36 For details see Hough and Fainsod, *How the Soviet Union . . .*, pp. 204–210.
37 See Pethybridge, *A Key to Soviet Politics* (1962), chapter 2. L. Schapiro, *The Communist Party . . .*, has a similar summary, pp. 561–7.
38 Radio Moscow's English Service (3 July 1957). Cited by R. Conquest, *Power and Policy in the USSR* (1961), p. 265.
39 L. Schapiro, *The Communist Party . . .*, p. 569.
40 *Pravda* (7 July 1957), cited by Conquest, *Power and Policy in the USSR* (1961), p. 311.
41 *Pravda* (19 December 1958), cited by Conquest, ibid., p. 314.
42 Jerry Hough, 'The Soviet Elite', *Problems of Communism*, vol. 16, no. 1 (Jan/Feb. 1967), pp. 29–30.
43 Robert Conquest, *Power and Policy in the USSR* (1961), p. 31.
44 *Kommunist*, no. 10 (July 1957), p. 5. Cited by Myron Rush, *Political Succession in the USSR* (1965), p. 60.
45 *Khrushchev and the Soviet Leadership 1957–1964* (1966), pp. 7–8.
46 *Power in the Kremlin*, pp. 429–60.
47 T.W. Wolfe, 'Political Primacy vs. Professional Elan', *Problems of Commun-*

ism, vol. 13, no. 3 (1964), p. 50. For a more detailed account of the changing role of the military, see Roman Kolkowicz, *The Soviet Military and the Communist Party* (1967), esp. pp. 345–6.

48 For an account see R.L. Garthoff, *Soviet Military Policy*, chapter 3.

49 *Pravda* (15 January 1960). Cited by Linden, *Khrushchev and the Soviet Leadership . . .* , p. 93n.

50 R.L. Garthoff, *Soviet Military Policy* (1966), p. 58.

51 *Pravda* (22 June 1961), cited by M.P. Gallaher, 'Military Manpower: A Case Study', *Problems of Communism*, vol. 13, no. 3 (1964), p. 64.

52 R.L. Gartoff, *Soviet Military Policy*, p. 60.

53 Matthew P. Gallaher, 'Military Manpower . . .', p. 62.

54 John A. Armstrong, 'Party Bifurcation and Elite Interests', *Soviet Studies*, vol. 17, no. 4 (1966), p. 418.

55 Armstrong, ibid., p. 426.

56 For the best account using Kremlinological methods, see Michael Tatu, *Power in the Kremlin* (1967) Part Four. For a case study of agriculture, Sidney I. Ploss, *Conflict and Decision Making in Soviet Russia* (1965).

57 Report of British Communist Party visit to Moscow, cited by L. Churchward, *Contemporary Soviet Government* (1968), p. 287.

58 J.A. Armstrong, 'Party Bifurcation and Elite Interests', (1966), p. 418.

59 Hough and Fainsod, *How The Soviet Union is Governed*, p. 236.

60 Terry McNeil, 'The Kosygin Succession – a One-Horse Race', Munich–Radio Liberty, RL 313/80, p. 3.

61 Hough and Fainsod, *How The Soviet Union is Governed*, pp. 252–6.

62 *Narodnoe obrazovanie, nauka i kul'tura v SSSR* (M. 1977), p. 7.

63 S. Bialer, *Stalin's Successors* (1980), p. 24.

64 Further biographical data have been summarized by H. Kraus, Radio Liberty Report, Munich, 1982 RL 452/82.

65 W.G. Hyland, 'Kto Kogo in the Kremlin', *Problems of Communism*, vol. 31, no. 1 (Jan.-Feb. 1982), p. 24.

66 Marc D. Zlotnik, 'Chernenko's Platform', *Problems of Communism*, vol. 31, no. 6 (Nov.-Dec., 1982), pp. 70–80.

67 See particularly the account in Zhores Medvedev, *Andropov* (1983), pp. 93–7.

68 Press Report, United Press International. (12 November 1982).

69 Peter Taylor, Radio Liberty Report, Munich 1983, RL 236/83, p. 2.

70 Michel Tatu, 'Andropov in Power: the Succession Reconsidered', Radio Liberty Report, Munich 1983, RFE 405/83, pp. 3–4.

71 Henry Shapiro, *United Press International Feature* (25 November 1982). Shapiro himself pours scorn on such views.

72 E. Teague, Radio Liberty Report, Munich 1982, RL 454/82, p. 5.

73 Jerry F. Hough, 'Andropov's First Year', *Problems of Communism*, vol. 32, no. 6 (1983), pp. 60–1; Vadim Medish, 'A Romanov in the Kremlin?', *ibid.* pp. 65–6.

Further Reading to Part I

This bibliography does not include all references cited in the text. It is intended to assist the reader who wishes to pursue further study. Under 'Introductory' are listed works dealing with general themes; under 'Basic' are articles and books which are reliable guides to particular topics; 'Specialized' includes literature involving a more detailed treatment, which might be consulted by the specialist.

Introductory

Avinieri, Shlomo. *The Social and Political Thought of Karl Marx*. London: Cambridge University Press, 1970.

Bialer, Seweryn. *Stalin's Successors* Cambridge: Cambridge University Press, 1980.

Bottomore, T.B. and Rubel M. (eds). *Karl Marx, Selected Writing in Sociology and Social Philosophy*. London: Penguin Books, 1963.

Buchan, A. *The End of the Post-War Era: A New Balance of World Power*. New York: Dutton, 1974.

Carr, E.H. *The Russian Revolution from Lenin to Stalin*. London: Macmillan, 1980.

Dobb, Maurice. *Soviet Economic Development Since 1917*. London: Routledge, 1966.

Kochan, Lionel B. *Russia in Revolution 1890–1918*. London: Paladin, 1970.

Lane, David. *Leninism: A Sociological Interpretation*. Cambridge: Cambridge University Press, 1981.

McLellan, D. *Marxism After Marx*. London: Macmillan 1980.

McLellan, D. (ed.). *Marx: The First Hundred Years*. London: Fontana, 1983.

Miliband, R. *Marxism and Politics*. Oxford: Oxford University Press, 1977.

Nettl, J.P. *The Soviet Achievement*. London: Thames and Hudson, 1967.

Nove, A. *An Economic History of the USSR*. London: Allen and Unwin, 1969.

Ulam, Adam. *The Rivals: America and Russia since World War II*. London: Allen Lane, 1971.

Werth, Alexander. *Russia at War, 1941–45*. London: Barrie and Rockliff, 1964.

Wolfe, Bertram. *Three Who Made a Revolution*. London: Thames and Hudson, 1956.

Basic

Beloff, Max. *The Foreign Policy of Soviet Russia, 1929–1941*, 2 vols. London: Oxford University Press, 1947 and 1949.

Bunyan, James, and Fisher, H.H. *The Bolshevik Revolution, 1917–18: Documents and Materials*. Stanford, California: Hoover Institute, 1934.

Carr, E.H. *The Bolshevik Revolution, 1917–1923*, 3 vols. London: Macmillan, 1950–1953.

Carr, E.H. *Socialism in one Country*, vol. 5 of *A History of Soviet Russia*. London: Macmillan, 1959.

Chamberlin, William H. *The Russian Revolution, 1917–1921*. New York: Macmillan, 1952.

Cohen, S.F. 'Bolshevism and Stalinism', in R.C. Tucker, *Stalinism*. New York: Norton, 1977, pp. 12–13.

Deutscher, Isaac. *The Prophet Outcast. Trotsky, 1929–1940*. London: Oxford University Press, 1963.

Eason, Warren W. 'Population Changes', in Cyril E. Black (ed.), *The Transformation of Russian Society*. Cambridge, Mass.: Harvard University Press, 1960, pp. 72–90.

Elleinstein,Jean. *The Stalin Phenomenon*. London: Lawrence and Wishart, 1976.

Ferro, Mark. *The Russian Revolution of February 1917*. London: Routledge, 1972.

Fitzpatrick, S. (ed.) *Cultural Revolution in Russia 1928–1931*. Bloomington: Indiana University Press, 1978.

Haimson, Leopold. *The Russian Marxists and the Origins of Bolshevism*. Cambridge, Mass.: Harvard University Press, 1965.

Harding, Neil. *Lenin's Political Thought*. London: Macmillan, vol. 1, 1977 vol. 2, 1981.

Hough, J. and Fainsod, M. *How The Soviet Union is Governed*, Cambridge, Mass.: Harvard University Press, 1979.

Kaplan, F.I. *Bolshevik Ideology and the Ethics of Soviet Labour*. New York: Philosophical Library, 1968.

Knei-Paz, Baruch. *The Social and Political Thought of Leon Trotsky*. London: Oxford University Press, 1978.

Kolko, Gabriel. *The Politics of War*. New York: Harper and Row, 1972.

Lenin, V.I. 'What is to be Done?' in *Collected Works*, vol. 5. Moscow: Foreign Languages Publishing House, 1961.

Lewin, M. *Russian Peasants and Soviet Power. A Study of Collectivisation*, translated by Irene Nove. London: Allen and Unwin, 1968.

Lorimer, Frank. *The Population of the Soviet Union*. Geneva: League of Nations, 1946.

Lyashchenko, P.I. *History of the National Economy of Russia*. New York: Macmillan, 1949.

Marx, K. 'Preface to the Critique of Political Economy', in *Selected Works*, vol. 1. Moscow: Foreign Languages Publishing House, 1958.

Marx, K., and Engels, F. 'The Manifesto of the Communist Party', in *Selected Works*, vol. 1. Moscow: Foreign Languages Publishing House, 1958, pp. 21–65.

Marx, K., and Engels , F. 'Critique of the Gotha Programme', in *Selected Works*, vol. 2. Moscow: Foreign Languages Publishing House, 1959, pp. 13–45.

Pethybridge, R. *The Social Prelude to Stalinism*. London: Macmillan, 1974.

Rashin, A.G. *Formirovanie rabochego klassa Rossii*. Moscow: Sotsekgiz, 1958.

Schapiro, Leonard. *The Communist Party of the Soviet Union*. London: Constable, 1970.

Stalin, J.V. *Foundations of Leninism*. Lectures delivered at the Sverdlov University at the beginning of April 1924. London: Lawrence and Wishart, 1942.

Stalin, J.V. *Problems of Leninism*. Moscow: Foreign Languages Publishing House, 1941.

Trotsky, Leon. *The History of the Russian Revolution*. New York: Simon and Schuster, 1936.

Tucker, Robert (ed.). *Stalinism: Essays in Historical Interpretation*. New York: Norton, 1977.

White, S. *Political Culture and Soviet Politics* London: Macmillan, 1979.

Specialized

Aron, Raymond. *Democracy and Totalitarianism*. London. Weidenfeld and Nicolson, 1968.

Aspaturian, V.V. *Process and Power in Soviet Foreign Policy*. Boston: Little, Brown, 1971.

Avrich, P. *Kronstadt, 1921*. Princeton: Princeton University Press. 1970.

Bergson, Abram. *The Real National Income of Soviet Russia Since 1928*. Cambridge, Mass.: Harvard University Press, 1961.

Bradley, John. *Allied Intervention in Russia*. London: Weidenfeld and Nicolson, 1968.

Brzezinski, Z.K. *The Permanent Purge* Cambridge, Mass.: Harvard University Press, 1956.

Carr, E.H. and Davies, R.W., *Foundations of a Planned Economy 1926–29*, vols. 1 & 2, London: Macmillan, 1969 and 1971.

Cohen, G.A. *Karl Marx's Theory of History: A Defence*. London: Oxford University Press, 1978.

Conquest, Robert. *The Great Terror, Stalin's Purge of the Thirties*. London: Macmillan, 1968.

Conquest, Robert (ed.). *The Soviet Police System*. London: Bodley Head, 1968.

Davies, R.W. 'Planning for Rapid Growth in the USSR', in *Economics of Planning*, vol. 5, no. 1–2, 1965, pp. 74–86.

Davies, R.W. *The Collectivisation of Soviet Agriculture*. London: Macmillan, 1980.

Davies, R.W. *The Soviet Collective Farm 1929–1930*. London: Macmillan, 1980.

Degras, Jane (ed.). *Soviet Documents on Foreign Policy*, 3 vols. London: Oxford University Pres, 1951–3.

Degras, Jane (ed.). *The Communist International, 1919–1943: Documents, I: 1919–1922*. London and New York: Oxford University Press, 1956.

Dunham, Vera. *In Stalin's Time*. Cambridge: Cambridge University Press, 1976.

Economic Bulletin for Europe, 'Regional Economic Policy in the Soviet Union: The Case of Central Asia', vol. 9, no. 3, Nov. 1957.

Ellman, Michael. 'Did the Agricultural Surplus Provide the Resources for the Increase in Investment in the USSR During the First Five Year Plan?', in *Economic Journal*, 85, December 1975, pp. 844–64.

Feis, Herbert. *From Trust to Terror: The Onset of the Cold War, 1945–1950*. London: Anthony Blond, 1970.

Ferro, M. *October 1917: A Social History of the Russian Revolution*. London: Routledge, 1980.

Garthoff, Raymond L. *Soviet Military Policy: A Historical Analysis*. New York: Praeger, 1966.

Garthoff, Raymond L. 'Mutual Deterrence and Strategic Arms Control', in *International Security*, vol.3, no. 1, 1978.

Gerschenkron, Alexander. 'The Rate of Industrial Growth in Russia since 1885', in *The Journal of Economic History*, vol. 7 (Supplement), 1947 pp. 144–74.

Getzler, I. *Kronstadt 1917–1921. The Fate of a Social Democracy*. Cambridge: Cambridge University Press, 1982.

Haimson, L. (ed.). *The Politics of Rural Russia, 1905–1914*. Indiana University Press 1979.

Hoffman, E.P. and Fleron, F.J. (eds). *The Conduct of Soviet Foreign Policy*, 2nd edn. New York: Aldine, 1980.

Johnson, D.G., and Kahan, A. *Comparisons of the United States and Soviet Economies*. Washington: Joint Economic Committee of US Congress, 1960.

Keep, J.L. *The Russian Revolution: A Study in Mass Mobilization*. London: Weidenfeld and Nicolson 1976.

Kemp-Welch, A. 'Stalinism and Intellectual Order', in T.H. Rigby, A. Brown and P. Reddaway, *Authority, Power and Policy in the USSR*. London: Macmillan, 1980.

Kennan, George F. 'The Sources of Soviet Conduct', in *Foreign Affairs*. vol. 25, July 1947, pp. 566–82.

Kennan, George F. *Russia and the West under Lenin and Stalin*. London: Hutchinson, 1961.

Khrushchev, N.A. 'Speech to the Twentieth Congress', reprinted in *The 20th Congress and World Trotskyism*. London: New Park, 1957.

Kolakowski, L. *Main Currents of Marxism*, 3 vols. London: Oxford University Press, 1978.

Lane, David. *The Roots of Russian Communism*. Assen: Van Gorcum, 1975.

Lenin, V.I. 'The Two Tactics of Social Democracy in the Democratic Revolution', in *Selected Works* (1936), vol. 3. Moscow: 1936.

Lenin, V.I. *Imperialism, The Highest Stage of Capitalism*. London: Lawrence and Wishart, 1948.

Lenin, V.I. *The State and Revolution*. Moscow: Foreign Languages Publishing House, 1958.

Lenin, V.I. 'The Tasks of the Proletariat in the Present Revolution', in *Collected Works*, vol. 24. Moscow: 1964, pp. 19–26.

McLellan, D. *Marx: The First Hundred Years*. London: Fontana, 1983.

Marx, Karl. *Capital*, 3 vols. Moscow: Foreign Languages Publishing House, vol. 1, 1958; vol. 2, 1957; vol. 3, 1959

Medvedev, R. *Let History Judge*. New York: Alfred A. Knopf, 1971.

Medvedev, R. *The October Revolution*. London: Constable 1979.

Melotti, Umberto, *Marx and the Third World*. London: Macmillan, 1977.

Moore, Barrington, Jr. *Social Origins of Dictatorship and Democracy*. London: Allen Lane, 1967.

Moore, Barrington. *Injustice: The Social Bases of Obedience and Revolt.* New York: M.E. Sharpe, 1978.

Nutter, G.W. *Growth of Industrial Production in the Soviet Union.* Princeton, N.J.: Princeton University Press, 1962.

Perrie, M. *The Agrarian Policy of the Russian Socialist Revolutionary Party.* Cambridge: Cambridge University Press, 1977.

Pethybridge, Roger. *The Spread of the Russian Revolution.* London: Macmillan, 1973.

Pintner, W.M. and Rowney, D.K. 'Officialdom and Bureaucracy: Conclusion', in W.M. Pintner and D.K. Rowney, *Russian Officialdom: the Bureaucratisation of Russian Society from the Seventeenth to the Twentieth Century.* London: Macmillan, 1980.

Rabinowitch, A. *The Bolsheviks Come to Power. The Revolution of 1917 in Petrograd.* New York: Norton, 1976.

Rattansi, A. *Marx and the Division of Labour.* London: Macmillan, 1982.

Reed, John. *Ten Days that Shook the World.* New York: Vintage Books, 1960.

Richardson, J.L. 'Cold-War Revisionism. A Critique', in *World Politics*, vol. 24, no. 4, July 1972, pp. 579–612.

Rigby, T.H. *Communist Party Membership in the USSR, 1917–1967.* Princeton, New Jersey: Princeton University Press, 1968.

Salisbury, Harrison E. *The Siege of Leningrad.* London: Secker and Warburg, 1969.

Shanin, T. *The Awkward Class.* London: Oxford University Press, 1972.

Skocpol, T. *States and Social Revolutions.* New York: Cambridge University Press, 1979.

Solzhenitsyn, A. *The Gulag Archipelago.* Glasgow: Collins/Fontana, 1974.

Stone, Lawrence. 'Theories of Revolution', in *World Politics,* vol. 18, no. 2, January 1966, pp. 159–76.

Tökés, R.L. (ed.). *Eurocommunism and Detente.* Oxford: Martin Robertson, 1978.

Trotsky, L. *The Permanent Revolution,* London: Plough Press, 1957.

Trotsky, L. *The Revolution Betrayed: The Soviet Union, What It is and Where It Is Going.* New York: Pioneer Publishers, 1958.

Trotsky, L. *The New Course,* translated by Max Schachtman. Ann Arbor, Michigan: University of Michigan Press, 1965.

Tucker, R.C. *Philosophy and Myth in Karl Marx.* Cambridge: Cambridge University Press, 1961.

Tucker, R.C. *The Soviet Political Mind.* New York: Praeger, 1963.

Ulam, Adam B. *Expansion and Coexistence: Soviet Foreign Policy 1917–1973.* New York: Holt, Rinehart and Winston, Second Edition. 1974.

Unger, A.L. 'Stalin's Renewal of the Leading Stratum', in *Soviet Studies*, vol. 20, Jan. 1969, pp. 321–30.

Venturi, Franco. *The Roots of Revolution: A History of the Populist and Socialist Movements in 19th Century Russia*, translated by Francis Haskell. London: Weidenfeld and Nicolson, 1960.

Von Laue, Theodore H. *Sergei Witte and the Industrialisation of Russia.* New York:

Columbia University Press, 1963.

Wheatcroft, S.G. 'On Assessing the Size of Forced Concentration Camp Labour in the Soviet Union, 1929–56', in *Soviet Studies*, vol. 33, no. 2, 1981.

Winner, Irene. 'Some Problems of Nomadism and Social Organisation among the Recently Settled Kazakhs', in *Central Asian Review*, no. 11, 1963.

Wolin, Simon and Robert M. Slusser. *The Soviet Secret Police*. Westport, CT: The Greenwood Press, 1975.

Zaleski, E. *Stalinist Planning for Economic Growth 1933–1952*. London: Macmillan 1980.

Zimmerman, William. *Soviet Perspectives on International Relations*. Princeton, New Jersey: Princeton University Press, 1969.

Zlotnik, Marc D. 'Chernenko's Platform', in *Problems of Communism*, vol. 31, no. 6, Nov.–Dec. 1982, pp. 70–80.

Part II
POLITICS

5

THE COMMUNIST PARTY

It is impossible to understand American or British politics without an understanding of the principles of democracy which legitimate the political institutions and processes of these two countries. The same is true of Soviet society. In this chapter we shall first examine the Soviet Marxist notion of communism and developed socialism; then we shall turn to consider the ways that the Communist Party is organized. In the next chapter the government structure will be outlined and we shall consider some Western objections to the Soviet model. In the following two chapters (7 and 8), the processes of Soviet politics will be studied.

Socialism and Communism in Soviet Theory

We have seen that, for Marxists, class relations are based on property relationships. We have noted that after the revolution, the 'dictatorship of the proletariat' ensured the domination of the working class through the party over the dispossessed bourgeoisie and aristocracy. In 1936, Stalin decreed that socialism had been achieved and that no 'contradictory' classes existed in the USSR. The nationalization of property, and planned production guided by the Communist Party, gave rise to a *socialist* society.

In socialist society these elements (the main elements of the production process – labour power and the means of production) are combined in such a way that those taking part in the production process collectively own the instruments of labour which they employ. This totally excludes the possibility of the means of production being converted by one part of society into a means of exploitation of the other part of society. Since they jointly own social property and jointly participate in the social production process, all people are equal and their relations are based on principles of comradely co-operation and mutual assistance.[1]

The point to be emphasized here is that this consensual view of Soviet society is based on the Marxist notion, described earlier, that social and political conflict derives from ownership relations which give rise to classes

141

and their antagonism. From Stalin's viewpoint the abolition of property-owning classes, therefore, entailed the elimination of the major forms of socio-political conflict.

In 1936 the 'Stalin' Constitution was decreed. It proclaimed direct election to the Soviets (or Parliaments), secret ballot and the enfranchisement of all social classes. There was, of course, no freedom for the organization of political parties: parties could only rest on a class basis, and, as there were no classes in Soviet Russia, there could be no basis for them. The state, in the sense of an institution of legitimate coercion and military power, still existed. This was justified by reference to the encirclement of the USSR by hostile war-like capitalist states. The USSR required a state to protect and extend socialist power.

According to Stalin's theory there was friendly collaboration between the three main social groups: intelligentsia, working class and peasantry. This did not mean that there was complete harmony: there were still some areas of strife. For example, practices and values, which were derived from previous non-socialist epochs, and the differences between town and country gave rise to groups with separate and specific interests. Such conflicts, however, could be contained within the parameters of the Soviet state system: they were 'non-antagonistic' contradictions, rather than the antagonistic ones of the capitalist system which could only be resolved by a fundamental change in the social order. While conflict existed on a world scale between the USSR and the leading capitalist states, internally the social order and social relations as a whole were viewed as basically harmonious. Soviet political institutions were constructed on these assumptions.

The Soviet theory of socialism is unlike that of contemporary Western social democracy. It is based on the nature of commodity production: for Lenin, socialism was 'the abolition of a commodity economy'.[2] Western social democracy is more concerned with the equality of the *distribution* of commodities and resources (such as income and education). As Lenin put it: 'General talk about freedom, equality and democracy is in fact but a blind repetition of concepts shaped by the relations of commodity production ... Long ago Engels in his *Anti-Dühring* explained that the concept of "equality" is moulded from the relations of commodity production; equality becomes a prejudice if it is not understood to mean the *abolition of classes*. This elementary truth regarding the distinction between the bourgeois-democratic and the socialist conception is constantly being forgotten.'[3]

Socialism, however, is but the first stage of communism, which is the highest form of society. Marx defined the features of communism in only general terms.[4] In the *Critique of the Gotha Programme*, he said:

In a higher phase of communist society, after the enslaving subordination of the individual to the division of labour, and therewith also the antithesis between mental and physical labour, has vanished; after labour has become not merely only a means of life, but life's prime want; after the productive forces have also increased with the all-round development of the individual, and all the springs of co-operative wealth flow more abundantly – only then can the narrow horizon of bourgeois right be crossed in its entirety and society inscribe on its banners: From each according to his ability, to each according to his needs![5]

As there are no classes in communist society, there can no longer be any coercive state or apparatus of oppression which, by Marxist definition, is essentially the executive of the ruling class. Economically too, communism differs from socialism. Under communism an abundance of goods is produced, money and prices disappear: for money is a means to distribute scarce goods. Perhaps the most succinct definition of social relations under communism is that in a classless society, 'one works according to one's ability and receives according to one's needs.'

On some component parts of his theory of society, Marx was ambiguous and his followers have reinterpreted his work. For example, Marx implied that the division of labour would be superseded under communism. Ali Rattansi, however, dismisses such 'romantic, almost visionary passages'[6] in Marx's early work. The mature Marx of *Capital*, he holds, recognizes that the complete abolition of the division of labour, even under communism, is not possible.

What is clear from his writings is that, under communism, goods and services will be produced for use – not for profit and exchange, as under capitalism. Some part of production, however, will be retained for renewal and investment. For this society as a whole will extract 'surplus' from the producers, and such 'surplus' is not the same as that extracted as 'surplus value' or 'profit' under capitalism. The distribution of goods and services will be according to need and not (as in the first stage of communism) according to the differential contribution to production. Alienation will disappear and the individual will be a 'free' person, being in unity with other people and with nature.

In Marxist theory, moreover, the abolition of capitalism and the advent of communism lead to the 'withering away' of the state. Lenin made this explicit in *State and Revolution:* 'So long as the state exists, there is no freedom; when freedom exists, there will be no state.' But in the USSR, at present a state apparatus is still necessary in theory for the organization of material construction, to 'exercise control' over work and consumption, to maintain 'law and order' and socialist property and to fortify the regime against external attack. Indeed, only with the 'triumph and consolidation' of socialism in the world arena will the state become unnecessary.

TABLE 5.1: COMMUNISM AS A MODE OF PRODUCTION

ECONOMY:	High capital intensive production (automation)
	Colletive ownership
	Rational system of production and exchange (planning)
	Production of use values
	Extraction of surplus (for renewal and investment)
	Division of labour – minimal or abolished
POLITY:	Classless society
	Administration of things (state 'withers away')
	Political process: co-operation, harmony, democracy
SOCIAL:	Distribution by need
	Liberation of dependent strata (e.g. women)
	Unity and freedom of individual
	Universal leisure
	Equality of treatment or consideration

It might be useful here to summarize some of the main features of the *communist mode of production* as reconstructed from Marx's own works. This is attempted in table 5.1. A communist economy has collective ownership and a rational system of the production of use values. The extraction of surplus product continues for purposes of renewal and investment. It is likely that some kind of division of labour will be necessary. The polity is a classless one. The state as the instrument of coercion of a dominant class will have 'withered away'. The political process is one of harmony, co-operation and democracy. Social relations will be characterized by the freedom of the individual. People will receive according to their needs. There will be universal leisure and equality of treatment or consideration.

Developed Socialism

Soviet society is not in theory or in practice a communist mode of production. Present leaders of the Soviet state define it as being in the stage of 'developed socialism' *(zrely* or *razvitoy sotsializm)*. This is different, in theory, from communism. It has four characteristics, derived from Stalin's notion of socialism:

1. The class *relations* of the means of production have been socialized following the seizure of power by the Bolsheviks and the nationalization of the means of production.
2. State planning has replaced the bourgeois market as a method of co-ordination of the economy and allocation of resources; competition

between capitals has been superseded and labour has lost its character as a commodity.

3. Once the industrialization process was completed (during the first Five Year Plan in Russia), the *level* of productive forces was sufficient to define the economy as being at the socialist stage.

4. Given the hegemony of the Communist Party and its control of the major institutional systems (ideology, science, education), the superstructure is socialist, and the remaining incongruities or 'left-overs' (religious views, personality cults, petty crime) from other modes of production will gradually disappear with the maturation of socialist society.

The notion of 'developed socialism' emphasizes the greater economic maturity of modern Soviet society.[7] This in turn enables a more 'harmonious' type of development to take place, with a move away from the concentration of resources in investment towards a greater emphasis on consumer welfare. This transformation is to be achieved by harnessing the benefits of the 'scientific-technological revolution' to the socialist system. A greater 'coming together' *(sblizhenie)* of the groups constituting Soviet society is occurring: differences between town and country will narrow, and the distinctions between manual and non-manual workers will decline. In short, a 'new historical community of people' is being created.[8] The preamble of the 1977 Constitution succinctly summarizes these goals: the tasks of the Soviet state are 'to build the material and technical foundations of communism, to perfect social relations and transform them into communist relations, to mould the citizen of communist society, to raise the living standards and cultural level of the working people, to ensure the country's security, to help strengthen peace and to promote international cooperation.'

In this essentially unitary and harmonious society, conflict continues. But such clashes are of a qualitatively different kind from those found under capitalism. As Kosolapov has put it:

... conflicts and clashes occur, but they are no longer an expression of the struggle of class against class, of labour against capital and capital against labour or of enmity between nations; as a rule, they are evidence either of disagreements *between individuals* or of the selfish interests *of an individual or group of individuals* as juxtaposed to the interests of all of society. Marxism–Leninism has always distinguished between *social antagonism,* which has no place under socialism, and *individual antagonism,* which will still be encountered for a long time, and it has always taken a critical attitude towards attempts to identify them as the same thing.[9]

In international relations the role of the Soviet Union under 'developed socialism' is to support the struggle of peoples for 'national liberation and social progress', and it also seeks to maintain peaceful relations with the leading capitalist states.[10] A major objective is to strengthen the position of world socialism and to prevent wars of aggression. Relations between socialist countries and the Soviet Union should be based on 'socialist internationalism'. This policy might be contrasted with the more aggressive version of Marxism (adopted by supporters of Chairman Mao) that emphasizes the antagonistic contradictions in the world.

The present stage of Soviet society falls for short of the ideal notion of communism described above. It is not contemplated that either the government or the party will 'wither away', and the need for political organization continues. This takes the concrete form of the institutions of the Communist Party (which provides political *rukovodstvo*, leadership), those of the Council of Ministers (which administers the country – the *upravlenie*) and those of the Soviets (which provide for the expression of popular demands, for oversight of the administration, and for public participation in affairs of state). Commodities and services are still distributed according to one's deserts (i.e. depending on one's work) and not according to need. Money will remain in use as a medium of exchange for a considerable time and the family, as a social institution, is 'under the protection of the state'. The divisions between town and country and between manual and non-manual labour also continue.

Having discussed the Soviet conception of developed socialism we shall turn to a description of the actual structure of contemporary Soviet society and the political processes at work in it. I shall outline the formal institutions, which are mentioned in the Constitution of the USSR and which are known through previous research to play a leading political role. These include the organization and membership of the party, and the forms of the Soviets (Parliaments) and their membership. Finally, at the end of the next chapter, I shall mention some Western criticism of Soviet institutions and an alternative view of the Soviet state. In subsequent chapters, the processes at work in Soviet politics will be analysed.

The Party Structure

In Soviet Russia after the October Revolution of 1917, the Communist Party became the authoritative source of values and now has a monopoly of political organization. It claims the right to make pronouncements in a wide range of fields. Its statements on science, education and the organization of the economy are more detailed and have more influence than party statements in liberal-democratic states. In the 1977 Constitution, the role of the·party was defined as follows:

The Communist Party of the Soviet Union is the leading and guiding force of Soviet society and the nucleus of its political system, of all state and public organisations. The CPSU exists for the people and serves the people.
The Communist Party, armed with Marxism–Leninism, determines the general perspectives of the development of society and the course of the home and foreign policy of the USSR, directs the great constructive work of the Soviet people, and imparts a planned, systematic and theoretically substantiated character to their struggle for the victory of communism.[11]

The CPSU is the only political party in the Soviet Union. It should be made clear, however, that the CPSU is not the government any more than the British Labour Party or the American Democratic Party, when in office, is the government of Great Britain or the USA. The government is organizationally separate. Here I may anticipate the next chapter by saying that the cohesion of the Communist Party of the Soviet Union is stronger and its influence more direct over the government than that of parties in liberal-democratic societies.

When we say that the party in the USSR has a monopoly over political power, this does not mean that every action taken in the USSR is determined by the party. Many decisions taken in social institutions like the family or in government departments are made without recourse to party authority. What is meant is that the party's values are dominant and solely legitimate: i.e. in Soviet terminology, only the party safeguards the interests of the working class. It decides the social, economic and political goals of the society: it fixes the relationship between people and property, shapes the dominant economic and political mores, and exercises control over the selection of the leading personnel in the government.

To understand the ideological role of the party in more detail it is helpful to look at its structure and the formal principles that officially govern it. The notion of democratic centralism as formulated by Lenin has already been discussed in chapter 2 (see pp. 41–2). The modern party's rules stipulate that the guiding principle of the organizational structure of the party is democratic centralism. This means:

(i) the election of all leading party bodies, from the lowest to the highest;
(ii) periodical reports of party bodies to their party organisations and to higher bodies;
(iii) strict party discipline and subordination of the minority to the majority;
(iv) the decisions of higher bodies are [binding on] lower bodies.[12]

The formal structure of the party embodying these formal organizational principles is shown in diagram 5.1.

The Communist Party of the Soviet Union covers the whole territory of

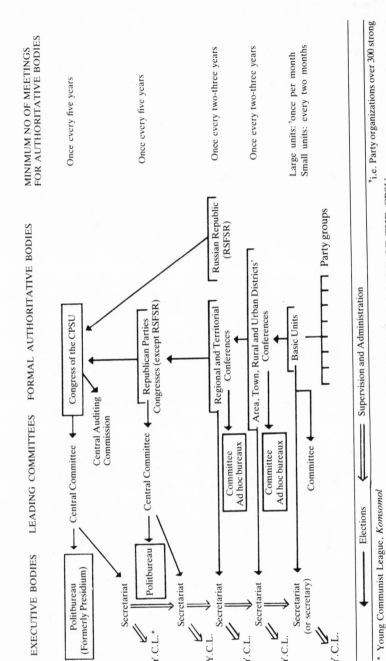

EXECUTIVE BODIES   LEADING COMMITTEES   FORMAL AUTHORITATIVE BODIES

MINIMUM NO OF MEETINGS
FOR AUTHORITATIVE BODIES

Once every five years

Once every five years

Once every two-three years

Once every two-three years

Large units: †once per month
Small units: every two months

Politbureau
(Formerly Presidium)

Central Committee

Congress of the CPSU

Russian Republic
(RSFSR)

Central Auditing
Commission

Secretariat

Y.C.L.*

Politbureau

Central Committee

Republican Parties
Congresses (except RSFSR)

Secretariat

Y.C.L.

Secretariat

Regional and Territorial
Conferences

Committee
Ad hoc bureaux

Y.C.L.

Secretariat

Area, Town, Rural and Urban Districts'
Conferences

Committee
Ad hoc bureaux

Y.C.L.

Secretariat
(or secretary)

Basic Units

Committee

Party groups

Y.C.L.

——— Elections

⇒ Supervision and Administration

* Young Communist League, *Komsomol*

† i.e. Party organizations over 300 strong

DIAGRAM 5.1: ORGANIZATIONAL CHART OF THE CPSU

the USSR and embraces the Communist Parties of the union republics, all of which, except the RSFSR,[13] have their own Republican Communist Party. The single arrows in diagram 5.1 show the elective processes within the party; double arrows denote supervision and administration. This diagram, of course, represents only what the rules define as the proper procedure.

At the bottom of the diagram are the party basic units, or primary party organizations. These are formed at the workplace in factories, state farms, collective farms, schools and the armed forces; they may also be formed at the place of residence – in villages or on housing estates. The minimum number required to form a branch is three. Those fifteen or more in number elect a bureau (or executive), those with less elect a secretary and deputy secretary. Party branches qualify for a full-time salaried official if branch membership exceeds 150. Branches with more than 300 members must meet at least once a month; those with less may meet every two months. Basic units may be sub-divided into branches, for example, in factories, by shift or workshop.

The upward–pointing arrows illustrate the first condition of the party's organizational structure: the election of all leading bodies. The centralization of political decision-making and the subordination of the members to the leaders are mainly enforced by the Secretariat which is responsible for day-to-day policy. The double lines stand for the processes linking the administration of the party at all levels and ensure that central policy is consistent throughout the party machine. The double lines pointing down and to the left show the links between the party and the youth organization, the Young Communist League (*Komsomol*). Here too are links with other bodies, such as the government and trade unions. As pointed out above, the party is the leading core of all organizations of the working people, both government and voluntary.[14] The party and its groups are expected to bring influence to bear over other bodies. This is done through party groups organized in them. (The example of party intervention in the administration is given in Chapter 7.)

The process· of election formally takes place at all levels of the organization. As shown in diagram 5.1, the basic units elect delegates to area, town or district conferences, which should meet once every two to three years. These in turn elect delegates to regional conferences, which (except in the RSFSR) elect to Republican Congresses, which again (together with the regional conferences of the RSFSR) elect to the Congress of the CPSU, the party's supreme body. At the Congress, the Central Committee is elected, which in turn elects the Politbureau[15] and the leading secretaries. The Politbureau is the chief deliberating and policy-making body; in July 1983 it had 19 members (11 full);[16] after the assumption of the General Secretaryship by Chernenko in 1984 there were 18 members (12 full). (See list below, pp. 166–8).

The decisions of higher bodies are binding on lower ones. The highest authoritative body is the Congress of the CPSU, which is equivalent to the national conventions of the major American parties, or the British Labour Party or Conservative Party annual conference. Next in order of importance come the Congresses of the Union Republics, the Conferences of regions and territories, followed by those of local territorial organizations (towns, rural and urban districts, etc.) and finally, the general meeting of the basic party groups.

The Congresses and Conferences elect a Secretariat, which administers the departments concerned with specific questions. The General Secretary, who heads the administration, is in a strong position to influence policy and its implementation. The Secretariat, which he controls, is responsible to the Central Committee for directing 'current work, chiefly the selection of cadres and the verification of the fulfilment of party decisions'.[17] As we shall see later, this gives the Secretariat considerable *de facto* power within the party. The departments themselves are of crucial importance, for they provide information and policy recommendations for the Politbureau and Central Committee of the CPSU. Though they are not now defined in the party rules,[18] Western research has established that there are the following specialized departments: party organs, propaganda and agitation, agriculture and food, science, higher educational institutes and schools, culture, heavy industry, light industry, machine construction, defence, economic development, chemical industry, fuel industry, construction, transportation, trade finance and planning organs, administration, foreign, liaison with parties of socialist countries, security, chief political administration of the Soviet army and navy, letters to the Central Committee, party commission, general department, and administration of the Central Committee of the CPSU.[19]

An important aspect of the Secretariat's work is the control of cadres, i.e. party membership and recruitment to non-party posts. The All-Union and Republican Party bureaux exercise control of recruitment to all the leading positions: heads of enterprises, editors and government deputies. A similar structure exists at the local level, where the Secretariat is regularly in contact with the top *apparat*. The Secretariat, shown in the diagram by arrows pointing leftward, administers policy and provides full-time party workers.

In the top left-hand corner of diagram 5.1 are the chief decision-making bodies within the party. The Secretariat has already been described. The Central Committee (at the Twenty Sixth Congress in 1981, it had a full membership of 319 and 151 candidates members) 'directs the activities of the party, the local party bodies, selects and appoints leading officials, directs the work of central government bodies and public organisations of working people through the party groups in them, sets up various party organs, institutions and enterprises and directs their activities, appoints the editors of the central newspapers and journals operating under its control and distributes the funds of the party budget and controls its execution'.[20]

Political Recruitment: Party Membership

Like all political parties, the CPSU recruits from the population political activists and trains professional politicians. Membership is open to 'any citizen of the Soviet Union who accepts the Programme and Rules of the Party, takes an active part in communist construction, works in one of the party organisations, carries out all party decisions and pays membership dues'.[21] Duverger has distinguished between *cadre* and *mass* political parties. 'A *cadre* party is small, and derives its power from the quality of members, bringing influence to bear on the basis of individual knowledge, prestige, riches or skill. A *mass* party has a large membership: its tactics are to make its influence felt by the strength of numbers of members.'[22] Duverger argues that parties 'based on cells ... are mass parties, but less definitely so'. One must distinguish between the different forms taken by the Russian Communist Party during its history. The activity and composition of the Bolshevik party were very different before the October Revolution from those of the CPSU today. The RSDLP (Russian Social Democratic Labour Party), the precursor of the CPSU and operating in the Russian underground before the revolution, was more of a cadre party based on members with a strong commitment to Marxism. The modern ruling party, particularly since the end of the Second World War, has had a mass character. The change may be gauged by the growth in membership[23] (excluding the *Komsomol* or Young Communist League) from about 390,000 in 1918 to 18.1 million in 1983, representing over nine per cent of the *adult* population. Since, however, many politically active people remain in the *Komsomol* until the age of 28 years, the 'political saturation' of the population by the Party is more like 15 per cent. In 1983, 1.17 million party members (6.4 per cent of membership) were under 25, in the 26 to 40 age group were 5.78 million (32 per cent), in the 41 to 50 age bracket were 4.6 million (25.4 per cent) and there were 6.54 million (36.2 per cent) over 50.

The membership of the CPSU is formally made up of Communist Parties of the Union Republics as shown in table 5.2.[24] The Russian Republic does *not* have its own separate party. In columns 2 and 4 is shown the party

TABLE 5.2: MEMBERSHIP OF REPUBLICAN COMMUNIST PARTIES

	Col. 1	Col. 2	Col. 3	Col. 4	Col. 5
Republican Party	Republican population (1980) 000s	Membership 1 Jan 1973 000s	Col.2 ——— Popn. 1970 %	Membership 1 Jan 1983 000s	Col. 4 ——— Col. 1 %
Ukraine	49,953	2,479	5.3	3,038	6.1
Byelorussia (White Russia)	9,611	461	5.1	626	6.5
Uzbekistan	15,765	450	3.8	606	3.8
Kazakhstan	14,858	609	4.7	762	5.1
Georgia	5,041	305	6.5	363	7.2
Azerbaidzhan	6,112	270	5.3	361	5.7
Lithuania	3,420	132	4.2	181	5.3
Moldavia	3,968	121	4.0	174	4.4
Latvia	2,529	134	5.7	167	6.6
Kirgiziya	3,588	107	3.6	135	3.7
Tadzhikistan	3,901	90	3.1	115	2.9
Armenia	3,074	134	5.3	173	5.6
Turkmenistan	2,829	73	3.4	102	3.6
Estonia	1,474	77	5.7	103	6.9
Total	126,123	5,492		6,896	
Total membership of CPSU		14,821		18,117	

Source: Party membership: 'KPSS v tsifrakh', Partiynaya zhizn,' no. 10, May 1973, p. 11 and Partiynaya zhizn,' No. 15, August 1983, p. 16.

republican membership for 1973 and 1983 respectively. The percentages in columns 3 and 5 are based on the total republican population data for 1970 and 1980. The table shows that in 1983 nearly 6.9 million or 38 per cent of the membership lay outside the Russian Federative Republic. Comparison of columns 3 and 5 shows the growing saturation of party membership in the Republics, as in the USSR as a whole.

This does not mean, of course, that the republican parties are wholly composed of non-Great Russians. The proportion of Great Russians in each republican party is not available. Columns 1 and 2 of table 5.3 show the number of each major national group in the CPSU in 1973 and 1983. Column 3 shows the data for 1983, expressed as a proportion of total CPSU membership. In column 4 is the share of each nationality group in the USSR population. Column 5 expresses membership by nationality (given in column 3) as a percentage of the relevant republican party membership, given in table 3.2. Study of columns 1 and 2 shows a growth in membership of all nationalities over the period. Column 5 further informs us that certain nationalities figure prominently in the membership, not only of the

TABLE 5.3: COMPOSITION OF CPSU BY NATIONALITY

	Col. 1	Col. 2	Col. 3	Col. 4	Col. 5
Nationality	1 Jan 1973 000s	No. in CPSU 1 Jan 1983 000s	% of party 1983	% of population 1979	% of republican party membership (1983)
Russians	9,025	10,809	59.7	52.4	—
Ukrainians	2,369	2,899	16.0	16.1	95.4
Byelorussians	522	684	3.8	3.6	109.2
Uzbeks	292	428	2.4	4.7	70.6
Kazaks	255	355	2.0	2.5	46.5
Georgians	246	303	1.7	1.4	83.4
Azerbaidzhanies	212	305	1.7	2.0	86.9
Lithuanians	97	135	0.7	1.0	74.5
Moldavians	59	98	0.5	1.1	56.3
Latvians	62	74	0.4	0.5	44.3
Kirgiz	46	70	0.4	0.7	51.8
Tadzhiks	59	80	0.4	1.1	69.5
Armenians	225	273	1.5	1.6	157.8
Turkmens	44	69	0.4	0.7	67.6
Estonians	46	58	0.3	0.4	56.3
Others	1,262	1,476	8.1	10.2	—
Total	14,821	18,117	100%	100%	

Source: 'KPSS v tsifrakh', *Partiynaya zhizn,'* no. 15, August 1983, p. 23.

party of their own republic but also outside – e.g. Byelorussians (White Russians) 109.2 per cent and Armenians 157.8 per cent. A low share of a given nationality in their own titular republic indicates a large number of *other* nationalities in that republic (e.g. Kazakh 46.5, Moldavian 56.3, Latvian 44.3, Kirgiz 51.8). One fact not shown by republican data is that the Jews have been the most 'party-saturated' nationality. In 1981, there were 257,620 Jews in the Party – 1.4 per cent of its membership[25] – whereas in 1979, Jews constituted 0.69 per cent of the total production. Though the representation of Jews has declined from 1.9 per cent of Party membership in 1976, their representation is still twice that of any other ethnic group.[26] Inferences from the percentages shown in columns 3 and 4 of table 3.3 can only be made with extreme caution. It could be concluded, for example, that Azerbaidzhanies and Kazakhs were under-represented in the party. This is incorrect. The data ignore age distribution, a young population being under-represented, and an old one having more party members being over-represented. Jones and Grupp have estimated party density by nationality when standardized for the numbers in the adult population. Their results are noted in table 5.4 (data for 1976). This shows that Azerbaydzhanis (Azeris), Kazakhs, Georgians and Armenians in fact represent a higher proportion of the *adult* population in the party than the Russians. The Baltic nationalities, by contrast, all have a low party participation rate.

TABLE 5.4: JONES AND GRUPP'S INDEX OF PARTY SATURATION BY NATIONALITY (AGE ADJUSTED), 1976

Slavic	Russians	111
	Ukrainians	90
	Byelorussians	94
Baltic	Estonians	71
	Latvians	65
	Lithuanians	62
Muslim	Uzbeks	77
	Kazakhs	112
	Azeris	113
	Kirgiz	75
	Tadzhiks	67
	Turkmens	70
Other	Georgians	127
	Moldavians	42
	Armenians	115

Source: Ellen Jones and Fred W. Grupp, 'Measuring Nationality Trends in the Soviet Union: A Research Note', *Slavic Review,* Spring 1982, vol. 41, no. 1, p. 116. See also; Ellen Jones and Fred W. Group, 'Modernisation and Ethnic Equalisation in the USSR', *Soviet Studies,* vol. 36, no. 2, 1984, pp. 159–184.

'Social position' in the USSR is based on an individual's relationship to the means of production: 'manual workers' work with their hands and are occupied in production, 'peasants' are engaged in productive work on collective farms (not state farms), 'employees' (or non-manual workers) use their brains and make up the administrative, secretarial and executive personnel.[27] As a proportion of the social category, this last group constitutes the largest single group of party members. Official Soviet statistics show the following divisions: (manual) workers, employees and collective farmers. These are shown in table 5.5, together with two estimates of the party's occupational composition by field of employment. It is claimed that manual workers and collective farmers constitute more than half the total party membership. This is a correct but misleading statement if one considers that these groups make up nearly three-quarters of the total population. The collective farm peasantry[28] is slightly under-represented, being, in 1983, 12.4 per cent of the party membership but 13.3 per cent of the population.[29] 'Employees', however, constitute a

TABLE 5.5: SOCIAL BACKGROUND OF PARTY MEMBERS AND CANDIDATES

	1961	1964	1983	% of total population (1982)
1. Manual workers	35.0	37.3	44.1	60.9
2. Non-manual or 'Employees'	47.7	46.2	43.5	25.8
3. Peasants on collective farms	17.3	16.5	12.4	13.3
Total	100%	100%	100%	100%

Source: 'KPSS v tsifrakh', Partivna zhizm', No. 15, Aug. 1983, p. 21. Narkhoz 1922–82 (1982), pp. 30, 48.

far larger proportion of the party – 43.5 per cent – than they do of the population – 25.8 per cent. Party policy is to increase the share of manual workers. Between 1976 and 1980, 59 per cent of new members were manual workers, 30.7 per cent non-manual and 10.3 per cent collective farmers; in 1981, 59.5 per cent and in 1982 59.4 per cent of new members were manual workers. Since 1969, more than ten per cent of manual workers have been Communist Party members, and in the large industrial areas since 1966 manual workers have made up between 60 and 70 per cent of new party members.[30]

The distribution of party members by branch of the economy is shown in table 5.6. These data are rather general, but tables 5.7 and 5.8 show the occupational background of collective farmers and non-manual workers respectively. (Table 5.7 refers only to candidates admitted to full party membership.)

TABLE 5.6: COMPOSITION OF CPSU BY FIELD OF EMPLOYMENT

Field of Employment	All Members in Employment	
	1966 %	1983 %
Government, economic, party etc. bureaucracies	8.9	8.9
Science, education, health, culture	16.7	16.0
Trade and materials-handling, public catering	4.6	4.7
Housing, public and personal services	1.3	1.9
Communications and transport	9.1	8.1
Industry and construction	36.3	39.2
Agriculture	22.3	20.0
Other branches of economy	0.8	1.2
Total	100.0	100.0

Source: 'KPSS v tsifrakh', Partiynaya zhizn', No. 15, August 1983, p. 26.

156

In 1981, the state and collective farms[31] accounted for 8.1 and 10.1 per cent respectively of all employed party members. A breakdown of membership by type of work within the sector, however, shows that in 1981, the largest group of candidate members from agriculture were operatives of farm machinery (or mechanics) who might, in a social sense, be more like urban workers than farmhands and should perhaps be included as far as their occupation is concerned, under the heading of manual workers. The remaining farm worker candidates ('others', 11.6p per

TABLE 5.7: OCCUPATIONAL BACKGROUND OF PARTY COLLECTIVE FARMER CANDIDATES 1976–1980

Branch of Production	Entrants to the Party 1976–1980 %
Tractor and combine harvester personnel and other mechanics	31.5
Field labourers, vegetable farmers and market gardeners	16.3
Stockmen	19.7
Agronomists, vets and other agricultural specialists including tekhniki	20.9
Others	11.6
	100.0

Source: 'KPSS v tsifrakh', 1981, p. 15.

TABLE 5.8: OCCUPATIONAL BACKGROUND OF NON-MANUAL PARTY MEMBERS AND CANDIDATES

	1 Jan. 1962 %	1 Jan. 1976 %	1 Jan. 1981 %
Leaders of organizations, institutions, factories, construction enterprises (stroyki), state farms and their subdivisions	10.0	8.9	9.4
Technical engineering workers, agricultural specialists	28.2	40.0	42.0
Scientific workers, education, health employees, literary and artistic personnel	21.6	24.2	23.4
Workers in trade institutions, supply, sales and public dining rooms	4.9	4.3	4.1
Inspection workers (rabotnikov kontrolya) accounting and secretarial	11.8	—	—
Others	23.5	22.6	21.1
	100.0	100.0	100.0

Source: 'KPSS v tsifrakh', Partiynaya zhizn', No. 10, 1976, Partiynaya zhizn', No. 14, 1981, p. 17.

cent) probably include officials and other 'non-productive' members of farms.

The various strata of 'employees', or those engaged in mental as distinct from physical labour, are shown in table 5.8. Again, some agricultural specialists (from state farms) included here are of similar occupation to others included on the 'collective farmers' table. The two largest categories, the technical specialists (42 per cent in 1981) and scientific workers (23.4 per cent in 1981), together make up over half the total of non-manual party members, giving substance to the party's claim of large membership among the intelligentsia. The group of 'others' is rather large (21.1 per cent non-manual members in 1981) and may include government or party functionaries.

An analysis by Rigby of the occupation and party membership of 2,500 government deputies confirms the high association between bureaucratic or professional status and party membership. He shows that 99 per cent of factory directors, 51 per cent of 'subdirectional management', 38 per cent of foremen and other junior supervisory jobs, and 27 per cent of 'specialists lacking administrative powers' were party members.[32] In 1983, for the population as a whole, every second writer, every fourth engineer, every fifth agronomist or animal specialist, every fourth teacher and every sixth physician and three quarters of all journalists were party members.[33] Moreover, in keeping with general trends among the population, the educational levels of party members are rising. In 1983, 54.7 per cent of all party members had received a higher or specialized secondary education; a third of all such 'specialists' were party members.[34]

Many of the figures refer to the *social position* of party members when they joined the party. Their actual work has not been defined and we are unaware, for example, of those working full-time in the party. Rigby, writing in 1957, has argued that Soviet figures underestimate the numbers in the political and administrative hierarchies which, he says, accounted, in 1954, for a million-and-a-half party members or about 20 per cent of the total membership.[35] Since the late 1950s an attempt has been made to increase the number of voluntary workers in administration and it is most probable that a fall in the number of full-time administrators has taken place. In 1983, only 8.9 per cent of party members (or under one million) in employment were engaged full-time in the apparatuses (see table 5.6). Some precise figures have been given for 1980–81, when 31,400 communists constituted the membership of the Central Committees of party and the leading district (*obkom*) and area (*kraykom*) committees; 2.37 million communists served as members or candidates in party groups; in all 4.8 million were in elected positions in party organizations.[36]

A finer occupational scale than these data can provide would be needed for a very detailed analysis of the party's stratification. But a few general conclusions can be made from them. First, among the non-manual party members, the highest proportion are technical specialists: a striking difference compared with members of British or American political parties. Second, the manual working class, especially in industry, transport and building, constitutes a very large part of present party membership. Under Brezhnev, for the first time in recent party history, the proportion of manual worker entrants to the party increased significantly. Third, support in the countryside has grown considerably and tends to be recruited from the more technically skilled farm workers. Fourth, party membership is changing with the social composition of the population, and the number of technically qualified members is rising, while the proportion of collective farmers is on the decline. Fifth, national identification is greatest among the Slavic groups and lowest among the Baltic.

The Primary Party Branch

The basic unit of party membership is the primary party branch (in Russian the *pervichnaya partiynaya organizatsiya*, or PPO). This unit admits members, organizes local party work, conducts education and propaganda, and disciplines members. In 1983, there were 426,000 primary groups with 18,118,000 members.[37] Such party groups, like those of Communist Parties in the West, are organized at the place of work; a small number – for pensioners, housewives – are located in residential areas. The division of party *groups* between various sectors of the economy in 1981 was as follows: 26.1 per cent in enterprises in industry, transport, communications and building, 5.1 per cent in state farms; 6.4 per cent in collective farms; 3.6 per cent in enterprises in trade and public catering; 17 per cent in educational establishments; 1.6 per cent in scientific institutions; 1.3 per cent in cultural establishments (e.g. museums, theatres); 4.0 per cent in the health service; 16.9 per cent in administrative establishments; and 18 per cent in living areas and rural settlements.[38]

In 1983, party groups were relatively small, 80.3 per cent having less than 50 members, though the larger groups were on the increase (see table 5.9). As one would expect, membership on the collective farms is low, but even so, the size of the average basic unit has grown over six times between 1946 and 1983 (from an average of 10 to 60). The largest units are in industrial enterprises (average 103), though when figures were given in 1965, scientific and educational institutions had very large branches (average, 86) (see table 5.10).

The rise in party membership has most probably been created by an

TABLE 5.9: SIZE OF CPSU PRIMARY ORGANIZATIONS

Size of group (members and candidates)	1 Jan. 1962 %	1 Jan. 1965 %	1 Jan. 1983 %
to 15	42.5	39.9	39.8
15–49	44.1	43.5	40.5
50–100	8.5	10.5	12.7
over 100	4.9	6.1	7.0

Sources: 'KPSS v tsifrakh' (1965), p. 16 (for 1962 and 1965). Partiynaya zhizn', 1983, No. 15, p. 28.

TABLE 5.10: AVERAGE SIZE OF PARTY PRIMARY UNIT IN DIFFERENT KINDS OF ESTABLISHMENTS

	1946	1 Jan. 1962	1 Jan. 1965	1977	1983
In industrial undertakings	38	62	78	95	103
In building and construction	27	37	42	39	39
On state farms	17	76	78	69	68
On collective farms	10	34	40	55	60
In scientific and academic institutions	—	76	86	—	—

Sources: KPSS v tsifrakh (1965), p. 16, 'KPSS v tsifrakh' (1977), p. 38, 'KPSS v tsifrakh' (1983), p. 28.

increase in new members aged between 26 and 40. On 1 January 1983 they constituted 32 per cent of all members and those under 25 years accounted for only 6.4 per cent of the membership, compared with 19.3 per cent in 1946.[39] The lower proportion of young people under 25 in the party reflects more the official policy of strengthening the *Komsomol* (Young Communist League) than a drastic decline in support among the young,[40] though the wartime generation of young communists was probably more idealistic than the post-1960 group who now see membership in a more instrumental and symbolic fashion. The growth of membership has meant that, by 1983, 88 per cent of party members were admitted after the Second World War.

The proportion of women in the party more than doubled between 1927 and 1983, rising from 12.2 to 27.4 per cent of membership.[41] Since, however, women outnumber men in the population, the figures still show a relative under-representation of women in the party's ranks: even so, compared to parties in other countries, a quarter of party membership is an extremely high figure. But as we analyse the place of women in the higher echelons of the party, we see that their share of the membership declines considerably: in 1975 they constituted 2 per cent of the full members of the Central Committee and none of the Politbureau; in 1976, not one of the 72 powerful regional secretaries was female, though, by 1981, 35 per cent of local secretaries were women.

We may conclude that the CPSU's membership shows a bias towards certain social groups in Soviet society. Party membership now is predominantly made up of people under 50 years of age who joined the party after 1945. Russians and Georgians figure prominently, some of the minor nationalities are under-represented. Women have a growing share, but are still very much in the minority compared with men. More significantly, the educated and scientifically trained strata of the population, which are growing in size and could possibly provide a challenge to the party's hegemony if excluded from it, are being absorbed into its ranks, while the traditional base, the urban working class, is very well represented. It can be seen that the party is in a very strong position in most sectors and this due to partly efforts to recruit particular groups and partly to a significant increase in the size of the party in recent years.

The Party Leadership

The Communist Party, with over eighteen million members, is a mass party. As noted above, it is hierarchically organized and, as in all organizations, those with positions at higher levels of the organization have greater influence and political power than the rank-and-file membership. In the next chapter we shall deal in more detail with the analysis of groups in the party and political system. Here I shall outline some of the main characteristics of the chief representative and executive bodies of the party. Its leading organs are as follows: the Politbureau, Central Committee, Congress, Secretariat, Central Auditing Commission.

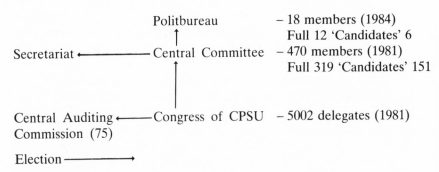

The Congress

The Congress is elected every five years by constituent party units as 'determined by the Central Committee' (Party Rules, para. 30). In turn it elects a Central Auditing Commission (75 members), and the membership of the Central Committee. The Central Committee has two types of members – elected at the Twenty Sixth Congress in 1981 were 319 full members having voting rights, and 151 'candidates', being non-voting members.

At the Congress the major interests in Soviet society are represented. Table 5.11 shows the occupational affiliation of the delegates at three Congresses over a twenty-year time span: 1961, 1971 and 1981. The number of delegates has grown somewhat during this time. The party apparatus (secretaries of party groups and other functionaries) accounted for 21 per cent of delegates at the Twenty Sixth Congress. The 'government apparatus' in 1971 came to only 11 per cent, the probable figure for 1981. It must be borne in mind that many of the officials from the 'government apparatus' were representatives of industry, and this sector, with 1728 delegates, was the largest single grouping (34.5 per cent of the delegates in 1981).

Congress deliberates for a good week. Its debates monopolize the mass media, rather like an intensive election campaign in Britain or the USA. The developments in Soviet society since the last Congress are summed up by the General Secretary, who plays a dominant role in the Congress. Foreign affairs are discussed and speeches are made by visiting foreign delegates. The economic plan for the coming five years is presented in general terms. The Party's own finances and composition are also the subject of discussion. Sometimes the Congress is used as a platform for a major policy statement – the denunciation of Stalinism by Khrushchev at

TABLE 5.11: AFFILIATION OF CONGRESS DELEGATES, 1961, 1971 AND 1981

	Congress		
	22nd 1961	24th 1971	26th 1981
Political			
Party apparatus	1158	1205	1077
Armed forces	350	300(+)	300(+)
Trade unions/Komsomol	104	126	⎰691
Government apparatus	465	556	⎱
Economic			
Industry	1391	1565(+)	1728(+)
Agriculture	784	870	877
Culture			
Education and the arts	?	120	⎰269
Science	?	138	⎱
Total	4813	4963	5002

Note: + Denotes incomplete figure.
Source: R.F. Miller and T.H. Rigby, *Twenty-Sixth Congress of the CPSU in Current Perspective,* Occasional Paper no. 16, Canberra ANU, 1982, p. 7.

the Twentieth Congress in 1956 and the announcement of the new USSR Constitution at the Twenty-Fifth in 1976 are cases in point. The Congress elects the Central Auditing Commission and the Central Committee. This is a somewhat formal happening, as a single list of candidates is voted on. There is a secret ballot and candidates are required to receive more than fifty per cent of the possible votes. The actual procedure is not open to the public and much of our knowledge is anecdotal. While delegates may comment on the suitability (or otherwise) of candidates, there is no choice between candidates. The nomination procedure here is crucial and the effective sifting of potential members is done by the cadres or the personnel department of the secretariat.

The Central Committee

The significance of the three types of Central Committee membership (full, candidate and auditing commission) lies in the status of members at the various levels. It marks out people who are eligible for top political office in the Politbureau and helps incorporate many groups into the wider political leadership. The occupational background of the voting members of the Central Committee for 1966 and 1981 is shown in table 5.12.

The table shows a 63 per cent rise in membership overall of the committee – an increase of 124 places. The Central Committee contains the chief party secretaries, those of the Union Republics; the leading members of the government, including the ministers representing the powerful industrial ministries, police chiefs, leaders of the armed forces, senior civil servants in the foreign office, the President of the Supreme Court, the First Secretary of the Young Communist League and the Chairman of the Trade Unions Central Committee. Leading writers, scientists and academics, as well as a few industrial workers and 'captains of industry', are also represented. In recent years there has been a marked increase in regional party officials, representatives from the government executive and the military chiefs. Symbolically, rank-and-file workers have increased four-fold, though they account for only 15 members out of a total of 319.

The Politbureau

The pinnacle of the Soviet polity is the Politbureau (political bureau). This is a body of men (there has only ever been one woman member, Furtseva, from 1956 to 1961) which is the effective decision-making body in the USSR. It is rather similar in size and status to the cabinet in British politics,

TABLE 5.12: AFFILIATION OF VOTING MEMBERS OF THE CENTRAL COMMITTEE OF THE CPSU, 1966 AND 1981

	1966	1981	% change
Party			
Secretaries of Central Committee	11	10	− 9
Other central officials	4	20	+ 400
Republic party secretaries	22	21	− 4
Regional/local party secretaries RSFSR	37	66	+ 78
Regional/local party secretaries other republics	10	20	+ 50
Government institutions			
Presidium USSR Council of Ministers	12	15	+ 25
Ministers and other central government officials	31	62	+ 100
Premiers and other republic government officials	8	12	+ 33
Regional/local government officials	1	2	+ 100
Foreign service	13	14	+ 7
Armed forces commanders	12	24	+ 100
Other organizations			
Officials of 'mass organizations'	5	8	+ 60
Press	1	3	+ 200
Union and Republic Supreme Soviet officials	8	9	+ 12
Legal officials	1	2	100
Academicians, scientists, technologists	2	2	0
Writers	2	2	0
Industrial executives	5	3	− 40
Industrial workers	3	15	+ 400
Agricultural executives	1	0	0
Agricultural workers	0	1	0
Retired top officials	3	0	0
Totals	195	319	63

Source: Derived from: R.F. Miller and T.H. Rigby, *Twenty-Sixth Congress of the CPSU in Current Political Perspective*, 1982, p. 77

with around two dozen members. As in the Central Committee there are two statuses of membership: full members and candidates. The General Secretary (a post occupied by Stalin, Khrushchev, Brezhnev, Andropov and Chernenko) has a similar role ('primus inter pares', first among equals) to the Prime Minister in British government. The Politbureau is elected from, and by, the members of the Central Committee. This election is formally carried out at the close of each Party Congress and subsequent changes may be made by plenums of the Central Committee.

The process of selection, promotion and demotion is shrouded in mystery. The Politbureau meets weekly and discusses the major national and international events. An account of its proceedings, as issued by the Soviet news agency Tass, is reprinted from *Soviet News*, 27 April 1983.

At the Political Bureau of the CPSU Central Committee

MOSCOW, April 21, 1983 TASS:

AT ITS REGULAR meeting the political bureau of the CPSU central committee has heard a report on the work of the CPSU delegation to the international scientific conference on "Karl Marx and our time: the struggle for peace and social progress" which was recently held in Berlin.

It was stressed that the conference had strikingly shown the viability of Marxist–Leninist theory, the role of socialism as the implementation of this theory, the unbreakable tie between socialism and the struggle for peace, and the importance of the internationalist solidarity of the communist movement and various movements for national and social liberation.

Contributing towards the accomplishment of the tasks set at the meeting of the first secretaries of the central committees of the communist parties of the USSR's union republics, territorial committees and regional committees of the party, which was held on April 18, the political bureau of the CPSU central committee discussed a number of questions concerning the further development of the country's agriculture.

Additional measures have been approved to ensure the gathering of the harvest, procurements for farm produce and fodder in the current year and to ensure the successful wintering of cattle in the period 1983 to 1984.

Measures have been decided upon to speed up the creation of facilities for the production of some types of farm machinery, thereby increasing their output at the enterprises of the Ministry of Tractor and Agricultural Machinery Building in the period 1984 to 1985.

Ways to improve the occupational instruction, education, and vocational guidance for pupils at rural general educational schools and vocational training schools, and to ensure that their graduates remain to work in agriculture has been discussed.

The meeting of the political bureau of the CPSU central committee has discussed the question of measures for the further development of the fuel and energy base in the areas beyond Lake Baikal and in the Far East in the period 1983 to 1985 and for the period up to 1990.

The political bureau of the CPSU central committee has approved the proposals of the USSR Council of Ministers to set up, at the Lenin Komsomol autoworks, facilities for the production of a new model of passenger motor-cars and its successive models on the basis of advanced achievements in the car industry.

The meeting of the political bureau of the CPSU central committee also discussed some other questions concerning the country's domestic affairs and foreign policy.

The Politbureau guides the various ministries which come under the government apparatus. It effects policy and decides priorities. It conducts a general oversight of foreign and domestic policy.

The Politbureau consists of the leading members of the most important and powerful institutions in Soviet society: the government apparatus, the Soviet parliament, the armed forces, the police, and the apparatus of the Party. At the Twenty Sixth Congress in 1981, 14 full members were elected and there were eight candidates. After the death of Andropov and with the coming to power of Chernenko there remained in 1984 twelve full members and six candidates. Their names, background and responsibilities are listed in table 5.13. The last two right-hand columns show the institutional overlap of membership and illustrate how the Politbureau incorporates the major interests in Soviet Society (discussed further in chapter 7).

The Politbureau is an ageing body, with an average age in 1984 of over 69 years. Death and ill-health regularly take their roll. While the leading personnel of Soviet politics are familiar figures and do not go out of office following regular elections as is often the case in the West, there is a considerable turnover of members in the Politbureau. Changes in the full members since 1971 are shown in table 5.14. Of the full members of the Politbureau elected at the Twenty-Fourth Congress in 1971, only three have survived until 1984. Guessing who will next take up the reigns of power as General Secretary is one of the major preoccupations of Western Kremlinologists. This dark art, however, is fraught with obstacles. Writing in 1982 after the Twenty-Sixth Congress, Miller and Rigby note that 'until fairly recently there was a near consensus that Brezhnev's probable successor was his most senior protégé Andrey Kirilenko ...' However, his age they (rightly) thought would be against him and Chernenko's 'meteoric rise' was noted.[42] Chernenko was adopted as heir apparent by Western writers and it was not perhaps unreasonable to back the nominee of the Party General Secretary. The subsequent rise of Andropov to the General Secretaryship, his death and the subsequent installation of Chernenko reminds us that we know relatively little of the political machinations and allegiances in the Polibureau (see above chapter 2). We are on more solid ground when we consider the social background of the leadership.

The Social Background of the Soviet Leadership

The party elite has been recruited from men with relatively modest social origins. For instance, the ten leading party secretaries in 1957 all came

TABLE 5.13: POLITBUREAU OF THE CPSU CENTRAL COMMITTEE

Full Members	Date of Election	Family Social Background	Party Membership since	Responsibility:	Other Positions
CHERNENKO, Konstantin Ustinovich	1978	Peasant	1931	Politbureau staff work. Ideology. Foreign Policy	Secretary, CPSU Central Committee; Chief, General Department, CPSU Central Committee
GORBACHEV, Mikhail Sergeevich	1980	Peasant	1952	Agriculture	Secretary, CPSU Central Committee
GRISHIN, Viktor Vasil'evich	1971	Manual	1939	Moscow administration	First Secretary, Moscow City Party Committee; Member, Presidium USSR Supreme Soviet
GROMYKO Andrei Andreevich	1973	Peasant	1931	International Relations Foreign Aid	USSR Minister of Foreign Affairs; Chairman, Diplomatic Publications Commission of the USSR Ministry of Foreign Affairs
KUNAEV, Dinmukhamed Akhmedovich	1971	Non manual	1939	Supervision of Kazakhstan	First Secretary, Central Committee, CP of Kazakhstan; Member, Presidium, USSR Supreme Soviet
ROMANOV, Grigorii Vasil'evich	1976	Peasant	1944	Supervision of Leningrad area	First Secretary, Leningrad Oblast Party Committee; Member, Presidium USSR Supreme Soviet
SOLOMENTSEV, Mikhail Sergeevich	1983	Peasant	1940	Economic Administration in RSFSR	Chairman, Party Central Committee
VOROTNIKOV, Vitali Ivanovich	1983	Manual?	1947	Economic Administration RSFSR	Chairman, RSFSR, Council of Ministers

Name	Year	Social Origin	Year	Responsibility	Official Position
SHCHERBITSKY, Vladimir Vasil'evich	1971	Manual	1941	Supervision of Ukraine	First Secretary, Central Committee, CP of Ukraine; Member, Presidium USSR Supreme Soviet
TIKHONOV, Nikolai Aleksandrovich	1979	Non manual	1940	Economic Administration	Chairman, USSR Council of Ministers
USTINOV, Dimitrii Fedorovich	1976	Manual	1927	Defence, Space, Military Aid	USSR Minister of Defence; Marshal of the Soviet Union
ALIEV, Geidar Alievich	1976	Manual	1945	Economic Administration	First Secretary, Central Committee, CP of Azerbaijan; Major General
Candidate Members					
DEMICHEV, Petr Nilovich	1964	Manual	1939	Culture	USSR Minister of Culture
DOLGIKH, Vladimir Ivanovich	1982	Non manual	1942	Economic Administration, Heavy Industry	Secretary, CPSU Central Committee, Chief, Heavy Industry Department, CPSU Central Committee
KUZNETSOV, Vasili Vasil'evich	1977	Peasant	1927	Legislative Organs Ceremonial style functions	First Deputy Chairman, Presidium USSR Supreme Soviet
PONOMAREV, Boris Nikolaevich	1972	Non manual	1919	Non-ruling Communist Parties, National Liberation Movements Foreign Affairs	Secretary, CPSU Central Committee; Chief, International Department, CPSU Central Committee
SHEVARDNADZE, Eduard Amvrosievich	1978	—	1948	Supervision in Georgia	First Secretary, Central Committee, CP of Georgia
CHEBRIKOV, Viktor Mikhailovich	1983	—	1944	Security	Chairman State Committee for Security (KGB).

TABLE 5.14: CHANGES IN FULL MEMBERS OF POLITBUREAU 1971–1984

Elected at 24th Congress (1971)	Deceased/ lost office	Subsequently joined	Elected at 26th Congress (1981)	Deceased/ lost office	Subsequently Joined	1984
Brezhnev			→ Brezhnev	+		
Voronov	+					
Grishin			→ Grishin			→ Grishin
Kirilenko	+		→ Kirilenko	+		
Kosygin	+					
Kulakov	+					
Kunaev			→ Kunaev			→ Kunaev
Mazurov	+					
Pel'she			→ Pel'she	+		
Podgorny	+					
Polyanski	+					
Suslov			→ Suslov	+		
Shelepin	+					
Shelest	+					
Shcherbitski			→ Shcherbitski			→ Shcherbitski
		Andropov (1973)	→ Andropov	+		
		Gromyko (1973)	→ Gromyko			→ Gromyko
		Grechko (1973) +				
		Romanov (1976)	→ Romanov			→ Romanov
		Ustinov (1976)	→ Ustinov			→ Ustinov
		Chernenko (1978)	→ Chernenko			→ Chernenko
		Tikhonov (1979)	→ Tikhonov			→ Tikhonov
		Gorbachev (1980)	→ Gorbachev			→ Gorbachev
					Aliev (1982)	→ Aliev
					Vorotnikov (1983)	→ Vorotnikov
					Solomentsev (1983)	→ Solomentsev

Source: Data adapted from Miller and Rigby, *Twenty-Sixth Congress of the CPSU in Current Perspective,* p. 85 and other sources.

from peasant or worker families. From information available on 148 of the 175 members of the Central Committee (1961), 49.3 were of peasant, and third of worker origin. Only two of the fathers were of known higher occupational strata.[43] It is quite probable, however, that many of the 'unknown' social origins were from the professions. By 1981, statistical data about social origins of the leaders disappeared from the reports of the CPSU Congress. A party career may be an avenue of social mobility for the children of lower social strata, who may find it more difficult to rise to the top in professional or ministerial sectors of Soviet society. In the earlier years of Soviet power this was not the case. For instance, of 15 members of the Politbureau between 1917 and 1927, 9 had 'middle class' social origins; but of 25 members between the years 1957 to 1967, only 3 hailed from a non-manual background. On the other hand, in the earlier period (1917–1927) 8 out of 15 had had higher education, whereas in 1967, the ratio was 9 to 11. The occupations of the fathers of the 1971–75 Politbureau were overwhelmingly worker or peasant: 5 had manual worker fathers, 6 hailed from the peasantry, one was an 'artisan' and the other two were non-manuals. Of the Politbureau in 1984, 6 were of working class origin, 6 peasant and 4 non-manual (3 were unknown). In 1939, only 40 per cent of the rural and urban party secretaries had even completed secondary education,[44] whereas in 1981, 57.4 per cent of secretaries of primary party groups had completed higher education. Illustrating the high level of educational qualifications of the local and Republican Party groups is the fact that in 1981 higher education had been completed by 70 per cent of candidates and members of the Republican Central Committees (and Auditing Commissions) and members of the regional (*oblast'*) and district (*kraykom*) committees.[45] At the level of secretaries of the Central Committees of the republican parties, of district and regional committees, in 1981, 99.9 per cent had completed higher education.[46] In terms of the kind of education received by the members of the Central Committee, of those with a complete higher education in 1981, 22 per cent had had an education in the humanities (16 per cent in 1966); the majority, 60 per cent, had attended colleges in the natural or technical sciences or mathematics (61 per cent in 1966); another 10 per cent had been educated in military academies; and 8 per cent in the Party's own institutions of higher education.[47]

Important in the training of the leading cadres is the party's own system of schools. These range from modest part-time evening classes to the Academy of Social Sciences, which is under the direction of the CPSU's Central Committee. Below this is the Higher Party School. Party members may work their way up the hierarchy until they have received the equivalent of a university education. Such graduates then occupy key positions in the party, government and media.[48] Here is an avenue, not only for political recruitment, but also for upward social mobility for those to whom other doors have been shut. Of the delegates to Twenty-Third Party Congress (1966), 24.9 per cent had been educated at party schools; and of a representative sample of Party Secretaries, Stewart estimates that 31.5 per cent had received such an education.[49] 'Placement' in the political hierarchy is carried out by the Party Secretariat. The party's schools have also played an important role in training Communist officials both for the Eastern Europe and the Third World.

We may make some obvious points about the social composition of the political leadership. It is composed of full-time officials of the government and party bureaucracies; and it is considerably older than the party membership as a whole. It is relatively well-educated and includes a high proportion of men (very few women) with scientific or technical backgrounds. The membership figures noted above provide us only with a quantitative index of party support. One should bear in mind that the statistical data tell us nothing about what membership means, of the intensity of party allegiance compared to other group allegiance (say to profession or to a government ministry).

NOTES

1 *Fundamentals of Marxism–Leninism* (1961), p. 695.
2 V.I. Lenin, 'The Agrarian Question', *Collected Works,* vol. 15, p. 138.
3 V.I. Lenin, 'Economics and Politics in the Era of the Dictatorship of the Proletariat', *Collected Works,* vol. 30, pp. 116–7.
4 See 'The Manifesto of the Communist Party', *Selected Works,* vol. 1 (1958), pp. 27–9.
5 'Critique of the Gotha Programme', *Selected Works,* vol. 2, p. 23.
6 Ali Rattansi, *Marx and the Division of Labour* (1982), p. xii.
7 For a discussion of trends see: A.B. Evans, Jr., 'Developed Socialism in Soviet Ideology', *Soviet Studies,* vol. 29, no. 3, (July 1977); V.S. Semenov, *Dialektika razvitiya sotsial'noy struktury sovetskogo obshchestva* (1977); R. Kosolapov, 'The "Wholeness" of Developed Socialism', translated in *The Current Digest of the Soviet Press,* vol. 35, no. 10 (6 April 1983), pp. 4–6.
8 See Semenov, *Dialektika...,* p. 103.
9 Kosolapov, 'The Wholeness...', pp. 5–6.
10 See also *Constitution of the USSR* (1977, chapter 4) and Appendix D, below.
11 Article 6, *Constitution of the USSR;* see Appendix D, below.
12 *Rules of the Communist Party of the Soviet Union,* English edition (1977), paragraph 19. For the complete rules, see Appendix C below.
13 Russian Soviet Federative Socialist Republic.
14 Article 6, *Constitution of the USSR.*
15 It is sometimes called the Political Bureau. This body was called the Presidium between October 1952 and April 1966. It should not now be confused with the Presidium of the Soviet Parliament (see p. 180).
16 In 1981, there were 25 members of whom 14 were full members.
17 Paragraph 37, *Party Rules.*
18 For Republican and lower bodies see *KPSS, Naglyadnoe posobie po partiynomu stroitel'stvu* (1969), pp. 37–45, and *Obshchestvovedenie,* second edn. (1964), p. 209. For a detailed exposition in English see: R.J. Hill and P. Frank, *The Soviet Communist Party* (1981).
19 A. Avtorkhanov, *The Communist Party Apparatus* (1966), pp. 209–11. *The Apparatus of the CPSU,* Radio Liberty, RL 9/78 (January 1978).
20 Paragraph 34, *Party Rules.*
21 Paragraph 1, *Party Rules.*
22 M. Duverger, *Political Parties* (1964), pp. 62–70.
23 See Appendix A for full statistics 1905–1983.
24 For an historical account and more detailed treatment see T.H. Rigby, *Communist Party Membership in the USSR, 1917–1967* (1968).
25 *Narodnoe khozyaystvo SSSR v 1922–1982* (1983), hereafter abbreviated to: *Narkhoz 1922–1982,* p. 49.
26 T.H. Rigby, *Soviet Studies,* vol. 28, no. 4, p. 615. R.F. Miller and T.H. Rigby,

26th Congress of the CPSU in Current Political Perspective, Canberra: ANU, Occasional Paper No. 16 (1982), p. 71.

27 The statistics on social background of party members usually refer to social position when joining the party.

28 That is, collective farmers and co-operative handicraftsmen; the figures here exclude all employed in state farms.

29 Population figures for 1982.

30 *Partiya i rabochi klass v usloviyakh stroitel'stva kommunizma* (1973), p. 37. *Partiynaya zhizn'*, no. 15 (August 1983), p. 18.

31 *Partiynaya zhizn'*, no. 14 (1981), p. 19.

32 This was in the period 1950–61. T.H. Rigby *Communist Party Membership . . .*, (1968), p. 433.

33 *Pravda*, 26 September 1983.

34 *Partiynaya zhizn'*, no. 15 (1983) p. 22 and *Pravda*, 26 September 1983.

35 T.H. Rigby, 'Social Orientation of Recruitment and Distribution of Membership in the Communist Party of the Soviet Union', *The American Slavic and East European Review*, vol. 16 (Oct. 1957), pp. 289–90.

36 *Partiynaya zhizh'* (1981), p. 22.

37 *Pravda*, 11 April 1983.

38 'KPSS v tsifrakh', *Partiynaya zhizn'* (1981), p. 20.

39 1946 figures cited by M. Fainsod, *How Russia is Ruled* (1963), p. 280. For 1983 see 'KPSS v tsifrakh' (1983), p. 25. The remaining statistics for 1983 are: members and candidates 41–50 years of age, 25.4 per cent; over 50, 36.2 per cent.

40 See 'Izmeneniya v ustave KPSS i vnutripartiynaya zhizn', *Kommunist*, no. 7 (May 1966), p. 5.

41 *Narkhoz 1922–82*, p. 48 and 'KPSS v tsifrakh' (1983), p. 24.

42 Miller and Rigby, *26th Congress of the CPSU . . .*, p. 89

43 Figures cited by Z. Brezezinski and S. Huntington, *Political Power USA/USSR* (1964), p. 135.

44 John A. Armstrong, *The Soviet Bureaucratic Elite* (1959) p. 31.

45 'KPSS v tsifrakh' (1981), p. 25.

46 Ibid., p. 23.

47 Full voting members only. Data cited in Radio Liberty Research, RL 159/81 (1981), p. 8.

48 See E.P. Mickiewicz, *Soviet Political Schools* (1967).

49 Philip D. Stewart, *Political Power in the Soviet Union* (1968), p. 143.

6

THE GOVERNMENT STRUCTURE

While the Communist Party is an authoritative source of values and political authority, the government has the legal power of enforcement: it has the right to apply physical force and sanctions. The party mobilizes the population towards the achievement of particular goals, whereas the government formally arranges the execution and enforcement of policy. We shall return to party–government relations below, after describing the organization of the government, and the background and work of the deputies, or members, of the Soviets.

'The government' is composed of two structures: a system of elected parliaments (or Soviets), which are something like Western legislative bodies and are organized territorially, and an executive, or ministerial structure, which in theory is responsible to the elected bodies. In constitutional theory, the Soviets 'constitute the political foundation of the USSR. All other organs of [the government] are under the control of, and accountable to, the Soviets of People's Deputies.'[1] Legitimate power lies in a series of Soviets, which perform a role similar to parliaments in Western states. Soviets exist at all levels of government: from town or rural (village) Soviets carrying out local government, to the Supreme Soviet of the USSR, which is the 'all-union' government. The executive arm of government is composed of various ministries and bodies coming under the Council of Ministers. For clarity, diagram 6.1 summarizes the leading bodies of the three main political institutions: parliaments, ministries and the Communist Party. The parliamentary organs are elected, and the members work part-time. In constitutional theory they are supreme, having authority, at the appropriate level, over the administration of ministries (shown in the second column). The ministries, and other committees, however, carry out the day-to-day policy; they are the effective government of the country. The Council of Ministers is a body with over 130 members (see Appendix 'E'). It is unwiedly for policy-making and there is an official Presidium composed of the chairman of the Council, his deputies and other leading

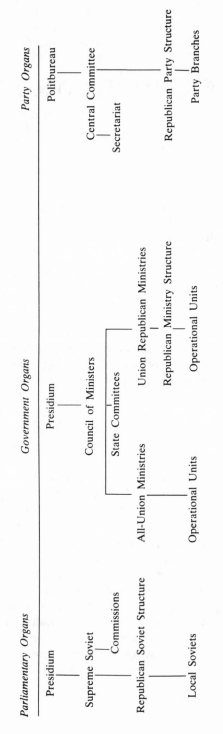

Parliamentary Organs *Government Organs* *Party Organs*

Presidium

Supreme Soviet
└─ Commissions

Republican Soviet Structure

Local Soviets
└─ Operational Units

Presidium

Council of Ministers
└─ State Committees

All-Union Ministries
└─ Operational Units

Union Republican Ministries

Republican Ministry Structure
└─ Operational Units

Politbureau

Central Committee
└─ Secretariat

Republican Party Structure
└─ Party Branches

DIAGRAM 6.1: CONFIGURATION OF PARLIAMENTS, MINISTRIES AND PARTY ORGANS members. Finally, on the extreme right of the diagram is the party organization. It seeks to lead and 'control' the other two structures at all levels. It is not, however, formally part of the administration (the *upravlenie*).

Soviet Federalism

We may begin our consideration of the formal organization of the Soviet system by describing the federal structure. The reader must bear in mind that here we are considering the 'legal charter' rather than actual practice. By 'federal' is meant that powers are divided between a central (or federal) government and regional (or republican) governments. The individual republican governments, in theory, should have authority over certain aspects of social life, while the central government has an overall authority over other aspects. Soviet federalism seeks to integrate the separate nations and areas into a single 'all-union' state and economic order while giving an element of autonomy to the individual nations. The advantages of a federal system generally are that it has the virtues of a large market, a single monetary system and a common army and allows for local diversity: separate language, religion, culture and 'way of life'. The integrating institution is the federal or, in Soviet terminology, the *All-Union* government of the USSR: the Soviet Republics promote local government. (See Appendix D, Constitution, Section VI.)[2]

The formal federal structure is illustrated in a very simplified form in diagram 6.2. The USSR is divided into fifteen Union Republics. In some cases these contain Autonomous Republics (of which there are 20),

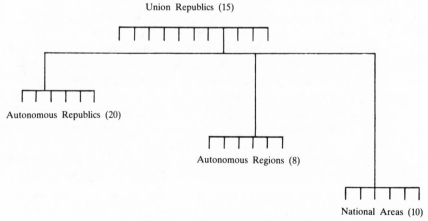

DIAGRAM 6.2: FEDERAL UNITS OF USSR (SIMPLIFIED)

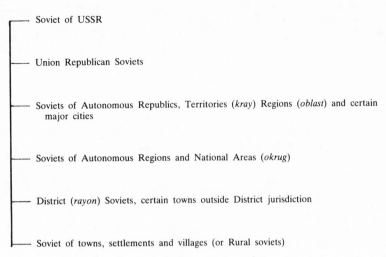

- Soviet of USSR

- Union Republican Soviets

- Soviets of Autonomous Republics, Territories (*kray*) Regions (*oblast*) and certain major cities

- Soviets of Autonomous Regions and National Areas (*okrug*)

- District (*rayon*) Soviets, certain towns outside District jurisdiction

- Soviet of towns, settlements and villages (or Rural soviets)

DIAGRAM 6.3: LEVELS OF SOVIET ADMINISTRATIVE UNITS

Autonomous Regions (eight) and National Areas (ten). How these lower units are divided among the Union Republics is shown in diagram 6.3. All these units are based on the existence of a homogeneous national group, having its own written language. The units vary in status: Union Republics have their own Constitution and more powers than National Areas. The significance of the federal units is that they give some authority and territorial integrity to a fairly well-defined national or ethnic grouping.[3] The federal or All-Union parliament is bicameral (with two chambers) having representatives both by density of population (Council of the Union) and by national areas (Council of Nationalities). All lower parliaments are unicameral (with one chamber).

The detailed powers of the All-Union and republican governments are defined in the Constitution (see Appendix D). We may summarize them here. The chief powers of the *All-Union* government are to issue currency, to declare war, to regulate external trade, and to develop a plan for the economic development of the Soviet Union. With the exception of the last condition, the formal constitutional powers of the All-Union government are similar to those of the federal government in the USA.

The Republics have the constitutional right to adopt and to amend their own constitution (as long as it remains consistent with the All-Union constitution), to approve a national plan and budget and to secede from the USSR. Each republic legally has the sanctity of its borders and the guarantee of republican citizenship.

Autonomous Republics are subordinate to the parent Union Republic in the establishment and interpretation of their constitutions. But a Union Republic has the right to suspend the laws of an Autonomous Republic and it may also intervene to ensure that economic planning is in conformity with the national plan.

The Autonomous Regions and National Areas are more limited in their powers. They are administrative bodies and do not have Supreme Soviets or constitutions like Republics. These units conduct business in the national language and like Republics they have the right to send delegates directly to the Supreme Soviet.

Within the federal structure are a number of administrative divisions on which local government is based. The exact configuration varies between republics, and the details need not detain us here. The skeleton of the structure is depicted in diagram 6.3.[4] Directly subordinate to the Union Republican government are certain large cities (equivalent, say, to British county boroughs), which in turn are subdivided into small administrative districts (*rayons*). Some republics are divided into large territories or regions and then subdivided into districts, towns and villages, others are directly divided into regions, towns and villages. At each lower level there is a Soviet or parliament which is directly elected every two-and-a-half years (Constitution, Article 90).

While election to the Soviet is direct, the administration is centralized and indirect. The Constitution defines democratic centralism as: 'the electiveness of all bodies of state authority from the lowest to the highest, their accountability to the people and the obligation of lower bodies to observe the decisions of higher ones' (Article 3). This results in a vertical chain of command with a strong element of centralization. Finance is centralized and apportioned to the Union Republics. The local units tend to be organs of administration, though local participation is encouraged.

The Supreme Soviet

The Supreme Soviet of the USSR is the highest body of government authority. Its powers include 'the adoption and amendment of the Constitution of the USSR; the admission of new republics to the USSR, endorsement of the formation of new Autonomous Republics and Autonomous Regions; approval of the state plans for economic and social development, of the budget of the USSR, and of reports on their execution; and the institution of bodies of the USSR accountable to it .... Laws of the USSR shall be enacted by the Supreme Soviet of the USSR or by a nationwide vote (referendum) held by decision of the Supreme Soviet of the USSR' (Constitution, Article 108).

It should perhaps be made clear that being the chief legislative and executive body does not give to the Soviets, even in Soviet constitutional theory, supreme *political* authority. This is claimed by the Communist Party which is 'the leading and guiding force of Soviet society and the nucleus of its political system, of all state organisations and public organisations ... The Communist Party, armed with Marxism–Leninism, determines the general perspectives of the development of society and the course of the home and foreign policy of the USSR, directs the great constructive work of the Soviet people, and imparts a planned, systematic, and theoretically substantiated character to their struggle for the victory of communism' (Constitution, Article 6).

The distinction between political authority, claimed by the party, and legislative and executive powers exercised by the parliament (Soviets) and the executive of government, is novel to the Soviet Union. The constitutional theory of Western liberal-democracy has no analogous principle.

The Supreme Soviet is composed of two houses: the Soviet of the Union and the Soviet of Nationalities.[5] The Soviet of the Union is elected by density of population, with one deputy per some 300,000 inhabitants. In the 1984 election, there were 750 deputies so elected. The Soviet of Nationalities is formed by representatives of the different federal units described above. Union Republics each send thirty-two delegates, each Autonomous Republic eleven, an Autonomous Region five and a National Area one: this gives a total of 750. The composition of the Supreme Soviet by place of origin of delegates is shown in table 6.1.

The left-hand column shows the number of deputies in the Soviet of the Union: the Russian Federative Republic accounts for more than half the delegates (405), followed by the Ukraine (144). Each Union Republic has the right to send 32 delegates to the Soviet of Nationalities, and in addition, the lower federal units also send delegates, as defined above. This procedure gives the Russian Federative Republic a total of 243, Uzbekistan 43, Georgia 59, Azerbaidzhan 48 and Tadzhikistan 37.

The Supreme Soviet is directly elected every five years on the basis of universal suffrage and by secret ballot. The two chambers are equal in their rights and usually meet separately. Joint sittings are presided over alternately by the chairperson of each house. Laws are adopted if passed by both chambers by a simple majority vote in each. In the inconceivable event of disagreement between them, questions are referred to a conciliation commission, formed by an equal number of members of each house. The problem of resolving formal disagreement by vote either within or between the houses in fact never arises. Differences are ironed out before meetings of the Supreme Soviet and, in keeping with the

TABLE 6.1: ELECTION TO THE USSR SUPREME SOVIET, BY PLACE OF ORIGIN OF DELEGATES

			⎧ 32 Deputies from ⎪ each Union Republic
	Supreme Soviet		⎪ 11 Deputies from ⎪ each Autonomous
1 Deputy per ⎫ 300,000 inhabitants ⎭	*Soviet* *of the* *Union*	*Soviet* *of* *Nationalities*	⎬ Republic ⎪ ⎪ 5 Deputies from ⎪ each Autonomous Region
			⎪ 1 Deputy from each ⎩ National Area

By Republics:
  Deputies Elected (Union)   *Deputies Elected (Nationalities)*

Russian Republic	405		⎧ 32 + 176 from 16 Autonomous Republics
		243	⎨ 25 from 5 Autonomous Regions, and
			⎩ 10 from 10 National Areas
Ukraine	144	32	
Byelorussia (White Russia)	28	32	
Uzbekistan	39	43	32 + 11 from one Autonomous Republic
Kazakhstan	41	32	
Georgia	14	59	⎰ 32 + 22 from two Autonomous Republics ⎱ 5 from one Autonomous Region
Azerbaidzhan	15	48	⎰ 32 + 11 from one Autonomous Republic ⎱ 5 from one Autonomous Region
Lithuania	9	32	
Moldavia	11	32	
Latvia	7	32	
Kirghizia	9	32	
Tadzhikistan	9	37	32 + 5 from one Autonomous Region
Armenia	8	32	
Turkmenistan	7	32	
Estonia	4	32	
	750	750	

assumption of the political homogeneity of the USSR, divisive votes are not taken. Debates on proposed legislation take place in one chamber, where calls for amendments are frequently put.

The sessions are public, and representatives from non-parliamentary groups (such as trade unions) and other specialists may take part in the proceedings. The agenda includes: discussion of the budget, extra-ordinary

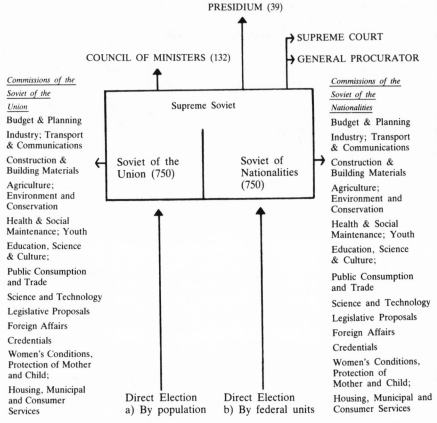

DIAGRAM 6.4: STRUCTURE OF THE SUPREME SOVIET OF THE USSR

legislation, approval of decrees of the Presidium. Reports (lasting 90 minutes) are presented to the sessions, participants in discussion are allowed 25 minutes and independent speeches 5 minutes.[6]

The Supreme Soviet at a joint sitting formally elects the Presidium, the Council of Ministers, the Supreme Court and the General Procurator; each house also elects 16 commissions (as shown in diagram 6.4.). These commissions do much of the work of the Soviet; they are described below.

The Presidium, headed by Chairman Chernenko, the Party's General Secretary, (as Andropov and Brezhnev before him), has the right to take decisions when the Soviet is not sitting. As the Soviet meets only twice per annum for a session, usually lasting three to five days, the Presidium's decrees, later approved by the Soviet, are quite numerous.[7] The Presidium technically may annul the decisions of the Council of Ministers, it can interpret laws, ratify treaties, declare war, proclaim martial law, dismiss and appoint ministers – all subject to subsequent confirmation by the Supreme Soviet. (For full details see Article 121 of the Constitution.) The Presidium is 39 in number: it includes a Chairperson, the First Vice-Chairperson, fifteen vice-chairpersons (one from each of the Union Republics), a secretary and twenty members. The Chairman is not in a strictly comparable position to the President of the USA and he is not directly elected by the public. In practice, he performs many of the functions of Head of State: he accepts foreign delegations, foreign ambassadors and signs official decrees. The assumption of this post by the party's General Secretary, Brezhnev, in 1977, Andropov in 1983, and Chernenko in 1984, gives to the party leader – as head of the legislature – a higher legal status than the chief of the executive or government apparatus. Chernenko, Andropov and Brezhnev were also made Chairman of the Defence Council giving control over the armed forces.

Elections

The franchise is universal: all citizens over 18 years of age have the right to vote with the exception of the mentally handicapped and insane. Formally, elections to government organs are direct and secret, and votes are cast on printed ballot papers. Any person over 18 is eligible for nomination to a local Soviet, over 21 to the Soviets of a Union or Autonomous Republic and over 21 years of age to the USSR Supreme Soviet.

Soviet elections, it should be added, are not the same kind of process as those held in liberal-democratic states. For the voter, there is no choice of candidate. He has, however, the opportunity to cross off the name on the official ballot paper. In this way, he can prevent the election of a candidate, who must receive more than fifty per cent of the votes on the voting register. In local elections such abstentions do happen: in 1982, 94 candidates failed to get the necessary number of votes.[8] In these elections, in the USSR as a whole, 2,288,885 deputies did get elected unopposed and an overwhelming majority of the population (over 99.9 per cent of the electorate) voted for the nominated candidate. Voters absent from their own constituency may vote in another, provided that they have a Voting Right Certificate. The sick and invalids may vote at home by dropping their ballot papers into a ballot-box brought specially to them. Booths are also erected on long distance trains and ships. In the March 1984 elections to the Soviet of the Union, 99.94 per cent of the voters supported the official candidate; 109,072 voted against and 17 votes were invalid.[9] Similar figures apply to the Soviet of Nationalities. The numbers voting in favour of the candidate have risen with time; in 1937, 98.6 per cent voted in favour of candidates to the Soviet of the Union; 632,074 people voted against and

636,808 spoiled their voting paper. Though voting can be done secretly – a booth is provided for crossing off the name and the ballot paper is valid if dropped folded into the ballot box – a person entering the booth is most likely to be voting against the candidate (by crossing out the name). This procedure has led to the accusation that the election cannot be 'secret'.[10] In the event of a candidate failing to get the necessary majority in the election, another election is called.

The crucial decisions over candidates are made at the selection stage. Nominations may be put forward to the government electoral commission by any public organization – for example, by the party or trade union, or by the meeting of a collective farm. A person named at a meeting is discussed by the organization concerned and, if approved, his name is put forward. All such nominated candidates are then discussed at a constituency 'pre-election meeting' attended by representatives from various organizations (party, unions) and a decision is reached on the candidate to be supported. As a Soviet source puts it: 'In order that collectives possessing the right to nominate candidates may come to an agreement on a general candidate, practice has developed such a form of consulting opinion at a meeting of representative persons of collectives. At this meeting, not only do they decide on which candidate to put up for balloting in a given electorate, but how to develop the campaign for that candidate.'[11] Those who do not receive support at this meeting either gracefully withdraw their nomination, or have it withdrawn for them by their nominating organizations. It is here that the merits and faults of particular candidates are discussed, and possibly conflicting group and individual interests are manifested. The successful contender is registered with the District Electoral Commission in the name of the *organization* nominating him.

The procedure of accepting nominations from organizations involves restrictions on the nomination of candidates. This may be illustrated by the attempt of Roy Medvedev, a human rights campaigner, to stand for election to the Supreme Soviet in 1979. (On Medvedev see chapter 9 below.) A group of citizens in the Moscow Sverdlovsk district sent in a nomination for Medvedev to the Electoral Commission. He writes: 'At first, the appearance of a group of workers with such a proposal prompted amused reactions among the electoral commission. The chairman of the electoral commission even asked the members of the group whether they knew what country they were living in and whether they would like to come down from the sky into this sinful land.'[12] After some days the leader of the self-styled '1979 Election Group' was summoned to the Electoral Commission and told that the documents were not in order: the organization was not registered with the local authority. The group tried to register with the authorities. This request was eventually turned down. The supporters of Medvedev, however, decided to cross out the name of the 'official candidate' and write in 'Medvedev'. This they did. Needless to say, the official candidate was overwhelmingly elected.

The Electoral Commission is probably strongly controlled by the party and ensures its control of *cadres* or, in political science jargon, it ensures political recruitment. As Barabashev and Sheremet have put it: 'In elections to the Soviets, the party works out and puts into effect general directions on such cardinal questions as basic ratios in the social composition of deputies, the problem of continuity and renewal, and so forth.'[13] After selection by the pre-election meeting, the candidate must appear in public before his constituents. It is possible for objections to be made about his unsuitability: facts about unsavoury morals or unsatisfactory past work record, for example, may be brought to light, and he may be forced to withdraw. If a majority present do not approve of the candidate, his/her name does not go forward. This does sometimes happen. An émigré has described the process:

Someone was reading off a piece of paper, such and such are the circumstances and we propose nominating so and so. Suddenly everyone is shouting, 'No! We don't want her.' Then suddenly someone suggests Kisseleva (a simple, but active and well-liked woman) and since no one else is nominated, Kisseleva is accepted unanimously with the exception of the first nominator who had come from the Party committee.[14]

These 'revolts' are unusual. But they are a safety valve for the expression of public disapproval. In 1965, there were some 2,000 cases of rejection in this fashion – about 1 in 1,000 of nominees.[15] The potential for revolt also has a constraining effect on the local political leadership.

As Hill has pointed out, the local party organization carefully examines comments made by voters on the ballot papers after voting day. 'The Party *obkom* acquainted itself with all the remarks, proposals and requests of the electors, written by them on the ballot papers on election day. The *oblispolkom* (district Party committee) was detailed to study them closely and take steps in response to them.'[16] These measures seem to have been successful. In the last twenty years or so, the number of seats has increased by 40 per cent, whereas the number of non-elected candidates has fallen by a third. Many Western commentators argue that Soviet officials now anticipate voters' performances and nominate more popular candidates for election.[17] Others contend, however, that 'disillusionment with the election system is widespread.'[18] Zaslavsky and Brym argue that about 25 per cent of the electorate, in fact, do not vote.[19] A more cautious and reliable estimate is that of Friedgut, who has estimated that among Moscow intellectuals, about ten per cent do not vote,[20] and overall, about 2.5 per cent abstain. There is over-registration of votes: when people are away, the agitator will vote for them and passports (to establish identity) are often taken collectively to the voting station. The election is certainly a legitimating device and serves as a symbolic public demonstration of loyalty. Like religious worship, the act of electing helps to create a political identity for the voter.

The Deputies

The election of representatives has the effect of directly involving large numbers of non-party people in public affairs. In July 1982, for example, there were 2,288,885 deputies elected in local government. Of these, only 42.8 per cent were members of the Communist Party. As a result, many are drawn into political activity who would not consider joining the party. At the March 1984 election to the Supreme Soviet, 28.6 per cent of those elected were non-party. Though non-party deputies are in a majority in *local* Soviets, it is unlikely that they are a powerful force in decision-making or serious opponents to the party. Leading positions are usually held by party members. Higher up the political hierarchy, the proportion of party members increases steadily. In 1984, all of the members of the Council of Ministers were party members. In the Pr sidium of the Supreme Soviet in the same year, two out of 39 members were non-party.[21]

As to the social background of the deputies, in the Supreme Soviet elected in 1979, 35 per cent were defined as 'manual workers', 16 per cent were collective farmers (of whom 62 out of 244 were farm chairpersons); factory managers and other specialists constituted 4.4 per cent; employees of government organs accounted for 14 per cent; party officials, 16.6 per cent, and officers of the trade unions and Komsomol, 1.3 per cent. Employees in science, culture, literature, art, education, health and the media came to 9 per cent and military personnel 3.7 per cent.[22] Lay representation drops considerably at the level of the Presidium. Of the 39 elected in 1979, 17 were government officials, 10 were officers of the party, 2 were employees of unions and Komsomol, 3 were heads of welfare (*obshchestvennye*) and voluntary (*dobrovol'nye*) organizations. The lay representation consisted of one writer, one doctor, and five manual workers and collective farmers.[23]

At the middle and lower levels of the parliamentary system one is struck by the very large number of elected representatives. In the elections held in 1980 to the Supreme Soviets of the Union Republics, Autonomous Republics and to local Soviets, a total of 2,274,699 people were elected.

There is a lack of detailed information about the social background of such delegates, but they appear to be fairly representative of the population as a whole. In 1980, 43.3 per cent were manual workers and 25.4 per cent collective farmers, 21.1 per cent were members of the Komsomol and 33.3 per cent were under 30 years of age.[24] Similar data may be cited for the local elections held in July 1982. A total of 2,288,885 deputies were elected: 44.3 per cent were manual workers and 24.9 collective farmers, and 34 per cent were under 30 years of age.[25] Women constitute a slightly higher proportion of members at the local level than they do in the national parliament. In local elections in 1982, 50.1 per cent of deputies were women, and at the 1980 elections to the Supreme Soviets of the Union Republics and Autonomous Republics, 49.5 per cent were women. In 1984, 32.8 per cent of the delegates to the Supreme Soviet of the USSR were women.[26] The last figure, representing a total of 492 delegates, is claimed to exceed the total number of women elected to all the parliaments of Western countries.

As with the Supreme Soviet, executive positions are held disproportionately by men and party members. Of the executive committees of local Soviets elected in 1977, of a total of 371,552 members, 67.1 per cent were men (51 per cent of the total number of deputies elected) and 71.6 were members of the CPSU (compared with 43.2 per cent of the total number of deputies.)[27]

Compared with those of elected representatives in advanced Western states, the occupation of Soviet deputies shows some striking differences. The largest group is made up of engineers and technicians (20.5 per cent), followed by farming specialists (11.7 per cent). Lawyers, who form a large contingent among American Congressmen, constitute only 0.9 per cent of deputies to the Supreme Soviet.[28] Taking these figures as a whole, the occupational spread is wider and the participation of women is much greater than in the West. Deputies, however, are not full-time parliamentarians. They continue in their jobs, though they must be given paid leave to attend the Soviet and deal with its affairs. They receive more than one hundred rubles per month to cover expenses and are entitled to free transport (by rail, ship or plane). However laudable the idea of a deputy being in constant contact with life at the bench or on the farm, it is probable that his or her effectiveness as a deputy is decreased by the need to work in another job.

Voters also have the right to 'mandate' their deputy to do something. Such mandates must command a majority of votes at an election meeting. Between 1973 and 1975, there were a total of 847,185 mandates.[29] They were to do with conditions in schools, post-offices and hospitals, with repairs to public property, with street lighting and with supplies of materials. This puts a certain pressure on deputies and, if they are unable to implement these mandates, they may be 'recalled' by their electors. In practice, over 85 per cent of mandates are fulfilled within a two-year period.[30]

Deputies are advised to report to the group that nominates them. If their work is unsatisfactory, a public meeting may be called and the local Soviet may be petitioned. A public meeting is then called and if a majority vote against the deputy, he is recalled and an election is arranged to elect a new deputy. Such occurrences happen 600 to 700 times per annum[31] (out of a total of over two million deputies).

The function of the deputy is to carry out political communication between government and the Soviet citizen. He is expected to deal with individual complaints from constituents and to keep the law-making organs informed of his constituents' wishes. He reports to groups of constituents on the work of the Soviet, justifies its actions and explains the reasons for proposed legislation.

I try to use any opportunity I have to inform my electors of the Supreme Soviet's decisions and to mobilise them for their implementation. My official reports to the constituency apart, I pursue this line at the sittings of the District and Village Soviets, at the different meetings and conferences and at my meetings with electors in collective and state farms and in factory shops.[32]

Deputies of the Supreme Soviet give regular reports of their work to party and union meetings, speak on the radio and appear on television. Elected representatives often put certain days aside to meet constituents who have suggestions or grievances. Here, the intervention by a deputy can often lead to results after the exposure of inefficiency in administration. A deputy, for example, must have a reply to an enquiry put to an official 'within the time-limit established by law'.[33] The existence of this regulation, of course, does not mean that he always gets a prompt or satisfactory reply. Examples of the things the deputy gets done are: putting right faults in buildings, speeding up cultural development (i.e. providing library facilities) and improving railway services. Of 118 requests received by a deputy to the Supreme Soviet, 15 called for greater efficiency in the work of collective farms, nine mentioned the need for help in factories, 27 wanted help for municipal institutions (schools, hospitals, canteens, etc.), 18 were on labour and citizen's rights, 27 were on housing problems and 22 asked for help in procuring building materials.[34]

All the activities described above give the citizen some degree of participation in decision-making. They are, however, not very powerful means of control over the administration. Officials and professionals are largely in control of the policy process and the values of centralized

TABLE 6.2: INCREASES IN BUDGETARY EXPENDITURE OVER MINISTER'S
PROPOSALS, 1974–1980

	Percentage Increases	
	1974–79	1979–80
Economy	0.00	0.00
Socio-cultural	0.14	0.13
Defence	0.03	0.02
Administration	0.11	0.04
Republican budget	0.12	0.11
Total	0.06	0.05

Source: Stephen White, 'The Supreme Soviet and Budgetary Policies in the USSR', British Journal of Political Science, vol. 12, Jan. 1982, p. 86.

authority persist. Deputies are part-timers and there is also a high turnover of deputies.[35]

Study of the activity of deputies also throws some light on the budgetary process in the USSR. Stephen White has examined the way the budget is constructed and has illustrated that deputies make claims which influence the level of expenditure planned by the government. White compared the government's budgetary proposals with the budgetary laws subsequently adopted. Some of the data are cited in table 6.2. Total expenditure is divided into the categories of use: economy, socio-cultural, defence, administration and republican budget. The table shows relatively small (but in total expenditure considerable) increases. Defence has hardly been increased, while socio-cultural expenditure and the finance given to republican budgets has risen. Such increases occur due to the pressure exerted by the deputies. As White puts it: 'There is a good deal of evidence that deputies do indeed seek to make use of such opportunities to press the claims of their constituents, their republics or the institutions in which they work, both in the formal sessions and in the committee meetings that precede them.'[36] A similar process concerning the expenditure proposed for the republican governments was detected by White: republican budgets rose by an average of 0.11 per cent in 1979–80 and 0.12 per cent 1974–79.[37] We should also note that internally generated taxes are variably kept in Union Republics: e.g. 100 per cent in the Turkmen Republic, 80.6 per cent in Lithuania and 41.8 per cent in Latvia.[38] These figures probably conceal a process of political bargaining and suggest that deputies act as articulators of regional interests. As Donna Bahry says,

Regional leaders take virtually every opportunity – including Congresses of the Communist Party of the Soviet Union (CPSU) and meetings of the Central

Committee and Supreme Soviet – to highlight local needs as they recite the achievements of socialism.[39]

Commissions of the Soviet

If we are to look for other pivotal points in the political structure where sectional interests are articulated, it would seem unlikely that the sessions of the Supreme Soviet are one of these. Its sessions are short and the number of delegates participating is small. However, one might expect that the various commissions of the Soviets play a more important role in interest articulation.

The standing commissions are made up of deputies to the respective Soviets. They examine proposals put to the Supreme Soviet and they supervise the work of the executive bodies.[40] They also put forward bills on their own initiative. The Soviet of the Union and the Soviet of Nationalities each has commissions on: youth, budget and planning, industry, transport and communication, construction and building materials, agriculture, health, environment, consumption, education, science and culture, trade and services, legislative proposals, foreign affairs, women and children, housing, municipal affairs and credentials (see p. 180). *Ad hoc* commissions may also be formed.

The commissions are set up during the first session of parliament and last for its duration. They function even when the Supreme Soviet is not in session and it is here that much of the aggregation of interests takes place. Again, a comparison may be made with the functions performed by parliamentary committees in Great Britain and the USA, though greater publicity is given to the work of the latter. The commissions provide specialist forums for the detailed study of various aspects of government work. In the 1979 session of the Supreme Soviet, the commissions had a total membership of 1,140, that is, 76 per cent of the total number of deputies. Commissions have 35 members in each chamber (except budget and planning which has 45 members in each chamber). Each one is made up of men and women with different regional and institutional interests and, as a result, it is very probable that the claims of various groups find their expression here. However, many of the permanent members are party and government officials, and worker and peasant deputies tend to be transient. Moreover, heads of ministries and departments are also members, and this may restrain the espousal of consumer interests (see table 6.3).

Certain aspects of the work of the commissions are specifically organized to ensure the representation of sectional interests. To ensure that interested parties involved in a bill have a chance to comment on it, a bill may be discussed in more than one commission.

TABLE 6.3: COMPOSITION OF PERMANENT COMMISSIONS OF THE SUPREME
SOVIET, 1979

Employees of government organs	75
Officials of party organs	228
Managers and chiefs of enterprises and other specialist sectors of the economy	62
Manual workers	418
Collective farmers	168
Employees in science, culture, literature, art, education, health and media	127
Officials of trade unions and Komsomol organs	17
Military	44
Women	355
Members and candidates of the CPSU	826
Members of the Komsomol	148
Total in permanent commissions	1,140

Source: Verkhovny sovet SSSR (1979), p. 44.

The bill on the Budgetary Powers of the USSR and the Union Republics is referred to the Budgetary Commissions of both chambers, and to the Economic Commission of the Soviet of the Nationalities. On the draft of the Fundamentals of Land Use Bill, the following commissions were involved: agriculture, industry transport and communications, construction and building materials, legislative proposals.[41] In the discussion of the government's economic plan and budgetary proposals in 1978, the various commissions held sixty-five meetings and considered 199 reports from various government bodies and about 200 expert government witnesses were called to report to the commissions.[42] It can be seen, therefore, that procedures are available through which proposals may be discussed and compromise made. On the other hand, in contrast to the legislative process in Western states, not all bills go before commissions.

The standing commissions have their parallels at all levels of the Soviet parliamentary system – from the Union to the local Soviets. In the Soviet of the Ukrainian Union Republic there are, for example, 17 standing commissions embracing 81.2 per cent of the total number of deputies. In local Soviets, after the 1977 elections, there were 329,052 permanent commissions, on which 1,797,016 deputies served – 80.6 per cent of the total.[43] Thus approximately four-fifths of all deputies are on commissions.

Like the committees in Western parliaments, the commissions draw into their work specialists on particular topics depending on the nature of the bill. Representatives of the party, trade unions and the Young Communists

League are also represented in the additional subcommissions, which are set up to deal with the analysis of particular problems.

The Council of Ministries

The Council of Ministers is the effective executive or government of the USSR. The Chairman of the Council, or Prime Minister, at the time of writing is N.A. Tikhonov. The Council of Ministers numbers over a hundred and thirty people, including the heads of all Soviet ministries and a number of other high ranking officials – the fifteen chairmen of the Union Republic Councils of Ministers, the chairmen of the specialist government committees. (For a list, see Appendix E.) These people are usually also members of the Central Committee of the party. The members of the Council, who need not be members of the Supreme Soviet (though they usually are), cannot be in the Presidium of the Supreme Soviet, as the Council is responsible to it when the Supreme Soviet is not sitting.

There are two main types of Ministry – All-Union and Union-Republican. (In addition, there are Republican Ministries which are directly subordinate to the Republican governments). The former have as their sphere of responsibility the country as a whole, whereas the latter operate from the Union Republics and are therefore more decentralized.

The state committees, whose chairmen are on the Council, are most important bodies for co-ordinating government policy. These include the USSR State Planning Committee (Gosplan), and those for Construction, Economic Relations with Foreign Countries, Labour and Wages, Materials and Technical Supplies, Planning, Timber Industry, Science and Technology and Vocational and Technical Education. Other important committees with chairmen in the council of Ministers are: the People's Control Committee, the Board of the USSR State Bank, the Central Statistical Board, the State Security Committee (KGB) and the Association for the Supply of Agricultural Machinery.

The tasks of the Council, as defined in Article 131 of the Constitution, are to direct and co-ordinate the work of the All-Union Ministries, to carry out the economic plan, to maintain law and order, to conduct foreign affairs, to organize the armed forces, and to set up state committees. With respect to those branches of the administration within its competence, it has the right to suspend the decisions and orders of the Councils of Ministers of the Union Republics and to annul the orders and instructions made by individual ministers of the USSR (Article 134, USSR Constitution). In practice, the Council and its Ministries are the main sources of legislation and issue decrees and regulations governing the whole of economic and social life. It should be noted here, moreover, that the

TABLE 6.4: COUNCIL OF MINISTERS

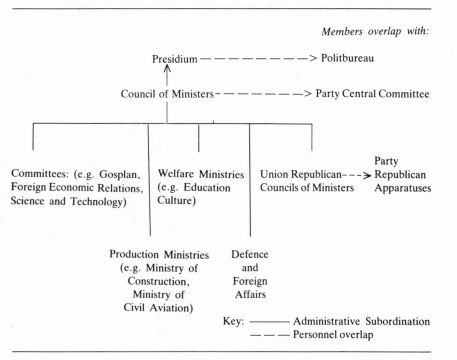

Members overlap with:

Presidium — — — — — — — —> Politbureau

Council of Ministers — — — — — — —> Party Central Committee

| Committees: (e.g. Gosplan, Foreign Economic Relations, Science and Technology) | Welfare Ministries (e.g. Education Culture) | Union Republican- - -> Councils of Ministers | Party Republican Apparatuses |

Production Ministries
(e.g. Ministry of
Construction,
Ministry of
Civil Aviation)

Defence
and
Foreign
Affairs

Key: ———— Administrative Subordination
— — — Personnel overlap

Note: For complete membership see below Appendix E.

executive arm of government is much stronger than its counterparts in capitalist countries. The whole economic activity of the country is directed by the government. This gives the Council of Ministers great economic and therefore political power.

Such a large body cannot effectively 'guide' the complex affairs of government. A smaller Presidium of the Council has operated for many years. Its position has been clarified in Article 132 of the 1977 Constitution. It is composed of the Chairperson of the Council, the First Vice Chairpersons and Vice Chairpersons: other Ministers may also be co-opted to the Presidium. Its relationship to the Council is shown in table 6.4. Its function is to act 'as a standing body of the Council of Ministers to deal with questions relating to guidance of the economy, and with other matters of state administration'. The Presidium, like the Politbureau, meets weekly. It is noteworthy that the coercive instruments of the state apparatus – the police and armed forces – are absent. The Presidium acts much more as an instrument of the *economy*, being

concerned with accumulation of capital and the production and distribution of goods and services. The Politbureau is more a dominant apparatus
of the state, i.e. being concerned with the defence and reproduction of the
political order. The economy, through the Council of Ministers and its
Presidium, aggregates and articulates demands of an economic kind, which
are then either translated into policy or brought to the attention of the
Politbureau. Because the government controls and operates the economy,
however, one should not conflate the economy with the state: their
functions and their institutions are differentiated.

Rule Enforcement and Adjudication: The Police and Courts

In all modern societies a division of labour takes place between
rule-makers (parliamentarians), rule-enforcers (executives) and rule-
adjudicators (lawyers). In liberal-democratic societies, a theoretical
autonomy exists between the legislative, executive and judiciary: this is
said to ensure the citizen a degree of independence from arbitrary
treatment. The courts adjudicate in cases of conflict between the individual
and the executive arm of government. The law-making process in the USA
is bounded by the judiciary, which can declare Acts passed by Congress to
be unconstitutional. This has not been the case in Britain, though
membership of the European Economic Community has restricted the
sovereign powers of the British Parliament.

In Marxist theory, the 'separation of powers' is an illusion. Law is not an
'independent' body of rules and the judiciary is not a group of persons in
any way independent of the ruling class. Laws, or the rules of society, are
made by the ruling class and are the expression of it. Enforcement is in the
interests of the ruling class. Justice is class justice. This Marxist viewpoint
has influenced the structure of law enforcement in the USSR, where it is
considered to be an instrument of the political arm of the ruling class (the
party), and has a political role: 'The formal law is subordinate to the law of
the revolution. There might be collisions and discrepancies between the
formal commands of laws and those of the proletarian revolution .... This
collision must be solved only by the subordination of the formal
commands of law to those of party policy.'[44] While this statement was
made during the 'dictatorship of the proletariat' in 1935, it still influences the
present Soviet approach to law.

As the extent of Soviet government is wide, so is the area of the
jurisdiction of the courts and police over the citizen. The existence of law,
or a set of rules binding on the members of a community, is held by liberals
to be one of the greatest safeguards of individual freedom. Regularized
processes of law depend to a large extent on a legal profession whose views

of justice and whose norms are congruent with those of the law-makers. In the USSR, even during the Stalin period, law 'was for those areas of Soviet life where the political factor was stabilised'.[45] Where it was not, the police arrested, tried, imprisoned, and executed suspects. With the renunciation of Stalinism, law and legal norms have begun to play a more important role in the Soviet state. As Brezhnev put it to the Twenty-Fifth Party Congress: 'The time has clearly come to issue a (uniform) code of laws of the Soviet state. This will make our laws more accessible to all Soviet citizens.'[46]

A modern statement of Soviet legal theory is: 'Soviet law is a system of rules established by the state to promote the consolidation of the social order which helps society advance toward communism.'[47] Consequently, the *adjudicating* role of the Soviet courts and law is weak, though it has been strengthened since the death of Stalin, whereas its rule *enforcement* role is strong. If one identifies the achievement of communism with the development of the individual's freedom, rights and dignity, then of course there can be no contradiction between law enforcement and individual interest. 'Soviet legislation is a juridical expression of the people's will and is designed to promote the fulfilment of the grand programme of communist construction.'[48] As we shall see below, however, the promotion of collective, or class, interests in practice often conflicts with the individual's perception of rights. (See section on human rights below, chapter 9). The destalinization campaign of Khrushchev led to a greater emphasis being placed on socialist legality. The state was no longer the expression of the 'dictatorship of the proletariat', but that of the 'whole people'. Legal statutes were created and law was seen to be a 'regulator of social relationships'.[49] In 1971, a Ministry of Justice was formed with the functions of 'organised guidance of the judicial organs of the union republics and military tribunals, guidance of the bar, of the State Notary,* and other agencies of justice; systematization and preparation of drafts of law codes; execution of other functions in accordance with the legislation of the USSR and of the union republics'.[50] Brezhnev in 1976 called for 'an improvement of our legislation and the consolidation of the socialist legal order. The passing by party and government organs and the adoption by the USSR Supreme Soviet and the Supreme Soviets of the republics of laws on some of the key problems of our life are of major socio-political importance .... We have adjusted our judicial rules to the new level to which our society has risen.'[51] Thus, on entering the stage of 'developed socialism', a greater emphasis has been accorded in the theory of Soviet society to the rights of the individual over the state.

---

* The State Notary is an office created to protect socialist property and citizen's interests, to strengthen legality and to prevent the violation of law.

A certain light can be thrown on these developments from another angle by looking at the changing role of the security forces organized under the Committee for State Security (the KGB). The control of the internal security organs by Stalin was a crucial factor in the maintenance of his power and the enforcement of his policies. The security forces were subordinate to Stalin himself and their actions were not subject to judicial review: they had the power to exile, confine and execute the accused without trial. The importance of the police and the role of terror has already been described in the historical part of this book (see above, chapter 3). Obviously, after Stalin's death, Beria, as head of the secret police (then called the MVD, Ministry of Internal Affairs) was in a powerful position *vis-à-vis* both party and government officials. He was, however, destroyed by them and, consequently, the powers of the security forces have been weakened. (Beria and five other police officials were executed in December 1953.) The Chairman of the Committee for State Security (KGB) was (and still is) in the Council of Ministers of the USSR. The KGB is now thought to be subordinate to the General Department of the Central Committee of the party. Under Khrushchev an attempt was made to give the security police a new positive image, and to bring it under the control of the party and the government. Since Khrushchev's fall, KGB activity seems to have been on the increase. But there is no evidence of police repression or a return to terror.

The KGB, during Brezhnev's ascendancy, was staffed at its highest levels by his former party associates. Andropov was for a long time a member of the Politbureau and joined its secretariat in May 1982, when he relinquished his KGB post. In December 1983, the Chairman of the KGB, Viktor Chebrikov, maintained its presence by being elected to a candidate's place in the Politbureau.

The KGB is responsible for preventing all major crimes against the state (espionage, ideological, subversion, political dissent – see chapter 9 below – and serious economic crimes) and for external intelligence. It has four Chief Directorates: the First conducts foreign operations, the Second deals with internal affairs, the Fifth (there are no Third and Fourth) has special responsibilities to detect internal treasonable acts by Soviet citizens.[52] It also has a Directorate controlling the border guards, and its own armed forces – the border gaurds, signal troops and the internal security troops of the Ministry of Internal Affairs.[53] The KGB can arrest and hold a suspect for 24 hours after which a procurator, who is a member of the government legal service, should sanction the arrest or discharge the accused. A person may be detained for two months pending the investigation of a charge. (This may be extended to six months by order of a senior procurator.)

Between 1962 and 1968 the ordinary police force, the militia, came under the Ministry for the Preservation of Public Order. Since 1968, the title Ministry of Internal Affairs has been restored to this Union Republican Ministry. It is charged with detecting crime, apprehending criminals, operating the internal passport system, keeping order, controlling traffic and so on.[54]

A system of courts parallels the parliamentary system. At the apex is the Supreme Court of the USSR, then come the Supreme Courts of the Union Republics. The Supreme Court judges and the Procurator General are formally elected by, and responsible to, the Supreme Soviet for a period of five years. The Procurator General is charged with the administration of the legal apparatus and his role is to ensure that acts committed by ministries and their subordinate units (enterprises, etc.) are legal. Excluded from the brief of the Supreme Court, as in English law, are acts or orders of the Council of Ministers and the Supreme Soviet. At the base of the system are the People's Courts, which have a professional judge and two lay assessors who are directly elected for a two-year period by 'general meetings of industrial, office and professional workers'.[55] The Supreme Court of USSR is a final court of appeal, resolving conflicts between the lower judicial organs, and deals only exceptionally with cases of first instance.

The procurators have power to call for documents from institutions and to initiate proceedings against individuals or bodies against whom there is a *prima facie* case. After an investigation the procurator prosecutes to the courts. Prosecution is based on the infringement of legal codes, which are classified by subject: the criminal code, labour law, family law and so on. The details of the codes cannot be considered here.[56]

In sentencing policy an attempt is made to attribute blame, to exact retribution for crime and to use penalties to 'reform' the accused. The law is used to adapt conduct and to mould behaviour to create the 'new Soviet man'. In sociological jargon, the Soviet process of law serves as a positive and negative part of socialization.

This will be clearer if we look at the theory behind Soviet forms of punishment. The criminal code lays down the following three aims of punishment:

(i) retribution for the committed crime;
(ii) correction and re-education of the convicted persons in the spirit of an honourable attitude towards labour, of strict compliance with the laws, and of respect towards communal life;
(iii) the exercise of educational influence on the offender and other people in order to deter them from committing criminal offences.[57]

Under the first category comes the death penalty, which can be given to criminals convicted of treason, espionage, banditry, intentional murder, speculation and theft of state property on a large scale. There are four kinds of 'correction colonies': general regime, used for first offenders convicted of minor crimes; strengthened regime, reserved for criminals sentenced for more serious crimes; strict regime for second or third offenders; special regime, for hardened criminals who have been convicted of violent and serious crime. Other penalties are deductions from wages (of from five to twenty per cent of earnings), fines, public censure and deprivation of medals, orders or other public titles.[58]

What is seen in terms of Marxist theory as the gradual reduction in the role of the coercive state apparatus – the 'withering away of the state' – has involved the transfer to social organizations of some legal tasks previously carried out by the state. The voluntary people's militia, formed through the trade unions and Komsomol, have been charged with the maintenance of public order. Minor crimes are tried by comrades' courts, which are elected at the place of work or place of residence. Their jurisdiction covers pilfering, hooliganism and labour relations, and fines of up to 50 rubles and reparation of loss up to the same amount may be imposed. Public reprimands may also be given. 'Law and order stations' were set up from the 1970s under the local Soviets and these are manned by local volunteers, who act rather like vigilantes in their efforts to prevent crime.[59]

Two points may be made to bring out the difference between the role of law in Britain and the Soviet Union. First, the pre-trial investigation of the alleged crime tends to diminish the importance of the court trial itself.[60] Medvedev has pointed out that: 'the fatal defect of the system is that in the majority of cases the defence lawyer is deprived of the opportunity to give the accused an explanation of his rights as a person who is presumed to be innocent. The lawyer has no chance of challenging the investigating officials' decision to order the detention of the accused before he is brought into court nor is he able to follow the course of the investigation and prevent possible abuses which unfortunately are by no means infrequent.'[61] Secondly, the Marxist and Bolshevik conception of law as the political arm of the state severely weakens the development of the courts as independent adjudicators (at least in criminal cases). The lack of a tradition of the presumption of innocence and the absence of a relatively autonomous legal profession help to strengthen the 'enforcement' elements in the Soviet political system, and weaken the function of adjudication.[62] As Juviler has pointed out: the measures of 'political and economic protection of the socialist state [are] still unusual by Western standards.'[63]

Having described, more or less in its own terms, the 'official' legal and political structure and its own view of the political process, we may turn to the criticisms often made in the West – objections on matters of fact, as it were, of the official view. I shall also outline briefly the Western concept of totalitarianism which seeks to interpret 'the facts' about the USSR in quite a different light to that of the Soviet notion of 'developed socialism'. In later chapters, we shall consider from a more behavioural point of view, the actual political process.

Criticisms of the Official Analysis

In the first place many would deny that the notion of socialist society is appropriate to the USSR. Raymond Aron has objected that: 'It is possible that the party leaders govern in the interests of the proletarian and peasant masses, but the regime is not one in which the proletariat itself is in power.'[64] The leadership rules 'on behalf of', rather than 'at the behest of', the working class. It is argued further that a distinction exists between the interests of the political leaders and those of the people. This criticism has been developed into various theories of bureaucratic and class rule.* The role of coercion and exploitation is at the centre of the Western critique of totalitarianism.

It must be admitted that Soviet theory is inadequate in some respects. It gives no adequate analysis of the distribution of power between different realms – economy, military, police and party. It also leaves unexplained such political processes as Stalin's 'excesses', which are put down by many Soviet writers to individual factors: 'the personality cult'. Another common criticism is that in Soviet theory it is recognized that there have been no 'antagnostic' classes or strata since 1936, yet in Marxist terms, it is objected, neither government nor the party are 'withering away' in any politically significant sense. If Soviet society is socially harmonious, then how can there be any justification for the continuing political domination by the Communist Party, which originally came into being to lead an under-developed working class? The criticism is often made in a slightly different form: that the Soviet description of Soviet society ignores political conflict, which is itself endemic. These criticisms, however, do not take account of Soviet writing on 'developed socialism', including that by its present political leaders, which recognizes the existence of conflict – though not of a system destabilizing kind.[65]

Another objection that is often made is that the CPSU plays a disproportionate, indeed illegitimate, political role at variance with the

* Various Marxist class conflict theories are discussed in my book *Soviet Society and Economy* (1984), chapter 3.

claim of rule through the elected Soviets. Pointing to the fact that a description of the Soviets takes up a considerable part of the constitution of the USSR, Leonard Schapiro asserts that 'behind the formal institutions of government ... stands the real source of both legislative and executive power, the party.'[66] But the wind has been taken out of such critical sails in the 1977 Constitution. As we noted above, Article 6 of the Constitution now defines the CPSU as the 'leading and guiding force of Soviet society and the nucleus of its political system, of all state and public organisations'. This would not confound followers of Trotsky, who in turn would argue that it is the party which is the facade and that the government bureaucracy is in control of the economy and is the effective ruler.

The formal description of the political processes within the party, given in its rules, has also been criticized in the West. Critics claim that the party in practice is not democratically organized on the basis of elections from the bottom up, but on the authoritarian method of control from the top down. It might be conceded that there is at least a tension in the theory of 'democratic centralism' between the democratic and the centralist components. The influence of party members over decision-making in the party is held to be very small indeed when compared with that of the political leadership and the secretariat. Obviously, the higher organs of the party and the secretariat are able to determine to a large extent the content of policy, its timing and implementation, and are able to bring pressure to bear to promote or expel personnel – they perform the aggregation function and thereby play a dominant role in forming party policy. The organs of the secretariat are enforcement agencies. The organizational structure, with a strong full-time secretariat and centralized finance, a diffuse membership banned from forming factions and an emphasis on strict discipline from the top downwards, strengthens the power of bureaucratic apparatus. Moreover, the indirect system of election within the party makes the control of higher bodies by lower ones more difficult. To view the party, therefore, as a structure which articulates the collective views of its total membership, a kind of 'general will' of the proletariat, is naive. In practice, the party can only act on behalf of the proletariat, and the full-time party secretariat (and with it the specialized departments of the Central Committee) indeed plays a decisive role both in aggregating and in articulating general policy goals.

The formal Soviet description of the organization of government – in respect of decentralization – has also been questioned in many respects. The federal system gives the republics relatively few powers and no major aspects of policy are left to the republics independently of the All-Union government. Indeed, the republics, regions and areas serve as units of administration whose role is the implementation of policy decided at the centre. Education, medical and social services, and welfare (for example, care of the old, child and maternity care) are the responsibility of the republics, but the control of foreign trade, economic planning and finance by the All-Union government means that, in practice, the government of the USSR is centralized. Lastly, the clause in the Constitution that states that the secession of a Union Republic from the USSR may take place is of little practical consequence.

Of course, centralization should not be thought of as characteristic only of the USSR. It is a general tendency of all modern large industrial states, and applies equally well to the USA. The main difference between liberal societies and the USSR lies in the extent of government power; the Soviet central government has much more power than do its Western counterparts. Direct local subordination to the central government does not generally take place in Western states (except in France), where more subtle methods of ensuring conformity, such as financial control and inspection, are usually used.

There are four main factors, political and economic, which have encouraged centralization in the USSR: the All-Union government's control of economic planning and the budget (which it appropriates to the lower units); the need for common technical standards in services throughout an enormous and highly differentiated society; the growth of a large complex economy, which has made all of its parts interdependent; and the highly centralized Communist Party.

Several other factors must be taken into account in arriving at a view of the workings of the Soviet State. While politics in general can be said to be about conflict and about alternative policies, the 'official' Soviet description of the workings of the state abjures any reference to major forms of antagonism. The sessions of the Soviets show no fundamental criticism of policies. The amendments, which are put and accepted and have been agreed to beforehand by the government and party, represent the end of a political process, rather than the initiation of one. This is said by many Western critics to demonstrate the absence of democracy in the USSR.

It is also argued that the role of the political police, in the shape of the KGB, is much greater than that of the security forces of Western states. Much of this is true. It does have a wider role, its powers are stronger and its personnel are probably greater in number. It is also a leading part of the effective government, its chief having normally a place in the Politbureau. The Soviet concept of political crime, the importance given to espionage and counter-espionage, puts the security services in a crucial position not recognized in the formal constitution. Lastly, it is often asserted that it is an open question to what extent the political police is controlled by the party apparatus.[67]

Totalitarianism

The most widely adopted stance to the Soviet power structure in the West is that it is held together by force and characterized by totalitarianism. Those who take this view, and they are the majority, see Stalin's crimes as symbolic of a malaise that infects the whole structure of the Soviet political apparatus. The role of coercion is given a prominent place in the concept of totalitarianism. Kornhauser defines totalitarianism as follows:

Totalitarian dictatorship involves total domination, limited neither by received laws or codes (as in traditional authoritarianism) nor even the boundaries of governmental functions (as in classical tyranny), since *they obliterate the distinction between state and society.* Totalitarianism is limited only by the need to keep large numbers of people in a state of constant activity controlled by the elite.[68]

In Kornhauser's theory the crucial factors are the wide control over the society exercised by the polity and the absence of any participation by the masses or of any constraints on the totalitarian dictatorship posed by law, custom or mores.

A second distinguishing feature of totalitarianism is the nature of the group structure. Intermediate groups, such as trade unions, parent–teacher associations, professional bodies and welfare groups, are both weak and 'inclusive' – 'weak' because they have little autonomy from the government and 'inclusive' because they organize many aspects of the individual's life. The ruling elite operates both directly on the population and indirectly through other structures which are effectively penetrated by it. Examples of such a society, argue the theorists of totalitarianism, are found in the USSR, Nazi Germany and Mao's China.

A more detailed model of totalitarianism specifically related to Soviet society has been devised by C.J. Friedrich and Z.K. Brzezinski, who not only accept Kornhauser's distinctions, but fill in the details of the role of ideology, party, leader, police and propaganda. In the first edition of their book (1956), totalitarianism is given six main characteristics:

1. an official ideology, consisting of an official body of doctrine covering all vital aspects of man's existence to which everyone living in that society is supposed to adhere, at least passively: this ideology is characteristically focused on and projected toward a perfect final state of mankind; that is to say, it contains a chiliastic claim, based upon a radical reflection of the existing society and the conquest of the world for the new one;
2. a single mass party led typically one man, the 'dictator', and consisting of a relatively small percentage of the total population (up to ten per cent) of men and women, a hard core of them passionately

and unquestioningly dedicated to the ideology and prepared to assist in every way in promoting its general acceptance, such a party being hierarchically, oligarchically organized, and typically either superior to, or completely intertwined with, the bureaucratic government organization;

3. a system of terroristic police control, supporting but also supervising the party for its leaders, and characteristically directed not only against demonstrable 'enemies' of the regime, but against arbitrarily selected classes of the population; the terror of the secret police systematically exploits modern science and more especially scientific psychology;

4. a technologically conditioned near-monopoly of control, in the hands of the party and its subservient cadres, of all means of effective mass communications, such as the press, radio and films;

5. a similarly technologically conditioned near-complete monopoly of control (in the same hands) of all means of effective armed combat;

6. a central control and direction of the entire economy through the bureaucratic co-ordination of its formerly independent corporate entities, typically including most other associations and group activities.[69]

In terms of Soviet society, the 'official ideology' obviously refers to Marxism–Leninism and its goal of a classless, free and harmonious society. The single mass party led by the 'dictator' controlling mass communications and the economy through terror is meant to sum up the Soviet regime under Stalin: hence the stress in many Western books on terror and dictatorship.

'Totalitarian' theory, particularly in its view of the Stalin period, has the merit of making the political system central. Ideology, mass communication, polity and economy are seen as integrated and operating to constrain the individual. But it is possible to criticize this theory on the grounds that there is no reason why only the six factors mentioned above have been selected. Indeed, in the second edition of Brzezinski's and Friedrich's book another two traits – expansion and the administrative control of justice and the courts – are added to the list.[70] Equally relevant and important to the Stalinist regime were rapid economic growth, full employment, the rise in educational standards, high population movement and mobilization, the growth of urbanism and the social relationships accompanying it.

Brzezinski's and Friedrich's typology was put to political use in the West during the Cold War, since it focused on the more horrendous and anti-liberal aspects of Soviet rule. As Herbert J. Spiro has suggested, the word 'totalitarian' became an 'anti-Communist slogan in the cold war'.[71] But the term has also been applied to Nazi society, and here it soon becomes evident that it is difficult to define the term in ways that make it suitable for sociological and comparative studies. Fascist and communist ideology are antithetical: communism postulates an ideal of man and a classless society quite foreign to fascism. The Soviet regime is founded on nationalized property and central planning, whereas the fascist regimes were based on private ownership and a much weaker control of the economy. The rates of economic growth and of social change were much lower in Nazi Germany than in Stalinist USSR.

One of the main criticisms of the theory of totalitarianism is that it is 'static'. It does not pay sufficient attention to the ends pursued by the Soviet political leaders. Simply emphasizing that the population is kept in a 'state of constant activity' and that the elite pursues a 'chiliastic claim' ignores the momentous changes accomplished by the Stalin regime. Moreover, the more extreme totalitarian models are unable to explain the facts of contemporary Soviet social and political life. It is doubtful whether a regime can last for long if it is completely impervious to demands made by the non-elite. The professional groups, which have grown significantly in size under Soviet power (e.g. scientists, managers, writers, journalists), cannot be ignored or regarded simply as forming 'front' organizations. They must in some important sense support the regime. The model also suffers from crudely lumping together the political elite with others of a different kind (social, economic, professional), and ignores the fact that the operation of the party through intermediary associations (of writers, trade unions, the police) does not ensure their subordination. In fact, such associations have acted to modify the party elite's demands and have articulated the wishes of interest groups.

The official description and the disclaimers made above are rather formal and do not show how the political system actually 'works'. This is one of the drawbacks of a formal 'institutional' approach. Constitutions have important ideological implications: they are concerned with how the political system *should work* and the political bodies defined in them are related to an ideal rather than to the actual state of the world. From the Soviet viewpoint, socialist society is socially and politically homogeneous and as a result, the institutional system does not recognize interest groups and conflict between them. As there is no fundamental antagonism between social groups, the logic runs, there is no need for competitive political elections or for political parties representing separate group interests. Whatever differences in priorities exist may be reconciled within the political institutions under the leadership of the Communist Party. The argument has further implications for the organization of institutions. When government represents a common interest, then there can by definition be no political repression of the citizens by the government. As a result, there is no need for a balance of power (between executive, judiciary and legislative). Thus there is a common theme – but with a different emphasis – between critical Western and 'official' Soviet accounts of Soviet society. Soviet writings focus on the unity of state and society and this unity is based on a concept of the common good which it in turn seeks to defend. Western critics of Soviet society also point to its unitary features – to the fusion of state, economy and society. But in these things they see only exploitation, manipulation and coercion – that is, the absence of what are considered the hallmarks of liberal democracy.

NOTES

1 *Constitution of the USSR*, Article 2.
2 For a Soviet account, see D. Zlatopolsky, *State System of the USSR* (n.d.), pp. 23–25.
3 National policy is discussed in detail in D. Lane, *Soviet Society and Economy* (1984), chapter 6.
4 For a full discussion of Soviet local government, see L.G. Churchward, *Contemporary Soviet Government*, second edition (1975), Chapter 12.
5 For a detailed description of the Supreme Soviet see: Peter Vanneman, *The Supreme Soviet: Politics and the Legislative Process in the Soviet Political System* (1977). Stephen White, 'The USSR Supreme Soviet', in D. Nelson and S. White (eds), *Communist Legislatures in Comparative Perspective* (1982).
6 Vanneman, ibid., p. 89.
7 During the Sixth Convocation (March 1962 to June 1966) 111 legislative acts were passed, including the approval of 60 decrees – which is roughly half the total.
8 See *Ekonomicheskaya gazeta*, 27 July 1982.
9 *Pravda*, 7 March 1984.
10 Robert Conquest, *The Soviet Political System* (1968), p. 44.
11 I.A. Azovkin, *Oblastnoy (kraevoy) Sovet deputatov trudyashchikhsya' (1982)*, p. 40. Cited by Lloyd Churchward, 'Soviet Local Government Today', *Soviet Studies*, vol. 17, no. 4 (April 1966), p. 449. See also: R.J. Hill, 'The CPSU in an Election Campaign', *Soviet Studies*, vol. 28, no. 4. (1976).
12 Reported in *La Stampa*, 14 January 1979.
13 G.V. Barabashev and K.F. Sheremet, 'KPSS i Sovety', *Sovetskoe gosudarstvo i pravo*, no. 11 (1967), p. 36. Cited by R.J. Hill, 'The CPSU in an Election Campaign', p. 594.
14 Cited by T.H. Friedgut, *Political Participation in the USSR* (1979), p. 87.
15 Ibid., p. 86.
16 R.J. Hill, 'The CPSU in an Election Campaign', p. 597. Quoted from *Barabashev and Sheremet, 'KPSS i Sovety'*, pp. 52–3.
17 See review of R.J. Hill's, *Soviet Politics, Political Science and Reform* (1980) by R.J. Brym in *Soviet Studies* (June 1982), p. 145.
18 V. Zaslavsky and R.J. Brym, 'The Functions of Elections in the USSR', *Soviet Studies*, vol. 30 (July 1978), p. 363.
19 Ibid., p. 366.
20 Friedgut, *Political Participation . . .*, p. 118.
21 *Verkhovny Sovet SSR* (1979), p. 41. *Pravda*, 7 March 1984. For more data in English on deputies see: E.M. Jacobs, 'Norms of Representation and the Composition of Local Soviets', in E.M. Jacobs (ed.), *Soviet Local Politics and Government* (1983), pp. 82–3.
22 Ibid., pp. 35–6.
23 Ibid., p. 41.
24 *Pravda*, 1 March 1980.

25 *Pravda,* 26 June 1982.
26 Data derived from relevant sources, cited above.
27 *Itogi vyborov i sostav deputatov mestnykh sovetov narodnykh deputatov* (1977).
28 *Verkhovny Sovet SSSR* (1974).
29 Friedgut, *Political Participation . . .,* p. 104.
30 L.G. Churchward, 'Public Participation in the USSR', in E.M. Jacobs (ed.), *Soviet Local Politics and Government* (1983), p. 44.
31 Friedgut, *Political Participation . . .,* p. 132.
32 Deputy V.P. Grishin, Director of Proshursky state farm, quoted in M. Saifulin, *The Soviet Parliament* (1967), p. 94.
33 See Article 105 of the Constitution.
34 Saifulin, *The Soviet Parliament,* p. 96.
35 Friedgut reports that in the late 1960s 81 per cent spent less than 10 hours per month on affairs of the Soviet, *Political Participation . . .,* p. 220.
36 Stephen White, 'The Supreme Soviet and Budgetary Politics in the USSR', *British Journal of Political Science,* vol. 13 (January 1982), p. 83.
37 Ibid., p. 89.
38 See Law on USSR State Budget for 1983, *Pravda,* 25 Nov. 1982. CDSP vol. 34, no. 49, 5 Jan. 1983, p. 27.
39 Donna Bahry, 'Political Inequality and Public Policy among Soviet Republics', in Daniel N. Nelson, *Communism and the Politics of Inequalities* (1983), pp. 109–10.
40 A. Zharkov and Y. Korolyov, *Standing Commissions of Soviet Parliament* (1982), p. 40.
41 Ibid.
42 White, 'The Supreme Soviet . . .', p. 81.
43 *Itogi vyborov i sostav deputatov mestnykh sovetov narodnykh deputatov* (1977), p. 6.
44 A. Vyshinski, *Sudoustroistvo v SSSR* (1935), p. 32. See also P.H. Juviler, *Revolutionary Law and Order* (1976).
45 H.J. Berman, *Justice in the USSR* (1963), p. 66.
46 L.I. Brezhnev, cited by Berman, ibid.
47 *Fundamentals of Soviet Law* (n.d.), p. 20.
48 Ibid., p. 22.
49 A.I. Korelev, 'Society, State and Law', *Sovetskoe Gosudarstvo i pravo,* no. 4 (1979), p. 23. Excerpt printed in: J.N. Hazard, W.E. Butler and P.B. Maggs, *The Soviet Legal System* (1977), p. 12.
50 'Edict on Creation of USSR Ministry of Justice', extract printed in J. Hazard et al., p. 68.
51 L.I. Brezhnev, 'Report of the CPSU Central Committee to the 25th Party Congress' (Feb. 24 1976), Extract printed in J. Hazard et al., p. 10.
52 John Barron, *The KGB* (1974), p. 75. Most information in this paragraph is taken from this book.
53 It has been estimated that at least half a million armed men come under its

jurisdiction. John J. Dziak, 'The "Action" Arm of the CPSU', *Problems of Communism,* no. 4, vol. 30 (1981), p. 54.

54 For details see E.L. Johnson, *An Introduction to the Soviet Legal System* (1969), pp. 138–142 and P.H. Juviler, *Revolutionary Law and Order* (1976).

55 For full details of elections of judges, see the Constitution, Articles 151–68, Appendix D below.

56 *The Soviet Legal System* (1977), edited by J.N. Hazard et al. Extracts from the various legal codes are printed in this source. See also the series, *Law in Eastern Europe,* published by W. Sijthoff, Leiden (1976). *The Civil Codes of the Soviet Republics.* Ye. Fleishits and A. Makovsky, *Soviet Statutes and Decisions* is a useful quarterly journal of translations of Soviet legislation, New York, M.E. Sharpe. See also W.E. Butler, *Soviet Law* (1983).

57 Cited by Ivo Lapenna, *Soviet Penal Policy* (1968), p. 87.

58 Special provisions exist for minors, see Lapenna, ibid., pp. 96–8.

59 See below, p. 249 and P.H. Juviler, *Revolutionary Law and Order,* pp. 81–2.

60 This has led to the assertion that the court becomes 'little more than a rubber stamp'. Leonard Schapiro, 'Law and Legality in the USSR', *Problems of Communism,* vol. 14, no. 2 (March–April 1965), p. 5.

61 R.A. Medvedev, *On Socialist Democracy* (1975), pp. 149–50.

62 For an example of a case which was utilized as a 'mass political measure', see Peter Juviler, 'Mass Education and Justice in the Soviet Courts', *Soviet Studies,* vol. 18, no. 4 (April 1967).

63 Juviler, *Revolutionary Law and Order,* p. 74.

64 R. Aron, *Democracy and Totalitarianism* (1968), p. 206.

65 Andropov recognized the role of 'selfish interests' in society, see his article on 'Socialist Democracy' in *Kommunist,* no. 3 (February 1983). Abstracted in CDSP, vol. 35. no. 10 (April 1983).

66 Leonard Schapiro, *The Government and Politics of the Soviet Union* (1965), p. 118.

67 See the case of Zhores Medvedev, below pp. 282–4.

68 William Kornhauser, *The Politics of Mass Society* (1960), p. 123.

69 *Totalitarian Dictatorship and Autocracy* (1956), pp. 9–10.

70 *Totalitarian Dictatorship and Autocracy* (1966), p. 22.

71 Herbert J. Spiro, 'Totalitarianism', *International Encyclopaedia of the Social Sciences,* vol. 16 (1968), p. 112.

7

THE POLITICAL PROCESS AND THE COMMUNIST PARTY

The political system of modern societies may be considered in terms of demands and supports, the articulation of inputs, the aggregation of interests, output and enforcement. The Soviet Union is like other modern societies in this respect, though the institutional arrangements and the balance of supports and demands, the ways that policy making is conducted have their own specific characteristics. 'Supports' represent sentiments approving of the 'regime' and more or less supporting its laws and structures through which inputs are converted into outputs. The 'demands' are expectations of action by individuals and groups; demands create stress in a society. 'Inputs' are demands which are communicated to a part of the political structure; they are claims of which the political system may take cognizance. Not all demands are articulated into 'inputs'; the system may be insensitive to certain claims made on it, or others may be ignored. Aggregation is the process by which inputs are collated; they may be either 'dropped' or turned into policies or decisions. The aggregation process consists of the interaction between political actors and groups in which policies are thrashed out. Decisions or laws or actions, decided on in the polity, are the 'outputs' which affect the population.

The stability or equilibrium of the social system as a whole will depend on the way in which the political system can handle the demands generated in the society. Demands dysfunctional to the continued maintenance of the Soviet system (such as, say, the denationalization of public property or the abolition of the Communist Party) are vigorously suppressed by the political leadership. Other demands, shared by a wide range of social strata (such as for better welfare facilities or more housing), may be channelled into 'outputs' which effectively reduce these areas of stress. The ability of a social system to flourish depends on the way the political system can adjust itself to the changing demands made on it. As Easton has put it: 'To persist, the system must be capable of responding with measures that are successful in alleviating the stress so created. To respond, the authorities at least must be in a position to obtain information about what is happening so that they may react insofar as they desire or are compelled to do so'.[1] One of the striking facts about the Soviet regime has been its capacity to persist and to change.

In this and the following chapter we shall consider the ways that interests are articulated and aggregated. Before discussing the demands made by various 'dissenting' groups that are largely outside the formal political system, we shall review the various generalizations made by Western political scientists about the Soviet political systems. At the core of the Soviet political system is the Communist Party.

Even in Western societies, where many political biographies and memoirs have been published and where party life is more accessible to observers, it is notoriously difficult to describe the internal workings of a contemporary political party. In state socialist societies the difficulty is compounded both by the general secrecy surrounding the political process and by the emphasis placed on party unity. Many Western studies have described the process of Soviet politics, but they have done so in terms of individuals and their factionalism in the party.[2]

We are fortunate, however, in having a good historical study of the party, based on original materials. The articulation of interests in the party has been described in Fainsod's study of Smolensk during the inter-war period. He shows that, while local secretaries played an important role in transmitting political instructions (or outputs) received from the centre, the process also worked the other way:

> There were also times when the *obkom** secretary had to be a middleman or broker, mediating between the rock-bottom needs of his constituents and the niggardly resources which the centre made available to meet them. As a representative of the interests of the *oblast'*, and indeed as a condition of his own survival, the *oblast'* secretary had to press for allocations of supplies to the *oblast'*, for budgetary appropriations which would enable him to fulfill the commitments which the centre imposed on him. In periods of distress, such as harvest failures, he had to plead for a lifting of the burden, for special assistance which was infrequently and only grudgingly forthcoming. What was required was negotiating skill of a high order, but it had to be supported by an overall record of successful performance of function. The long reign of Rumyantsev in Smolensk (1929–37) testifies to his adroitness in navigating between central and local pressures, though when disgrace finally came, it was complete and crushing.[3]

Written reports were sent to the Central Committee Secretariat on all aspects of the local party's work. Officials frequently travelled to Moscow to make oral statements. Sometimes special reports of failures were called

*Regional or province party committee; similarly, *oblast'* refers to region or province.

for; here Fainsod cites an example of the local secretary asking for grain quotas to be reduced.[4] In the past, the local party organs tended to 'hush up' deficiencies, and it is interesting to note that the secret police provided its own reports direct to Stalin and 'not infrequently they stimulated drastic intervention by the centre in the affairs of the oblast.'[5]

John Armstrong's study of the Ukrainian Party apparatus in the post World War II period throws some light on the political process in the regions and the role of the party. Armstrong points out that 'types of training, career lines, and association in common activities tend to form cross-institutional alignments which, as power groups, may often be more important than formal structural divisions.'[6] The Ukrainian Party convened Congresses and Central Committee meetings regularly, even after the Great Purge. The Ukrainian Party elite tended to consult with other interested and affected groups when decisions were being made. Though rather circumspect on this score, Armstrong concludes: 'Whatever the reasons for the peculiarities of Ukrainian apparatus operation before 1953 as compared to other segments of the Soviet apparatus, they did tend towards the oligarchic, as contrasted to the autocratic system of rule.'[7]

Philip D. Stewart in an analysis of a party committee in the Stalingrad *obkom* concludes: 'The evident tendency of the party secretaries to consult with interest groups in the policy-making process indicates that now many of these institutional interest groups may be able to translate their potential influence into actual influence.'[8] Channels of access to decision-making are controlled by the First Secretaries. Conferences are transmission belts to convey top policy to the masses and access to the decision-making process: 'It does appear', continues Stewart, 'that a certain amount of criticism is directed by the speakers at particular officials, or at the way particular policies are implemented, or at the failure of the party officials to deal effectively with particular problems. At the same time, and this is the crucial point, the participants in the conferences . . . speak from a position of extreme weakness.' But other non-party groups are consulted 'in open and frank discussions in bureau sessions'.[9] The party articulates other group interests: of particular potential influence, says Stewart, are the Soviets, industrial managers, Komsomol and trade-union leaders, cultural-educational groups and the police. The Party Secretaries are key men in the interest articulation process: '. . . the observed tendency of the party secretaries to consult with interested groups, to listen to them, to encourage their participation in at least the public aspects of *obkom* activity must not be overlooked. Compared to the period of the thirties, more institutional interest groups now appear to have the opportunity to exert some influence in *obkom* decision-making.'[10]

T.H. Rigby's discussion of the role of the party in modern Russia makes clear that the lower levels of the party organization, party branches and regional committees, for instance, discuss issues and make recommendations. 'In these various ways, new ideas and facts are brought to the attention of the policy makers and they learn something about group preferences.'[11] The party apparatus acts as an information-gathering and processing machine: it receives messages from the rank and file members and party groups, which are acted on at higher levels of the Party Secretariat. At this stage, the aggregation of interests is performed. The Central Committee, during Khrushchev's leadership, was an arena for interest articulation and aggregation. Zbigniew Brezezinski writes: 'Khrushchev's practice of holding enlarged Central Committee plenums, with representatives of other groups present, seems to have been a step toward formalising a more regular consultative procedure ... Such enlarged plenums provided a consultative forum, where policies could be debated, views articulated and even some contradictory interests resolved.'[12]

Brezhnev would seem to be endorsing such a view when he said that 'the party's policy brings the required results when it precisely takes into account the interests of the whole people, and also the interests of the classes and social groups that compose it, and directs them into one common stream.'[13]

Some examples of interest articulation in the party are available from studies of party congresses. Wolfgang Leonhard, for instance, has shown that at the Twentieth Party Congress (1956) many interested parties spoke about the reform of educational policy. The Chairman of the *Komsomol* (Young Communist League) said that insufficient training was given in practical skills. Khrushchev advocated the setting up of boarding schools, presumably to reduce the influence of family background in children's socialization. The President of the Academy of Sciences spoke against an 'excessively "practical approach"'. Another scientist advocated a closer link between theory and practice.[14] These are only glimpses of political reality which may be caught by the observer. In the party behind the scenes, many interests – teachers, regional authorities, industry, universities and the Academy of Sciences – articulated their views before the leadership finally put forward the educational reforms. H.L. Biddulph, in a study of speeches at the 24th to 26th Congresses of the CPSU (1971, 1976 and 1981), has shown that the articulation of local demands has steadily increased between these dates. Most of the requests were about agriculture, followed by the topics of energy and fuels, water resources and transport.[15]

The Central Committee of the party is an arena in which various interests may be voiced. It is composed of members of the CPSU

Politbureau and secretariat, the first secretaries of the republican communist parties, the chairman of the Council of Ministers and some of the chairmen of the republican Councils of Ministers; in addition some other government ministers, the first secretary of the Komsomol, the chairman of the Trade Union Council and the president of the Academy of Sciences are also members. The meetings of the Central Committee serve for the various interests of these groups to be articulated. Gehlen has shown that under Khrushchev speakers at Central Committee plenums were specialists and many were not even members of the Central Committee; under Brezhnev, however, party secretaries were more conspicuous.[16] The meetings are, to use Gehlen's term, 'information forums' and though different points of view are expressed, no opposing sides are publicly taken. The Central Committee then may be regarded as one of the important bodies in which information is articulated which is necessary for effective decision-making in the USSR. While the Central Committee enables the articulation of interests to take place, its size (in 1981 there were 319 full members and 151 candidates) and the shortness of its duration as a deliberating body (it usually has about two or three sessions a year, each lasting not more than a week) weaken it as an instrument in the aggregation process.

The Politbureau

It is at the highest levels of the party apparatus that policy decisions are aggregated and factional differences finally resolved. The Politbureau is a crucial organ. To accommodate the greater activity in Soviet society, it grew in size from five (1979–21) to eleven in 1966–67; in 1981 it had fourteen members, and in 1984 twelve.[17] The Politbureau is technically elected by the Central Committee. Western writers have attempted to identify the members of the Politbureau (patrons) with interests in the Central Committee (clients). By studying their careers, forms of advancement, various groupings and differences in political constituencies are delineated. John P. Willerton has studied the linkages between Politbureau members and Central Committee members in the post-Khrushchev period (1966–1976).[18] The main interests he identifies are Party (P), Komsomol (K), State Security (police) (St.S), Heavy Industry (HI), Agriculture (A), Trade Unions (UT), Light Industry (LI) (see table 7.1). The party is clearly the major stepping stone to success. The constellations of interests and pressures on candidates once they have arrived in the Politbureau are such to invalidate any simple correlation of interests of a member with his 'client' group. Ex post facto, this analysis has not been very useful in identifying candidates for high office. Andropov, for instance, did not

TABLE 7.1: POLITBUREAU 1966–1976: CLIENTS AND NON-CLIENTS

	No. of Clients		Sector Institution	Client in Same Sector	Client in Different Sector
	Party	Non-Party			
Andropov	1	2	P St.S K	2	1
Brezhnev	17	9	P H I	22	4
Grechko	—	5	Military	5	0
Grishin*	7	2	P T U	6	2
Gromyko	—	2	Foreign Service	2	0
Kirilenko	4	5	P H I	9	0
Kosygin*	—	7	L I, Ministry work	6	0
Kulakov	2	—	P A	2	0
Kunaev	2	5	P H I	4	3
Mazurov	9	4	P K H I	12	1
Pelshe	4	5	P ideology-pol.	8	1
Podgorny	9	11	P L I	12	8
Shcherbitsky	5	3	P H I	7	1
Suslov	1	5	P ideology	2	4
4 deposed	18	12		26	4
TOTAL	79(51%)	77(49%)		125	29

Note: *Totals do not tally, presumably due to missing data.
Source: Data based on Willerton, C. 'Clientelism in the Soviet Union ...' (1979), pp. 175, 177.

score very high in terms of his previous associates. Joel Moses in 1976 analysed the subsequent advancement of some of Brezhnev's former colleagues. He claims that 75 per cent of Brezhnev's Dnepropetrovsk cohort has advanced politically compared to only 18 per cent of Podgorny's Lvov and Kharkov cohorts.[19] This may have helped secure Brezhnev's own position but it did not ensure that his preferred successor, Chernenko, advanced after his death to the pinnacle of the party's power structure. Similarly, though Andropov in turn is said to have advanced his own supporters, his earlier opponent, Chernenko, succeeded him (see above, chapter 4).

Some useful information about the operation of the Politbureau has been collected by Henry Brandon following an interview with an official (Valentin Falin) of the Central Committee. In describing the decision-making process, the official said:

Our decision-making system differs from the American in that it is more centralized. In international or national security affairs American Secretaries of State and Defence can take a good many decisions on their own. In our case all foreign policy and national security questions must be discussed and decided in the Politbureau.

The process is about as follows: the Ministry of Foreign Affairs prepares a paper that deals with the issue in question on the basis of concrete facts. If the issue includes national security aspects then the Ministry of Defence and possibly other ministries are drawn into the preparation of the paper and a summary of views is drawn up. This summary is then handed to the relevant department in the central committee which employs its own experts and consulting staff, who check the facts before it is submitted to the Politbureau.[20]

As to the actual conduct of business in the Politbureau, Falin describes it as follows:

Brezhnev presides over the Politbureau meetings and when he is absent a central committee secretary performs that function. From my own experience I know that the General Secretary first gives the floor to every member and they then each express their point of view. Then he sums up the course of the debate and defends the view which he considers to be the correct one. Issues or differences are not decided by vote; there must be a consensus. If several members have a different opinion on the same matter, then Brezhnev sums up those differences and suggests a postponement of the decision for further study. If, however, a member feels that there are still some unanswered questions, then the paper under discussion is returned to the body which presented it, for further elucidation and a week later, or if it is an urgent matter, the next day, the issue is once again discussed in the Politbureau.

Experts and other officials often participate in the work of the Politbureau. Brandon cites the testimony of Nikolay Inozemtsev, the Director of the Institute for World Economics. After emphasizing the importance of scientists' participation in government, Inozemtsev is reported as saying, 'It has not only increased in the economic field, but in the state ruling system and in its decision-making process. Take the position of Mr. (Anatoly) Alexandrov, the President of the Academy of Sciences. He is also the head of the Commission which deals with our energy development for the entire country. His conclusions, presented by him to the Politbureau, no doubt have practical consequences in shaping political decisions.'

When Falin was questioned about the role of the military he replied:

[The Western media] attribute powers and possibilities to them [the military] which they do not have in the decision-making process. The only military person in the Politbureau is the Minister of Defence, Mr. Ustinov, and he is not really a professional soldier. Nor is Brezhnev, although he fought in World War II and three years ago was given the rank of Marshall. The important military decisions are taken in the Defence Council, also chaired by Brezhnev, but even there, although the military are represented in greater strength, they are not in the majority.

In the course of the discussion, Falin pointed out that prior to meetings of the Politbureau, a long series of discussions had taken place between various interested parties – in the Central Committee of the Party, in the Council of Ministers, in various ministries and within special commissions.

The Central Committee is seen normally as a sounding board, though its members can bring influence to bear on various decisions. Particularly in foreign affairs, the Politbureau is the effective power. Soviet officials are reported by Temko as saying that the Central Committee did not meet before the sending of Soviet troops to Afghanistan, nor before a protest was sent, in the Committee's name, to the Polish communist leadership following its handling of the *Solidarity* movement; (i.e. before the clampdown in 1982). The note, officials said, was 'shown' to all committee members after the final drafting by the Politbureau. (*Christian Science Monitor*, 23 February, 1982).

The Party Apparatus

The Politbureau is serviced by a secretariat of the party. Technically, this secretariat is subordinate to the Central Committee of the Party and elected by it. The officials and staff of the Central Committee are often called the apparatus, or the Party *apparat*. It is generally believed in the West that the secretariat is dominant in the party. As Leonard Schapiro has put it: a feature of the party (in 1952) was 'the predominance within the party of the apparatus of officials and secretaries who formed a small minority of around three per cent...these officials could dominate elections, discussions and decisions inside all party organisations throughout the country.'[21] But the role of the secretariat in decision-making is obscure.

Western researchers have constructed a very informative table in which the departments are defined. This is reproduced in table 7.2.[22] It seems likely that these departments may articulate specific interests. (The members of the Politbureau with their chief responsibilities are listed above, table 5.13.) They define and clarify policy proposals for the Politbureau. We do not know how this advice is received, or whether it conflicts or augments that of other institutions and groups, such as the police, army or industrial ministries.

Some light in this political process has again been shed by Western commentators. Ned Temko has questioned Soviet officials about the role of the secretariat. He reports[23] that in 1982 the secretariat met weekly and was chaired by Brezhnev – in his absence it was taken by Kirilenko or

TABLE 7.2: THE APPARATUS OF THE CENTRAL COMMITTEE OF THE CPSU

Administration of Affairs	Department for Liaison with Communist and
Administrative Organs Department	Workers' Parties of Socialist Countries
Agriculture and Food Department	Light Industry and Goods for Popular Con-
Agricultural Machinery	sumption
Department for Cadres Abroad	Letters to the Central Committee
Chemical Industry Department	Machine Building Department
Construction Department	Organizational Party Work Department
Culture Department	Planning and Finance Organs Department
Defence Industry Department	Propaganda Department
Department for Economic Collaboration	Science and Educational Institutions Depart-
with Socialist Countries	ment
Economic Department	Soviet Publica(tions)
General Department	Trade and Domestic Services Department
Heavy Industry Department	Transport and Communications Department
Information Department	Main Political Directorate of Soviet
International Department	Army and Navy

Other organizations under the Central Committee: Party Control Committee, Academy of Social Sciences, Institute of Scientific Atheism of the Academy of Social Sciences, Higher Party School, Higher Party Correspondence School, Institute for Raising the Qualifications of Leading Party and Soviet Cadres of the Higher Party School, Institute of Marxism-Leninism, Institute of Social Sciences, Novosti, Chief Editors of the Newspapers and Journals of the Central Committee of the CPSU: *Pravda, Ekonomicheskaya gazeta, Sel'skaya zhizn', Sotsialisticheskaya industriya, Sovetskaya kul'tura, Sovetskaya Rossiya; Agitator, Kommunist, Partiynaya zhizn', Politicheskoe samoobrazovanie, Voprosy istorii KPSS.*

Note: This is not a complete list. Data based on Radio Liberty, RL 9/1978 (1978, updated 1983).

Chernenko. In addition to the secretaries, other leading communists also participate – the editors of the leading newspapers and broadcasting authority, the heads of the Central Committee's specialized policy departments, 'and other people, from outside are called in according to the particular issue or issues being discussed ...'. At its meetings, said one official, 'no-one really asks for the floor, in any formal manner ... Suslov or Brezhnev, or whoever, just looks around. You raise your hand and speak.' The secretariat 'frames policy decisions ... , by the time an issue reaches the Politbureau, the framework is usually already there' (Soviet official).

An official who has attended both Secretariat and Politbureau meetings is reported by Temko as saying:

The secretariat does not have competence in areas of [government], as opposed to Party, fundings and expenditure. Moreover, in the Party hierarchy, the Secretariat cannot give directives to the Government, while the Politburo can ...

Thus a number of economic questions must technically be decided by the

Politburo. Even on some decisions that fall in this category, the secretariat will, in effect, work everything out and pass it up to the Politburo just to be looked at.

The aggregation of interests in the USSR is a more intractable problem than in liberal democracies. No *open* institutional channels exist to resolve fundamental disagreements. Bargaining occurs between various interests in the ways described above and only exceptionally with publicity. The party plays an important role in articulating and aggregating interests. Informal contacts between administrative elites are effected through the party structure.[24] But the absence of institutionalized popular and effective elections gives rise to internal struggles within the party elite, which have the character of personal rivalry.

An attempt may now be made to summarize interest articulation at the top levels of the Soviet political system. The Politbureau is seen to be institutionally linked to the Secretariat, the Central Committee and to the government ministries (see diagram 7.1). Interests are articulated and aggregated in the party's Central Committee, in the government apparatus and in the Secretariat. Inputs are passed for policy-making to the Politbureau. Final binding decisions are made in the Politbureau and these are executed by the government and the Party Secretariat.

The Articulation of Values: Ideology

We have discussed above the role of the party apparatus in the framing and articulation of political interests. A second important dimension of the party's power is in the sphere of ideological control. Ideology is a form of normative power for it may inculcate certain responses in the individual towards his environment – towards the legitimacy of the rulers, or the powerful, and towards the legitimacy of the rewards and privileges enjoyed by certain groups. Ideology is, in Mannheim's terms, a pattern of beliefs which justifies the social order and which explains to man 'his historical and social setting'.[25] But it is not simply an instrument used by the political rulers to ensure compliance; ideology also acts as a constraint on their own activity, for it gives rise to expectations on the part of the governed which the rulers must try to fulfil. Ideology defines the terms of legitimacy on which rule is conducted.

In earlier chapters of this book the main 'stages' or ideal types of society defined by Marxist thinkers were described. We have seen that Soviet Russia has passed through the 'dictatorship of the proletariat' to the stage of building a socialist society. One of the chief roles of the party is the articulation of policies and programmes for the creation of a communist society. In policy-making, the party must take into account a number of

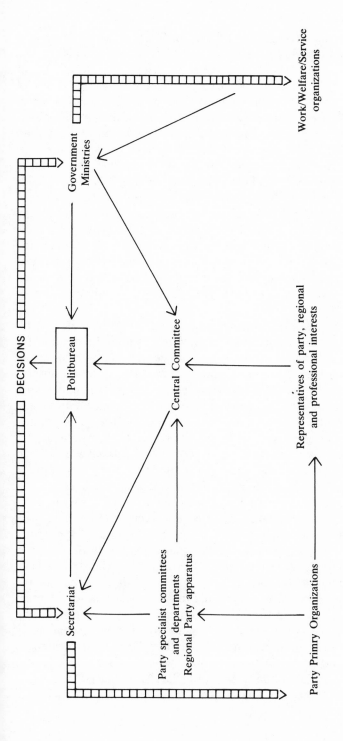

DIAGRAM 7.1: POLITICAL INPUTS TO THE POLITBUREAU

Key: Political inputs ⟶
Decisions ▭▭▭⟩

DECISIONS

Politbureau

Government Ministries

Central Committee

Secretariat

Work/Welfare/Service organizations

Representatives of party, regional and professional interests

Party specialist committees and departments
Regional Party apparatus

Party Primry Organizations

factors. Ideological values (say the primacy of Marxism) generated in the past cannot be ignored, but neither can specific popular demands (say for better housing). The last programme, published in 1961,[26] is an example of the width and nature of the party's ideological output. It has, of course, been modified by subsequent development and 'brought up to date' by the 1977 Constitution and the notion of 'developed socialism' (discussed above, chapter 5). *The New Programme of the CPSU* was an attempt by Khrushchev to spell out some of the general goals deriving from the communist belief system. It is instructive to study them, not because they are 'true' in a philosophical sense, but because they indicate the kinds of expectations generated by the political leadership, and their view of social change. (*The New Programme* is regularly republished. In the mid-1980s another version is under discussion in the Secretariat.)

Khrushchev emphasized the role of the Soviet people in 'building communism': the Soviet Union, it was claimed, would create 'the material and technical basis of communism' and would surpass the United States in per capita production (of 1961) by 1970. By 1980, 'communist' society would 'be built in the USSR'.

No radical changes were envisaged in the 'coming of communism'. Money as a means of exchange was to continue. Income differentials for specialized and skilled work would persist but decline. Some services and commodities were planned to be taken out of the price system, transport and public catering being important in this regard. In the economic sphere, the practice of 'one-man management' was to be augmented by the institution of various advisory committees within the factory. The position of women was to be improved by the provision of collective services, but the monogamous family as a unit was to continue. Khrushchev advocated the development of boarding schools to reduce the disparities between various social groups, but this policy has since been modified.

The apparatus of government would continue: it was necessary to assist in the organization of material production, to 'exercise control' over work and consumption, to maintain 'law and order', to secure socialist property and to fortify the regime against external attack. Only with the 'triumph and consolidation' of socialism in the world arena would the state become unnecessary. Until such a time, however, some of the functions of the existing government would be transferred for administration to voluntary bodies. Trade unions, and the Young Communist League (Komsomol) would take over responsibility for aspects of the management of enterprises, for supervising personal conduct and for the enforcement of law and order. The 'withering away' of the state was to begin with greater participation in administration at the lower levels. Soviet policy here, if implemented, would certainly have meant an increase in participation in the decision-making processes (see below pp. 246–8). Also, the provisions were intended to give much more power to the party at the expense of the government apparatus.

The notion of 'developed socialism' has added new dimensions and changed the emphasis somewhat from that of the 'New Programme'. As noted above (chapter 5), developed socialism mentions the importance of harnessing the 'scientific-technical revolution' to achieve communism; the stress on the 'withering away' of the state apparatus has been replaced by greater emphasis on the importance of government and party providing correct guidance, organization and management. Present writers are more cautious than Khrushchev about the timing of the arrival of the second phase of (full) communism. As Andropov put it: 'We must soberly consider where we stand: running ahead means setting impossible tasks, while resting on our laurels means failing to utilize our full potential. At present our country finds itself at the beginning of the lengthy historical stage of improving developed socialism and, as we do so, gradually moving towards communism. Naturally, this stage itself will have its own periods and substages.'[27]

The ideology of Soviet communism, as summarized in the Constitution and in statements about 'developed socialism', marks a shift in role of Marxist theory. In chapter 2, we saw that under capitalism Marxism–Leninism emphasized the values of social class war. Now the official Soviet doctrine is one of social harmony; the vision of a Utopia has to a great extent been replaced by the goals of higher standards of living and a striving for world peace. Daniel Bell has remarked that the notion of the transformation of the world, an important aspect of Marxist theory, has become exhausted (at least in the 1950s).[28] In the USSR ideological trends seem to confirm Bell's views.[29] Developments under the leadership of Brezhnev, Andropov and Chernenko have minimized the emotional appeal of communist ideology; the communist Utopia was replaced by the more pragmatic, utilitarian and practical policy of the political leadership. At the Twentieth Congress (1956), Stalin and the personality cult were denounced; at the Twenty-Second (1961), the *The Programme of the CPSU* tried to redefine goals into the 1980s; the 1977 Constitution attempted to consolidate existing achievements. These changes over time also indicate a different emphasis given to the kinds of sanctions – coercive, ideological and remunerative – which the political leadership may utilize. In destroying Stalin's reliance on terror and coercive sanctions, Khrushchev sought to replace them with normative controls. Under Brezhnev, in the early years, utilitarian rewards were increased. Towards the end of Brezhnev's leadership, social solidarity was enhanced by the greater store placed on the charismatic appeal of Brezhnev. In the very short period of Andropov's rule, more weight was given to the efficient operation of the economy, to a stress on material incentives and to greater conformity to socialist legality. Around Chernenko has again begun to develop a minor personality cult.

Looking at Soviet ideology over a longer period of time, Barrington Moore has remarked that: 'On the whole, one is likely to be more impressed with the flexibility of Communist doctrine than with its rigidity.'[30] The established ideology is not politically neutral: it supports those in positions of power, and behind ideological statements are social groups whom ideology serves. Since Khrushchev's replacement first by Podgorny, Kosygin and Brezhnev, second by the ascendancy of Brezhnev and then by Andropov and Chernenko, there have been accompanying shifts in the emphasis of doctrine. This suggests that there may be group interests in Soviet society which emphasize different elements in Marxism–Leninism. It is worthy of note that Chernenko has written much about the importance of the leading role of the party over the apparatus of government and Soviets; he favoured paying attention to public opinion and he also stressed the importance of detente.[31] His rival, Andropov, before coming to power was less vocal on these subjects. During his short period of power Andropov dwelt more on the need for efficiency and greater discipline. His stress on the importance of the 'scientific-technical revolution' meant that greater cognizance be given to the groups (administrative, scientific and military) involved in the management of modern society.

There can be no doubt that, since the October Revolution, the dominant official ideology of Soviet Marxism has changed. It has adapted itself to a new world: from challenging a *status quo* to defending it. The content of the ideology has also altered in response to the modern technical-industrial structure of Soviet society and to the groups thrown up by it: now there is not only a party-political leadership but also other institutional groups (the armed forces, industrial ministries, the Academies of Sciences, republican and regional interests) which the party ideologists connot ignore.

The Party as an Agency of Political Control

The party not only aggregates interests in the formulation of ideology and policy, but also seeks to assert its priorities over other institutions and interests. It does this by the control of personnel, or cadres (*the nomenklatura*), and through the security police (KGB) the party may exert direct supervision (or *kontrol'*) over other 'non-party' institutions (such as factories, schools and the government administration). The enforcement activity of the Soviet political system, however, is less a function of the party than of the government apparatus. (The courts of law and the ordinary police come under the Supreme Soviet.)

The recruitment and placement of personnel in the highest decision-making posts remain the party's prerogative. The list of ministers presented to the Supreme Soviet for its consideration has been approved by the party's Central Committee. In this respect the CPSU is not unlike ruling parties in Western societies, though membership of the party is necessary for a much wider range of jobs in the USSR than here. How far party membership is merely a formal requirement, demanding no firm ideological position or political conviction, cannot at present be accurately assessed. Much depends on the post: for engineering and scientific work, party membership is probably a formality, but for leading jobs in literary journals or foreign affairs, or the security police, not only party membership, but also reliable political beliefs are necessary.

At all levels, the party organization is responsible for the supervision of the selection of personnel to leading positions – in factories, unions, collective farms, administration. Under Stalin, between 1934 and 1939, party organs selected and promoted to leading government and party posts over half a million Bolsheviks and others 'standing close to the party'.[32] Harasymiw has estimated that in the 1960s about three million administrative and executive positions were subject to ratification or approval by party organs.[33] To take an example from the field of education, a Soviet writer has described the process as follows: 'Since the Twenty-Fourth Congress of the CPSU, the *nomenklatura* controlled by the Moscow town and district committees has been made more exact. The town committee *nomenklatura* now contains 304 persons – all the rectors, VUZ (i.e. higher educational institutions) party committee secretaries and most of the heads of social science faculties. The secretaries of VUZ party bureaux at faculty level and all social science teachers are on the district committee *nomenklatura* ... Within the VUZy a *nomenklatura* of leading members of staff whose appointments are confirmed at meetings of the party committees and bureaux has also been fixed.'[34]

The party, however, is confronted with the personnel (or 'cadres') departments of ministries and enterprises, which are responsible for recommendations for appointments in their respective fields. The party may veto a nomination on political criteria, but it seems doubtful whether this is necessary now in the large majority of cases. Though it does sometimes happen that 'party men' may be rewarded with sinecures, appointments in industrial ministries are made on functional grounds and it is in the interest of both party and ministry to select the most efficient person. This may be demonstrated by examining the background of party secretaries and government administrators.

Jerry F. Hough's path-breaking study of the party and industry[35] shows that the leading administrators in ministries tend to be men of a different type from the party secretaries in ideological and even industrial posts.

The available data on USSR ministers and deputy ministers (a total of 63) appointed in the 1950s showed that they joined the party on average at the age of 28 or 29 years, and that all had had an engineering education. 'By the 1950s the men rising to ministerial rank increasingly came to have characteristics indicating that political factors were becoming even less of an influence on promotion within the industrial hierarchy.'[36] On the other hand, party first secretaries (25 in all) of the studied *industrialized* regions (*oblasti*) had entered the party on average at 23 years of age, and only 12 out of 22 had had an engineering education.[37] But Hough points out that the position is not as bad as it would appear from Bulganin's statement in 1955 that, 'The industrial departments of the party organs are frequently staffed by inexperienced officials, who do not have the necessary technical and economic knowledge and who cannot deeply analyze the work of the enterprise.'[38] Since the mid-1950s the party has seen an improvement in the educational standards of its full-time personnel and many secretaries have moved into the party after a period of service (at a junior level) in industry. By 1976, the leading cadres of the party (those serving in the Central Committees of the republican parties and in regional and district executive committees) had a majority of people (69 per cent) with a higher education. Of the secretaries of district and city organizations, 99 per cent had higher education.[39] Ths tendency has continued into the 1980s (see data above, pp. 169–70).

The creation of Regional Economic Councils (*sovnarkhozy*) in 1957 was hailed as an attempt by Khrushchev to increase party control over the industrial ministries. But it is interesting to note that the leading officials of the *sovnarkhozy* were recruited from the industrial ministries. Of 97 *sovnarkhoz* chairmen, only six had previously been party officials; the remainder were men who had been senior state administrators (8 had been USSR ministers, 30 USSR deputy ministers, 9 lower ministerial officials, 8 deputy chairmen of a republican council of ministers, 16 republican ministers, 6 republican deputy ministers and 14 directors of plants or combines).[40] Industrial ministers are men with outstanding industrial experience. In 1965, 88 per cent of the ministers had been enterprise directors or above for at least 15 years, and 55 per cent of them for at least 20 years. Senior ministerial staff have security of tenure and are promoted from within the government, rather than from the party structure. Of 33 USSR industrial and construction ministers appointed in 1965, 12 had been USSR ministers in 1957, 10 had been deputy ministers, 4 had been in charge of industrial boards and one had been a minister in the Russian Federation. As Hough concludes, 'Even if the top Soviet industrial officials may not be ideally equipped to carry through any revolution in industrial planning and administration, they remain men with great technical authority and they remain formidable opponents in bureaucratic struggles on planning and technical questions.'[41]

At the regional levels of administration, there is greater overlap between party and government posts. Joel C. Moses has analysed the career paths of 614 officials in 25 representative areas of the Russian and Ukrainian republics from 1953 to 1979. He concludes that party and government administrators have distinct but overlapping career paths and that one may detect 'five quite different functional subgroupings': these are agricultural specialists, industrial specialists, ideological specialists and mixed generalists.[42] Within these functional divisions at the regional level there is movement for administrators (governed by the *nomenklatura*) between party and government institutions. Moses concludes, correctly I think, that the policy of functional specialization is an important factor in creating institutional diversity in the political system. Officials develop a professional 'mental set' and identification with certain interests or 'functional subgroups'.

In local government there can be no doubt that party cadres policy plays a most important role. The attempts by the government to increase voluntary participation in local government activity have led to the local party branches taking the initiative.

Only the party can unite and give correct political direction to all forms of organisation of the public, hasten the development of socialist democracy in the work of Soviets, raise their role as mass organisations. Thus the development of socialist statehood into communist self-administration is impossible without the development of the leading role of the party in the work of all mass organisations of workers both state and social.[43]

The party exercises supervision (or *'kontrol'*) over the Soviets through factions of its members, which influence the appointment of the leading officials of the Soviets (Chairman, Vice-Chairman and Secretary).[44] Local government elections too are regulated by the Communist Party. While many nominations do not originate in party groups, no candidate can receive the mandate of the electoral committees without party approval. 'The central party organisations decide the social and political ... composition of the Soviet.' The party also controls the agencies which nominate candidates.[45]

In Soviet (parliamentary) and trade-union elective posts, party nomination and oversight are most important. Here specific techniques are less relevant than in ministerial posts and personal and 'political' considerations may be taken more into account. Party activists may sometimes be rewarded for their energy. In these spheres the party performs the political recruitment role.

The Committee for State Security (KGB) is a crucial institution, having at its command the agency of force. The KGB is ostensibly the sword and shield of the party, but the history of the USSR under Stalin illustrated that the police could act independently of the party. Under Khrushchev and Brezhnev an attempt was made not only to curb the KGB's arbitrary powers, but also to appoint party men to its top ranks. The 'mixed generalists' referred to by Moses are important here. Andropov, its former chief, for instance, came from the Party's Secretariat, was a member of the Politbureau, until he returned to a leading role in the Secretariat prior to his elevation to General Secretary in 1982. This is how John Barron describes the relationship of the KGB to the Politbureau.

...[It] answers to the Politburo. Andropov [when KGB chief], himself more of a Party bureaucrat than a professional intelligence officer, reports directly to..., Brezhnev. The Politburo approves, and in many cases initiates, major KGB operations. It oversees the KGB's daily functioning through the Administrative Organs Department* of the Central Committee. The KGB may not hire anyone as a staff officer without permission of this department. All assignments of KGB personnel abroad, and all but the most inconsequential assignments within the Soviet Union, must be sanctioned by the department. So must all promotions. ...Virtually every officer must become a Party member, submit personally to Party discipline, attend interminable indoctrination sessions and fulfil his communist duty to inform on colleagues. The watchdogs of the Soviet people are themselves forever watched.[46]

The KGB is almost certainly a conservative grouping at the top echelons of power. Barghoorn generalizes that the KGB favours 'relatively repressive "anti-imperialist" domestic and foreign policies'.[47] It is often said that the KGB advocates more traditional and severe policies for the treatment of dissidents and opposes the widening of cultural contacts and greater liberalization. This is a matter of conjecture, and others claim that the top echelons of the KGB are staffed with the more intelligent and even progressive forces in Soviet society. It is probably that the KGB is an important group within the party, bringing its power to bear in all areas of the party's activity. Rather than thinking of the Committee for State Security as an 'interest group' which influences the state, it should be seen as an integral part of the coercive state apparatus. As such it is not simply the executive arm of the party, but it has also a certain autonomy. It is linked to the government apparatus by its chief having a place in the Council of Ministers.

As noted above (pp. 194–5), the KGB is not the only police apparatus. The Ministry of Internal Affairs (MVD) also has a presence. In the Georgian Republic in the early 1970s, the MVD, suspecting corruption at

*Now called 'General Department'.

the highest levels and collusion between the top party leadership and the KGB, carried out surveillance of the leading government and party functionaries (and their families). If an émigré account is to be believed, the chief of the MVD secured sufficient evidence to ensure the dismissal by Brezhnev of the local political leadership.[48] (On the role of the KGB in suppressing dissent, see below pp. 274–5.)

Party and Government: Kontrol' *of the Administration*

In the sphere of political output and enforcement, the party is now probably less important than the government ministries. General political pronouncements, 'propaganda' and political education are the most important elements of party activity. Government output in quantitative terms is predominant: it is made up of ministerial decrees, orders and everyday ministerial activity. Enforcement is largely a state affair under the surveillance of the police and courts. The party also has a role to play here. The party has the right to 'supervise' (*kontrol'*) the activity of the government administration. Its groups operating through the primary party organizations (PPOs) are required to 'check up' on the letter and spirit of the activities of an organization. They may ask for explanations from the heads of institutions and they have the right to inspect their books. Party groups, however, have no rights to perform the tasks of government organizations. Should they find irregularities, they are required to report findings to higher party bodies which in turn may intervene at an appropriate position in the government apparatus. Chernenko, in 1981, writing as a Politbureau member and Secretary of the Central Committee, emphasized the role of the party under developed socialism. In an article in *Kommunist*, the party's theoretical journal, he wrote:

Realising its leading role in practice, the party certainly does not take the place of government or of public organisations. The principle of the clear-cut delineation of the foundations of party and government organs is recorded in the CPSU rules and was reflected in the new USSR Constitution. Operating within its framework, the party exercises political leadership of government and public organisations, determining the main directions of domestic and foreign policy, mobilising the masses to realise it and organising broad public control over the fulfillment of adopted decisions.

The party's policy and its decisions serve as reference points which enable government organs and public organisations to keep to the correct course and avoid a narrow departmental approach to the matter, as well as manifestations of parochialism . . .

Monitoring and verification of the execution of decisions is an important part of all our party work . . .

It is through the primary party organisations that the party explains the meaning and significance of its policy to the Soviet people. Not only explains but mobilises them to implement it. It is through the primary party organisation that the CPSU Central Committee, union republic Communist Party central committees and local party committees maintain constant contact with working people, discover their feelings, needs and concerns and obtain on-the-spot information about the state of affairs, achievements and shortcomings, production difficulties and day-to-day difficulties. This enables the party to listen sensitively to the people's voice and make amendments to its policy on the spot as the need arises.[49]

Voluntary control commissions, formed of party activists, supervise the execution of laws. Such groups attempt to 'control' production in the factories and keep order in the streets. The party has a long history of 'control' of non-party organizations. In the 1960s regulations were published defining the party's rights (see Reading No. 12 in D. Lane, *Politics and Society in the USSR,* second edition (1978) pp. 335–8). In 1971, the party asserted its right over supervision of the government ministries. In the 1980s the Party Central Committee has called for party organizations to raise

the standard of the monitoring and verification of execution in the primary party organizations, which have the paramount role in resolving the tasks involved in the building of communism ....
.... It is decreed that Party organisations in ministries, departments and economic organs should make fuller use of the right granted to them to monitor the work of the apparatus in fulfilling party and government directives.[50]

The Central Committee reiterated the importance of party control. An editorial in *Pravda* called upon party organizations 'to display greater principledness and to pursue firmly the party line, whether it is on a question of personnel problems, of fulfilling economic plans or of improving people's working and everyday living conditions'.[51] In 1982, the Central Committee passed regulations strengthening the role of primary party organizations in their control function. They were called upon to set up special commissions, composed of non-managerial staff, to exercise such supervision. Reports of such commissions are to be made to the party's primary groups; if its recommendations are not complied with, appeal may be made to the Central Committee of the CPSU or to the USSR Council of Ministers. (The new regulations are printed below, Appendix F.)

The tenor of the Central Committee's injunctions to primary party organizations may be indicated by the following article in the party's journal which appeared in November 1982.

Certain party committees continue to underestimate monitoring practices as an important means for eliminating inadequacies, developing initiatives by communists, for encouraging criticism and self-criticism and improving the state of affairs. When discussing issues related to the resolution of economic and social problems, they frequently forget about the role and responsibility of primary party organisations, and about the need for them to implement more fully their statutory right to monitor...

The CPSU Central Committee requires the party organisations to use forms and methods for monitoring the activities of the administration, which have shown themselves to be effective; and it points out the need for every employee of an enterprise, regardless of the position which he occupies, to answer for his work and actions before, first of all, the party organisations and the collective where he works. Regardless of whether the discussion concerns personnel issues, the fulfilment of economic plans or improvements in the living and working conditions of people, the party organisations must adhere to their principles, they must not be under the administration's thumb; when the latter acts incorrectly, they must take a firm party line.[52]

What makes it difficult for the party to exercise power at the higher reaches of the industrial ministries is its small staff. The Leningrad *sovnarkhoz*, for instance, had a staff numbering over a thousand, whereas the industrial department of the Leningrad Party Committee had only 25 officials.[53] The party relies to some extent on part-time auxiliaries but, in practice, the sheer volume of work, its technical character, and the lower competence of party officials, must leave the government bureaucracies with considerable power.

The industrial ministries possess their own chain of command. They have specific tasks on which their criteria for success are determined. To maintain morale and to increase output, the ministries and increasingly industrial enterprises must be allowed considerable independence. Their specialist technical expertise gives them a strong bargaining position against purely 'political' interests (say party secretaries) located in other structures. At the top levels of policy-making the ministries are faced by the specialized bureaux of the Central Committee, which probably have a large say in the final aggregation of policy (we do not really know how they interact). In the articulation of their own interest and in the carrying out of plans, the ministries are in all probability highly independent of party direction. Also, the top levels of leadership have to act on the information and proposals put to them by the government ministries.

There is often a tendency for party groups and their secretaries to identify with their work organizations. Ivan Kapitonov, Secretary of the Central Committee in 1978, complained in *Sotsialisticheskaya Industriya* (18 October 1978) that party branches were supporting the pleas of factory managers to have the provisions of their economic plans reduced and thereby were violating discipline. In another article in the party's journal, A. Veretennikov, in discussing the work of party control commissions, pointed out that

solving the enterprise's basic problems would be more effective if the party organization utilized more fully its authority to oversee management activities. The party relies in its work on these commissions, staffed by six or seven people. These are: quality control, technological innovation and capital construction ... It becomes obvious from conversations with activists on the commissions that they sometimes do not have a clear understanding of the purpose, forms and methods of party checking on management activities. In addition, the commissions with the task of overseeing management ... are sometimes headed by persons who, by virtue of their position, are responsible for such activities.[54]

Another party secretary, N. Drunov, in the journal of the Soviet of People's Deputies, called for greater vigilance over the government apparatus. In February 1982 he said, 'It has to be acknowledged that quite a large number of primary party organisations of government institutions are still not making full use of their rights and duties. Poor control is being exercised over the work of the apparatus, shortcomings are overlooked, and cases of indiscipline tolerated.'[55]

Party organizations, however, should not be lightly dismissed as agents of central policy at lower levels of the administration. Party Secretary D.A. Kunaev, in calling for the enhancement of party control over the government administration, pointed out that, in 1982, 14,500 commissions had been formed to help party primary groups to monitor administrative Activity.[56] *Pravda*, in an editorial on 29 January 1983, described the work of primary party organizations in production as follows:

Much is being done by, for example, the Tashkent Obkom to insure that labour collectives cope efficiently with 5-year plan targets. By the end of each 10-day period the party regional executive committee (*obkom*) has data on the work results of every city and district (*rayon*), enterprise, collective and state farm. Steps are promptly taken if work is not proceeding properly. The best experience is consistently propagated. They are waging a real struggle against the notorious downward amendment of plans, not just paying lip-service to such a struggle. In 1982, 122 enterprises amended plans in this way. But as a result of the principled attitude and persistence of the obkom the plans were restored and the collectives not only managed to avoid hitches, but did their utmost to exceed the targets.

Negligence may be penalized by the party sacking officials. In 1981, a Deputy Minister in the Ministry of the Petroleum Industry was dismissed for allowing 'negligent use of equipment and materials intended for increasing oil output ...'.[57]

A Goal-Directed Society?

The presence of autarchic tendencies and tensions between party and government organs places in doubt the view that the USSR is a 'goal-directed' society pursuing the quest for a communist society. T.H. Rigby has argued that 'The (Soviet) regime is primarily concerned not with regulating activities but with directing them.'[58] From this viewpoint, the distinction about the Soviet system is that it is (in theory, through the party) geared to the attainment of a general goal of a communism: *all* action is supposedly consistently related to this aim.

In practice, however, there is no 'regime' directing or regulating activities to the achievement of an abstract goal of communism. Individual parts of the system operate to fulfil specific tasks – the Ministry of Automobile Production to make cars, the KGB to root out subversives and to contain dissents, the Ministry of Secondary and Higher Education to train graduates. These parts (organizations and associations) operate to sustain a formal rationality, i.e., they seek to achieve their own goals which may conflict with the goals of others and systemic goals. 'Substantive rationality' (i.e. a rationality concerning ends) is the province of the Communist Party: its direct and indirect involvement in the activity of the economy and other organizations is meant to ensure that they operate to achieve the goals of communism. It cannot be assumed that it is successful in this quest as advocates of the 'goal-directed society' would claim.

The notion of a goal-rational society also ignores the role of personal and institutional interests which may interpret and distort general political goals.[59] The activity of the security police may altruistically be intended to further the goals of communism, but it may on the other hand be linked to the interests of the security services to preserve its own field of endeavour and *its* own definition of communism. The trouble with 'mono-organizational' theories of society such as Rigby's is that organizations are not monistic but contain conflicting parts, some of which may even seek to displace the explicit organizational goals.[60] This is the crux of the problem of a party which seeks to rule on behalf of the working class, but delegates the activity of ruling to the government bureaucracy. In attempting to ensure conformity between the party's goals and government activity, it has sought to influence the selection of personnel (the *nomenklatura*) and to intervene in the administration through party groups.

Party–government relations are bedevilled by a fundamental role conflict. The party seeks a diffuse, particularistic role, whereas the ministries have specifistic and universalistic tasks. Under conditions of urban-industrial society, specifistic, universalistic and performance relationships result from the highly specialized division of labour and differentiation of relationships. Soviet writers point out that the impact of the 'scientific-technical revolution' in the USSR should lead to more scientific management.[61] This leads to the professionalization and greater independence of ministries, research units and work organizations and concurrently acts as a constraint on central planning and the overall control of the party. As illustrated in some of the case studies that follow in the next chapter, there can be no specific 'party' explanation on drunkenness, hooliganism, or any legitimate ruling on the *effects* of short prison sentences. Khrushhev recognized that the party had to be strengthened and he encouraged the recruitment of technical specialists. He and Brezhnev in the late 1970s and early 1980s much strengthened the party but the ministries must remain very powerful administrative and political institutions.

It would be wrong, however, to view party, government and economy as being locked in continual conflict. We must not overlook the fact that there is also much consensus between them. This is founded on a unity of an ideological kind: all accept the structure of Soviet society—the goal of communism, the nationalization of property, the system of stratification, of a one-party state. In this context the Central Committee of the party acts as a kind of market in which various interests (of government ministries, regional groups, and specialist interests, such as academics) are articulated. It is in this forum that major policy decisions are increasingly legitimated, and important exchanges between its members take place behind the scenes. R.J. Hill has succinctly summarized the party's role as becoming 'one of adjudicator, assessing which broadly aggregated demands are compatible with the ideological aim of building a communist society'.[62] But the Politbureau remains the source of effective leadership and ultimate interest aggregation.

Some Conclusions about the Role of the CPSU

We have seen earlier that the Communist Party articulates an ideology to which social and economic life should conform; it shapes the structure of the political system, and the form in which inputs should be made. But the party's incapacity both to aggregate inputs and to perform specialist output functions has in my view led to its decline as a dominant power, and has increased the power of the government apparatus, though the party covets its hegemonic political legitimacy and both Khrushchev and Brezhnev tried to enhance its power. There has developed a tendency towards greater differentiation of activities and the rise of spheres of interest or competence between factions of the ruling elites – the security police, the military, the leading industrialists and economists are examples. The notion of 'institutional pluralism' coined by Jerry Hough (see below pp. 257–8) entails not only greater automony to such interests, but also a diminution in the role of the party as a hegemonic force in Soviet Soviety. Unlike the view taken by many contemporary writers, the CPSU is not regarded as a Soviet 'power elite'. Such writers exaggerate the party's power: they tend to ignore or minimize the real powers of social forces and institutions outside it;[63] they too readily accept Soviet and 'totalitarian' ideological beliefs. On the other hand, we should not, like Casinelli, relegate the party to a position of obscurity, excluding it even from the most important instruments of rule.[64] The party retains its power by virtue of normative controls – it articulates an ideology. It defines what is and what is not legitimate. It has considerable powers in political mobilization, recruitment and placement. It plays an important role in input articulation. While much aggregaton of interests takes place within and between the ministerial apparatus, the final aggregation process occurs in the Politbureau. This is a party body. This in itself, however, does not 'prove' that the party, as such, rules. The Politbureau is influenced by institutions and social forces outside it; it is internally differentiated. From the time of Khrushchev it has *taken* the final decisions, but it is quite another thing to say that it *makes* the decisions at the behest of the party. The ministries and government committees seek to exert their interests on the party and they are often in practice relatively autonomous from party bodies. The importance of the party is that it seeks to establish a form of substantive rationality in bureaucratic structures which, as Weber pointed out, tend to act, if unchecked, in an instrumental fashion, being concerned with their own specific goals. Attempts to strengthen party control of the ministerial system are an attempt to deal with the problems of bureaucratic structures which also confront Western capitalist societies.

From a political and Marxist viewpoint, the party seeks to represent the interest of the dominant class, the working class. Marxists distinguish between the dominant class that rules and the executive of that class that governs. The Soviet concern with 'party control' expresses the view that the party should rule, but not directly govern. The executive bodies – the Soviets and ministries – should carry out the policy of the party. In practice, however, the executive (parts of the government apparatus) asserts its own view of what the class interest is. The party authorities move from moralistic cajolery to more direct control – to the setting-up of various 'watch-dog' committees operating through primary party organizations.

I would suggest that the Soviet political leadership is characterized not by the rule of a unitary power elite, but by the interaction of a number of elites both between themselves and with other groups. Rather than viewing the party or the government bureaucracy as a monistic structure 'ruling' the USSR, both are seen as providing an apparatus through which interests are articulated and aggregated and outputs are enforced. It is sometimes said that the distinctive character of 'totalitarian systems' is to 'suppress demands coming from the societies' and to be 'unresponsive to demands comiríg from the international environment'.[65] The view adopted here is that the Soviet political system functions in a similar way to Western ones. While *there is a difference* in the degree of suppression of demands on the system, in any system demands which threaten its integrity are suppressed or suppression is attempted. Another important difference between it and liberal-democratic societies is the stronger distributive capability of the Soviet polity (government and party): the boundaries between it and other social sub-systems are weak and the polity is able to exert its power in areas of social life from which it is excluded in the West – except in times of emergency such as war. As we shall distinguish below, the wide extent of the government in policy-making is a separate issue from the process of decision-making.

The State under Socialism

The above analysis of political institutions may be generalized in a discussion of the state as a theoretical concept. Liberal-democratic writers on the Soviet Union regard the Soviet state to be qualitatively different from that under capitalism. In *liberal* theory the state is an institution which 'organizes the will of a people, politically constituted, with respect to its collective interests';[66] it is the political organization of society. The liberal-democratic state is an expression of multiple group interests and its activity is limited. There is a boundary between those activities which are private and those which are public. In the Soviet Union, there is no clear distinction of this kind. Public control of media, education, welfare, public ownership of the economy, and party penetration of associations lead Western liberal-democrats to deny the distinction between state and society, between public and private; hence 'totalitarianism'. As Rigby has put it:

The state (partly disguised as 'voluntary' or 'co-operative' organisations) takes over and runs nearly all spheres of social action; ... the market is reduced to a minor role in the overall co-ordination of social action, which is now handled administratively, through the bureaucracies of state and state-party.[67]

Many Marxist writers also share this position. For them almost every institution in Soviet society is conflated into the 'state apparatus'. David Law has defined the Soviet state as 'political apparatuses, legislative, executive, judicial, coercive and cultural both on the national scale and at the local level, including the productive enterprise'.[68] If one takes this position, then one cannot separate out state, economy and society.

A distinction should be made between state and economy in terms of their function. The *economy* carries out the processes of accumulation and production. All economies perform these functions whether they be privately or publicly owned. In the USSR, in concrete terms, these activities are performed by ministries and committees (and their subordinate units) concerned with production, distribution and exchange of material goods: these include the industrial ministries, the banks and planning committees (Gosplan).

I would define the *state* as being composed of those institutions which function to produce, or to reproduce, or to create certain social relations to the means of production. The state acts essentially to secure the allegiance of the population; it strives to provide cohesion to the system. This it does through coercive and ideological apparatuses – through penal sanctions, socialization and ideology. The socialist state, however, takes a more active and hegemonic role than the capitalist: it seeks to turn public property relations into socialist social relations. The relationship between state and economy in the Soviet Union is not the same as in modern capitalist societies. Writers like Ralph Miliband regard the state under capitalism as 'primarily and inevitably the guardian and protector of the dominant economic interests.'[69] The capitalist state is predicated on the economy. This is not the case, however, in the Soviet Union. The Soviet state in the form of its political apparatuses created a modern economy and defines and safeguards the public form of ownership relations to the means of production. The party seeks to preserve the interests of the working class. It acts on behalf of the working class. While coercive and ideological apparatuses may work in harness, there are undoubtedly differences in emphasis, and on the means to be pursued between, say, the security police and the literary intelligentsia.

One can discern conflicts of interests and differences of priorities between the economy concerned with production and accumulation and the state's role in defining and striving for ideal socialist relationships – the prerogative of party, police and media. The constellation of major interests might be listed as follows:

State Apparatuses	*Economy*
Ideological – party apparat	Production – industrial ministries
Socialization – education, propaganda	Finance – state bank
Coercive – KGB, legal system, armed forces	Planning – Gosplan and co-ordinating committees

The interests of state and economy may clash when the latter emphasizes the necessity to produce – often on the basis of experience borrowed from capitalism. The state for its part sometimes stresses as a priority the need for security, or for idealistic imperatives – ideal incentives or the importance of combating ideological subversion. On any given issue alliances may arise ranging across state/economy boundaries. There is a relationship of tension between the various functional interests both within and between the state and economy: these are often manifested, as noted above, in the Central Committee and the Politbureau.

The state then may be conceptualized as being made up of different apparatuses having specific functions. Groups guiding them may differ over priorities and means to achieve goals. In the economy, there may be similar conflicts of interests between planners and producers. The very bureaucratic nature of the system may induce a kind of formal rationality, with executives pursuing their particularistic notions of the public good. It certainly cannot be assumed, as does Rigby, that the 'achievement of tasks' compared to the 'application of rules' is a characteristic difference between state socialism and capitalism[70] – though perhaps it should be.[71]

NOTES

1 David Easton, *A Systems Analysis of Political Life* (1965), p. 33.
2 Some of the interests involved in the rise and fall of Khrushchev and the ascendance to power of Andropov have been discussed above in chapter 4.
3 Merle Fainsod, *Smolensk Under Soviet Rule* (1958), p. 76.
4 Ibid., p. 82.
5 Ibid., p. 84.
6 John A. Armstrong, *The Soviet Bureaucratic Elite, A Case Study of the Ukrainian Aparatus* (1959), p. 146.
7 Ibid., p. 149.
8 Philip D. Stewart, *Political Power in the Soviet Union* (1968), p. viii.
9 Ibid., pp. 195, 197.
10 Ibid., pp. 200, 213. See also S. Bialer, *Stalin's Successors* (1980).
11 T.H. Rigby, *Communist Party Membership in the USSR 1917–1967* (1968), p. 40.
12 Zbigniew K. Brzezinski, *Ideology and Power in Soviet Politics* (1967), p. 119. See M.P. Gehlen, *The Communist Party of the Soviet Union* (1969) pp. 66–70.
13 *XXIV S'ezd KPSS* (Moscow 1971), vol. 1, p. 97. Cited by R.J. Hill and P. Frank, *The Soviet Communist Party* (1981), p. 14.
14 W. Leonhard, *The Kremlin Since Stalin* (1962) pp. 149–50.
15 H.L. Biddulph, 'Local Interest Articulation at CPSU Congresses', *World Politics*, vol. 36, no. 1, (October 1983). pp. 28–52.
16 Gehlen, *op. cit.,* pp. 63–6.
17 For membership 1971 and 1984, see table 5.14 above.
18 John P. Willerton, Jr. 'Clientelism in the Soviet Union: An Initial Examination', *Studies in Comparative Communism*, vol. 12, nos. 2, 3. (Summer/Autumn 1979).
19 J. Moses, 'Regional Cohorts and Political Mobility in the USSR: the Case of Dnepropetrovsk. *Soviet Union*, vol. 3, pt. 1 (1976) p. 82.
20 *Washington Star*, 16, July 1979.
21 Leonard Schapiro, *The Communist Party of the Soviet Union* (London, 1960), p. 548.
22 See also for an earlier version: Abdurakhman Avtorkhanov, *The Communist Party Apparatus* (Chicago, 1966), pp. 201–5.
23 *Christian Science Monitor,* 23 February, 1982.
24 For an example from Moldavia, see: R.J. Hill, *Soviet Political Elites* (1977), p. 173.
25 K. Mannheim, *Ideology and Utopia* (1936), p. 239.
26 *The Programme of the CPSU* (adopted at the 22nd Congress 1961), reprinted in *Soviet Booklet,* no. 83 (1961).
27 Yu. Andropov, *Kommunist,* no. 3, February 1983. Abstract in *CDSP,* vol. 35, no. 10 (6 April 1983).
28 See *The End of Ideology* (1961), pp. 396–7.

29 See his 'Marxism – Leninism: A Doctrine on the Defensive', in M.M. Drachkovitch, *Marxist Ideology in the Contemporary World* (1966).
30 Barrington Moore, Jr., *Soviet Politics–The Dilemma of Power* (1965 edn), p. 416.
31 See, for example, his articles in: *Kommunist*, no. 17 (1980); *Voprosy istorii KPSS*, no. 2 (1982); *Kommunist*, no. 13, (1981); *Kommunist*, no. 6 (1982).
32 J. Stalin, *Problems of Leninism* (1941), p. 652. Cited by Louis Nemzer, 'The Kremlin's Professional Staff', *American Political Science Review*, vol. 44 (1950), p. 64.
33 B. Harasymiw, 'Nomenklatura', *The Canadian Journal of Political Science*, vol. 2, no. 3, 1969, p. 511.
34 *Iz opyta ideologicheskoy raboty partii* (1973), pp. 304–5. Cited by M. Matthews, *Education in the Soviet Union* (1982), p. 112.
35 Jerry F. Hough, *The Soviet Prefects: The Local Party Organs in Industrial Decision-Making* (1969).
36 Ibid., pp. 47–8.
37 Ibid., p. 51.
38 *Pravda*, 17, July 1955, p. 6, cited by Hough, ibid., p. 52.
39 *Partiynaya zhizn'*, no. 10 (1976).
40 Hough, *The Soviet Prefects . . .*, pp. 58–9.
41 Ibid., pp. 78–9.
42 Joel C. Moses, 'The Impact of *Nomenklatura* in Soviet Regional Elite Recruitment', *Soviet Union*, vol. 8, pt. 1 (1981), p. 64.
43 G. V. Barabashev and K. F. Sheremet, *Sovetskoe gosudarstvo i obshchestvennost' v usloviyakh razvernutogo stroitel'stva kommunizma* (1962), p. 57. Cited by Lloyd Churchward, 'Soviet Local Government Today', *Soviet Studies*, vol. 17 (4) (April 1966), p. 443n.
44 Lloyd Churchward, ibid., pp. 443–4.
45 Ibid., p. 451.
46 John Barron, *The KGB* (1974), p. 73.
47 F.C. Barghoorn, 'The Security Police', in H.G. Skilling and F. Griffiths, *Interest Groups in Soviet Politics* (1971), p. 115.
48 See report by Konstantin Simis, *The Sunday Times* (London), 19 September 1982, and his book, USSR, *Secrets of a Corrupt Society* (1982).
49 K. Chernenko, 'Leninskaya strategiya rukovodstva', *Kommunist*, no. 13 (1981).
50 *Pravda*, 16 August 1981.
51 *Pravda*, 9 March 1981.
52 *Partiynaya zhizn'*, no. 21 (Nov. 1981).
53 Hough, *The Soviet Prefects . . .*, p. 69.
54 A Veretennikov, *Partiynaya zhizn'*, no. 11 (June 1982), p. 69.
55 N. Drunov, *Sovety narodnykh deputatov*, no. 2 (Feb. 1982).
56 *Partiynaya zhizn' Kazakhstana*, no. 10 (Oct. 1982).
57 V. Sevastyanov, *Sotsialisticheskaya industriya*, no. 4 (Oct. 1981) p. 2.
58 'A Conceptual Aproach to Authority, Power and Policy in the Soviet Union', in T.H. Rigby et al. (eds), *Authority, Power and Policy in the USSR* (1980), p. 19.

59 Study of the Soviet educational system may illustrate the conflicting interests and goals, see D. Lane, *Soviet Society and Economy* (1984), chapter 8.
60 The best example of this in the West is that of managers who may seek to maximize salaries or size of plant rather than profit of the firm. In the Soviet Union under Stalin, an example would be the role of the security police apparatus in displacing the party.
61 See the excellent discussion by Eric P. Hoffman, 'Changing Soviet Perspectivices on Leadership and Administration', in S.F. Cohen, A. Rabinowitch and R. Sharlet, *The Soviet Union Since Stalin*, (1980), pp. 71–92.
62 R.J. Hill, 'Party-State Relations and Soviet Political Development', *British Journal of Political Science,* vol. 10 (1980), p. 161.
63 T.H. Rigby, 'Traditional, Market and Organisational Societies and the USSR', *World Politics,* vol. 16 (1964); Allen Kassof, 'The Administered Society', *World Politics,* vol. 16 (1964).
64. C.W. Casinelli, 'The Totalitarian Party', *The Journal of Politics,* vol. 24 (1962).
65 G.A. Almond and G.B. Powell, *Comparative Politics* (1966), p. 28. Later in the book, however, they describe the political conversion process in group terms (pp. 277–9).
66 L.V. Ballard, *Social Institutions* (New York, 1936), p. 153.
67 T.H. Rigby, 'A Conceptual Approach to Authority . . .', pp. 18–19.
68 *Critique,* no. 7 (1976), p. 144
69 R. Miliband, *The State in Capitalist Society* (1973), p. 123.
70 On the role of the state as a component in the social formation of state socialism, see Lane, *Soviet Society and Economy*, chapter 3.
71 My thanks to E. Teague for some useful references to sources used in this chapter.

8

POLITICAL PARTICIPATION

The political leadership has for long been the principal concern of Western students of Soviet society. This focus has been too narrow to ensure a balanced political analysis. One must also consider the middle ranges of power, the role of public opinion and the participation of the masses in the political system.

I shall outline empirical studies which describe the process of politics at the middle level and at that of the masses. The empirical studies should prepare the reader for the discussion which follows on the notion of political particiption, democracy and legitimation.

The Middle Ranges of Power

Discussion of group influence in the Soviet political system is relatively recent. The notion that the Soviet Union was 'totalitarian' in nature effectively precluded any analysis of pressures or influences on the government. As H. Gordon Skilling has put it in the introduction to a seminal study of interest groups in the USSR: 'The uniqueness of a totalitarian system was deemed to lie in the very totality of its political power, excluding, as it were, by definition, any area of autonomous behaviour by groups other than the state or party, and still more, preventing serious influence by them on the process of decision-making.'[1] Political scientists in the West in the late 1960s questioned this viewpoint and numerous studies identified empirically various groups with specific interests who sought to influence the top decision makers. In reviewing such work, Skilling concluded in 1983 that 'This research, while not neglecting the role of the official authoritative organs of state and party, confirmed, to the satisfaction of many, that interest groups contributed important inputs to the process of decision-making.'[2]

By the 'middle ranges of power' we refer to those groups or institutions which operate within the system of values sustained by the political

238

leadership; they mediate between the political elites and the masses. The interests discussed above such as the security services (KGB) or Party Secretaries would not be considered to be part of the 'middle ranges' of power: they constitute the political leadership. Interests characterizing the 'middle ranges' of power are regional groups (such as republican-based interests) and professions. Here we may give some examples of their activity: first is the case of regional interests who opposed educational changes in language requirements in several non-Russian republics; second is a study of industrial managers as an interest group; third is the campaign of an 'environmentalist lobby' and fourth is a study of the role of criminologists in decision-making.

Regional Interests and Language Requirements

The Council of Nationalities of the Supreme Soviet is composed of representatives of different areas of the USSR. As indicated earlier in chapter 6 above, business is conducted without polemic and strife. Regional interests, however, are voiced. This was particularly the case over proposed reforms of language teaching in the national republics.

In 1959 the reforms proposed by the Central Committee and the Council of Ministers recommended that non-indigenous pupils of various republics would have the right to opt out of the republican language (i.e. Estonian in Estonia); also the indigenous population, attending Russian-language schools, were no longer to be obliged to learn the language of the republic.[3] This proposal threatened the non-Russian speaking nationalities. Dissent was expressed in the Supreme Soviet. Some republics, the Ukraine, Georgia, Armenia, Azerbaidzhan and the Baltic states, vigorously championed their rights and the obligation they had to teach the indigenous language. 'We must not set up the Russian and the local indigenous language one against another by allowing people to choose between them. For us both languages are native languages, both of them are indispensable, and both are obligatory.'[4] The spokesmen of the Central Asian Republics and Moldavia were less hostile.

The upshot of this pressurizing was that the recommendations were left out of the all-union law. Each republic could decide the issue for itself. In the Russian Republic (RSFSR), the original proposals were incorporated in the laws and similar proposals were introduced in Uzbekistan, Tadzhikistan, Turkmenistan and Kirgizia. In the Ukraine, Russian was to be compulsory. In Armenia, Estonia and Georgia the laws would be 'implemented so as to strengthen the native languages rather than Russian'.[5] In Azerbaidzhan and Latvia the importance of the indigenous languages was emphasized. The point to be made here, is that regional interests were articulated within the framework of the federal system. The central authorities had the last word, as Aspaturian puts it: 'the elites of the various nationalities are forced to play two social roles, each responding to different pressures and constituencies, often pulling in opposite directions. Since the political constituency of the non-Russian Soviet official is in Moscow, though his natural constituency is his national republic, he is more likely to be responsive to the interests of Moscow than to those of his republic.'[6]

Industrial Managers

The role of the technical and managerial groups in politics has been long debated. The importance of professional groups and particularly of 'economic technicians' has been noted by Myron Rush in his study of political succession.[7] The works of Jeremy Azrael, and John P. Hardt and Theodore Frankel have focused on industrial managers as an interest group.[8] These writers consider industrial managers both at the time of Stalin and at the present time.

Even under Stalin, managers had opportunities to articulate interests and to put demands. 'Enterprise directors ... confronted their superiors in the industrial ministries in the protected bargaining that constituted the planning process. While the bargaining was cast in terms of specific input and output figures, it must have solidified a cognizance of shared and opposed interests on both sides.'[9] In the study of contemporary managers, the authors identify channels of interest articulation and mention in this respect the meetings of managerial personnel (9,000 managers took part in 10 zonal conferences in the RSFSR, and an All-Union Conference brought together 5,000 planners, administrators and economic managers). Interestingly, Hardt and Frankel argue that managers may be divided into sub-groups on the basis of age, education and function. They point out that the rising generation of managers have a management and economic orientation compared to the old-style 'production-engineer' type.

Jeremy Azrael has generalized about the role of managers as follows:

the available data confirm that the managers have played [a significant role in Soviet political development] in a manner that justifies their treatment as a political group rather than as an aggregate of discrete political actors. In the first place, it is evident that managerial status has had an important influence on the political behaviour of the men concerned ... In addition, most industrial executives have consciously recognised that they have important interests in common ... Finally, there is good reason to believe that the managers have sometimes collectively engaged in more or less discplined and co-ordinated political action. So far as one can judge on the basis of the available evidence, they have never emerged as a formally organised 'faction', but they do seem occasionally to have developed a common political strategy for the purpose of influencing public policy in a pre-determined direction.[10]

For the Khrushchev period he shows that the demands made by the managerial group did not transcend the boundaries defined by the political elite. While they gained by the curbs on police action and the greater freedom of expression, they sought to preserve their privilege and did not want a full-blooded destalinization.[11]

It is difficult to find evidence of the articulation and aggregation of a *managerial* interest; rather the findings seem to point to fragmentation and particularization of managerial concern. The ministerial industrial system gives managers a loyalty to their industry in a way similar to that which managers give to their firm in the West. Soviet managers tend to be specialists tied to a production process rather than generalists, which reinforces institutional loyalty. As industries compete for resources, then managerial interests too tend to be divided.

In the post-Stalin succession struggle, 'the managers' did not play a direct part in either Khrushchev's rise or fall. It is more likely that they played a supporting part, and that potential political leaders advocated policies which would appease managers. According to Azrael, Malenkov indicated 'that he was acutely aware of the need for more realistic planning. Nor was the appeal of his position on planning diminshed by his simultaneous advocacy of greater investment in light industry.'[12] Party control was opposed by the ministerial leaders and managers, and therefore Malenkov might also be regarded as a spokesman or articulator of managers' interests. The point must be made, however, that the managers were unable formally to aggregate and articulate such an interest themselves – this was left to members of the political leadership.

The reorganization of industrial ministries into a hundred or so economic regions (*sovnarkhozy*) again provides an indication of the ways a managerial interest has been manifested. In 1955 George Glebovsky, the director of Uralmash, had publicly opposed the dismantling of the industrial ministries, and he too came out against Khrushchev's decentralization plan. Other 'extremely influential directors' also opposed Khrushchev on this issue.[13] The managers tended to support the 'anti-party' political faction.

At the time of Khrushchev's fall, the managers *as a group* do not seem to have played a very direct part in the succession struggle though their hostility to Khrushchev's economic policies and support for ministerial (as against party) power no doubt provided considerable backing for the anti-Khrushchev counter-elites. Certainly policy since Khrushchev's departure has been geared more closely to their interests – for instance, the strengthening of the ministerial system, the greater powers of managers over factory-level decisions and the emphasis now put at enterprise level on profit maximization.

The foregoing discussion illustrates that managers have interests which are voiced and of which cognizance is taken by the political leadership. In the crucial areas of group interest articulation and aggregation we lack adequate information to show how effective managers are as an interest group.

The Campaign over Lake Baikal

Concern with the environment, particularly pollution, has brought into the open the activity of many interested parties and study of it may illustrate the interaction of ministerial, top party, scientific and media interests. Thane Gustafson has pieced together the complex political infighting related to the siting of an industrial complex on Lake Baikal.[14]

Baikal is the largest freshwater lake in the world and is a naturalist's paradise. In the late 1950s it was planned to build a rayon cord factory on its shores: the lake provided water and the nearby forests an ample supply of wood. Protests were voiced by scientists and journalists. In 1963, the conservative journal *Oktyabr'*, and the paper of the Union of Soviet Writers, *Literaturnaya Gazeta,* published articles exposing the proposed development. At the Twenty-Third Congress of the Party, Sholokov spoke publicly in support of preserving the lake.[15]

Demands were made that adequate treatment of industrial waste be carried out, and consequently a test plant was set up. Such a process is not normally observed in the Soviet Union and Gustafson suggests that 'the project was under unusual behind-the-scenes pressure from the start.[16] Opposition to the scheme was expressed by the State Committee for Scientific Research and the Siberian Department of the Academy of Sciences. Construction of the plant continued and little progress was made on the treatment of waste. In 1965, workers on the site wrote to *Literaturnaya Gazeta* reporting that the waste pipe was being laid straight to the lake. In 1966, a letter appeared in the newspaper of the Young Communist League, *Komsomol'skaya Pravda,* advocating the abandonment of the scheme. It was signed by a vice-president of the Academy of Sciences and other Academicians, Heroes of Socialist Labour and a section head of the Russian State Committee on Construction. This was followed by Gosplan organizing a commission of experts to review the project.

This commission supported the scheme which went ahead despite further protests. Concessions were achieved, however – in 1966, seven additional waste-treatment units were constructed. But a report in *Pravda* in 1969 pointed out that sewage was not being properly processed. In the 1970s various decrees were issued by the Council of Ministers and the Party Control Committee dealing with pollution. They have been effective. Gustafson writes:

The flow of orders and regulations since 1971 has finally produced real results. In the view of American experts from the Environmental Protection Agency who have visited the waste-treatment facilities at Baikalsk, they are the most elaborate in the world (when they operate). In short, the lake's defenders can boast of no mean achievement, for they raised a nationwide scandal, gained top-level attention for the lake for a span of more than fifteen years, and turned the lake's preservation into a Soviet showpiece that the government now eagerly displays to foreigners.[17]

The studies on the Baikal issue suggest that groups do *independently* articulate their interests and seek to influence the priorities of political elites. Kelley identifies two centres of operation in the Baikal affair: the formal bureaucratic channels, dominated by the industrial ministries, and a larger arena 'in which top-level Soviet officials were being urged on by an *ad hoc* environmental coalition to override the decisions of their ministerial subordinates'.[18]

We do not know about the extent of interest group pressure. Much activity occurs behind the facade of unanimity which the political system projects to the outside world. This in itself has many undesirable consequences for the effective operation of Soviet government. The barriers to the flow of information may make the leadership adopt the wrong policies 'because of a lack of open, expert, countervailing criticism'.[19] As Gustafson has pointed out: 'as technical issues grow ever more complex and interconnected, the usefulness to the leaders of having them thrashed out publicly will increase, for only a wide airing will preserve the leaders from the biased information "interested" ministries may provide or from one-sided advocacy of specialist-entrepreneurs and regional "patriots".'[20] It is important to note also that the government departments, in the cases discussed above, had the last say. Their policy may be modified, but in this case the established institutions were decisive in the influence they brought on the top decision-makers.[21]

Criminologists in Decision-making

A more ambitious of political interests has been conducted by Peter H. Solomon, Jr.[22] He not only analyses empirically the participation of Soviet criminologists in the policy process, but he also compares such participation with that of criminologists in the USA and Britain.

Solomon pursues three case studies: delinquency prevention; alcoholism and hooliganism; and parole and recidivism reforms. In these areas he attempts to assess 'the scope, quality and impact' of specialists on policy. He shows that, in respect of commissions attached to city and regional Soviets which were set up as voluntary bodies in the 1960s, Soviet criminologists were instrumental in directly shaping policy as regards their composition and functions. They participated in meetings of the chair persons of such commissions, convened by the Presidium of the Supreme Soviet of the RSFSR. They undertook detailed study of the operation of the commissions which 'documented and analysed their shortcomings'.[23] Under the USSR Procuracy they participated in commissions to improve juvenile crime prevention. Solomon identifies the views of particular criminologists (Minkovski and Pronina) particulary on the need for full-time qualified staff. They put their views in the government newspaper, *Izvestiya*, and also in legal journals. Their proposals were included in the reforms. They also wrote extensive book-length commentaries on the statutes. Solomon concludes that 'questions of substance were left almost entirely to the discretion of criminologists and officials and controversies over details, like the question of incentives for public guardians, were resolved through quiet bargaining within the confines of the *ad hoc* commissions.'[24]

On the question of the treatment of hooliganism and alcoholism, Solomon distinguishes the groups with opposing policies. In attempting to reduce infractions of public order, the minister V.S. Tikunov (Minister for Defence of Public Order) advocated the enforcement of existing laws – 'a campaign against hooligans'. On the pages of *Pravda* he advocated 'increased sanctions' for hooligans.[25] The other group, composed of criminologists, proposed dealing with the causes rather than treating the symptoms of crime. In *Izvestiya* they advocated 'educational work rather than repression [as] the most effective means of reducing crime'.[26] They pleaded for compulsory treatment in special centres (*profilaktori*) and restrictions on the sale of alcohol. They proposed and drafted a comprehensive anti-alcoholism law. Tikunov, however, wrote in *Izvestiya* that intensified repression of hooligans was called for. The Minister of Trade also had reservations about curtailing sales of alcohol – the sale of vodka and liquor contributed more than ten per cent of turnover tax. Rather than a law for alcoholism, one on hooliganism was enacted: this had been drafted by officials from the Ministry of Public Order.[27] The law, subsequently adopted in 1967, ignored the recommendations of the criminologists, i.e. a voluntary society for fighting alcoholism, restrictions on liquor sales, anti-alcoholic propaganda.

This is not the end of the story, however, for the enactment proved difficult to enforce and the incidence of alcoholism and hooliganism did not appreciably decrease. In 1972, an edict on alcoholism prevention was issued.

The third issue addressed by Solomon is that of parole and recidivism. The problems which arise here are concerned with the effects on prisoners of different prison sentences and early release. Though it is an oversimplification to point to two viewpoints on these issues, there is one school which emphasizes the role of law as deterrence and retribution and correction of the criminal and another that puts more stress on the rehabilitation of the offender. In the 1960s, Solomon relates, many officials and citizens 'expressed contempt' for early release: as a rank and file policeman put it 'if you get fifteen years, you should sit fifteen'.[28] On the other hand, liberals in the legal profession argued that parole would lead to improvement in future behaviour. In discussion of policy in the plenum of the Supreme Court, the deputy director of the Procuracy Institute argued that the effectiveness of parole was not a matter of opinion, but should be studied scientifically.

As a result of this and other discussions, which surfaced on the pages of *Izvestiya*, scientific research on early release and the effects of short sentences was put in hand. Arising from this work, done by criminologists, a number of recommendations were put forward concerning the criteria for parole, the procedure to be used concerning the selection of parolees and the terms of parole. The details need not concern us here.[29] The Supreme Court Advisory Council sponsored a conference to discuss the topics attended by three hundred judicial officials and scholars. *Ad hoc* commissions were also formed to discuss the issues. The upshot were changes in the *Fundamental Principles of Criminal Legislation*. These contained amendments in line with many (not all) of the recommendations of the criminologists.

In explaining the changes to the public, in the Supreme Soviet, R. Nishanov of the Uzbek Communist Party, announced: 'This draft law was originally drawn up by a commission of the Supreme Soviet. On the commission's instructions, sociological and criminological research was conducted with the participation of the central departments and scientific institutions ... the purpose of the research was to establish the categories of individuals to which the provisions contained in the draft law would be applied in the future'.[30]

These studies of decision-making in law amply portray the role of specialists in shaping decisions. Solomon concludes his study by arguing that during the 1960s 'participation by scholars [i.e. criminologists] became a regular feature both of criminal policy-making and of the scholars' own work roles'.[31] Under Brezhnev, the process of participation was institutionalized. Compared to the position of criminologists in the USA and England, *'Soviet criminologists seemed to have had about as much influence on criminal policy as did their counterparts...'*[32] Finally, Solomon concludes that the role of specialists in policy-making in the USSR is limited, but that the constraints on them 'were not peculiar to the Soviet setting; similar limitations also affected criminologists and other specialists who took part in policy-making in the USA.'[33]

These studies would indicate that professionals do influence policy-making. They are, however, subject to constraints: executive officers, politicians, the press and 'public' opinion are also important determinants of policy outcomes.

Participation by the Citizen

The leaders of the Soviet Union espouse a form of participatory democracy. As Brezhnev put it to his electors in a speech in 1979: 'every Soviet citizen can feel his involvement in state affairs, be sure that his opinion [and] his voice will be heard in the making of large and small decisions.'[34]

Mass participation takes place through the party, the Soviets, through the organs of People's Control, through elections and through the articulation of 'public opinion'. The party is the most important institution because it is here that the politically most competent people are located. The party in recent years has been strengthened in two ways: it has been given greater rights to 'control' the administration, and it has increased in membership. However, little is known about the ways that party groups have influence on higher level policy. They 'parallel' the government administration and have the right to be consulted, they have rights to the access of information and they can question the administrators running various organizations. At lower levels such groups are often an effective check on the administration and many are involved in the work of the primary party organization. Participation in elections and in the government organs has been outlined above in chapter 6.

People's Control

The notion of organs of 'people's control' is a particularly Soviet concept. After the revolution, control or monitoring of the administration was introduced not only to encourage people to participate, but to check that the administrators were not sabotaging the affairs of the new Soviet state. The organs have been revived first under Khrushchev and then under

Brezhnev and their aim is to involve the rank and file in the running of affairs. As N.A. Tikhonov put it when introducing the draft law on people's control to the Supreme Soviet in 1979:

Guided by Lenin's teaching, our party is constantly improving control as a means of enlisting the broad masses into the construction of communism ... The very title "people's control" exhaustively expresses the essence of control of the new, socialist type. In the shape of the people's control organs there has been found one of the effective forms of the implementation by workers, peasants and the intelligentsia of their right to daily control over all aspects of the work of the government and economic organs and enterprises and organizations. The living, practical business of millions and millions of people's control workers, the active assistants of the Party and government, lies behind the provisions of the bill.[35]

Khrushchev had been particularly active in reviving people's control in his efforts to weaken the government bureaucracy, and in 1965 he set up the Party-Government Control Committee, which was outside both apparatuses. The People's Control Committee (PCC) (*Komitet narodnogo kontrolya*), which grew out of it, was formed in December 1965. It is formally subordinate to the Soviets, though the primary party organizations often initiate the formation of local groups. The committees, along with party commissions on control, attempt to replace the Stalinist process of 'control from above' with that of 'control from below'. While the removal of Khrushchev from his party post in 1964 led many Western commentators to anticipate a counter-revolution of the 'clerks' against popular participation, this has not been the case.[36]

The membership of the commissions has grown steadily from 1965 when it numbered around five million to 9.5 million volunteers in 1976; membership has continued at this level up to 1980 when there were 'around 10 million members'.[37] These were organized in institutions as shown in table 8.1. By social background the volunteers are manual workers (47 per cent), collective farmers (15 per cent), white collar workers (36 per cent), students (0.4 per cent), pensioners and house wives (1.8 per cent). Party members play a big part (being 38 per cent) in membership. Most prominent in the committees are people from party organizations (4,652 in 1980), Soviets (5,073), trade unions (4,430) and the Young Communist League (4,538). There were 7,667 full-time officers of the organization, the remainder being voluntary activists.[38] In the top Committee of the PCC, elected in April 1979, were 19 men (no women).[39] The chairman, Aleksey Shkol'nikov, had been a party official until 1966 when he became a first deputy chairman of the Russian Republic Council of Ministers. The other members are representatives from government and party bodies, the

TABLE 8.1: GROUPS AND POSTS OF PEOPLE'S CONTROL (ELECTED 1980)

In industrial enterprises	347,012
In enterprises and organizations of transport and communications	81,747
In construction enterprises and organizations	115,923
In collective farms, state farms and other agricultural organizations	345,411
In trade, public catering and services	123,123
In science, research and planning	40,109
In educational institutions	72,958
In culture and health	58,480
Under the local Soviets in villages and settlements	44,872

Source: 'Sistema organov narodnogo kontrolya v SSSR', *Politicheskoe samoobrazovanie*, no. 5 (1981), p. 82.

apparat of the Young Communist League, regional Committees of People's Control and newspapers.

As to the activity of the groups of the PCCs, *Pravda* publishes a weekly report on their activities.[40] The committees investigate complaints made in letters concerning inefficiency and slackness, they participate in the planning process, they intervene in ministries to rectify infringements of planning. The committees have examined such topics as the use of fertilizers in agriculture and the quality of output of synthetic fibres. Government plans are passed for comment to the committee whose role is presumably to expose hidden resources. Its members are co-opted on to planning committees, and to standing commissions of the Soviets. The committees intervene to try to prevent shortages, waste and losses in the economy caused by inefficiencies. They procure reprimands for inefficient and careless factory managers and, by intervening with the minister, have secured dismissals for incompetence. Accounts in the Soviet press claim large savings from the activities of the committees and the yearly participation in their work of some six hundred thousand citizens (in 1979).

Western critics of the committees argue that many of the claims are exaggerated. An account by Boris Bochshtein (an émigré Soviet journalist) has pointed out that findings are suppressed (e.g. levels of radioactivity in the Moscow air) for fear of offending 'some influential person'.[41] Even such accounts, however, concede that the PCCs do expose inefficiency and cheating. The role of the party in their activity is also emphasized. Committees of People's Control undoubtedly involve many citizens in political activity; one might be a little sceptical, but certainly not dismissive of their effectiveness.[42]

Self-administration

In addition to the Committees of People's Control, attempts have been made to involve the citizen in the direct administration of affairs. Khrushchev particularly advocated self-administration which he saw as providing a means by which the state would 'wither away'. Some of the main activities are involvement by citizens in comrades' courts and voluntary units of militia (*druzhiny*). The intention here is to have a self-policing community. The comrades' courts deal with disputes between residents, drunkenness, petty pilfering, hooliganism, arrears of rent, 'parasites', and family disputes. In 1980, some 2.6 million people took part in the courts' activities. The *druzhiny* also deal with petty crime and the control of public order: hooliganism, manifestations of immoral behaviour and drunkenness come under their purview. In 1980, there were some ten million members of the *druzhiny*. They wear armbands, carry out street patrols and have the power of arrest.[43]

The trade union organization also depends on the goodwill of volunteers who perform a wide range of tasks. They play an important role in administering social security benefits: they participate in commissions which decide levels of disability, they help with checking up on malingerers, and they also pay social visits to sick members. In the early 1980s there were some four million trade union members helping to administer benefits. In addition, many union committees in the factories are concerned with improving production and implementing the economic plan: such committees are responsible for innovation, quality control and organization of work. Unions also organize sports and leisure activities.

Friedgut has suggested that a function of direct administration is to meet deficiencies in the administrative apparatus. What this amounts to is that volunteer self-help groups carry out various services which are either not done, or are badly done, by the statutory bodies. Such activities include repair gangs and building maintenance. Also organized on a community basis are children's nurseries and play groups. In addition, street and house committees are formed which check up on the occupants of flats by rooting-out illegal tenants; they also see to the cleanliness of the flats, tend the gardens and organize libraries. One should not interpret these activities cynically. They provide meaningful and useful things to do for many people. Interviews conducted by Friedgut with 300 Soviet émigrés found that the attitudes of the overwhelming majority were positive to such groups: for instance, of volunteer groups under the Soviets, 32 per cent said that they were 'of some use', 41 per cent 'useful' and 6 per cent 'very useful'; of community activities, the respective figures were 35 per cent, 43 per cent and 4 per cent.[44] They help to create a sense of community and mutual obligation between citizens. In a modest way, the voluntary work discussed above helps to overcome the professionalism and bureaucratic tendencies inherent in welfare states.

'Public Opinion'

In addition to the formal processes of election and administration, the Soviet citizen is able to voice his criticism of (or respect for) the system of government by writing to or communicating with the press or other media. This form of participation is generally ignored by Western commentators, though Adams, Mickiewicz and White have correctly emphasized its importance.[45] In the post-Khrushchev period, the political leadership has advocated that greater attention be paid to letters to the media and to public authorities as a way of strengthening links with the people. The Central Committee of the party has set up a special department to deal with such communications. As Chernenko pointed out in 1981 in *Kommunist*,

In the period between the 25th and 26th Congresses the Central Committee of the CPSU received more than three million letters ... Our Party and its Central Committee attach great significance to work with these letters. A thorough analysis of letters in Party committees at all levels makes it possible to reach a better understanding of the thoughts and sentiments of Soviet people – communists and non-party men and women. It enables one to make objective judgements on the effectiveness of decisions adopted and to reveal and eliminate the causes of shortcomings.

At the same time ... many letters are indicators of serious local shortcomings ... It must be said that often questions raised in letters can and must be resolved by the leaders of the enterprises concerned and by district and city organisations. There are still not infrequent instances of a formal, unconscious examination of letters, failures to respond to them in good time and unjustified rejection of requests ...[46]

The main Soviet newspapers (*Izvestiya* and *Pravda*) receive around half a million letters each per year.[47] Mickiewicz has calculated that *Izvestiya* is sent ten times the number of letters received by the *New York Times* and, if one controls for circulation, the Soviet paper receives twice as many letters as the American paper.[48] *Izvestiya* has a large staff (about 60) processing the letters. All letters should receive a reply. The Soviet press features letters extensively. Of those letters received by the central press (e.g. *Pravda, Izvestiya*), from one to five per cent are published; in local newspapers the figure rises to about a third. The organ of the Young Communists, *Komsomol'skaya Pravda* publishes between 2,100 and 2,600 letters per year – seven to nine per issue.[49] Such letters are often the centre of discussion and they spark off lively exchanges and investigatory visits by the newspapers' journalists. On particular issues a nation-wide discussion is conducted and newspapers often augment their staff to deal with the deluge. In the discussion of the 1977 Constitution, more than 400,000 amendments were sent in, and 150 were accepted. Brezhnev reported that 140 million citizens took part in the discussion of the new Constitution.[50]

In a study of seven Soviet newspapers appearing in 1977, Adams found that 68 per cent of issues in letters were devoted to 'consumer' and the remainder to 'producer' topics. Of the 'consumer' complaints, the largest group, 39 per cent, were about consumer goods and services – their availability and quality. Next came communal and cultural facilities (29 per cent), followed by 'housing and office space' (22 per cent) (mainly on the subject of upkeep and repair).[51] Relatively few (8 per cent) were on topics of personal rights. In the area of complaints about production, the largest number of complaints were about the quality of personnel (28 per cent), followed by another group (27 per cent) of general complaints about 'the unjust outcome of arbitration, misuse of trade-union funds, inferior or erroneous management practices, faulty construction regulations, lagging industrial construction and ... unworkable economic plans'.[52] The content of the letters appearing in the press reflects the interests, to a large extent, of the papers' editorial staffs. There were no letters, with targets of criticism, on the political leadership, the party and foreign policy.[53] Government ministries, however, come under criticism, as do the 'unworkable' elements in the Five-Year Plan.

Letters may be utilized not only to criticize agencies, but also to 'strengthen the moral fibre' of Soviet society. A group of army officers. serving in Afghanistan, wrote the following to the army newspaper, *Krasnaya zvezda*.[54]

Quite recently the Blue Guitars vocal and instrumental ensemble, a by no means unknown collective, gave some concerts for us. We assumed that, like our previous guests who had come here to perform for fighting men in the limited Soviet contingent in Afghanistan, these artists had a pretty good idea of where they were going and for what purpose. But both the concerts and the behaviour of these guests convinced us of exactly the opposite . . . .

The programme's ideological and artistic aspect will not stand up to criticism – it was simply a pale copy of by no means the best western originals. Granted there were a few numbers in which one heard lofty words, but the form in which they were clothed in no way corresponded to the content. These words were pitiable as were the barbarically interpreted, distorted songs 'Pedlars' and 'Along the Petersburg Road' . . .

Didn't the Moscow concert organisation know what sort of musical baggage the Blue Guitars were bringing us? . . . .

The reply in the issue of 12 January reported that the Director of the Moscow Concert Organization and the Secretary of the party committee had written to the editors conceding that 'the criticism directed at the Blue

Guitars ... was correct.' The leader of the ensemble had also admitted that the criticism was justified. The reply also said that 'The Blue Guitars ensemble was removed from the planned schedule of foreign tours and was forbidden to give concerts in Moscow. Administrative sanctions were imposed on the ensemble's leader ...'

As to the effectiveness of the letters in righting wrongs or changing the priorities of the system, we have no direct knowledge. From the citizen's point of view, this is a means of outlet for frustration and expression of grievance. The institutions of Soviet society also probably fear adverse press comment. Many letters on the same subject are often amalgamated into a general article – with a ministry or local Soviet bearing the brunt of the paper's criticism. For *Pravda* and *Izvestiya*, the letters' department is the paper's largest. It subjects the contents of letters to computer analysis of themes which are passed monthly to the relevant authorities. The letters are also an effective source of information for the authorities. Mickiewicz has pointed out that the 'official' channels of communication feedback in the various bureaucracies are dominated by the selective perception of party members, whereas readers' letters and meetings with the public are more representative of the real feelings of the population. Hence the authorities are learning to pay particular heed to such sources of information.[55] The papers forward their own analysis to the Presidium of the Supreme Soviet, to the chairman of the Council of Ministers and to the Central Committee of the party and its Control Committee.[56] Many Western scholars now believe that the authorities do respond to citizen complaints – as far as is possible.[57] No political system – East or West – it may be noted, is responsive to all citizen demands and many are regularly ignored or repressed.

It is an indication of the changing political style of the party leadership that Chernenko, when Central Committee Secretary in 1979, called for greater attention to be given to public opinion in the forming of policy.[58] Public opinion polls carried out by sociological institutes are also means by which the authorities keep in touch with popular grouses and complaints.[59] Stephen White has quite reasonably suggested that the letters' departments of newspapers – and the role of investigative journalism – operate rather like an Ombudsman in dealing with criticisms and grievances in the Soviet Union.[60]

POLITICAL PARTICIPATION AND POLITICAL LEGITIMACY

Political participation is a crucial dimension in the modern state for two reasons. First, political legitimacy – the right of the leadership to rule – rests on consent expressed through participation by the citizen. Second, participation has a psychological dimension: various performances bind citizen to society, regardless of the political effects of the citizen's activity on the leadership. In our thinking about participation, it may be useful to distinguish between the 'normative' and the 'behavioural' approaches.

Normative theories specify in ideal terms what the desired relations between citizen and government should be. These theories emphasize that democracy can only occur when there is a positive citizen 'input': that is, the citizen actually shapes or at least controls what the government does. Writers taking up this position invoke classical theorists of democracy, such as Mill, Rousseau and G.D.H. Cole. They define 'real' participation as direct involvement in the making of decisions. In the policy process, there is no one group of rulers or leaders who make the decisions, but a 'symmetrical' system[61] in which each member of a society should have an equal chance of determining (or influencing) decisions. Many such theorists (particularly socialists) also require that participation be effective not only in the national government, but also in other groups and associations – the work-place and voluntary associations.

Behavioural theorists, by contrast, place at the centre of their analysis the actual practices of modern democratic states – usually the USA, Britain and France. The 'essence' of democracy is distilled from the processes of these states and presented as defining characteristics of 'participatory democracy'. Such theories focus on the ways that social cooperation is achieved, on how various forms of political and social activity lead to incorporation of the citizen, to its popular acceptance. Hence 'legitimacy' of government has to do with its acceptance by the masses. This approach concedes that popular 'participation' may have no real effects as political 'inputs' to the system. The relationships between rulers and ruled may be asymmetrical; but this may be taken for granted and even welcomed by the citizen. For him or her, voting may be a ritual, having a minimal effect on decisions, it may replace one team of leaders by another, but the ritual has the effect of identifying the citizen with political leadership, with accepting it as right and proper.

In contrast to the normative theory of democracy, many political scientists accept as a legitimate form of democracy a low threshold of public political awareness, and emphasize the political culture and institutions in which the citizen is located – 'public opinion', a free press, competition between political parties resolved through elections, and forms of exchange, through pressure groups, between rulers and ruled. These may be largely symbolic, and sociologists regard political legitimacy in a behavioural sense as resulting from diffuse inputs of mass loyalty. A 'legitimation crisis' occurs when the 'legitimising system does not succeed in maintaining the requisite level of mass loyalty'.[62]

Until the 1970s the notion that Soviet-type societies could be legitimate in terms of citizen participation would have been considered as ludicrous by political commentators in the West. But the reproduction of the Soviet system, its stability over time, its capability to adapt to change, the decline in the role of coercion, as well as a change in emphasis by political scientists as to what constitutes the basis of legitimacy in the West, has led to a re-examination of participation in the USSR. Discussion of participation and legitimacy has shifted from comparing the process of the Soviet Union with normative liberal-democratic theory, to comparing it with how Western democracies actually operate.

Compared with normative theories of democratic participation, or even with the 'essence' of Western democratic societies, the Soviet Union is deficient. The relationship between rulers and ruled is asymmetric: the citizens and social interests do not equally decide the outcomes or decisions of government. There is a weak political input by the citizen. Western critics of Soviet society would say that such inputs are arranged by the rulers: there are no competitive elections either between parties or candidates. The political culture does not support the articulation of individual or group interests: there is no free press, trade union activity is controlled by the government, voluntary associations are under the tutelage of the dominant political party. Dissent is repressed by force.

While it must be conceded that there is a kernel of truth to the above critique, political scientists have recognized that Western countries too have low participation inputs. The much vaunted choice of ruling party has been termed an 'alternocracy' – the masses are excluded from effective political participation in key decisions.[63]

Soviet-type Participation

The Soviet system, in turn, has been conceived of in terms of asymmetric participation, having its own democratic 'essence' derived from its political processes. Marxist–Leninst ideology gives greater power to the centre: democratic centralism has, in practice, been highly centralized. Taking part in 'party, state, parliamentary (*sovetskoy*), trade-union and controlling (*inspektsionnoy*) work'[64] occurs within the context of 'the centralisation of administration'.[65] The Soviet notion of participation has emphasized taking part in the 'outputs' of the government. This is in direct contrast to the position in Western liberal-democratic regimes where voting for the political leadership is the essence of participation. The Soviet idea is summed up in Lenin's statement that 'Our aim is to ensure that every toiler, having completed his eight hours' task in production, shall perform state duty without pay.'[66]

The Soviet system is one of mass mobilization in the carrying out of decisions, rather than one in which democracy is seen to involve symmetric participation in decision-making. Rather than in terms of 'inputs' to the political system, participation in the Soviet Union must be considered in terms of 'outputs' from the political system. This conception is at variance with both the normative and behavioural theorists considered above. Neither would consider the Soviet polity to be 'democratic'. Soviet forms of participation, however, must be considered dynamically and in the context of Russian culture.

It need hardly be repeated that the Soviet government inherited an authoritarian and parochial political culture from Tsarist Russia. The Soviet regime was rooted in centuries of absolutism. There was no tradition of inputs from society determining government policy. The population was backward and largely illiterate. Soviet policies of economic growth and industrialization required as their social counterpart a population with a 'subject' political culture. That is, one that would be able, when called on, to implement actively government decisions.

Soviet policy has been to engender supportive sentiments to the regime, to mobilize the population to build a unitary political system. The charismatic image of Lenin and Stalin was similar in character to that of Nkrumah, Nasser, Ghandi and the Ayatolla Khomeini in other twentieth-century developing states. It facilitated the identification of a mobilized population with the new Soviet state. Socialist ceremonies, such as May Day parades, rituals of 'Lenin corners' (corners in public buildings where various paraphernalia about Lenin are collected), and the pervasive image building of Stalin were essentially integrative. This was a type of audience participation.

The electoral process which has evolved in the Soviet Union should be evaluated against this background. It is an attempt to involve the masses in public activity, to break down the parochial political culture. The actual election has no political input, in the sense that it represents a choice of a candidate by the electorate. It is meant to be an affirmative act of social solidarity and approval of the regime. The high participation rate (99-plus per cent) of the population voting gives legitimacy to the Soviet system. Rather than an election in the Western sense, it is much more like a religious ceremony – like Roman Catholics affirming their allegiance to their faith. Roman Catholics, after all, do not elect their Pope, or their local priest, but the lack of popular election does not weaken legitimacy in their eyes. The Soviet election process is completely lacking in conflict. There is an emphasis on unity – of people, government and party.

One might question, however, whether the present system is effective in its goals and whether a more highly educated population is not cynical about the ceremonial aspects of the electoral system. A Soviet commentator has noted that 'the artificial forcing of mass participation does not yield effective results.'[67] More politically competent people are aware that elections lack political significance. White, in summarizing émigré reports, writes:

As many as 91.9 per cent [of a study of émigrés in Israel] believed that the average Soviet citizen could exert no significant influence upon the government ... and only 8 per cent, in another study, regarded the Soviet government as acting in the interests of the mass public ... As many as two-thirds of a group of Soviet emigres in the USA, ... believed that even individual party members could have no effective influence at all upon its internal workings (among those with higher education there was nearly unanimous agreement – 92 per cent-on this point).[68]

Émigré accounts, however, must be treated with caution; they are not representative of the population as a whole: they are derived from people who are ideologically opposed to the USSR, who are drawn disproportionately from minority groups such as Jews, from predominantly non-manual and professional employees living in the large cities. For loyal Soviet citizens – and especially among the workers and peasants – the electoral process probably has legitimating and integrating effects. As White has shrewdly observed, there is a blend of 'genuine commitment to the Soviet system and pride in its achievements combined with considerable cynicism with regard to those presently responsible for its management ...'[69] The intention of the electoral process is not, as in the West, to provide mechanisms for rule by 'alternocracy', but to politicize Soviet life with the aim of creating a moral environment conducive to people accepting government controls.

In terms of the normative theory of participation discussed above, the Soviet Union is not democratic. There is an asymmetrical relationship between rulers and ruled. The Soviet system also does not fit the approach of 'asymmetric' democracy associated with writers like S.M. Lipset, who stress the importance of 'regular constitutional arrangements for changing the governing officials and a social mechanism which permits the largest possible part of the population to influence major decisions by choosing among contenders for political office'.[70] Political participation in the Soviet Union is of a different kind. It is assumed that there is a systemic unity of interest between masses and the political elite. Political participation mainly takes the form of the people being mobilized into the political *outputs* of the government. This has had the effect of identifying the masses with the political system. Minagawa is one of the few Western commentators on the Soviet political system who has noted the positive psychological effects of direct and indirect ritual in the operations of the Soviet parliamentary system.[71] The political culture has changed over the years of Soviet power from a parochial one to a subject one. In the last two decades of the twentieth century one is likely to witness an increase in the levels of participation in political inputs. This will follow from the higher educational levels and greater political consciousness of the population. Democratic centralism contains a tension between normative democracy – an activist political input – and centralism – a directing role encouraging the carrying out of decisions. As expectations arise, a more mature population will articulate demands and these are likely to be incorporated through the existing institutional system.

Western theorists of democracy would not consider the Soviet political system to be legitimate in their ideal terms. In ideal terms, however, Western systems also leave a lot to be desired, for input participation on the part of the mass of the population is also often ineffective. As Dahl has remarked, '... in the United States generally one of the central facts of political life is that politics – local, state, national, international – lies for most people at the outer periphery of attention, interest, concern and activity.'[72] If legitimacy is viewed in terms of a psychological commitment on the part of the citizen to accept the structures and processes of government, then the Soviet system is as 'legitimate' as Western ones. It has to be understood from the standpoint of its own history, culture and traditions. 'Real' democracy does not exist in the real world.

Support for the Soviet regime has increased. It is no longer held together by the coercion which characterized the Stalin epoch. The fact of time itself has helped to legitimate the Soviet system. Generations have been born under the existing value system and have been come to 'take it for granted'. The advance of the Soviet Union as a world power gives a sense of pride and achievement to the citizen. There has been a gradual and steady improvement in the standard of living, welfare and education. This is what is experienced in the USSR – and not the model of superior consumerism of the West.

Socialist Pluralism?

The greater legitimacy (in a behavioural sense) of the Soviet political system, an increase in popular involvement together with the evidence afforded by the pressure group analysis mentioned above, has led many political scientists to reject the paradigm of 'totalitarianism' as an appropriate description of the contemporary USSR. Rather than elite domination, some writers have considered the Soviet system to be one of 'pluralism'. Such writers are influenced by the empirical studies we noted above, which show that interests are articulated within the system.

Jerry Hough is the best-known advocate of an interest group approach of 'institutional pluralism'.

The political leadership has not been intervening against the interests of major groups in the system; decisions do largely seem to be those that the specialised ministerial-party-scientific complexes could be expected to favour in the various policy areas; a wide range of proposals for incremental change are observable in the press, as is a great deal of interest representation by specialised figures within a broadly defined "leadership echelon"; the bargaining mentality seems deeply embedded in the political and administrative actors.[73]

In such a system, he says:

One can speak of "complexes" ... and of "whirlpools" ... of specialised party, state, "public", and scientific personnel working within the respective policy areas. The definition of goals formally remains the responsibility of the party leadership, but except for ensuring that the Marxist goals in social policy are pursued, the leadership is not to act with "voluntarism" – that is, it generally should follow the advice of the specialised "complexes" or "whirlpools" in their respective areas, limiting itself to a mediation of the conflicts that arise among them. In practice, policy-making power informally comes to be delegated to these complexes.[74]

It is germane to point out here that Hough is not equating 'institutional pluralism' with that of an idealized American system. His approach acknowledges conflict within Soviet society: not just in terms of the quest for power between individuals, but in terms of the assertion of influence between parts of the social and political system. It should be noted that this focus on interests and conflict does not ignore the role of a political elite, or of political leadership. The political leadership, as in Western societies, has a role of 'steering'; it also allocates the 'authoritative values in society'. Hough here is outlining a type of institutional pluralism with specialists articulating particular demands on the system. Such a process would be more comparable to the 'behaviourists' study of the political process in the USA and is open to the objections noted above. Hough leaves as 'an open question'[75] the impact of citizen participation in decisions. This viewpoint comes closer to the Soviet's own denotive view of the 'essence' of socialist democracy: the absence of economic class struggle; the leadership of the Communist Party on the principles of democratic centralism; and a socio-political identity of state and individual impossible under capitalism.[76]

The notion that the Soviet Union may be considered as 'pluralist' and that the group process of politics derived from American political science may apply to the USSR has in turn been criticized by Western political scientists. Adoption of this model of politics and its implied parallels with Western liberal-democracy has also led to objections by Soviet Marxists.[77] Alexander Groth has summarized these viewpoints when he asserts that the 'pluralist approach has only obscured major differences between political systems'.[78]

Franklyn Griffiths rejects an 'interest group' approach to the study of Soviet politics. He suggests that the political culture of the USSR does 'not greatly favor a view of interest groups as coherent units which possess a human capacity to pursue ends'. He argues that in the Soviet Union the 'aggregates' of individuals which form 'groups' are diffuse, lacking 'a will and purposes of their own in making claims'.[79] Thus Griffiths regards interest group activity as occupying at most a secondary place in the analysis of the Soviet political process. Archie Brown echoes these sentiments when he points out that groups in the Soviet Union lack 'autonomy'. Pluralistic interpretations of Soviet politics, he argues, 'tend to stress the fact that the Soviet party and state leadership does not make up a unified elite, that it is a body in which there are numerous cleavages based, for example, upon the functional and geographical division of responsibilities among different sectors of the all-Union and republican leaderships'.[80] He goes on to point out the fallacy of equating 'any influence on the party or state leadership from outside the ranks of that leadership' with a concept of pluralism. Brown faults pluralistic approaches to Soviet society on the grounds that they 'have little, if anything, to say on the question of autonomy'.[81]

The retort that may be advanced against such conceptions is that a view of 'pluralism' is adopted which is appropriate to a very limited number of Western political systems. As Brown notes: 'Western *theorists* of pluralism ... tend to stress (as a central feature of pluralism) the relative autonomy of society generally, and of organisations and groups specifically, *from* control by the government.'[82] Also Griffiths defines 'interest groups' as 'an aggregate of persons who possess certain common characteristics and share certain attitudes on public issues and who adopt distinct positions on these issues and make definite claims on those in authority'. Such discussion defines 'pluralism' and interest group activity in ways that are associated with the development of Western liberal-democratic societies. It is not the only form of 'pluralism' and interest group activity. In Western societies the degree of 'autonomy' of groups and the role of interest groups, as such, to influence the government may also be questioned as empirical facts. The power of political elites, the power of economic interests, the difficulty of non-elites to organize *effective* opposition, the prevalence of areas of effective 'non-decision-making'[83] have led many commentators to abandon the concept of pluralism as applied to Western politics.

In my view, there is an ideological element in the refusal of many political scientists to equate the Soviet political process with a type of 'pluralism' derived from Western political science. To accept such group activity on a comparable scale would seriously weaken the legitimacy and institutional supports of *Western* parliamentarianism in the shape of private property, the market, competing political parties, the division of powers, the limited role of the state and free elections. If there are similarities in terms of the process of politics, then the massive defence expenditure justified in terms of sustaining Western democracy would seem to have little point. (The same argument may also be applied in the USSR.) There is a tendency for Western critics of the Soviet system to compare the political ideal of pluralism – 'true pluralism' – in the United States with the actual nature of affairs in the USSR. In reality, 'pluralism' in the West refers to (a) the interaction between elite interests – in parties, government ministries, labour, industry and commerce; (b) the relatively open entry to such elite positions and (c) periodic and limited accountability of the political elite to the non-elite.

In attempting to grapple with a political system which is not totalitarian and does not fit the model of Western pluralism, in the late 1970s political scientists turned to the notion of corporatism to help conceptualize the Soviet system.

Corporatism

'Corporatism' is a type of institutional pluralism, rather than being an alternative to it.[84] In the late 1970s proponents of 'corporatism' reacted against both 'pluralistic' and ruling 'power elite' conceptions of advanced *Western* industrial society. Writers advocating corporatism see the rise of a new kind of socio-political 'balance'. Gone are the days of free competition in politics and economics – the people's will represented by political parties operating through parliaments, and consumers' preferences by business firms competing through the market. Corporatism attempts to take account of a balance or compact between dominant economic and political interests standing over the people in the shaping of public policy. Such dominant interests include business, trade unions and government bodies. Corporatism, as a theory of society, has three dimensions: (i) it describes the structure of dominant institutions, (ii) it defines a set of values which integrates society, and (iii) it posits an exchange relationship between the dominant groups which ensures the compliance of the masses. Panitch has defined corporatism as 'a political structure within advanced capitalism which integrates organised socio-economic producer groups through a system of representation and co-operative mutual interaction at the leadership level and of mobilization and social control at the mass level'.[85] This emphasizes the third dimension.

Winkler brings out the characteristic of values: 'Corporatism is an economic system in which the state directs and controls predominantly privately-owned business according to four principles: unity, order, nationalism and success.'[86] He points not only to the directive role of the state but also to the values of the corporatist leadership in stressing the need for collaboration for the common good, for the success of the national community.

Corporatism, in terms of the first dimension mentioned above, is a theory which is explicitly linked to capitalism: it differs from socialism in that it accepts private ownership of the means of production. It also is less unitary in conception; it concedes that there are endemic conflicts of class interests but denies the inevitability of class conflict. It assumes that there is a functional interdependence between labour and capital and that they may collaborate for mutual advantage. Competition between economic and political units may be harmful – leading to political crises and unemployment. There is a responsibility of the corporate interests to work 'in harmony' and to promote the good of society as a whole. Expansion and growth of the national community are key criteria in attributing success. The corporatist elites therefore are not 'power elites', exploiting or manipulating the non-elites, but have established a compact with them; they make concessions and ostensibly act on their behalf. The leaders of the 'constituent units' of corporatism also use their influence and power to discipline their members. This feature has been emphasized by Colin Crouch: 'What is distinctive about corporatism is that leaders are prepared to enforce on their members compliance with the terms of the agreements they have reached with their *contraparti*.'[87] Distinct from pluralist theory in which there is a multiplicity of competitive interests and in which government is a reflection of a kind of moving constellation of interests, corporatism has a limited number of constituent units. They are given recognition by 'the state' and have a monopoly over certain areas of social life. In exchange they observe certain limitations in their demands; they act as agents for the state and they 'control' their constituent parts.

This line of thinking has been applied to the Soviet Union under Brezhnev, but only in a rudimentary way.[88] Writers adopting this standpoint reject the notions of 'totalitarianism' (elite rule) and 'pluralism' as apt descriptions of the contemporary USSR. Bunce and Echols consider 'the core' of corporatism to be 'a decision-making structure in which major functional interest groups are incorporated into the policy process by the state and its leaders'.[89] The system of corporatism 'is designed to provide something for everyone, especially for those crucial to the system's operation and most particularly for those at the top. It is a system for preservation and protection, *with* growth, through planning, co-optation, and the sharing of benefits. It is, *ideally*, a comfortable and convenient coalition of interests, achieving growth and influence without stress.'[90]

Bunce and Echols have only a partial conception of 'corporatism' which is indistinguishable from a benevolent polyarchy. It is, in fact, quite reconcilable with Hough's notion of institutional pluralism – for Hough does not accept the Western normative democratic theory of a multiplicity of interest groups, passive state behaviour, and the 'unseen hand of group competition'.[91]

In corporatist theory, the state is a 'neutral' set of institutions carrying out the policies of the corporate elites. For Bunce and Echols, in the Soviet case, the state is defined as 'the state [sic] and the party'.[92] The party's role 'is not to dominate wholly, but to be the activist, the catalyst, in leading and co-ordinating the various sectors of the Soviet system. There is no doubt that the party is primary.'[93] This seems to me to undermine the corporatist notion of a number of equal and interacting, though dominant groups, whose independent and mutually adjustable interests are mediated by the government.

A second difficulty lies with the politico-economic structure of the USSR as a corporatist society. Corporatism was invented as a concept to explain the politics of a *capitalist* society. Corporatism is distinct from socialism in having *private* ownership of the means of production conjoined with public control.[94] The corporatist economy still embraces the profit motive, the circulation of capital, the extraction of surplus value and unionized labour of a kind, and the government apparatus provides a framework for profit. Thus business interests have a quite different role in a corporatist state from that in Soviet society.

The structure of corporatism also implies that the trade union leadership becomes a component of the politically dominant groups. This is not the case in the USSR. While some 50 per cent of top trade union secretaries were members of the Central Committee in 1976,[95] participation in the Politbureau is not usual. Alekandr Shelepin was the first trade union chief to hold a position in the Politbureau since the early years of the Revolution, and he held it before taking on his trade union responsibilities. Blair Ruble goes further than most Western specialists in concluding that the All-Union Central Council of Trade Unions, its departments and staff 'are one of several important political institutions involved in the formulation of Soviet labour policy'.[96] Even so, he would not claim that unions have the dominant position entailed in corporatist theories.

Hough makes the point that corporatism may be faulted as a theory because, 'like pluralism,, [it] deals almost exclusively with the input side of politics.'[97] This may be true of those writers who have applied the term to the USSR. Much writing on corporatism, however, does include reference to socio-economic structures, values and processes. (But Hough is correct to point out that democracy also has to do with 'output' in the sense of 'what society wants and which rests on consent'.[98]

What Bunce and Echols[99] correctly bring out is that the Soviet Union has a form of planning (made more pragmatic since Brezhnev). The Soviet Union also is a welfare state and has growing tendencies to consumerism.[100] But this hardly adds up to a 'corporatist state' on the West European model. What is a new dimension to our thinking about Soviet society are Winkler's principles of operation – unity, order, nationalism and success. By 'unity' is meant the achievement of economic goals through co-operative effort – not competition. Order has to do with planning and government control; the labour force has to accept discipline in return for stability in employment and a rise in living standards. Nationalism emphasizes the well-being of the nation-state: it is above individual or sectional interest. Finally, 'success' places a value on the achievement of national collective goals: there is an emphasis on effectiveness rather than efficiency. The achievement of society's goals takes precedence over individual and legal rights.[101]

An objection may be made that such stipulated values are also common to other societies such as de Gaulle's France, and Adenauer's Bundesrepublik, and they have been put forward in various degrees by other politicians such as Harold Macmillan and John Kennedy.

The major differences between the structures of traditional capitalism, corporatism and Soviet socialism may be summarized in table 8.2. The following distinctions are made: ownership is public or private; control is administrative or pluralistic; the economy is planned or competitive; and labour is strongly or weakly organized. Corporatism is seen to differ from state socialism both in terms of labour organization and kind of ownership. Its type of political control and forms of economic planning have similarities with a corporatist model. State socialism is distinguished (a) by public ownership, (b) by a planned economy, (c) by weak labour organization, and (d) by administrative control. In this context, the party provides political leadership and the various interests articulate demands.

TABLE 8.2: TYPOLOGY OF CAPITALISM, CORPORATISM AND SOVIET SOCIALISM

Control	Ownership		Economy
	Private	Public	
Administrative	Corporatism	State Socialism	Planned
Pluralistic	Capitalism	'Market' Socialism	Competitive
	Strong	Weak	
	Labour Organization		

Writers on corporatism are ambiguous as to whether it is a mode of production (an alternative to, or supercession of, capitalism), a type of government (an alternative to parliament), or a process of 'interest intermediation' (an alternative to pluralism, institutional pluralism or monism).[102] It is the last that has exercised the minds of the writers on Soviet society (Hough, Bunce and Echols, Brown). In the sense of the ways that interests are expressed and aggregated, corporatist theorists do rightly point to the two-sided nature of the leading interest organizations. These I would define as party secretariat, security police, industrial apparatus, defence/foreign affairs interests. On the one hand, they form part of the dominant political elites: they exchange with each other in the determination of public policy. On the other hand, they are also responsible to their members: they seek to defend their interests and also to control and regulate them. The writers on Soviet politics we have considered above emphasize only one aspect of political reality: those, like Bunce and Echols, who bring out the political *inputs,* and those like Brown who point to the extent of *control.* Corporatism as a theory of *interest intermediation* neatly combines both. As a theory of a mode of production or as a form of government, it is not very usefully applied to the USSR. I shall take up some of these points in the final chapter after discussing dissent and human right.

NOTES

1 H. Gordon Skilling and Franklyn Griffiths, *Interest Groups in Soviet Politics* (1971) p. 3.

2 H. Gordon Skilling; 'Interest Groups and Communist Politics Revisited', *World Politics*, vol. 36, no. 1. October 1983. p. 25. The following have been particularly influential studies. Donald Barry, 'The Specialist in Soviet Policy-Making: The Adoption of a Law', *Soviet Studies*, vol. 14 (1964) pp. 152–65. Articles by H. Morton, p. Juviler, L. Graham in Peter H. Juviler and Henry Morton (Editors), *Soviet Policy-Making* (1967). J.Schwartz and W. Keech, 'Public Influence and Educational Policy in the Soviet Union', in Roger Kanet (Ed.). *The Behavioural Revolution and Communist Studies* (1971).

3 Vernon Aspaturian, 'The Non-Russian Nationalities', in Allen Kassof, *Prospects for Soviet Society* (1968). For an excellent study of groups in education, see P.D. Stewart, 'Soviet Interest Groups and the Policy Process', *World Politics*, vol. 22, no. 1 (Oct. 1969) and J.J. Schwartz and W.R. Keech, 'Public Influence and Educational Policy in the Soviet Union', *American Political Science Review*, LXII (1968). On the voicing of other regional demands at the sessions of the Supreme Soviet, see Bess Brown, 'Concerns of the Central Asian Republics Aired at USSR Supreme Soviet', Radio Liberty RL 378 (Dec. 1979).

4 Speech at Supreme Soviet, cited by Aspaturian, p. 170.

5 Aspaturian, ibid., p. 171.

6 Ibid., p. 173.

7 *Political Succession in the USSR* (1968), pp. 85–6.

8 Jeremy Azrael, *Managerial Power and Soviet Politics* (1968), pp. 85–6; John P. Hardt and Theodore Frankel, 'The Industrial Managers', in H. Gordon Skilling and F. Griffiths, *Interest Groups in Soviet Politics*.

9 Hardt and Frankel, ibid., p. 187.

10 Azrael, *Managerial Power...*, p. 8.

11 Ibid., chapter 5.

12 Ibid., p. 125.

13 *Pravda*, 4 April 1957, cited by Azrael, ibid., p. 135.

14 *Reform in Soviet Politics* (1981). In this book Gustafson considers a wider range of policies in the environmental sphere. By the same author, 'Environmental Policy under Brezhnev: Do the Soviets Really Mean Business?', in D.R. Kelley (ed.) *Soviet Politics in the Brezhnev Era* (1980). See also: D.R. Kelley, 'Environmental Policy-Making in the USSR: The Role of Industrial and Environmental Interest Groups', *Soviet Studies*, vol. 28, no. 4 (1976).

15 Cited by Gustafson, *Reform in Soviet Politics*, p. 41.

16 Ibid., p. 41.

17 Ibid., p. 45.

18 Kelley, 'Environmental Policy-Making...', p. 589.

19 Gustafson, *Reform in Soviet Politics*, p. 158.
20 Ibid., p. 158.
21 Different interests have voiced their opinions concerning the diversion of the Siberian rivers *Irtysh* and *Ob* from the Arctic to Central Asia. On the one hand scientists have expressed concern about the environmental effects – particularly on life in the Arctic and influences on the weather. Articles in the Uzbek and Kazakh press, however, have vigorously argued in favour of the scheme, as water shortages will be acute in Central Asia by the end of the century. For a brief treatment see: 'Possible Environmental and Demographic Problems from Diversion of Siberian Rivers', Radio Liberty RL 196/83 (1983).
22 *Soviet Criminologists and Criminal Policy: Specialists in Policy-Making* (1978).
23 Ibid., p. 72.
24 Ibid., p. 79.
25 Ibid., p. 87.
26 G.Z. Anashkin, cited by Solomon, ibid., p. 82.
27 Ibid., p. 87.
28 Cited by Solomon, ibid., p. 94.
29 See ibid., pp. 96–100.
30 *Izvestiya*, cited by Solomon, ibid., p. 103.
31 Ibid., p. 149.
32 Ibid., p. 152. Italics in original.
33 Ibid., p. 160.
34 L.I. Brezhnev, *Leninskim kursom*, vol. 7 (1979), p. 616. Cited by Stephen White, 'Political Communications in the USSR', *Political Studies*, vol. 31 (1983), p. 59.
35 *Pravda*, 1 Dec. 1979, p. 4.
36 This is the term used by Brzezinski. *The New Republic*, vol. 151, no. 20 (14 Nov. 1964), cited by J. Hough, 'Political Participation in the Soviet Union', *Soviet Studies*, vol. 28, no. 1 (1976) p. 3. Hough provides a useful analysis of participation and shows the continuity in policy.
37 For details to 1977 see Jan S. Adams, 'Institutional Change in the 1970's: The Case of the USSR People's Control Committee', *Slavic Review* (Sept. 1978), p. 460. Figures for 1980, 'Sistema organov narodnogo kontrolya v SSSR', *Politicheskoe samoobrazovanie*, no. 5 (1981), p. 80.
38 Ibid., p. 81.
39 *Izvestiya*, 19 April 1979.
40 The following is based on J. Adams, 'Institutional Change ...', 'Sistema organov ...' and *Pravda*, 18 Feb. 1982.
41 'The Reality of "People's Control"', Radio Liberty, RL 3/80 (27 Dec. 1979), p. 2.
42 For a more detailed study, see Jan S. Adams, *Citizen Inspectors in the Soviet Union: The People's Control Committee* (1977).
43 For further details on *druzhiny* and comrades courts, see T.H. Friedgut, *Political Participation in the USSR*, pp. 249–261.
44 T.H. Friedgut, 'On the Effectiveness of Participatory Institutions in Soviet

Communities'. Paper presented at World Congress of Slavists, Garmisch (1980), p. 16.

45 Jan S. Adams, 'Critical Letters to the Soviet Press: An Increasingly Important Public Forum', in D.E. Schulz and J.S. Adams, *Political Participation in Communist Systems* (1981); Stephen White, 'Political Communications in the USSR: Letters to Party, State and Press', *Political Studies*, vol. 31 (1983), pp. 43–60. On the media generally, see E.P. Mickiewicz, *Media and the Russian Public* (1981); also, by the same author, 'Feedback, Surveys and Soviet Communication Theory', *Journal of Communication* (Spring 1983), pp. 97–110.

46 K. Chernenko, 'Leninskaya strategiya rukovodstva', *Kommunist*, no. 13 (1981).

47 For data 1952 to 1981, see White, 'Political Coomunications in the USSR ...' (1983), p. 52.

48 Mickiewicz, *Media and the Russian Public*, p. 68.

49 Data cited by White, 'Political Communications ...' (1983), p. 53.

50 Cited by S. White, *Political Culture and Soviet Politics* (1979).

51 Adams, 'Critical Letters to the Soviet Press ...', p. 112, 114.

52 Ibid., pp. 116–7.

53 Ibid., p. 129.

54 4 Dec. 1982. Translated in *CDSP*, vol. 35, no. 9 (30 March 1983), pp. 2–3.

55 Mickiewicz, 'Feedback, Surveys ...', p. 100.

56 Adams, 'Critical Letters to the Soviet Press ...', p. 133.

57 See discussion in: D.E. Schulz, 'Political Participation in Communist Systems: The Conceptual Frontier', in Schulz and Adams, (See Reference 45) esp. pp. 11–12.

58 *World Marxist Review*, no. 5 (May 1979).

59 See W.D. Connor, 'Public Opinion in the Soviet Union', in W.D. Connor and Zvi Y. Gitelman (eds), *Public Opinion in European Socialist Systems* (1977).

60 White, 'Political Communications ... ' pp. 57–60.

61 See H. Eckstein, 'Authority Patterns: A Structural Basis for Political Enquiry', *American Political Science Review*, vol. 67 (Dec. 1973).

62 J. Habermas, *Legitimation Crisis* (1976), p. 46.

63 See W.R. Schonfield, 'The Meaning of Democratic Participation', *World Politics*, vol. 29 (1976), pp. 146–9.

64 V.S. Semenov, *Dialektika razvitiya sotsial'noy struktury sovetskogo obshchestva* (1977), p. 143.

65 P.N. Fedoseev, 'Aktual'nye problemy obshchestvennykh nauk', *Kommunist*, no. 5 (1975), p. 33

66 Cited by T.H. Friedgut, *Political Participation in the USSR* (1979), p. 279.

67 Cited by Friedgut, ibid., p. 283.

68 S. White, *Political Culture and Soviet Politics* (1979), pp. 110–11.

69 Ibid., p. 111.

70 S.M. Lipset, *Political Man* (1963), p. 27.

71 S. Minagawa, 'The Functions of the Supreme Soviet Organs and Problems of their Institutional Development', *Soviet Studies*, vol. 27. no. 1 (January 1975), p. 52.

72 R. Dahl, *Who Governs? Democracy and Power in an American City* (1971), p. 279.
73 *The Soviet Union and Social Science Theory* (1977), pp. 9–10. See also his 'Pluralism, Corporatism and the Soviet Union', in Susan S. Solomon (ed.), *Pluralism in the Soviet Union* (1983), esp. pp. 43–5.
74 J.F. Hough and M. Fainsod, *How the Soviet Union is Governed*, (1979), p. 526. (Hough is referred to in the text as he is responsible for the passages cited.)
75 Ibid., p. 123.
76 For a comparison of Western political pluralism and socialist democratic centralism, see: G. Shakhnazarov, 'O democraticheskom tsentralizme i politicheskom plyuralizme', *Kommunist*, no. 10 (July 1979), pp. 96–104.
77 Ibid.
78 Alexander J. Groth, 'USSR: Pluralist Monolith?', *British Journal of Political Science*, vol. 9 (1979), p. 464.
79 H.G. Skilling and F. Griffiths, *Interest Groups in Soviet Politics* (1971), pp. 341, 343.
80 Archie Brown, 'Pluralism, Power and the Soviet Political System: A Comparative Perspective', in S.G. Solomon (ed.), *Pluralism in the Soviet Union* (1983), p. 69.
81 Ibid.
82 Ibid., p. 62.
83 P. Bachrach and M. Baratz, 'Decisions and Non-Decisions; An Analytical Framework', *American Political Science Review*, vol. 57 (Sept. 1963).
84 Cf. A. Brown, 'Pluralism, Power and the Soviet Political System: A Comparative Perspective', pp. 75–8.
85 L. Panitch, 'The Development of Corporatism in Liberal Democracies', in P.C. Schmitter and G. Lehmbruch, *Trends Towards Corporatist Intermediation* (1979), p. 123.
86 J.T. Winkler, 'Corporatism', *European Journal of Sociology*, vol. 17, no. 1 (1976), p. 103.
87 Colin Crouch, 'Pluralism and the New Corporatism: A Rejoinder', *Political Studies*, vol. 31, no. 3 (Sept. 1983), p. 455.
88 Valerie Bunch and John M. Echols III, 'Soviet Politics in the Brezhnev Era: "Pluralism" or "Corporatism"', in Donald R. Kelley (ed.) *Soviet Politics in the Brezhnev Era* (1980).
89 Ibid., p. 3.
90 Ibid., p. 7. Italics in original.
91 See Bunce and Echols, p. 4. Hough, in fact, in commenting on the article by Bunce and Echols concedes that 'corporatism' as they define it is better than their notion of 'pluralism', but he argues that the utility of the notion of institutional pluralism is not diminished by Bunce and Echols. 'Pluralism, Corporatism and the Soviet Union', in Susan G. Solomon (ed.) *Pluralism in the Soviet Union* (1983), esp. pp. 39–40, 55–6.
92 Bunce and Echols, 'Soviet Politics in the Brezhnev Era ... ', p.7.

93 Ibid., p. 11.
94 Winkler, 'Corporatism', p. 113.
95 In 1956, the figure was 33 per cent and in 1971, 57 per cent. Blair Ruble, *Soviet Trade Unions* (1981), p. 38.
96 Ibid., p. 41.
97 Hough, 'Pluralism, Corporatism...', pp. 46, 55.
98 Ibid., p. 44.
99 See Bunce and Echols, 'Soviet Politics in the Brezhnev Era...', pp. 12–13.
100 Ibid., pp. 15–16.
101 For a more detailed account, see Winkler, 'Corporatism', p. 106–108.
102 See discussion in L. Panitch, 'Recent Theorisations of Corporatism: Reflections on a Growth Industry', *British Journal of Sociology*, vol. 31, no. 2 (1980).

9

DISSENT AND HUMAN RIGHTS

The different political structure and ideology of capitalism and socialism have important consequences for the manifestation of dissent and opposition. Under Western liberal democracy, dissent and opposition are recognized and institutionalized, and this may involve neutralizing rather than accepting critical policy; it may be acknowledged, but respectfully ignored. Groups advocating policies which the political elites consider to be harmful to the integrity of the existing order are excluded from the formal political arena. The stuff of democratic Western politics is about different solutions to accepted political problems. In Britain, topics such as the legitimacy of the monarchy, workers' management of industry, the operations of the intelligence and prison services, animal rights, the sanctity of private property and the effects of nuclear war are publicly discussed and often cause embarrassment to the incumbents of political power. Such issues, however, are at present the concern of articulate minorities and the government does not feel threatened by them. In the theory of liberal democracy, the legitimacy of the political order entails tolerence of minorities to campaign for their objectives. Mass demonstrations are a safety value for political protest. They allow for the expression of critical comment without seriously hindering the activity of the established political elites.

In the Soviet Union, opposition and dissent cannot be ignored by the state; they are not recognized as legitimate and institutionalized. Marxism–Leninism defines Soviet society as 'developed socialism' which allows no place for 'dissent' or 'opposition'. As the party is the expression of the will of the people, opposition to party rule defines dissidents as enemies of the people. The activity of dissidents seeks to make illegitimate the claim that the institutions of the Soviet state reflect the political unity of Soviet society, and it weakens the state's authority to resolve differences. The activity of groups acting outside the legitimate channels criticizing the leadership and its policies is considered to be harmful to the integrity of the

270

Soviet order. Such groups are suppressed in a more systematic and ruthless way than in Western democracies. What may be innocuous political activities in terms of the practice of Western democratic states become in the Soviet Union manifestations of 'dissent' involving penal sanctions. This is because the party is the leading political institution and is seen as *the* legitimate articulator of group interests. Activity outside of its purview undermines its authority. Under pluralism, a tenet of the democratic process is the freedom of associations to campaign publicly to assert their own definition of their interest. Under democratic centralism, as interpreted in the Soviet Union, such interests have to be manifested within the context of the leading role of the Communist Party.

In the study of Soviet politics in the West, the suppression of dissent figures largely as an area of concern, whereas Western political scientists pay little attention to comparable activity (i.e. revolutionary and 'system-rejective' groups) in their own society. This is not solely because of the international competition between capitalism and communism, but because the capitalist state's tolerance of dissent does much to disarm it, and the dissident does not become more alienated and hostile to society. Under the Soviet system, harsh treatment of the dissident and his stigmatization make him more alienated, magnify his deviance and lead him to define his identity around the facts of deviance.

The Dissenters

The 'dissent' movement in the USSR is small and of very little political significance *internally*. Roy Medvedev has rightly cautioned Western correspondents not to exaggerate the extent of disaffection. 'The overwhelming majority of the population unquestionably sanction the government's power and show no particular wish to have a run-in with the authorities by voicing grievances.'[1] In 1979 he estimated that 'the number of former dissidents livings abroad... is much greater than the number of dissidents remaining in the USSR.'[2] In 1980, defining 'dissidents' as people who work 'outside the system' in order to change it, he estimates that there were only a 'handful of dissidents'.[3] The various forms of protest have declined significantly since the 1970s. He makes the telling point that 'barely twenty' people 'all of them with one foot in the courtroom' signed a petition on behalf of Sakharov, whereas for the trials of the 1960s 'there were thousands of signatures, hundreds for Sinyavsky, Daniel, Ginzburg and Galantsov.'[4] This is due to the twin effects of repression by the authorities and emigration of many dissidents.[5]

The dissident groups are heterogeneous in outlook, and it would be erroneous to conceive of them as providing a single or consistent critique of

Soviet society: they range from Solzhenitsyn's opposition to large-scale secular society, to Medvedev's demands for intellectual freedom within a reformed Marxist–Leninist framework. The 'democratic opposition' is based on concern for human rights, freedom of information through the media and the maintenance of legality.

Rudolf Tökés, following a review of the literature, has defined 'Soviet dissent' as '[A]n ideologically heterogeneous political reform movement that is motivated by both shared and constituency-specific grievances with which the dissidents have sought to promote change by making demands on the political leadership to alleviate or eliminate unacceptable conditions'.[6] This definition applies to many different positions, some of which would not be defined as 'dissent' or 'opposition' by the political leadership in the USSR, and their advocates would not be subject to penal sanctions. Jerry Hough has aptly pointed out that the use of the word 'dissent' has expanded to a point beyond all recognition. 'People striving to achieve personal goals are engaged in dissent; consumerism is dissent; proposals to increase the use of market mechanisms are dissent; a failure to work conscientiously is dissent; the advocacy of efficiency and professionalism is "an obviously dissident ideology" ....'[7]

One defining characteristic needs to be added to take account of Hough's structures: such views must be expressed as demands outside the legitimate political system. 'Dissent' is not just concerned with the content of criticism, but with the manner and style of its execution. It must also be perceived by the regime to be a threat – real or potential – to its legitimacy, stability and coherence. This is why 'dissent' in the USSR has such a wide connotation.

Many dissenting writers in the USSR could be considered as 'loyal critics' rather than 'dissidents'. Some, such as Evtushenko, have at times received official approval. His poem 'The Heirs of Stalin'[8] was published in *Pravda* (the official party newspaper) and condemned those who had supported him. The official party attitude to writers with critical thoughts about certain aspects of Soviet society (political corruption, anti-Semitism, individual morality) has fluctuated. At one time Khrushchev gave his blessing to anti-Stalinist literature. But after the initial cultural thaw initiated by the publication of Dudintsev's *Not By Bread Alone* and Solzhenitsyn's *One Day in the Life of Ivan Denisovich*, the Soviet cultural authorities clamped down on the more outspoken criticism of the regime associated with the works of Sinyavski, Voznesensky, Nekrasov, Akhmadulina, Vinokurov and others. Khrushchev came out strongly against them: 'Anyone who advocates the idea of political coexistence in the sphere of ideology is, objectively speaking, sliding down to positions of anti-communism. The enemies of communism would like to see us ideologically disarmed.'[9]

The trial of Daniel and Sinyavski is instructive in showing the way that estranged groups are prevented from articulating their interests: they are suppressed because their activity threatens (at least in the eyes of the elites) the integrity of the system. The charge against the two authors was that they broke article 70, section 1 of the Criminal Code of the RSFSR:

Agitation or propaganda carried out with the purpose of subverting or weakening the Soviet regime or in order to commit particularly dangerous crimes against the state, the dissemination for the said purposes of slanderous inventions defamatory to the Soviet political and social system, as well as the dissemination or production or harbouring for the said purposes of literature of similar content, are punishable by imprisonment for a period of from six months to seven years and with exile from two to five years, or without exile, or by exile from two to five years.[10]

The public prosecutor argued that the work of the 'so called "Soviet literary underground" was a form of "ideological subversion" in the interests of the "imperialist reactionaries" '. Sinyavski, it was alleged, had ridiculed the Soviet system and the principles of Marxism–Leninism; he had 'maliciously slandered Marxist theory and the future of human society'. Similar charges were made against Daniel who had depicted 'Soviet society as being in a state of moral and political decay'. His story suggested that the entire Soviet people is to blame for the cult of personality, that 'our prisons are within us', that 'the Government is unable to give us our freedom', that 'we sent ourselves to prison'.[11] Sinyavsky and Daniel, like Solzhenitsyn, were harshly dealt with because they allowed their criticisms to be published in the West under the pseudonyms of Abram Tertz and Nikolay Arzhak. These in turn were broadcast back to the USSR by Radio Liberty. Sinyavski was sentenced to seven years and Daniel to five years in a labour camp.

Hospitalization

Enforced hospitalization is often said to be a means used to silence and rehabilitate critics of the regime. It is important to bear in mind that our knowledge of the process of confinement to mental hospitals is based on the testimony of ex-patients and their supporters. There is then an inherent bias in the sources. Even when inmates are freed and subsequently examined in the West and found to be cleared of mental illness, it may be said to be consequent to the treatment and not indicative of the patient's mental state before it. However, so much information has been collected which points to abuse of power, that it cannot be dismissed.[12] Bloch and Reddaway document 210 cases of 'mentally healthy dissenters compulsorily confined to psychiatric hospitals'.[13] This count was for the period 1962 to 1976. Fireside estimates that between 1,000 and 2,000 people are 'forcibly treated in institutions for the criminally insane to "cure" them of their urges for free expression'.[14]

The case of the internment of Zhores Medvedev has been well documented and may be used to illustrate the process. It appears to be a sincere and honest account.

Zhores Medvedev wrote a critical study of Lysenkoism[15] in the early 1960s. This circulated in *samizdat* (i.e. illegally produced publications) form in 1962. Medvedev's work was publicly criticized and he was dismissed from his post. His work was considered 'ideological sabotage' by Lysenko's supporters and critical notes appeared about him in the *Agricultural Gazette* and *Pravda*.[16] Medvedev's book was taken to the West and appeared under the title of *The Rise and Fall of T.O. Lysenko* in 1969 (Columbia University Press). Medvedev also dabbled in politics (in a general sense), and a copy of his *Fruitful Meetings Between Scientists of the World*, which he completed in 1968, came into the hands of the KGB in February 1970. Here Medvedev detailed the controls over scientists at conferences abroad and he exposed the postal censorship. This was the immediate prelude to the forcible detention of Zhores in a psychiatric hospital. On 29 May 1970, he was seized in his flat and sent for examination at the Kaluga mental hospital. No court proceedings were involved. It is assumed that the authorities wished to punish Medvedev, but felt that a public airing of his case would give him publicity. Roy Medvedev asserts that the villains behind the forcible confinement were the local party officials and the KGB. 'The Obninsk authorities were not powerful enough by themselves to induce the Kaluga mental hospital to take such a radical step. The whole thing, of course, must have been co-ordinated with the Kaluga Party Committee and the Kaluga branch of the KGB.... Most likely of all [the whole operation was under the control of] some leading official of the regional Party Committee or the KGB.'[17]

If Roy Medvedev's account is correct, the KGB acted without recourse to the Central Committee of the Party. He writes: '.... at the offices of the Central Committee, [one] of their officials, Comrade N., listened to me attentively and took copious notes as I talked.... After speaking to someone on the 'phone he assured me that nobody on the Central Committee had anything to do with the events.... or, indeed, knew anything about them. "It sometimes happens that certain officials act on their own", N. said and promised that all I had told him would be reported to the leadership of the Central Committee as soon as possible.'[18] Later in the book, it was reported by Zhores Medvedev that the KGB had denied any involvement in the affair and that 'the whole episode was the work of the local authorities.'[19]

We have no account from the authorities' side as to why he was referred for psychiatric analysis. Roy Medvedev writes that the diagnosis was said to have revealed a 'psychopathological personality' with 'paranoid tendencies'. The symptoms were 'an exaggerated opinion of himself' and 'poor adaptation to the social environment'; Zhores 'showed "excessively scrupulous" attention to detail in his general writings'.[20] Such diagnoses do not account for the apprehension of the subject and do not explain the motives of the authorities.

Complaints were probably made about Zhores Medvedev by those riled by his criticisms: the Lysenkoist institutions, the Censorship Department of the Post Office, organizations responsible for international scientific exchanges and tourism.[21] Zhores Medvedev believed that the KGB was responsible for the action. 'The main reason for mounting this operation must have been my manuscript about international scientific co-operation ....'[22]

Following internal agitation and international expressions of concern, Medvedev was released. He subsequently left the USSR, was stripped of Soviet citizenship for 'actions discrediting the high title of citizen of the USSR'. He now lives in England.

The above discussion of the processes of the courts and confinement to mental hospitals illustrates the fact that individual liberties are not protected against the state machinery. While *all* police forces repress activities which threaten the political order, in terms of socialist values many of the Soviet practices may be condemned. There is some circumstantial evidence that the KGB is not effectively controlled. Before generalizing about the significance of dissent, the phenomenon may be further analysed by considering the different objectives of the dissenting groups and individuals.

Types of Dissent

Tökés has identified two 'basic intellectual tendencies' among Soviet dissenters: competing conceptions of *rationality* and those of *morality* on the basis of which they hope to undermine the regime's authority.[23] In analysing the diverse nature of dissent in the USSR, Tökés has suggested that it may be divided into three basic ideological positions: the 'moral-absolutist', the 'instrumental-pragmatic' and 'anomic-militant'.[24]

By *moral-absolutist* is meant 'programs and programmatic statements that represent alternative conceptions of morality and ethical validity and an unconditional reaffirmation of spiritual values over expedient, pseudo-scientific philosophies justifying man's inhumanity to man in the name of modernisation and technical progress or the attainment of a utopian end-state of political development'. Such a grouping includes religious critics, philosophers, poets and writers such as Bukovsky, Galantsov, Amalrik, Solzhenitsyn.

Instrumental-pragmatic ideologies are 'programs, statements, and other forms of public or semi-public communication that represent competing interpretations of the Marxist classics (particularly Lenin); alternative methods of modernisation and scientific progress; and a commitment, expressed in language ranging from the aesopian to the most explicit, to experimentation free of political control, pursuit of scientific (that is, empirically verifiable rather than ideologically orthodox) truths, and, most importantly, demands for the unconditional official endorsement of the principle of intellectual autonomy in scientific matters'. Soviet academics are the main occupational group in this category. They seek to persuade the political elite to act in accord with their views. Examples here are: Sakharov, Medvedev, Dzyuba.

The *anomic-militant* ideologies include 'programs and statements that represent affirmations of national identity or spiritual autonomy or expressions of extreme alienation from the political philosophies, institutions, laws and governing practices of the Soviet system'. Groups advocating these ideas are combative and confrontational. They include spokesmen for national and religious rights. They often seek a more authoritarian type of government of a pre-modern type.

It is impossible here to discuss all the various groups and individuals.[25] As examples we shall describe the critiques of Solzhenitsyn, Sakharov and Roy Medvedev and, in the context of a discussion of claims for human rights, the Free Trade Union Movement.

'Moral Absolutists': Solzhenitsyn

Aleksandr Solzhenitsyn was born in December 1918 and reared under Soviet socialism. His birthplace was Kislovodsk in the Caucasus. His family were rich landowners before the revolution when their property was confiscated.[26] He studied at Rostov University and (by correspondence) at the Moscow Institute of Philosophy, Literature and History. He then served in the war and was decorated twice while serving in the artillery. In February 1945, Solzhenitsyn was arrested, tried and found guilty of anti-Soviet agitation and of organizing an anti-Soviet group. He was sentenced to eight years' imprisonment, ostensibly because he was disgruntled with conditions and criticized Stalin in a letter to a friend.[27] His experience in prison is a major concern of his early novels.

The political position of Solzhenitsyn has changed from 'a radical opposition to the Soviet bureaucratic regime into an authoritarian moralising'.[28] His writing in *One Day in the Life of Ivan Denisovich* (1962), *For the Good of the Cause* (1971), *Cancer Ward* (1968) and *The First Circle* (1968) was a critique of bureaucratic mis-deeds in Soviet society. Here the author bitterly and sceptically contrasts the ideology of Soviet socialism with its reality. He caricatures the social elites and Stalinist political leadership and exposes the rhetoric and privilege of those in established positions. The contrast is always made with those who are the objects of authority – prisoners and patients. In these early novels, the socialist framework is accepted critically and Solzhenitsyn advocates democratization and ethical renewal. Only *For the Good of the Cause, One Day in the Life*... and three short stories were published in the Soviet Union, though *Cancer Ward* was once set up in type. The biting satire and political cynicism caused offence to the political authorities; in these books there was also, in an undeveloped form, an ideology of a Russian populism and of an ethical critique of the Soviet system.

It is quite possible that greater tolerance by the censors and the security police (KGB) would have led him to work within the regime as a loyal critic exposing corruption, degeneration and lawlessness. A point I made above is that the suppression and intimidation of criticism does not eradicate it, but creates greater alienation and resentment. In 1965 his personal papers, including a draft of *The First Circle*, were seized by the police. His *One Day in the Life of Ivan Denisovich* was not given official recognition by the award of a Lenin prize. It became impossible for his work to be published in the USSR.

Solzhenitsyn's early cynicism turned to pessimism, his ethical socialism was transmitted into a religious morality, his anti-bureaucratic anti-Stalinism developed into anti-communism, his populism became an extreme Russian nationalism. He clearly was alienated and hostile to the Soviet regime. These sentiments were expressed in his *Letter to the Fourth Writers' Conference* (1967), *August 1914* (1972), *Gulag Archipelago* (1974, 1975), 'Letter to the Soviet Leaders' (1974), *One Word of Truth* (Noble Prize speech) (1972) and *Lenin in Zurich* (1975).

In 1969, Solzhenitsyn was expelled from the Writers' Union of the USSR. Of the many denunciations of Solzhenitsyn in the USSR, the statement by the Secretariat of the Board of the RSFSR Writers' Union is indicative of such criticism:

... It is evident from his actions and his statements that he has actually joined the opponents of the Soviet system.

During the last two years a number of letters, statements, manuscripts and other writings of Aleksandr Solzhenitsyn have been delivered abroad through illegal channels. This material was published in thousands of copies in different languages,

Russian included, by many foreign newspapers, magazines and publishing houses, among them the *Posev* and *Grani*, two white-guard, openly anti-Soviet publishing houses.

...

It is noteworthy that the centres abroad, which engage in anti-Soviet activity, use Solzhenitsyn's works not only in their political struggle against the Soviet Union but also for financing the programmes of various subversive organisations.

...

To judge by his letter, he sees nothing shameful in the fact that his work has become a weapon in the hands of our class enemy. He denounces the very notion of class struggle, in fact he jeers at it . . . .'[29]

His 'Letter to the Soviet Leaders' (written in September 1973, published in *The Sunday Times*, 3 March 1974)[30] summarizes his ideological position. He makes it clear that he is not a socialist; he rejects and opposes Marxism, though in fact he is concerned with the ideology of Soviet Marxism–Leninism. He singles out two major 'failures' of the Soviet Union's policy: opposing world imperialism, and supporting communist movements abroad. These faults stem from 'exact adherence to the precept of Marxism–Leninism'. Russians, says Solzhenitsyn, have been and are being asked to 'die in an ideological war – and mainly for a dead ideology!' He rejects Marxism as being a 'primitive, superficial economic theory':

It was mistaken when it forecast that the proletariat would be endlessly oppressed and would never achieve anything in a bourgeois democracy . . . . It missed the point when it asserted that the prosperity of the European countries depended on their colonies . . . . It was mistaken through and through in its prediction that socialism could only ever come to power by an armed uprising . . . . And the picture of how the whole world would rapidly be overtaken by revolutions and how states would soon wither away was sheer delusion, sheer ignorance of human nature . . . Marxism is not only not accurate, not only not a science, has not only failed to predict a single event in terms of figures, quantities, time scale or locations . . . .

Solzhenitsyn rejects the whole ideology of Marxism–Leninism. Such an ideology is 'intolerable', 'nothing constructive rests on it, it is a sham, cardboard, theatrical prop – take it away and nothing will collapse, nothing will even wobble.'

What, then, does Solzhenitsyn seek to put in the place of (Soviet) Marxism–Leninism? He has no programme but rather asserts a set of values. He is a Russian patriot: '. . . it is the fate of the Russian and Ukrainian peoples that preoccupies me above all . . . .' He is an (orthodox) Christian: 'I myself see Christianity today as the only living spiritual force capable of undertaking the spiritual healing of Russia.' He seeks to reassert traditional values: 'A civilisation greedy for "perpetual progress" has now choked and is on its last legs.' Solzhenitsyn is opposed to more than the rule of the Communist Party: he rejects the doctrine of progress originating in the Enlightenment – 'The whirlwind of progressive ideology swept in on us from the West ... has tormented our soul quite enough ....' He is against the large-scale urban-industrial order, against rapid economic growth. 'The urban life under which by now as much as half our population is doomed to live is utterly unnatural.... An economy of non-giantism with small-scale, though highly developed, technology will not only allow for but will necessitate the new building of towns in the old style.' Solzhenitsyn is a traditionalist, a populist, a nationalist and is opposed to Marxism and modern large-scale industrialism.

Solzhenitsyn's politics involves a return to a patriarchial authoritarian order. He wants 'kindness' added to the existing state apparatus. His earlier democratic aspirations have gone. He acknowledges the absence of a democratic tradition in Russia. An authoritarian regime can only guarantee stability; unlike its communist counterpart such an 'authoritarian order' would be based on 'a strong moral foundation ... not the ideology of universal violence but Christian Orthodoxy'.

Since his exile to the West, he has become critical of Western democracies.[31] There is a flabbiness, lack of will and moral inertia in Western society. '... I could not recommend your society in its present state as an ideal for the transformation of ours. Through intense suffering our country has now achieved a spiritual development of such intensity that the western system in its present state of spiritual exhaustion does not look attractive.'[32]

Solzhenitsyn's opposition is a curious almost mirror-image of the present Soviet system. Perhaps because of this it is taken so seriously by the KGB. Its authoritarianism, its links with Russian tradition, its (Christian) religiosity together with an opposition to liberal-democratic and parliamentary procedures have a resonance in common with the established Soviet (and Stalinist) right-wing.

'Instrumental Pragmatists': Sakharov and Medvedev

Andrei Sakharov, who was born in 1921, is another critic of Soviet power reared under socialism. The son of a Moscow physics professor, he attended Moscow University and graduated in 1942. He served in the war and then became a leading participant in research on nuclear power. He was elected a full member of the Academy of Sciences in 1953 and awarded the Order of Socialist Labour (the highest civilian honour) on three occasions. Sakharov then is a person who has been accorded fame and prestige under and by the Soviet regime.

Until 1966, Sakharov was an 'internal critic' of aspects of Soviet policy.

He opposed nuclear tests and Khrushchev's policy of requiring university students to have pre-university experience. He campaigned against Lysenkoism. In 1966 he signed a letter to the Twenty-Third Party Congress opposing the rehabilitation of Stalin. He protested against the Soviet law of slander of the state.

In 1968 was published in the West his monograph *Reflections on Progress, Co-existence and Intellectual Freedom* (London, 1968). Here Sakharov argued that 'socialism and capitalism are capable of long-term development, borrowing positive elements from each other and actually coming closer to each other in a number of essential aspects.' Like Khrushchev, Sakharov regarded the prevention of world war and nuclear conflict to be the foremost task of modern government. He advocated co-operation between capitalist and socialist states to work out a 'broad programme of struggle against world hunger'.[33] He opposed 'irrational and irresponsible' censorship, the violation of all human rights; he wanted an amnesty for political prisoners and the complete 'exposure of Stalin'. All these proposals, to my mind, are in keeping with political developments under Khrushchev. The only exceptional programmatic statement was his suggestion that the Soviet Union move in the direction of a Western-type democratic system.

The clamp-down on dissenters in the Soviet Union, the military intervention in Czechoslovakia and the withdrawal by the authorities of Sakharov's clearance for scientific work further alienated him from the Soviet system. In 1970, he became a founder of the Moscow Human Rights Committee. He advocated the cause of the Crimean Tatars,[34] and he took up the cause of dissidents such as Amalrik and Bukovsky. In 1973 he was publicly decried in *Literaturnaya Gazeta*, the journal of the Writers Union, and denounced in the Academy of Sciences.

His work thereafter took a more virulent and hostile form to the Soviet authorities. In his essays *My Country and the World*[35] he likened the USSR to a totalitarian state and criticized the lack of vigilance in the West in 'its stand against totalitarianism'.[36]

He equated Soviet socialism with 'a one-party system, power in the hands of a grasping and incompetent bureaucracy, the expropriation of all private property, terrorism on the part of the Cheka or its counterparts, the destruction of productive forces, with their subsequent restoration and expansion at the cost of countless sacrifices by the people, and violence done to free conscience and convictions'.[37] In his conclusion Sakharov called for twelve major reforms of the Soviet system: the widening of the economic reforms of 1965 involving 'full autonomy for plants, factories, etc. in matters of economics, production and personnel policy; partial denationalisation of all types of economic and societal activity, probably excluding heavy industry, major transportation, and communications ... especially in the area of services ... partial decollectivisation and government encouragement of the private sector'; full amnesty for all political prisoners; a law giving the freedom to strike; 'a series of legislative acts guaranteeing real freedom of convictions, freedom of conscience, and freedom to circulate information; ... legislation providing that the adoption of the most important decisions ... be publicly disclosed and subject to public accountability'; 'a law assuring the freedom to choose one's place of residence and of employment within the country; legislation guaranteeing the freedom to leave the country ... and to return to it; banning all forms of Party and official privileges .... Equal rights for all citizens ...'; the rights of Soviet republics to secede; a multiparty system; currency reform, the convertability of the ruble; and the abolition of the foreign trade monopoly by the government.[38]

From the mid-1970s, Sakharov took up the cause of many Soviet people whom he felt were discriminated against. In his Nobel Prize speech in 1975 (*Peace, Progress and the Rights of Man*) he championed the cause of Soviet political prisoners and exiles. He publicly supported the claims of Jews and Germans who wanted to emigrate, the claims of Crimean Tatars who sought to return to the Crimea, and many other groups.[39] In 1979, he signed a document on the anniversary of the Molotov–Ribbentrop Pact which said that the latter had 'denoted the end of the independence of Estnia, Latvia, and Lithuania .... As supporters of the principle of equality, and self-determination of peoples, respecting the right of every people to decide independently its own destiny, we consider that in the given historical situation the question of self-determination for Lithuania, Latvia and Estonia should be decided by means of a referendum conducted in each of these countries under conditions guaranteeing the free expression of the will of the people.'[40]

In January 1980, Sakharov was arrested and sent into 'administrative expulsion' to the town of Gorky.

On January 22 (1980) in Moscow, KGB agents forcibly took me to the deputy prosecutor general, Alexander M. Rekunkov, who informed me that I was being stripped of my awards and would be sent into exile. He produced only the decree of the Supreme Soviet concerning the awards, giving an impression however, that the decree also called for exile. But that was not so.

I still do not know which branch of government or who personally made the decision to have me exiled. All my enquiries meet only with silence. In any event, the decision is illegal and is in violation of the constitution. In two letters to Rekunkov and in a telegram to the chairman of the KGB, Yuri V. Andropov, I demanded revocation of the illegal exile order and said I was prepared to face an open trial ....[41]

The Soviet justification for Sakharov's expulsion from Moscow was that his activity was in 'increasingly open, clear and ostentatious conflict with the demands of Soviet legislation and our criminal code'. A Soviet commentator complained that he had spread 'slander against Soviet reality and Soviet policy'. He had advocated

a boycott of scientific and cultural contact ... [He was] an accomplice of imperialist organs in their activity directly aimed ... [at] the vital interests of all Soviet people.... He approved the American administration's decision to employ economic sanctions against the Soviet Union ... [He] acted as though he were an official of an imperialist state's apparatus and expressed the readiness to serve its interests.... He had conveyed, or tried to convey, abroad a number of pieces of information relating to the most serious problems of our defence capacity ... He had also made attempts to set up a kind of organization of so-called 'dissidents' ... an organisation that could coordinate their activity aimed against the socialist countries' interests.[42]

Sakharov's case illustrates a number of points about dissidents in the Soviet Union. First, 'within-system' demands, wrongly handled, as in this case, snowball into criticisms of the system. Further, police reaction leads to dissent becoming not just a dimension of a person's life, but the centre of life. Second, the KGB takes the political and social system seriously. Criticism of the system and its leaders is slander, which involves sanctions in the loss of individual freedom. Third, administrative measures are largely the prerogative of the security police. The order of the Presidium of the Supreme Soviet did not involve his exclusion from Moscow. Sakharov was never charged or made to defend himself before a court. The KGB has considerable discretion and power to act in what it thinks is in the defence of the Soviet political order. Such activity in practice can go quite unchallenged in any public Soviet forum.

The Case of Roy Medvedev

Roy Medvedev, the twin brother of Zhores, was born in 1925. His father was a Marxist and was a teacher of dialectical materialism at the Tolmachev Military-Political Academy; he was arrested in 1938 and died in Kolyma labour camp in 1941. Like Solzhenitsyn and Sakharov, Roy Medvedev was reared under Soviet power, but unlike them he came from a family which had a positive commitment to its ideology. He studied philosophy and education at Leningrad University, became a teacher and head of a secondary school and then a research fellow at the Academy of Pedagogical Sciences where he published two books on vocational education. In 1956, after the Twentieth Party Congress, he joined the Communist Party and then began to study the history of the Stalin period.

He completed his book in 1968. It was submitted for publication to a Soviet publishing house but rejected.[43] That year a reappraisal of the (negative) activities of Stalin was being conducted by the party. In opposition to what he considered rehabilitation, Medvedev wrote to the editor of the party's theoretical journal, *Kommunist.*

Unknown to Roy Medvedev, this letter was later published in the émigré journal *Posev*. It is alleged that the Soviet security police was responsible for communicating this letter, thereby discrediting Medvedev and, by implication, his anti-Stalinist views.[44] What might have been permissible in a Soviet publication was regarded as subversion when published by the émigrés. Medvedev was subsequently expelled from the party. His position was further weakened by another letter published in *Posev* which Medvedev later disavowed. The reasons given for expelling him from the party were that he 'considered erroneous everything the party had done between 1920 and 1940, that [he] denied it was building socialism in our country, that [he] borrowed [his] views mainly from bourgeois sources, that [he] had maligned the party's achievements in strengthening the army and preparing the nation for war; ... on the pretext of criticizing the cult of Stalin, [he] had defamed the entire Soviet people, together with the State and social system.'[45] Following his expulsion from the party in 1969, he resigned his appointment in 1971, and has since been working on his own account.

Medvedev's interpretation of Stalin was an extension of Khrushchev's and could well be accommodated in a Soviet critique of Stalin.[46] He regards Stalin as a criminal guilty of crimes against humanity. His support for Marxism–Leninism, however, is unqualified and he applauds the ideology and will of the Communist Party; like Khrushchev he regards the Soviet system as basically sound. In commenting on the process by which his brother had been wrongly put into a psychiatric hospital, he noted: 'it must be stressed that the defects of our political structure are in no way distinctive features of the Soviet socialist state or inherent to it. These defects can and must be corrected within the framework of Soviet socialist society, and this will give our political and economic system not only more flexibility, but also make it stronger and more stable.'[47] He argues for free debate and greater rights for 'within-system' criticism: '.... A reasonable opposition is necessary in any well-organised society. This is especially true in highly complex modern societies, in which any important decision requires free debate and consideration of different points of views and independent opinions.'[48] Such freedom of criticism, of socialist 'pluralism', he sees as fundamental to Marxism–Leninism. A one-party totalitarianism 'is basically anti-Marxist and anti-Leninist'.[49]

If the above accounts are true, the KGB actively turned a legitimate 'within-system' critique into the status of dissent. Though unable to gain publication in the USSR, the views expressed in 'The Problem of Democratisation and the Problem of Detente'[50] are system-supportive rather than destructive. He writes that the Soviet dissidents are provocative, guided more by emotion than political acumen. He explicitly criticizes both Sakharov and Solzhenitsyn. He argues that change is likely to come from within the Soviet Party and not from being thrust upon it by pressures from without. Especially counter-productive are appeals made by the Western media. In his view, it is the internal political right-wing in the Central Committee and police, those continuing a Stalinist policy and having a Stalinist mentality, that have to be removed – as a result of pressure 'from the inside'. '.... [A] reorganisation of the methods and forms of leadership in social affairs and the economy, an expansion of political and civil rights, i.e. expansion of socialist democracy, cannot, we repeat, be the result of evident pressure from the popular masses and the intelligentsia but rather the result of an initiative "from above".[51]

Medvedev has brought upon himself the wrath of his political adversaries not only by his criticism of Stalin voiced in the USSR and abroad, but also for his opposition to the KGB. Part of his criticism of Stalin fell also on the police executive. The KGB he regards as a major maker of policy – independently of other groups in the party.[52]

Medvedev, while critical of the leadership of the USSR, still regards Soviet socialism to be a system superior to capitalism. More free discussion and the dissemination of information from the West, he argues,

would consolidate Soviet power and render it more attractive and flexible. It would make it possible to distinguish between socialism as a political system and Soviet power, between the government structure of socialist society in general and the particular regime that now rules the USSR, which is only one variant ... and not the best, by far ... of state socialism. Socialism and Soviet power have the potential capacity to refute any criticism from the west because, theoretically, socialism represents a higher stage of human advancement than capitalism does. The Soviet Union hasn't yet achieved advanced socialism, only a complex mixture of socialism and pseudo-socialism.[53]

HUMAN RIGHTS AND THE MOVEMENT FOR HUMAN RIGHTS

The ideological positions discussed above are criticisms by individuals of the present Soviet political system. These tendencies are part of the dissident protest, but they do not constitute a political movement. One of the most vocal and important dissenting groups in recent years has been that concerned with the implementation of human rights. Such demands are put by people who are self-defined as Marxists or democrats. The civil rights movement seeks to change the balance of forces between state and citizen and argues that citizens have independent rights under socialism. By 'rights' here we mean 'a cluster of ethical liberties, claims, powers and immunities that together constitute a system of ethical autonomy possessed by an individual ... vis a vis the state'.[54] This definition is a liberal conception of rights and is implicit in the dissenters' claims for the implementation of their individual rights against the government.

The Soviet political leadership does not deny that human rights have a legitimate role in the Soviet Union. Indeed, socialism, it is argued, ensures the fulfilment of 'real' rights rather than the sham rights characteristic of capitalism. The acceptance and definition of rights by the rulers has important consequences: not only does it limit what they can legitimately do, it also provides a basis of demands by those whose rights are infringed. Such rights, however, are defined in the context of Soviet society and do not correspond completely to Western liberal conceptions of rights.

The Soviet View of Rights

In the first Constitution of the RSFSR, published on 3 July 1918, the general principles of rights were articulated. These shared certain sentiments in common with the lists of rights declared as objectives in the American and French Revolutions. They included the 'equality of all citizens before the law, irrespective of race or nationality'[55] (art. 22); it opposed the repression of national minorities 'or in any way to limit their rights' (art. 22). The working classes were given 'effective liberty of opinion' in the promotion of which were transferred to the workers and peasants 'all the technical and material resources necessary for the publication of newspapers, pamphlets, books, and other printed matter'. Their 'unobstructed circulation throughout the country' (art. 14) was guaranteed. The workers were ensured 'complete freedom of meeting' (art. 15) and 'full liberty of association' (art. 16). To ensure '... effective access to education, the RSFSR sets before itself the task of providing for the workers and poorer peasants a complete, universal and free education' (art. 17). In addition, it reiterated the obligation for all citizens to work, the duty to perform military service and to defend the Republic. Workers and peasants resident in Russia were given the right of citizenship. Forms of discrimination on grounds of race or nationality were legally abolished. Persecuted foreigners were given the right of asylum.

Leaving aside for one moment the fulfilment of the rights promised in the Constitution, we may outline how these provisions differ from constitutional rights proclaimed in the West.

First, rights in the USSR have been defined collectively not individually.

In the West, in the seventeenth and eighteenth century, rights were seen to inhere in persons, in individuals. These included freedom of the person, the right to political consultation through Parliament, freedom of conscience, and also important economic rights for the individual to own property, to conduct economic enterprise unconstrained by the government.

The Russian Revolution was a catalyst in the development of social rights; it changed and extended the notion of economic rights. Explicit rights to work, to social security, and to education have been proclaimed. In the economic order individual rights to enterprise, to ownership of property have been abolished and freedom from economic exploitation, and rights to employment have been decreed; government ownership, control, and planning of the economy have been introduced. In addition, the individualist and 'market' conception of political rights expressed through competition of political parties and interest groups has been replaced by the idea of a collective political interest articulated by one political party.

Second, from the earliest days of the revolution, the emancipation of men and women and the development of their human rights were regarded as being dependent on the interests of the working class, as expressed through the Communist Party and as activated by the government. Unlike, then, in Western states, where rights are expressed as inalienable attributes of individuals, and are claims which the state cannot (or cannot lightly) override, human rights in the Soviet Union have been bound up with what the state can (or should) do to liberate the working class.

The third difference between rights in the USSR and in the West has to do with the role of government. Positive government action now is widely accepted in the West as a means to achieve individual and group rights of a social and economic kind. Despite the developments which have occurred here since the Second World War, there is still a strong residual belief that rights are about individual freedoms and that the government has a supportive, though essentially a limited, role in promoting rights. In the Soviet Union the emphasis is different. The state (party and government) has played a dominant role in defining and implementing rights. Obligations and duties of the state to the citizen are specified and effectively limit individual action. (Planning secures full employment but the absence of a market and the abolition of private property eliminates the rights of individual production and trade.) The Soviet state, in terms of the party and government, has always played a greater role in defining and implementing rights. Rights have been defined in post-1917 Russia *by* the government – not as claims *on* the government. The Bolshevik Party and the CPSU sees itself acting on behalf of the working class. Where an individual's right and class or social rights conflict, priority is given to the group or to society. Unlike in Western liberal conceptions of rights, where individuals are seen as having rights *qua* individuals to life and happiness, in the Soviet Union these rights are limited by the incumbents of political power when they conflict with the state's interests.

Fourth, this process has to be viewed in historical perspective. The law in Russia was never the protector of individual rights, as in Western Europe. As Pintner and Rowney have put it: '... [T]he widespread Western assumption that the guide for common social behaviour and the protector of the individual was, and ought to be, a legally controlled polity (*Rechtsstaat*) never took root in Russia. Faced with the same demands for social stability and reliable social organisation as any other society, Russia responded typically with extension of officialdom, but an officialdom disciplined and limited only by bureaucratic rules.'[56]

Constitutional Rights

Soviet constitutional developments have also recognized individual rights. There is now less prominence given to class struggle and to the class basis of human emancipation and much more to individual rights. The scope of social and economic rights has been extended. The Constitutions of 1936 and 1977 explicitly define a wide range of 'fundamental rights and duties of citizens'. There are twice the number of articles on the rights and duties of citizens in the 1977 than in the 1936 Constitution. It should be borne in mind that we discuss here normative rights, not empirically effective rights. The intention of the 1977 Constitution is to extend and 'strengthen the legal position of the individual'.[57] There is much greater concern in the 1977 Constitution with law and legality: in 1936 there were only 12 such references, in 1977 there are 70.[58] Rights are comprehensive and are undoubtedly now wider in scope than comparable lists to be found in the constitutions of liberal-democratic states. I have attempted to summarize the formal statements of rights in table 9.1, which is divided into economic, social and political rights.

Rights, however, have to be seen in a political context. Rights are claims on resources and values, and the definition and fulfilment of rights have to do with the distribution of power in society. The *individual* articulation of rights is circumscribed by the *collectivist* control claimed by the Communist Party. It is worth referring again to Article 6 of the Constitution:

The leading and guiding force of Soviet society and the nucleus of its political system, of all state organisations and public organisations, is the Communist Party. The CPSU exists for the people and serves the people. The Communist Party, armed with Marxism–Leninism, determines the general perspective of the foreign

TABLE: 9.1: RIGHTS OF CITIZENS IN THE SOVIET CONSTITUTIONS OF 1936 AND 1977

	1936 Constitution	*1977 Constitution*
Economic:	Right to work, to 'guaranteed employment'. Right to own, as personal property, income and savings derived from work, to own a dwelling house and supplementary husbandry, articles of household and articles of personal use and convenience, the right to inherit personal property. (Art. 10).	Socialist system ensures enlargement of the rights … and continuous improvement of living standards. Rights to work, to choice of trade or profession.
Social:	Right to rest and leisure, seven-hour day, annual vacations with pay, Maintenance in old age, sickness or disability. Education – free in all schools, in the native language.	Right to housing. Right to education, including teaching in native language. Right to cultural benefits. Right to freedom of scientific, technical and artistic work. Rights of authors, inventors and innovators protected. Right to leisure and rest, working week of 41 hours, paid holidays, extension of social service and sport. Health protection. Maintenance in old age, sickness or disability.
Political:	Rights of women on an equal footing with men 'in all spheres of economic, cultural, government, political and social activity'. Freedom of conscience, freedom of religious worship and freedom of anti-religious propaganda. Freedom of speech, press, assembly, street processions and demonstrations. The right to unite in mass organizations. Right of inviolability of the person, of the homes of citizens and the privacy of correspondence. Right of asylum to foreign citizens. Right to vote in elections, to nominate candidates through mass organizations and societies.	Equality before law. Men and women have equal rights. Equality of rights of different races and nationalities. Equality of rights of all citizens. Right to participation in management and administration of the state, to vote and be elected to Soviets, to submit proposals to state bodies, to criticize shortcomings. Freedom of speech, press, assembly, meetings, street processions and demonstrations. Right to asylum. Right to associate in public organizations. The right to profess any religion, to conduct religious worship. Inviolability of the person, of the home. Right of privacy, of correspondence, telephone conversations and telegraphic communications. Right to protection by state bodies. Right to complain against actions of officials, state bodies and public bodies.

policy of the USSR, directs the great constructive work of the Soviet people, and imparts a planned, systematic and theoretically sustained character to their struggle for the victory of communism.

Claims for *individual* rights against the state may be seen to weaken party hegemony which in turn enfeebles the class character of the state – and its role in defining the path to socialism. Assertions of individual rights against the state (the essence of rights in liberal democracy) can be conflated into attacks on the state. This gives rise to a major dilemma of individual rights under state socialism. While the state in building socialism claims to enhance individual rights, demands for individual rights may weaken the state's organizing capacity. Thus the role of the party, as developed in the USSR, is likely to be a major impediment to the legitimacy of rights claims as practised in Western liberal states.

Infringements of Rights

In practice, some rights of some individuals are infringed in Soviet society. Such violations are seen by some writers to be evidence of the de facto absence of rights in the USSR. A sympathetic commentator on the USSR, Alice Erh-Soon Tay, regards the repression of Stalin's rule as being 'based on sustained and systematic disregard of law and any respect for human dignity or human rights'.[59] John Lewis, a Western Marxist writer on Soviet rights, recognizes the 'disappearance of freedom of expression and political liberty under the Stalin regime'.[60]

Liberal Western writers cite in support of this viewpoint the suppression of dissent. As noted above, contemporary dissenters in the Soviet Union are harassed by the police, independence of thought is denied and foreign travel, writing and residence restricted.[61] Chalidze and other dissidents have pointed to the ways that fundamental freedoms of speech, communication, person, association and movement are restricted.[62] Ken Coates, in a lecture prepared for a Conference at Columbia University, has asserted that ... [F]or all the limited progress towards "socialist legality", we are bound to observe that some men and women are still forcibly confined in lunatic asylums, because they disagree; that state prisoners are held on charges which, in every other advanced country, would be laughed out of consideration; that writers are banished because they wished to express themselves freely; and that distinguished men are robbed of their citizenship ... without benefit of any judicial process whatever.'[63] But condemnation of the USSR must be tempered by the realization that human rights in all societies are on occasion infringed. The United States has used civil rights as an agency of its foreign policy to condemn the Soviet Union.[64]

One must also consider whether the Western concept of human rights is not an ethnocentric one and whether the Soviet Union in some way compensates for the infringement of individual political rights against the state by the implementation of social ones. The denial of some rights to 'dissidents' may not apply to other rights to other citizens. Additionally, one must discuss whether the infractions of human rights in the Soviet Union are likely to be a permanent feature of the society, or have been associated with the peculiar evolution of the Soviet state and may change with time.

Marxist Advocates of Human Rights

Marxist advocates for the effective implementation of human rights in the USSR would argue that such rights are a component of a Marxist theory of society. John Lewis has argued that it is a mistake to belittle the achievements of liberalism and to regard 'human rights and democratic liberties as "so many bourgeois prejudices, behind which lurk in ambush just as many bourgeois interests." This is a serious error ...'[65] Marxists often point to the fact that bourgeois freedoms of the person, of speech, association, of the press cannot be fulfilled because of the limitations imposed by the bourgeois freedom of property ownership. They would argue that the Soviet political leadership has tended to neglect the importance of such freedoms and has identified other goals (say of economic development) as being of greater importance. To this extent the leadership has been more concerned with measures to promote indus-trialization, security and defence rather than the development of socialist norms.

The recent history of the Soviet Union and some of the socialist states of Eastern Europe illustrates that political subcultures are being created which are coming into conflict with the more traditional ones. Here is a dynamic or contradiction in these societies. The traditional pattern of legitimacy, of the ideology of Stalinism, of central direction and control is being challenged by what Weber called the legal-rational. This involves a greater role being played by the legal system, by civil liberties and civil rights.[66]

Soviet legal theory has changed significantly since the death of Stalin and has paralleled the conception of an all-people's state and developed socialism (zrely sotsializm). In 1959, M.I. Kalinin called for strengthening the rights of workers, collective farmers and enterprises.[67] Since the mid-1960s Soviet lawyers have called for the formulation of a 'socialist conception of rights',[68] and for a 'concept of the rights of the individual'.[69] This is part of a tendency initiated by Khrushchev for greater regard for socialist legality, it has led to 'a considerable upgrading of basic rights in Soviet legal theory'.[70]

The reason for greater emphasis on legal norms is that the growing differentiation of society, its complexity, together with a more urbane and educated population, calls for a system of integration through exchange between various institutions and groups.[71] Such exchanges, however, involve greater autonomy and 'rights-claims', on the one side, and a decline in the hegemony of the state apparatus, on the other. The scientific and cultural intelligentsia (of whom Sakharov and Medvedev are 'dissident' representatives) is a major force in this movement. The ideology of Marxism–Leninism may be utilized, at a normative level, to endorse and legitimize such claims. The values underpinning socialist states – at least under conditions of 'developed socialism' – provide a basis for claims to be made by aggrieved citizens and groups in defence of their rights. The salience of such values, however, has to be studied in the context of the evolution of the Soviet Union and its political culture.

Dissident Civil Rights Groups: the Case of Free Trade Unions

Since the 1960s a number of explicitly human rights groups have been founded: notably, the Initiative Group for the Defence of Human Rights in the USSR, the Human Rights Committee, the Moscow Branch of Amnesty International.[72] These groups advocate to various degrees the rights incorporated in the UN Universal Declaration of Human Rights; they are particularly concerned with freedom of the press, freedom of movement (both within and out of the USSR) and with the rights of various social groups, nationalities and religions. The movement, while qualitatively important, has been relatively isolated and on a very small scale. On admittedly inadequate data, Kowalewski estimates that the number of groups demonstrating rose from 6 in 1965 to 13 in 1976.[73] This is an index of the scale of the movement. The movement is largely intellectual in composition.[74] There is no involvement by rank and file communists.

Rights claims have been made also by workers for trade union rights. Soviet workers have a legal right to employment, safe working conditions and an appropriate wage. Rather than competition through the market and the assertion of workers' rights by unions against capital, Soviet labour legislation assumes that workers have a duty to labour for which they will be justly rewarded; the unions also have legal rights for the participation of labour in planning and the administration of welfare.[75] Wage negotiations take place, and the role of labour has to be seen within the context of the economic plan. Unions have the right to initiate legislation and Soviet writers claim that government legislation on labour is never adopted if there is objection by the All-Union Central Council of Trade Unions.[76] Unions are said to have the following rights: they participate in government decisions concerning labour in Gosplan proposals on labour; 'they issue binding interpretations' and implement 'regulations regarding questions of labour law and social insurance law; they establish rules for the safety inspections carried out by regional and local unions.'[77] Unions have the dual role of helping to secure production and defending workers' interests.

The extent to which they do the latter is a contentious matter. Many examples may be cited from dissident sources such as *Chronicle of Current Events* concerning the infringement of rights. Luryi has documented a case of wrongful dismissal from a post of school teacher. The person was dismissed on evidence from the security forces (KGB) that his activity (and sympathy for the Soviet civil rights movement) discredited the Soviet system and was incompatible with a post as teacher. Luryi shows that the trade union committee was unable effectively to defend the person against dismissal.[78] There is, however, a danger of generalizing from individual cases of the abrogation of rights. In comprehensive scholarly studies of dismissal procedures both McAuley and Ruble have concluded that the rights to employment are protected and that the role of unions has been strengthened in this respect in recent times. Blair Ruble has concluded that workers' rights, though sometimes infringed,[79] are generally effective with respect to their jobs: 'Court decisions ... suggest that Soviet labor legislation not only guarantees citizens the right to work but also a seemingly inflexible right to their present jobs. This right remains secure even when a dismissal of an employee may prove economically beneficial to the plant as a whole.'[80]

The right to strike would be seen by Soviet authorities to be harmful: workers' rights are secured by a legal process and strikes would deprive other workers of employment (through lack of components) and deny products to consumers.

It is in this context that 'unofficial' trade unions have arisen in the USSR in opposition to the existing unions. In November 1977, Vladimir Klebanov, an ex-miner, announced 'that a group of disaffected, unemployed workers intended to form an independent trade union'.[81] A group of people around Klebanov issued press statements expressing dissatisfaction with the existing unions and their own conditions. They founded the Association of Free Trade Unions of Workers in the Soviet Union (AFTU). Its members argued that the 'official' unions are unable to defend effectively workers' rights because of their involvement in production, in securing the goals of the economic plan. The Charter of the Association (dated 1 February 1978) defines membership to be open to 'any worker or employee whose rights and interests have been violated by administrative, governmental, party, or judicial agencies'.[82] The purpose of the unions is 'to carry out obligations reached by collective bargaining; to induce workers and employees to join free trade union associations; to carry out those decisions of the Association which concern the defense of rights and the seeking of justice; to educate members in the spirit of irreconcilability towards deficiencies, bureaucracy, deception, inefficiency and wastefulness, and a negligent attitude to national wealth'.[83] These latter aims are wider in scope than those of Western unions and illustrate a parallel with the 'official unions'. The group applied to the International Labour Organization (ILO) for recognition and enclosed a list of 110 candidates for membership. But this union was short-lived. AFTU activists were quickly apprehended: some were arrested and others sent to psychiatric hospitals.[84]

AFTU was followed by the formation in October 1978 of the Free Interprofessional Association of Workers (SMOT).[85] This claimed a membership of approximately a hundred comprised of eight groups. By June 1979, it had expanded to ten groups with two hundred members.[86] SMOT defined its goals as follows:

The defense of its members in cases of the violation of their rights in various spheres of their daily activities: economic, social, cultural, spiritual, religious, domestic and political. This defense is to be carried out by all possible means within the framework of the constitution and international agreements signed by the Soviet government. Furthermore, SMOT intends to look into the legal bases of the complaints of workers; to ensure that these complaints are brought to the notice of relevant organisations; to facilitate a quick solution to workers' complaints; and, in cases of negative results, to publicise them widely before the Soviet and international public. In order to give stronger assistance to workers who are not members of SMOT, a working commission is also being organised.[87]

It had a similar fate to AFTU: its leaders were harassed and arrested. In all cases, however, the Soviet authorities have not brought actions against such dissidents on the grounds that establishing, or the membershsip of, a trade union is illegal. They were prosecuted for 'slander'.[88] Neither organization was able to organize and neither was able to recruit many members. This has led to criticism of the USSR by the ILO that workers were being persecuted for attempting to form free trade unions. A similar fate has befallen other 'rights' groups which have been set up in opposition to the authorities.

It is difficult to gauge just how much support exists for these independent unions. Whilst one may concede that the 'official' union organization is often lacking, it has in recent years taken a more active and powerful role in securing workers' rights. Since 1970, the powers of the union have been extended.[89] Osakwe's conclusion is that: 'Even though the present Soviet trade union leadership continues to demonstrate strong loyalty to the CPSU and subservience to the Soviet government, the inescapable fact of contemporary Soviet labour relations is that the traditional antagonism between labour and management (under capitalism) has been considerably blunted, and that Soviet trade union organisations are slowly but surely assuming a more meaningful role as protectors of the interests of Soviet workers'.[90]

It would also be naive to regard the inception of free trade unions in the Soviet Union as merely an expression of workers' interests. Their case is weakened by their small size, by the fact that they do not advocate the interests of employees in a particular trade or industry and by the diverse political aims of the unions. They have important effects in delegitimating the Soviet state. John C. Michael has pointed to the 'loss of prestige' suffered by the Soviet Union in its international labour policy; to the ways that the free trade unions have called into question the 'political unity of Soviet society' and to the role of the unions in impugning 'the economic paternalism of the Soviet state and its entire network of trade-union and industrial administration'.[91]

Dissent and Control

It cannot be denied that suppression of certain activities is a characteristic of the modern Soviet state. Harsh treatment of dissidents by the political authorities, however, may paradoxically help to perpetuate dissent. Sociologists of deviance point out that society's reaction to deviance has an important effect on the nature of the deviance itself. In many cases the political elites can define sanctions and may segregate the deviants. If societal support is given to the elite's sanctions, the deviant may be stigmatized and he may have no alternative but to organize his own life and define his identity around the facts of deviance.[92] Consequently, the deviant may become more alienated from, and hostile to, his society. The law-makers and law-enforcers may thus magnify the social (and political) costs of deviance; 'social control' and repression may institutionalize it.

Both Solzhenitsyn's and Sakharov's early protests were within the framework of Soviet values and practices. Solzhenitsyn opposed – as did Khrushchev – the 'excesses' of Stalin; Sakharov agitated quite legally against Soviet tests of nuclear weapons. But the regime's response in clamping down on dissent led to these critics becoming further enmeshed in 'deviant' activities. What was only marginal to their behaviour was transformed into a dominant feature of their life-style: their 'life and identity are organised around the facts of deviance.'[93] The action of the

Soviet state in the shape of the security police (KGB) not only penalized the offenders, but unintentionally sustained the deviance. It created a sense of distrust, of stigmatization – the deviant becomes aware that his life chances are restricted, his interactions with other people are inhibited. Solzhenitsyn, Sakharov and Medvedev all lost their formal work position and were socially ostracized by their colleagues.

Why does such control and repression occur and take the form that it does? All complex societies exert social control. The ruling groups define behaviour and values which are socially desirable and specify what is deviant and subject to legal sanctions. Societies undergoing rapid social change particularly face problems of ensuring solidarity. The political leadership actively defines goals, beliefs and ways of acting to which people must conform. In state socialist society, 'official' Marxism–Leninism is an ideology which acts as a social cement. The ideology of 'developed socialism' has no place for 'dissent'. It defines those things that are 'sacred': the October Revolution, Lenin, the Party, Communism. It also has other values which it shares with Western societies – the belief in progress, in industrialization, science, and the nation state. To attack such values and beliefs is to attack the political leadership, because the leadership shapes such ideology. But it is more than that: it weakens the integrity of the social order and its forms of social integration, and it weakens faith. Penal sanctions are used against opposition which is seen as an agency of capitalism. This is analogous to the suppression of dissent by dominant Christian churches in the Middle Ages – heretics could only work at the behest of the devil.

It must be emphasized that it is not being argued here that the USSR is a pluralist liberal-democratic state. The treatment of dissident protest is much more severe than in the contemporary United States and Britain. The Soviet state uses its massive resources to deflect, prevent or eradicate opposition. Prevention takes the form of systematic political socialization in schools and through the media. Censorship is pervasive. Vladmirov has estimated that 70,000 people under the Central Committee are engaged in carrying out censorship.[94] To some extent, the development and greater access to foreign media has reduced the effectiveness of these processes; but it does prevent the articulation of an alternative form of mass political socialization. The force of the law to suppress critical ideas is frequently used. As noted above, this takes the form of imprisonment for slander against the social and political system. Confinement in mental hospitals has in some cases been used to 'resocialize' political dissidents.[95] Others are subjected to interviews with the police.[96] In some cases, sanctions may involve loss of one's job, the acceptance of lower status employment[97] and a prohibition on foreign travel. Internal exile, as for Sakharov, and exclusion from the USSR have been the fate of Solzhenitsyn and many others. Such activities by the authorities are harsher than those in the more liberal Western capitalist states: though even here the record of the state, as events in Ulster and sentences of imprisonment for blasphemy in Britain have shown, is by no means always in keeping with liberal theory. If the number of 'prisoners of conscience' estimated by Amnesty International is around 10,000,[98] then, as Juviler has observed, the Soviet Union is 'nowhere near the top of the world list', and the salience of such dissent *in the USSR*, rather than *in the West*, must be relatively small. As Stephen White has reminded us: 'At least three-quarters of the country's population ... given the hypothetical opportunity of doing otherwise, would vote for the existing system. The great mass of the Russian people (in the words of one émigré dissident) "simply do not have the same liberal values and interests as the great mass of the West Europeans".'[99] The Soviet system has its own *traditional* bases of authority: these are the revolutionary tradition, the patriotic tradition and the labour tradition.[100] They provide alternative sources of authorization for the Soviet political leadership; the Western notion of *individual* rights has no place as a source of legitimation for the Soviet political leadership.

In stable societies socialization is passive: the family, school, media, church largely reproduce what has been customary practice: in so doing the individual is subject to social control. In the West, particularly England, social development has occurred slowly over centuries; the 'disruptive' elements are less of a problem to the maintenance of the political order because the values of the system are widespread, and are deeply ingrained. The legitimation of private property, of the market in politics and the economy is very deep-seated, especially in the older industrialized systems.

The Individual and Society

A capitalist market-type exchange system puts many kinds of behaviour outside the formal political arena. Physical repression is less salient than ideological control. Alternative value orientations are well integrated or incorporated through trade unions and parliamentary-type political parties. Under these circumstances the individual is considered to be the primary unit and society is seen as the emanation of the individual's interests; in other words, in liberal-democratic theory, the individual takes precedence over society. But even here, when custom breaks down, society exercises penal sanctions on deviants. Those who make nuisances of themselves by aberrant behaviour may find themselves in psychiatric hospitals, or those who conduct illicit business (counterfeiters, drug sellers, tax dodgers and prostitutes) may find themselves in prison. In collectivist Bolshevik social theory (Soviet Marxism–Leninism) the relationship between man and society is reversed. Society is the dominant unit: the individual has no interest independently of society. Claims for the assertion of individual rights are claims against society; they are demands for a particular kind of community. The leaders of the Soviet Union have had to carry out industrial development in the face of resistance from the carriers of traditional values; the political elites have had to establish their legitimacy after revolution and war. They have had to shape traditional orientations to their dominance and therefore feel more insecure when faced with dissension and opposition.

The denial of human rights must be seen as a negation of socialism as an ideal, and cannot be legitimated in Marxist–Leninist terms. The lack of fulfilment of rights in the past history of the USSR has to do with the lack of a stable international political environment (civil and foreign wars) and with the absence of many of the preconditions for the evolution of certain rights. In this context, elements of Marxist theory which are alien to bourgeois society (e.g. to bourgeois class rights) were fused with traditional values and led to the imposition of a political system which placed little, if any, emphasis on individual human rights. This process seems to me to be an episode in the evolution of the Soviet state and should not be regarded as endemic to socialism. The extent and methods of the abrogation of individual rights under Stalin cannot be justified ex-post even in terms of 'nation building' and economic growth.[101] As has been pointed out, the values of the Soviet Union derive from an autocratic state in which orthodoxy prevailed. Both the state structure of pre-1917 Russia and the traditions of the Orthodox Church gave no role to individual political rights. Individualism was a creed bound up with the Renaissance and Reformation, which had little influence on Tsarist Russia. Such ideas did not penetrate because of the isolation of Russia from Europe due to its size and inhospitable land mass.

The integrative structures of Russia were more communal than individualistic. The traditional Russian *mir* or *obshchina* (commune) was essentially a collectivist body. Sentiment emphasized interdependence and mutual support. Vasily Belov, in a novel about pre-revolutionary village life, graphically portrays such values: [102] '[In old Russia] to refuse to give alms to a begger was considered a great sin in the village community or *mir* ... The *mir* always helped people to get back on their feet again. Soldiers who had served out their twenty years in the army and received their discharge would return home on foot, the journey taking them several months, and they would always be given food in Christ's name. If someone had been robbed on the highway, if a pilgrim was returning home, they would always be fed by the community.' The village assembly had powers of collective ownership of property given to it under the terms of the emancipation of the serfs in 1861. The Russian serf, from being bound to the land, became bound to the commune. The American negro, on the other hand, from being owned by one master was given his or her individual freedom. If one can talk of a general *Weltanschauung,* or world view, comparativists would depict Russians as being collectivist and affective, as accepting of authority, and as having a group rather than an individual identity.

This traditional background did influence the evolution of the Soviet state. But also I would argue that there was a symbiosis between traditional values and practices and those of the ideology guiding the Soviet state. The Soviet leaders had developmental goals. Soviet Marxism-Leninism became a kind of 'Protestant ethic' of industrialization.[103] Priority was given to the provision of employment and also to the fulfilment of life needs – for food, shelter, health and education. Also, these rights were to be implemented through the state apparatus. Violations of state policy (presumably geared to fulfil human rights) were considered by the political leadership as transgressions of human rights. There was a different ranking of goals compared with those of the French Revolution. This does not, however, entail the rejection of democratic rights.

The dynamic of human rights in the USSR is to be found in 'within-system' changes rather than in the dissident movement. The emergence of 'dissident' groups in the USSR, together with a movement since Khrushchev towards greater legality by the political leadership and the claims of the 1977 Constitution, all point to the evolution of civil rights under state socialism. The dissident tendencies indicate that civil rights are by no means a dead issue either in Marxism or in the politics of the socialist states. They are, however, only the sharp end of rights-claims. In a less dramatic and less publicized form, civil rights may be given greater recognition by process of law, by a recognition of the rights-claims of citizens requiring the officers of state to perform their constitutional duty. It is in the evolution of a more rational legal system which explicitly recognizes the duties of the state to fulfil rights, and the role of the individual in claiming them, that the realization of human rights is likely to be achieved in the USSR. If I may speculate as to further developments in the Soviet Union, demands for the implementation of rights are likely to originate from interests already (weakly) established – regional/republican, professional, religious, trade-union, and party. With the greater maturation of the society, and given relative international security, interest-demands are likely to multiply. Such demands in the assertion of 'rights' claims cannot be easily resolved in the fashion of an economic and political market exchange with the state, as in the West. In the Soviet Union legitimacy is sought by the party to define whose and which rights are fulfilled. This is a cardinal assumption on which the political system is organized and creates a fundamental dilemma for rights-claims.[104]

NOTES

1 R. Medvedev, *On Soviet Dissent* (1980), p. 36.
2 Ibid., p. 122.
3 Ibid., p. 141.
4 Ibid., p. 147.
5 See further: D. Kowalewski, 'Trends in Human Rights Movement', in Donald R. Kelley (ed.), *Soviet Politics in the Brezhnev Era* (1980), p. 158.
6 R. Tökés, 'Varieties of Soviet Dissent: An Overview', in R. Tökés (ed.), *Dissent in the USSR: Politics, Ideology and People* (1975), p. 19.
7 J.F. Hough, 'Thinking About Thinking About Dissent', in *Studies in Comparative Communism*, vol. 12, nos. 2–3 (1979), p. 270.
8 'The Heirs of Stalin', published in Patricia Black and Max Hayward, *Half-Way to the Moon* (1964), pp. 220–1.
9 Cited by Patricia Black, 'Freedom and Control in Literature 1962–63', in A. Dallin and A.F. Westin, *Politics in the Soviet Union* (1966), p. 188.
10 Cited in *On Trial*, edited by Leopold Labedz and Max Hayward (1967), p. 149.
11 Ibid., pp. 152–4.
12 S. Bloch and P. Reddaway, *Psychiatric Terror: How Soviet Psychiatry is Used to Suppress Dissent* (1978); P.S. Grigorenko, *The Grigorenko Papers* (1976); A. Podrabinek, *Punitive Medicine* (1980); L. Plyushch, *History's Carnival: A Dissenter's Autobiography* (1977); Zhores and Roy Medvedev, *A Question of Madness: How a Russian Scientist was put in a Soviet Mental Hospital and how he got out* (1971).
13 *Psychiatric Terror...*, p. 258.
14 H. Fireside, 'Psychiatry and the Soviet State', *Problems of Communism*, vol. 30 (July–August 1981), p. 58.
15 Briefly, the doctrine of Lysenko rejects modern genetics and insists that changes may be brought about in plants by environmental influence. Under Stalin Lysenko's views dominated Soviet biology and other views were suppressed. He was criticized by Khrushchev in 1953 and dismissed as President of the Academy of Agricultural Sciences. However, he and his supporters remained in the Academy and he was defended by Khrushchev in 1958.
16 Z. and R. Medvedev, *A Question of Madness*, p. 52.
17 Ibid., p. 49.
18 Ibid., pp. 59–60.
19 Ibid., p. 168.
20 Ibid., pp. 119–20.
21 Ibid., p. 76.
22 Ibid., p. 91.
23 R.L. Tökés, 'Dissent: The Politics for Change in the USSR', in H.W. Morton and R.L. Tökés, *Soviet Politics and Society in the 1970s* (1974), p. 10.
24 R.L. Tökés, *Dissent in the USSR* (1975), pp. 14–5.

25 In addition to literature cited in this chapter, see also: Stephen F. Cohen (ed.), *An End to Silence: Uncensored Opinion in the Soviet Union* (1982); S.P. de Boer, E.J. Driessen and H.L. Verhaar (eds), *Biographical Dictionary of Dissidents in the Soviet Union, 1956–1975* (1982); Vladimir Bukovsky, *To Build a Castle – My Life as a Dissenter* (1979); Michael Meerson-Aksenov, Boris Shragin (eds), *The Political, Social and Religious Thought of Russian 'Samizdat' – An Anthology* (1977).
26 *Literaturnaya gazeta*, 12 Jan. 1972. Cited in *The Last Circle* (1974), pp. 22–23.
27 N. Vitkevich in *The Last Circle*, p. 140.
28 F. Barker, *Solzhenitsyn: Politics and Form* (1977), p. 1.
29 *Literaturnaya gazeta*, 26 Feb. 1969. Printed in *The Last Circle* (1974), pp. 9–13.
30 Also published in London by *Index on Censorship* (1974).
31 A. Solzhenitsyn, *Détente. Prospects for Democracy and Dictatorship* (1980), p. 8.
32 Ibid., pp. 9–10.
33 A. Sakharov, *Reflections on Progress, Coexistence and Intellectual Freedom* (1968), p. 86.
34 This nationality was deported to Central Asia in 1944 for alleged collaboration with the Germans.
35 London: Collins, 1975.
36 Ibid., p. 89.
37 Ibid., p. 91.
38 Ibid., pp. 101–2.
39 For details see: 'Sakharov and the Non-Russian Peoples of the USSR', RFE-RL 41/80 (1980).
40 Ibid., p. 4.
41 A. Sakharov, 'A Letter from Exile' (1980) (Press Statement).
42 N. Tolin, in *Novoe Vremya*, no. 5 (Feb. 1980), pp. 22–23.
43 A later version of it was published in the West as *Let History Judge* (1971).
44 See *Let History Judge*, p. x.
45 R. Medvedev, *On Soviet Dissent* (1980), p. 27.
46 See D. Lane, *Leninism: A Sociological Interpretation* (1981), pp. 80–2.
47 Zhores and Roy Medvedev, *A Question of Madness* (1971), p. 206.
48 *On Soviet Dissent*, p. 136.
49 Ibid., p. 146.
50 Reprinted in Radio Liberty, *Special Report*, RL 359/73 (19 November 1973).
51 'The Problem of Democratisation ....', p. 9.
52 *On Soviet Dissent*, p. 96.
53 Ibid., p. 13.
54 Carl Wellman, 'A New Conception of Human Rights', in E. Kamenka and A. Erh-Soon Tay, *Human Rights* (1978), p. 56.
55 Quotations from the 1918 Constitution are taken from the version printed in A. Rothstein (ed). *The Soviet Constitution* (1923). The various Soviet constitutions are conveniently collected in A.L. Unger, *Constitutional Development in the USSR* (1981). The following sections on rights draw from my

article, 'Human Rights Under State Socialism?', *Political Studies*, vol. 32, no. 3 (September 1984).

56 W.M. Pintner and D.K. Rowney, 'Officialdom and Bureaucratization: Conclusion' in W.M. Pintner and D.K. Rowney, *Russian Officialdom: The Bureaucratization of Russian Society from the Seventeenth to the Twentieth Century* (1980), pp. 379–80.

57 V. Kudryavtsev, 'The New Constitution and the Development of Socialist Law' in *The Development of Soviet Law and Jurisprudence* (1978), p. 13.

58 Ibid., p. 10.

59 Alice Erh-Soon Tay, in E. Kamenka and A. Erh-Soon Tay, *Human Rights*, (1978), p. 109.

60 John Lewis, 'On Human Rights', in *Marxism and the Open Mind* (1957), p. 72.

61 See R.L. Tökés, *Dissent in the USSR: Politics, Ideology and People* (1975), esp. contributions by R.L. Tökés and W.D. Connor.

62 Valery Chalidze, *To Defend These Rights: Human Rights and the Soviet Union* (1974).

63 'Civil Liberty and Socialism', in J. Pelikan et al., *Civil and Academic Freedom* (1975), p. 6. Ironically, Coates was denied an *American* visa to give his speech. See ibid., pp. 4–5.

64 Marnia Lazreg, 'Human Rights, State and Ideology: An Historical Perspective', in A. Pollis and P. Schwab, *Human Rights: Cultural and Ideological Perspectives* (1979).

65 John Lewis, 'On Human Rights', p. 72.

66 By rational-legal is meant a mode of legitimation resting on the belief that the exercise of authority, the substance and mode of command, are in accordance with a more general rule or rules. See T.H. Rigby, 'A Conceptual Approach to Authority, Power and Policy in the Soviet Union', in T.H. Rigby et al. (eds), *Authority, Power and Policy in the USSR* (1980), esp. pp. 11–12.

67 Cited by Gordon B. Smith, 'Developments of "Socialist Legality" in the Soviet Union', in F.J.M. Feldbrugge and W.B. Simons, *Perspectives on Soviet Law for the 1980s* (1982), p. 87.

68 V.M. Chkhikvadze, 'XXIV s"ezd KPSS i dal'neyshee razvitie sovetskoy yuridicheskoy nauki', *Sov. Gos. i Pravo*, no. 7 (1971). p. 3. Cited in G. Brunner, 'Recent Developments in the Soviet Concept of Human Rights', in F.J.M. Feldbrugge and W.B. Simons, *Perspectives on Soviet Law for the 1980s* (1982), p. 37.

69 V.N. Kudryavtsev. Cited by Brunner, ibid.

70 Brunner, p. 41. Brunner points out that within the Soviet Union the dominant instrumental view of the state has been challenged by some Soviet writers who seek to put the role of human personality at the centre of law.

71 Support for this may be found in many statements by Soviet writers on the role of law: 'The new social conditions imperatively demand strengthening the role of law and its prestige in the life of socialist society, and technological, economic, social and political processes have to be given legal consolidation and stimulation'. V. Zabigailo, 'The Modern State: Growing Law-Making Functions', in *The Development of Soviet Law and Jurisprudence* (1978), p. 74.

72 For a useful review see: David Kowalewski, 'Human Rights Protest in the USSR: Statistical Trends for 1965–78', *Universal Human Rights*, vol. 2, no. 1 (Jan.–March 1980), pp. 5–29.
73 Ibid., p. 18.
74 Ibid., p. 19. That is the 'human rights' movement. The religious groups such as Baptists and Lithuanian Catholics have a wider social base.
75 For an exhaustive treatment of Soviet labour rights and legislation see: Christopher Osakwe, 'Soviet Trade Union Organisations in Legal and Historical Perspectives', in D.B. Barry, F.J.M. Feldbrugge et al., *Soviet Law After Stalin* (1979).
76 Osakwe, p. 281.
77 Ibid., p. 281–2.
78 Y.I. Luryi, 'Three Years of the New USSR Constitution: The Soviet Approach to Human Rights', in Feldbrugge and Simons, *Perspectives on Soviet Law...*, pp. 63–68.
79 Safety regulations are particularly laxly enforced.
80 Blair Ruble, *Soviet Trade Unions* (1981), p. 71. See also, A. Kahan and B. Ruble, *Industrial Labour in the USSR* (1979); M. McAuley, *Labour Disputes in Soviet Russia 1957–1965* (1969).
81 John C. Michael, 'The Independent Trade-Union Movement in the Soviet Union', Radio Liberty, RL 304/79 (1979), p. 1. See also: John C. Michael, 'Independent Worker Movements in the USSR: A Primer', *Workers Under Communism* (Winter 1983), pp. 31–5.
82 Reprinted in A. Karatnycky et al. (eds), *Workers' Rights, East and West* (1980) Article 1, p. 97.
83 Ibid., Article 9.
84 Ibid., p. 56.
85 For an account of its activities see: 'An Interview with Vladimir Borisov, Founding Member of the Soviet Independent Tade Union, SMOT', Radio Liberty, RL 372/81 (1981).
86 Data cited by Michael, 'The Independent Trade-Union Movement...', p. 3.
87 Cited by Michael, ibid., p. 4.
88 Luryi, 'Three years...', p. 58.
89 Osakwe, 'Soviet Trade Union Organisation...', p. 305.
90 Ibid., p. 291.
91 Ibid., p. 1.
92 See E.M. Lemert, *Human Deviance, Social Problems and Social Control* (1972), p. 63.
93 Ibid., p. 63.
94 L. Vladmirov, 'Glavlit: How the Soviet Censor Works', *Index* (1973).
95 S. Bloch and P. Reddaway, *Russia's Political Hospitals* (1977).
96 See F.C. Barghoorn, 'The Post-Khrushchev Campaign to Suppress Dissent', in Tökés, *Dissent in the USSR...*, p. 64.
97 Ibid., p. 66.
98 P.H. Juviler, *Revolutionary Law and Order* (1976), p. 106.
99 S. White, 'The USSR: Patterns of Autocracy and Industrialism', in A. Brown

and J. Gray, *Political Culture and Political Change in Communist States* (1977), p. 42.

100 Christel Lane, 'Power and Legitimacy in the Soviet Union Through Socialist Ritual', *British Journal of Political Science*, vol. 14, pp. 207–17 (1984).

101 See, for example, discussion in R. Medvedev, *On Stalin and Stalinism* (1979); S.F. Cohen, 'Bolshevism and Stalinism', in R.C. Tucker, *Stalinism* (1977). For a review of different approaches, see D. Lane, *Leninism: A Sociological Interpretation* (1981).

102 *Nash sovremennik*, nos. 10–12 (1979); 1, 6, 7 (1981). Cited by Mary Seton-Watson, 'Myth and Reality in Recent Soviet Fiction', *Coexistence*, vol. 19 (1982), p. 228.

103 See D. Lane, 'Leninism as an ideology of Soviet Development', in E. de Kadt and G. Williams (eds), *Sociology and Development* (1974).

104 My thanks to Christopher Lane for some useful comments on an earlier version of this chapter.

10

POLITICAL CHANGE
IN THE 1980s

We have seen that the USSR is far from being a stereotyped form of totalitarian society with a dictatorial monistic ruling elite. As a state socialist political system, it has structural characteristics which differentiate it from liberal-democratic states: the government has a larger share of public ownership and a wider range of formal institutions of social control; there are no formal checks and balances between political institutions; there are restrictions in the ways that social group interests may be articulated. While the structures differ, the political *process* is essentially similar to other modern industrialized states. The group structure of modern society and the demands engendered by it require the reconciliation of diverse interests. The presence of a single political party with a monopoly of formal power is a quality that the USSR does not share with liberal societies. Communist ideology derived from Marxism–Leninism and the formal goals of a classless society too are unique characteristics.

Ideology in practice limits the options open to the political leadership. The party has changed from a narrow vertically integrated unit – the 'vanguard' of Lenin's socialist revolution – to a mass-based dominant party with primary organizations located in all institutions. The party seeks to rule but it does not govern. The modern party operates in a society criss-crossed with specialized group and institutional interests. One of its main current functions is to integrate Soviet society; it seeks to promote a consensus conducive to the 'building of communism'. To do this it articulates a social programme, it aggregates interests and it seeks to adjudicate between conflicting groups and institutions. In these respects it acts like ruling parties in other large-scale industrialized states, but on a much wider scale.

The Soviet Union in the latter part of the 1980s is faced with different kinds of problems of tension-management and system integration than in the past under Stalin and Khrushchev. The Soviet population is now more highly educated and urban and the demands it makes are more sophisticated than was the case in the days of Stalin's rule: to adopt Stalin's style in the contemporary USSR would be about as appropriate as an Oliver Cromwell attempting to rule contemporary Britain.

This has led to a changing balance between state and society, to an attempt to reach a new equilibrium of social and political forces. Such changes in the style of leadership have appeared to some commentators as signs of instability and indecisiveness. Brzezinski has asserted that there was 'no one in effective power in the Soviet Union' and he predicted that the effect of the (then) collective leadership of Brezhnev, Kosygin and Podgorny would be 'a kind of partial policy paralysis'.[1] Similarly (ten years later), Hillel Ticktin argued that the Soviet Union in the late 1970s was 'inherently unstable' and 'unviable'.[2] The political leadership is not, according to this school, in effective control. But the Soviet government's activities do not tally with such views. Just after Brzezinski's prognostications had been printed in 1968, the Soviet Army and those of other Warsaw Pact countries forcibly occupied Czechoslovakia. This was no evident lack of effective power, or paralysis of decision-making. In the late 1970s and 1980s, the completion of the Helsinki Agreement, exclusion of Podgorny from the Politbureau, assumption of Brezhnev as Head of State, publication of a new Constitution, military intervention in Afghanistan, Andropov's drive against corruption and Chernenko's boycott of the Olympics were not indicative of the paralysis of decision-making on the part of the Politbureau.

Hough has cogently argued that Soviet government operates in a similar 'incrementalist' fashion to Western governments.[3] Brezhnev continued many of the positive policies of Khrushchev, though in a less exotic style: he broadened participation in decision-making, reduced wage differentials, improved agriculture and strengthened the constitutional system. Such incrementalism has entailed a diminution in the powers of the central bodies, and has led to greater 'localism'.[4] Andropov and Chernenko represent continuity in policy.

Parkin is representative of many writers who attempt to generalize about the nature of opposition under state socialism. He postulates that there is a 'system contradiction' between the political and administrative apparatus of the state which has 'effective legal guardianship of socialised property' and an 'ascendant class' which is the intelligentsia.[5] The 'legal and political order' of state socialism becomes a fetter, he argues, on the intelligentsia which is the modernizing force. Such views are based on faulty analysis of the structure of Soviet society. The intelligentsia is highly integrated into the state apparatus in the shape of institutions such as the various Academies of Science, the Communist Party, and the Writers' Union. While 'dissident' intellectuals do not like and even oppose the party, this does not amount to a class contradiction. Such dissidents must be seen in the context of over half of the Candidates and Doctors of Science, and over 60 per cent of the creative writers being in the Communist Party. Churchward seems to be much more realistic when he concludes that '... most Soviet intellectuals seem to accept the socialist system and are prepared to work within the Communist political system, to observe its rules and to respect its restraints.'[6] This does not, of course, preclude disagreements about who is best fitted to run the system, or conflict within and between different institutions. But, as argued above, it does mean that the regime 'is now a substantially legitimate one' in terms of citizens' attitudes, and we must concur with White's conclusion that 'there is little evidence of dissonance between its political culture and its political system.'[7] This view is corroborated by the Soviet dissident Aleksandr Zinoviev, who says: 'The majority of the Soviet population has no use whatsoever for [Western democracy and liberalism] ... Our society is altogether different from Western society. It produces a different type of person who is satisfied by different kinds of values ... For the greater part of society, the reality, that is, today's "actually existing socialism" is a desirable one.'[8]

The Soviet political system has passed through a number of stages which may be described in terms of their dominant styles of political power. Etzioni distinguishes between coercive, remunerative and normative power.[9] In the Stalin era, coercion and normative sanctions were predominant and the political institutions which were supreme were the police and the industrial ministries. The cult of Stalin was developed to build on the traditional loyalty of the masses to a leader. Under Khrushchev, the forms of sanctions changed to bring them into line with the more complex social structure. The police lost their arbitrary power and the role of the party was enhanced. The sanctions utilized by Khrushchev depended more on remunerative factors: on providing individual material rewards, a higher level of goods and services and more and greater financial incentives in industry. The *Programme of the CPSU* (1961) was a blueprint for catching up materially with the West. In the 1970s the emphasis moved to accommodation with the West in the policy of detente: the Peace Treaty with Germany and the Helsinki Agreement. To be sure, coercion continued, as it does in all modern states, but it was not the predominant pattern. Khrushchev, too, attempted to revive normative sanctions: people were to be guided in their activity by reference to the norm of the 'new Soviet person'. This was very much a secondary and not very effective mechanism of gaining compliance. The 'cult of personality' was attacked.

Under the leadership of Brezhnev and Kosygin, the use of sanctions changed slightly. The predominant pattern was remunerative. Somewhat greater use has been made of coercive powers. 'Dissident' intellectuals have been repressed, and many have been allowed to emigrate. Internal stress has declined. Abroad military intervention has occurred in Czechoslovakia and Afghanistan. In 1977, a new Constitution was proclaimed emphasizing the continuity of Soviet policy, the importance of the party and normative controls. In the latter periods of Brezhnev's leadership, a distinct personality cult was fostered. One might well argue that under Brezhnev the political system was more remunerative and slightly more coercive and the leader sought to project a distinctive style of personal leadership. During Andropov's short rule, a leadership style was beginning to emerge of greater collegiality, of a more modest personality. The greater reliance placed on discipline and concern with economic efficiency indicated a greater stress being placed on remunerative sanctions. This has continued under Chernenko, albeit at a slower pace.

These changes in political style illustrate the adaptive capacity of the Soviet political system, of its attempts to grapple not only with the problems of revolutionary change, as during and after 1917, but also to come to grips with the control and direction of a complex modern economy and social structure.

Many commentators believe that in the future the Soviet Union will need to adapt considerably to meet the challenge of its differentiated occupational structures and the higher levels of educational attainment of its population. Roy Medvedev in declamatory fashion has insisted: 'The democratic rights and freedoms of Soviet citizens, especially freedom of speech and press, freedom of access to information and ideas, and also freedom to circulate information and ideas, must be consistently extended. Only in this way is it possible to ensure the rapid development and extension of the creation of the spiritual values which the Soviet people need no less than they need more and better material benefits. A truly socialist culture cannot develop within the rigid framework of restrictions by censorship and bureaucracy.'[10]

Medvedev, however sincere his socialist vision, has a great many shortcomings as a political analyst when we consider how such a programme of democratization may be put into effect. Medvedev holds to the view that the political is determinant in Soviet society. Individual leaders, he argues, do *not* have minimal capacities. They can influence not only the style and composition of the elite but also 'the tempo and forms of economic development and the character and specific features of foreign and domestic policy'.[11] This, however, is far too simplistic. It ignores the structural constraints on the leadership provided by party, government and a host of other interests.

No political leadership has a great deal of political space in which to manoeuvre. Indeed, it is not as simple to say that 'new leaders mean new policies and old leaders mean the continuation of old priorities ...'[12] As I suggested in chapters 5 and 7, the Politbureau is composed of different interests on which the General Secretary relies for support. The Soviet leader may have *less* political space than the American or British. The latter can and do choose the government executive and regularly select people who will follow their political line. The Soviet leader can only bring influence to bear at the margin in influencing the election of people to the Central Committee and Politbureau; and even then (as noted above), clients do not always repay their patrons.[13] Also, Medvedev avoids the question of how a political elite backing democratic reform will evolve. He notes that the next set of leaders are likely to be 'technocrats rather than bureaucrats' – they 'will be pragmatists rather than dogmatists'. But the maturation of Soviet society and its higher levels of education will not necessarily lead to a more democratic or tolerant leadership. Technocrats and pragmatists do not necessarily favour tolerence, conciliation, democracy and (socialist) spiritual values: rather the contrary. Medvedev also pays scant attention to the context in which the political elites have to rule: the policy of foreign powers and their own economic endowment, for example, are outside their control. Western analysts of political change in the Soviet Union in the post-Brezhnev period have been much more cautious. Jerry Hough in particular has pointed to the political obstacles in the way of reforms.[14]

In order to demonstrate the complexities involved in a prognosis of change, I have hypothesized three scenarios in table 10.1: A. the Soviet Union will stay more or less as it is; B. it will move to the Right; C. it will move to the Left (become more democratic). (These scenarios do not exhaust all possibilities.) Different policy outputs are linked to a number of related social, economic and political factors. First, there is the underlying world view of people supporting one of the three courses: those wishing to keep things as they were under Brezhnev emphasize the stability and successes of that period; Soviet right-wingers would perhaps be mainly concerned with the division and weakness of the communist world – in China, Poland, Hungary, the critique of the Eurocommunist movement in Western Europe – and with the hawks of the capitalist camp; democrats and leftists would stake their claims on 'modernizing' tendencies in the USSR, like rising levels of education and expectations – these they would see giving rise to a more profound and critical political consciousness. Second, I have postulated two different kinds of 'inputs' – those concerning the economy and foreign affairs (see details in table 10.1). Third, three 'instrumentalities of rule' are indicated – the values on which each scene is likely to be based (consumerism, Stalinist Marxism – Leninism, democracy with consumerism). These are coupled to the political leadership likely to

TABLE 10.1: PROSPECTUS FOR CHANGE IN THE USSR

	A. Stay as it is	B. Move to the 'Right' ('Stalinizers')	C. Move to the 'Left' ('Liberalizers')
1. Underlying Perceptions:	Stability and 'success' of Brezhnev period.	Weaknesses and division of communist world. Decline of 'true' Marxist–Leninist principles.	Modernizing tendencies of rising levels of education and expections.
2. Political Inputs: Internal (Postulated)	Economic growth steady but slow.	Decline/standstill in economy.	Increase in rate of growth.
External (Postulated)	Detente, arms limitation.	Right-wing hawkish foreign states, use of economic and political sanctions by the West.	Detente, disarmament and 'appeasement' by the West.
3. Instrumentalities of Rule: Values	Consumerism	Stalinist Marxism–Leninism.	Democracy/consumerism.
	Welfare	Russian patriotism, Soviet traditionalism.	'True' Marxism–Leninism.
Political leadership	Corporate elites	Police/Military.	Professionals, party intelligentsia.
Social Supports	Working class, Established intelligentsia.	Slavic ethnic groups. Army, Police.	Humanistic Intelligentsia, youth.
4. Policy Outputs: Economic	Minimize wage differentials.	Strengthening of defence, heavy industry. Central planning.	Market mechanisms, Consumer industries.
	Full employment, Low wage policy.	Full employment, Low wage policy	Increased wage differentials, labour mobility and unemployment.
Political	Social compact, Limited liberalization.	Russification, increase in censorship, coercion. Strengthening of law and order.	More liberalization, human rights. Curbing of police.
Foreign Policy	Limited detente.	Greater political intervention.	Support of 'Eurocommunist' policies.

achieve each position, and its relevant social support. Fourth and finally, I define the kinds of policy or 'outputs' which are likely to be associated with each leadership.

Given steady economic growth and an absence of excessive East–West tension, the most probable course under Chernenko and his successors is that of stability, of a continuation of the policies begun by Brezhnev. It is unlikely, even with the fulfilment of the 'inputs' postulated in table 10.1, that there will be a 'move to the Left'. The missing ingredient for this is political leadership. Even Medvedev concedes that 'there can be little hope that [the new generation of Soviet leaders] will also be more democratic or more tolerant of criticism or dissent, although even this possibility cannot be wholly excluded.'[15] While professionals and intellectuals in the party and other institutions may espouse democratic change, knowledge is not power. It is possible that there will be realignments among the 'corporate elites' (government, party, police and military) – the mix of outputs may then change. Continued economic problems may lead to more dependence on market mechanisms, greater labour mobility and an increase in unemployment.

A 'move to the Right' (as defined in the table) is also not very probable. Even with an internal economic standstill and confrontation with an external 'hawkish' foreign policy, such as that pursued by Margaret Thatcher and Ronald Reagan, it is improbable that the police and military will be able to breach party and government interests and return to a Stalinist-type political system. Unless there is a major war, no political leadership can replace (for long) the values of consumerism and welfare which are widely accepted by the Soviet population. The most probable scenario is that defined in the 'stay as it is' column (though there may be borrowings from the other two – an increase in Russification and coercion, or more consumerism and a greater role of the market).

It has been argued that the Soviet political and social system is legitimate in a behavioural sense: people have come to accept its practices and its fundamental structures. It is secured by an admixture of charismatic, traditional and legal-rational authority. With the passing away of Brezhnev, it is likely that the charismatic elements – small as they are – will decline even more. (The advanced age of Chernenko precludes a lengthy build-up for an effective charismatic leadership.) Legal-rational authority may be linked to the performance of the regime. There is evidence of a long-term development of legal norms, of a greater reliance on written rules and regularized procedures. If economic growth falls and the population is faced with declining living standards, it is likely that traditional values may be strengthened to ensure solidarity. The point must be made that the Soviet Union has its own pattern of traditions – the values and symbols of the revolution, of patriotism running from Ivan the Terrible to Stalin, the victor over Nazi Germany – of *Soviet* national strength and glory.

But all this does not mean the absence of considerable problems in the Soviet political system. In terms of interest articulation, many groupings cannot effectively make their claims known. The existence of a single candidate and the suppression of alternative candidates at elections does not encourage vigorous political activity at the grass roots. Popular rumours about corruption[16] among the elites and the inability of the party and police to control it leads to alienation and a weakening of the compact between leadership and masses. Western parliamentary-type elections do not raise fundamental criticism of capitalism, but they do allow criticism of government policy to be forcefully articulated and critics are allowed to vent their concerns, and corruption and moral turpitude is sensationally exposed (excepting, perhaps, that in Britain concerning the Queen and her immediate court). In Russia, interest aggregation is also less effective in the process of reconciling divergent views than in advanced Western states. The appraisal and re-appraisal of policy outside the political leadership is not always frank because the participant may be said to question the authority of the party. This may be considered disloyal and lead to intervention by the police. Lack of vigorous and wide-ranging public criticism may have the advantage to the political leadership that the public tends to follow government policy (say over dissidents) and it avoids the impression of division and weakness. But policies change and individual politicians fall from favour. Such changes and the sudden departure of leaders (such as Podgorny)* do not promote the confidence of the masses. The fact that individual and group rivalries are not recognized and institutionalized means that almost everything becomes politicized. In an institutionalized system of political conflict, interests are recognized and individuals and groups are consulted through the relevant mechanisms. Without such institutionalization, political conflict becomes more bitter; one must continually be on guard to defend one's interest.

The economic 'outputs' of the regime have had a tendency to fall short of public expectations: the ideology legitimates the system in terms of the greater efficiency of communism compared with capitalism. There is a possibility that legitimacy may decline due to an obvious gap between promise and performance. Finally, the enforcement policy of the Soviet state appears crude, though it is effective in the short run. The trials, hospitalization and exile of dissidents are examples of the resort to coercion which cannot in the long run achieve the intended reduction of political

* Podgorny's resignation as Head of State was announced by Brezhnev in a footnote to a speech.

stress. Indeed, they weaken the ideological sanctions entailed in the notion of 'the building of communism'. Here the political elites appear bound by the legacy of coercion, by previous responses, by the experience of the era of Stalin in which they were nurtured.

Soviet politics is *effective* politics: major interest groups within the system are able to articulate their needs. It is a *united* government: decisions are not questioned – in public. One should not, in discussing personality differences between leaders forget that the collective leadership shares many objective and sentiments. It is an accepted *government*: its process and structure are legitimate in the sense of being 'taken for granted by the masses'. Organized political dissent has little public salience: it is comparable to that of the communists in Britain or the USA. It is unlikely to have more than very marginal effects on the political system, and political changes are more likely to ensue from changes in the power relations of various groups within the power structure: party, academic, industrial, administrative, police, military and national.

How then may we generalize about the nature of the political system? Soviet state socialism as a political system cannot be characterized by conflated models of ideal socialism, pluralism, corporatism or totalitarianism. It contains elements of all four. It is perhaps best considered as a hierarchical structure of political incorporation. In table 10.2 five major

TABLE 10.2: STATE SOCIALISM AS A POLITICAL SYSTEM.

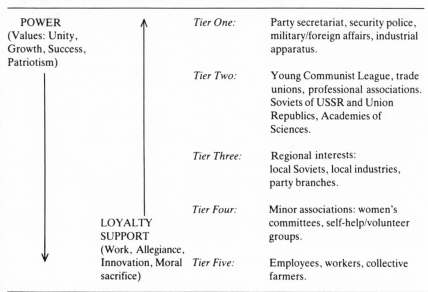

POWER (Values: Unity, Growth, Success, Patriotism)		*Tier One:*	Party secretariat, security police, military/foreign affairs, industrial apparatus.
		Tier Two:	Young Communist League, trade unions, professional associations. Soviets of USSR and Union Republics, Academies of Sciences.
		Tier Three:	Regional interests: local Soviets, local industries, party branches.
		Tier Four:	Minor associations: women's committees, self-help/volunteer groups.
	LOYALTY SUPPORT (Work, Allegiance, Innovation, Moral sacrifice)	*Tier Five:*	Employees, workers, collective farmers.

levels are distinguished. There is a hierarchy of interests. At the top, the four major groupings are: the party secretariat, the security police, foreign affairs/military, the industrial apparatus. It is the equivalent of the Western corporatist bloc of industry, government and labour. On Tier Two come the Soviet, Young Communist Leagues (Komsomol), trade unions and professional/academic associations. On Tier Three are regional interests: local Soviets, local industries, local party organizations. On Tier Four come minor associations: women's committees, self-help/volunteer groups and finally on Tier Five come social groups: rank and file manual and non-manual workers and peasants.

The relations between them are not exploitative, but are based on complicated sets of exchanges with Tier One setting and enforcing the major values (unity, patriotism, growth, success). Power is seen to run from the top down. Lower organizations face 'outwards' to their members whom they seek to defend and represent, and 'inwards' to the system of political power. They exert sanctions and control on behalf of the political leadership (Tier One). They pledge loyalty to Soviet power. This is expressed in willingness to labour, to give allegiance, to innovate and experiment, to give sacrifices of time, effort and (in war) life. But this loyalty is in exchange for benefits of a moral and material kind (membership of a strong world power, moral superiority of the claims of communism over capitalism, the delivery of material goods and services). The elites have to fulfil the expectations of the population: this they seek to do, within the constraints imposed by resources, organization and ideology. In so far as growth and expansion are achieved, support and loyalty at lower levels are secured; unity is established and the compact between levels is ensured. A condition of loyalty and support is the effective performance of the system – both ideologically and materially. The political leadership, therefore, is judged and will only continue to flourish on the basis of achievements.

NOTES

1 See Zbigniew Brzezinski, 'The Soviet Political System: Transformation or Degeneration?', *Problems of Communism*, vol. 15, (1966); and articles on the same theme in the subsequent numbers of this journal. The final article appeared in the May–June issue 1968, 'Reflections on the Soviet System', vol. 17, no. 3.

2 H. Ticktin, 'The Contradictions of Soviet Society and Professor Bettelheim', *Critique*, no. 6 (Spring 1976), p. 40.

3 J. Hough, 'The Man and the System', *Problems of Communism*, vol. 25 (1976).

4 See Gordon B. Smith, 'Bureaucratic Politics and Public Policy in the Soviet Union', in G.B. Smith, *Public Policy and Administration in the Soviet Union* (1980), pp. 10–13.

5 F. Parkin, 'System Contradiction and Political Transformation', *European Journal of Sociology*, vol. 13 (1972), p. 50.

6 L.G. Churchward, *The Soviet Intelligentsia* (1973) p. 128. See also D. Lane, *Soviet Economy and Society* (1984) chapter 5.

7 Stephen White, 'The USSR: Patterns of Autocracy and Industrialism', in A. Brown and J. Gray, *Political Culture and Political Change in Communist States* (1977), p. 44.

8 Cited by R. Medvedev, *On Soviet Dissent* (1980), p. 123.

9 Amitai Etzioni, *A Comparative Analysis of Complex Organisations* (1961), chapter 1. These are similar to C. Wright Mills's distinction between coercion (the use of force), authority (power justified by the beliefs of the voluntary obedient) and manipulation (power wielded unbeknown to the powerless). C. Wright Mills, 'The Structure of Power in American Society', *British Journal of Sociology*, no. 3 (1958). Charisma and traditional authority are not considered by these writers, but they are also important.

10 Roy Medvedev, 'USSR After Brezhnev', *Marxism Today* (September 1982), p. 24.

11 Ibid., p. 19.

12 Valerie Bunce, 'Do New Leaders Make a Difference?', *Executive Succession and Public Policy under Capitalism and Socialism* 1981, p. 255.

13 See useful discussion in A. Brown, 'Leadership Succession and Policy Innovation', in A. Brown and M. Kaser, *Soviet Policy for the 1980's* (1982), pp. 227–32.

14 Jerry F. Hough, 'Issues and Personalities', *Problems of Communism*, vol. 31, no. 5 (1982), pp. 20–40. See also Stephen F. Cohen, 'The Friends and Foes of Change: Reformism and Conservatism in the Soviet Union', *Slavic Review*, vol. 38 (June 1979), pp. 197–202.

15 Roy Medvedev, 'USSR After Brezhnev', p. 25.
16 K.M. Simis, *USSR: Secrets of a Corrupt Society* (1982), esp. pp. 34–37. Zhores
   Medvedev also describes action taken by Andropov (before becoming General
   Secretary) against some of Brezhnev's associates; see *Andropov* (1983)
   pp. 93–97.

Further Reading to Part II

Introductory

Brown, Archie and Kaser, Michael. *Soviet Policy for the 1980s*. London: Macmillan, 1982.

Brown, Archie and Kaser, Michael. *The Soviet Union Since the Fall of Khrushchev*. London: Macmillan, 1978, 2nd edn.

Butler, W.E. *Soviet Law*. Sevenoaks: Butterworth, 1983.

Churchward, Lloyd G. *Contemporary Soviet Government*. London: Routledge, 1975, 2nd edn.

Friedrich, Carl J., Curtis, M. and Barber, B.R. *Totalitarianism in Perspective: Three Views*. New York: Praeger, 1969.

Hill, R.J. and Frank, P. *The Soviet Communist Party*. London: Allen and Unwin, 1981.

Jacobs, Everett M. (ed.) *Soviet Local Politics and Government*. London: Allen and Unwin, 1983.

Juviler, P.H. and Morton, H.W. (eds). *Soviet Policy-Making: Studies of Communism in Transition*. London: Pall Mall Press, 1967.

Kelley, D.R. (ed.). *Soviet Politics in the Brezhnev Era*. New York: Praeger, 1980.

Lane, D. *The Socialist Industrial State: Towards A Political Sociology of State Socialism*. London: Allen and Unwin, 1976.

Spiro, Herbert J. 'Totalitarianism', *International Encyclopedia of the Social Sciences*, vol. 16. London: Macmillan, 1968.

Tökés, R.L. 'Dissent: The Politics for Change in the USSR', in H.W. Morton and R.L. Tökés, *Soviet Politics and Society in the 1970s*. London: Macmillan, 1974.

Basic

Adams, J.S. *Citizen Inspectors in the Soviet Union: The People's Control Committee*. New York: Praeger, 1977.

Amalrik, Andrei. 'Will the USSR Survive until 1984?', in *Survey*, no. 73, Autumn 1969, pp. 47–79.

317

Azrael, J.R. *Managerial Power and Soviet Politics*. Cambridge, Mass. Harvard University Press, 1966.

Bell, Daniel. 'Ten Theories in Search of Reality: The Prediction of Soviet Behaviour in the Social Sciences', *World Politics*, vol. 10, no. 3, April 1958, pp. 327–65.

Bialer S. *Stalin's Successors. Leadership, Stability and Change in the Soviet Union*. Cambridge: Cambridge University Press, 1980.

Biddulph, H.L. 'Local Interest Articulation at CPSU Congresses', *World Politics*. vol. 36, no. 1. October 1983 pp. 28–52.

Brown, A. 'Pluralism, Power and the Soviet Political System: A Comparative Perspective', in Susan G. Solomon (ed.), *Pluralism in the Soviet Union*. London: Macmillan, 1983.

Bunce, Valerie and Echols, John M. III. 'Soviet Politics in the Brezhnev Era: "Pluralism" or "Corporatism"', in Donald R. Kelley (ed.), *Soviet Politics in the Brezhnev Era*. New York: Praeger, 1980.

Churchward, Lloyd G. *The Soviet Intelligentsia*. London: Routledge, 1973.

Connor, W.D. and Gitelman, Zvi Y. (eds). *Public Opinion in European Socialist Systems*. New York: Praeger, 1977.

Djilas, Milovan. *The New Class: An Analysis of the Communist System*. London: Unwin Books, 1966.

Fainsod, Merle. *Smolensk Under Soviet Rule*. London: Macmillan, 1958.

Friedrich, Carl J. and Brzezinski, Z.K. *Totalitarian Dictatorship and Autocracy*. New York: Praeger, 1966, revised edn.

Friedgut, T.H. *Political Participation in the USSR*. Princeton: Princeton University Press, 1979.

Gehlen, Michael. *The Communist Party of the Soviet Union*. Bloomington: Indiana University Press, 1969.

Gustafson, Thane. *Reform in Soviet Politics*. Cambridge. Cambridge University Press, 1981.

Hill, Ronald J. *Soviet Political Elites*. Oxford: Martin Robertson, 1977.

Hough, Jerry F. *The Soviet Prefects: The Local Party Organs in Industrial Decision-Making*. Cambridge, Mass.: Harvard University Press, 1969.

Hough, Jeery F. *Soviet Leadership in Transition*. Washington: The Brookings Institution, 1980.

Hough, Jerry F. 'Pluralism, Corporatism and the Soviet Union', in Susan G. Solomon (ed.), *Pluralism in the Soviet Union*. London: Macmillan, 1983.

Hough, Jerry F. and Fainsod, Merle. *How the Soviet Union is Governed*. Cambridge, Mass.: Harvard University Press, 1979.

Juviler, P.H. *Revolutionary Law and Order*. New York: The Free Press, 1976.

Kautsky, John. *Communism and the Politics of Development*. New York: Wiley, 1968.

'KPSS v tsifrakh'. '*Partiynaya zhizn*'. no. 14. July 1981.

Lane, D. 'Human Rights Under State Socialism?', *Political Studies*. vol. 32, no. 3, 1984.

Lane, D. *Leninism: A Sociological Interpretation* Cambridge: Cambridge University Press, 1981.

Linden, Carl A. *Khrushchev and the Soviet Leadership, 1957–1964*. Baltimore, Maryland: Johns Hopkins University Press, 1966.

Mandel, E. 'Ten Theses on the Social and Economic Laws Governing the Transition Between Capitalism and Socialism'. *Critique* 3, 1974.

Medvedev, R.A. *On Socialist Democracy*, New York: Alfred A. Knopf, 1975.

Medvedev, R. A. *On Soviet Dissent*, London: Constable, 1980.

Mickiewicz, E.P. *Media and the Russian Public*. New York: Praeger, 1981.

Poss, Sidney I. *Conflict and Decision-Making in Soviet Russia: A Case Study of Agricultral Policy, 1953–63*. Princeton, New Jersey: Princeton University Press, 1965.

Rattansi, Ali. *Marx and the Division of Labour*. London: Macmillan, 1982.

Rigby, T.H. 'Traditional, Market and Organisational Societies and the USSR', *World Politics*, vol. 16, 1964.

Ruble, Blair, *Soviet Trade Unions* Cambridge: Cambridge University Press, 1981.

Rush, Myron. *Political Succession in the USSR*. New York: Columbia University Press, 1975, Third edn.

Saifulin, M. (ed. & tr.) *The Soviet Parliament*. Moscow, Progress Publishers, 1967.

Sakharov, A. *My Country and the World*. London: Collins, 1975.

Skilling, H. Gordon and Griffiths, Franklyn. *Interest Groups in Soviet Politics*. Princeton: Princeton University Press, 1971.

Steel, Jonathan and Abraham, Eric, *Andropov in Power*, Oxford: Martin Robertson, 1983.

Stewart, Philip D. 'Soviet Interest Groups and the Policy Process: The Repeal of Production Education', *World Politics*, vol. 22, no. 1, October 1969.

Tatu, Michel. *Power in the Kremlin: From Khrushchev's Decline to Collective Leadership*. London: Collins, 1969.

Ticktin, Hillel. 'The Contradictions of Soviet Society and Professor Bettelheim', *Critique*, no. 6, Spring 1976, pp. 17–44.

Tökés, Rudolf L. *Dissent in the USSR: Politics, Ideology and People*. Baltimore, Maryland: Johns Hopkins University Press, 1975.

Tökés, R. 'Varieties of Soviet Dissent: An Overview', in R. Tökés (ed.), *Dissent in the USSR: Politics, Ideology and People*. Baltimore, Maryland: Johns Hopkins University Press, 1975.

Trotsky, L. *The Class Nature of the Soviet Union*. London: W.I.R. Publications, n.d.

Tucker, R.C. *Stalinism*, New York: Norton, 1977.

Unger, A.L. *Constitutional Development in the USSR*. London: Methuen, 1981.

Vanneman, Paul. *The Supreme Soviet: Politics and the Legislative Process the Soviet Political System*. Durham, NC: Duke University Press, 1977.

White, S. 'Communist Systems and the "Iron Law of Pluralism"', *British Journal of Political Science*, vol. 8, 1979.

White, S. *Political Culture and Soviet Politics*. London: Macmillan, 1979.

White, S. 'The USSR Supreme Soviet', in D. Nelson and S. White (eds), *Communist Legislatures in Comparative Perspective*. London: Macmillan, 1982.

Willerton, John P., 'Clientelism in the Soviet Union: An Initial Examination,' *Studies in Comparative Communism*, vol. 12, 1979.

320   POLITICS

Winkler, J.T. 'Corporatism', *European Journal of Sociology* vol. 17, no. 1, 1976.
Zharkov, A. and Korolyov, Y. *Standing Commissions of Soviet Parliament.*
Moscow: Novosti, 1982.

Specialized

Adams, Jan S. 'Institutional Change in the 1970's: The Case of the USSR People's
Control Committee', *Slavic Review,* Sept. 1978.
Adams, Jan S. 'Critical Letters to the Soviet Press: An Increasingly Important
Public Forum', in D.E. Schulz and J.S. Adams, *Political Participation in
Communist Systems,* New York: Pergamon, 1981.
Amalrik, Andrei. 'Will the USSR Survive Until 1984?', *Survey,* no. 73, Autumn
1969, pp. 47–79.
Avtorkhanov, Abdurakhman. *The Communist Party Apparatus.* Chicago: Henry
Regnery and Co., 1966.
Barabashev, E.V. and Sheremet, K.F. *Sovetskoe gosudarstvo i obshchetstvennost' v
usloviyakh razvernutogo stroitel'stva kommunizma.* Moscow: 1962.
Barghoorn, F.C. 'Factional, Sectoral and Subversive Opposition in Soviet Politics',
in R.A. Dahl (ed.), *Regimes and Oppositions.* New Haven, Conn: Yale
University Press, 1973.
Barker, F. *Solzhenitsyn: Politics and Form.* London: Macmillan, 1977.
Barron, John. *The KGB.* London: Hodder and Stoughton, 1974.
Barry. D.B. Feldbrugge, F.J.M. et al. *Soviet Law After Stalin.* Leiden: Sijthoff
and Noordhoff, 1979.
Berman, H.J. *Justice in the USSR.* Cambridge, Mass.: Harvard University Press,
1963.
Berry, Donald. 'The Specialist in Soviet Policy-Making: The Adoption of a Law',
Soviet Studies, vol. 14, 1964.
Bloch, Sidney and Reddaway, Peter. *Russia's Political Hospitals.* London:
Gollancz, 1977.
Bloch, S. and Reddaway, P. *Psychiatric Terror: How Soviet Psychiatry is Used to
Suppress Dissent.* London: Future Publications, 1978.
Bociurkiw, Bohdan R. 'Political Dissent in the Soviet Union', *Studies in
Comparative Communism,* vol. 3, no. 2, April 1970.
Bourdeaux, M. *Religious Ferment in Russia: Protestant Opposition to Soviet
Religious Policy.* London: Macmillan, 1968.
Brown, Archie. *Pluralism, Power and the Soviet Political System: A Comparative
Perspective,* in S.G. Solomon (ed.), *Pluralism in the Soviet Union.* London:
Macmillan, 1983.
Bunce, Valerie. *Executive Succession and Public Policy under Capitalism and
Socialism,* Princeton: Princeton University Press, 1981.
Carlo, Antonio. 'The Socio Economic Nature of the USSR', *Telos,* no. 21, Fall
1974, pp. 42–86.
Chalidze, Valery. *To Defend These Rights: Human Rights and the Soviet Union.*
New York: Random House, 1974.

Churchward, L.G. 'Soviet Local Government Today', *Soviet Studies*, vol. 17, no. 4, April 1966, pp. 431–52.

Cohen, Stephen F. 'The Friends and Foes of Change: Reformism and Conservatism in the Soviet Union', *Slavic Review*, vol. 38, June 1979, pp. 187–202.

Conquest, Robert. *Russia after Khrushchev*. London: Pall Mall Press, 1965.

Crouch, Colin. 'Pluralism and the New Corporatism: A Rejoinder', *Political Studies*, vol. 31, no. 3, Sept. 1983.

Dziak, John J. 'The "Action" Arm of the CPSU', *Problems of Communism*, vol. 30, no. 4, 1981.

Evans, A.B. Jr. 'Developed Socialism in Soviet Ideology', *Soviet Studies*, vol. 29, no. 3, July 1977.

Feldbrugge, F.J.M. and Simons, W.B. *Perspectives on Soviet Law for the 1980s*. Nijhoff, The Hague: 1982.

Grigorenko, P.S. *The Grigorenko Papers*. Boulder: Westview Press, 1976.

Groth, A. 'USSR: Pluralist Monolith?', *British Journal of Political Science*, vol. 9, 1979.

Harasymiw, Bohdan. 'Nomenklatura', *The Canadian Journal of Political Science*, vol. 2, no. 3, 1969, pp. 493–512.

Hazard, J.N., Butler, W.E., & Maggs, P.B. *The Soviet Legal System*. New York: Oceana Publications, 1977.

Hill, R.J. *Soviet Political Elites*. Oxford: Martin Robertson, 1977.

Hill, R.J. 'The CPSU in an Election Campaign', *Soviet Studies*, vol. 28, no. 4, 1976.

Hill, R.J. 'Party-State Relations and Soviet Political Development', *British Journal of Political Science*, vol. 10, 1980.

Hill, R.J. *Soviet Politics, Political Science and Reform*. London: Martin Robertson, 1980.

Hoffman, E.P. 'Changing Soviet Perspectives on Leadership and Administration', in S.F. Cohen, A. Rabinowitch and R. Sharlet (eds), *The Soviet Union Since Stalin*. London: Macmillan, 1980.

Hough, J.F. 'The Soviet System: Petrification of Pluralism?', *Problems of Communism*, March–April 1972.

Hough J.F. 'Political Participation in the Soviet Union', *Soviet Studies*, vol. 28, no. 1, January 1976, pp. 3–20.

Hough, J.F. *The Soviet Union and Social Science Theory*. Cambridge, Mass.: Harvard University Press, 1977.

Hough, J.F. 'The Generation Gap and the Brezhnev Succession', *Problems of Communism*, vol. 28, July–August 1979.

Hough, J.F. 'Thinking About Thinking About Dissent', *Studies in Comparative Communism*, vol. 12, nos. 2–3, 1979.

Hough, J.F. 'Issues and Personalities', *Problems of Communism*, vol. 31, no. 5, 1982, pp. 20–40.

Hough, J.F. 'Pluralism, Corporatism and the Soviet Union', in Susan S. Solomon, (ed.), *Pluralism in the Soviet Union*. London: Macmillan, 1983.

Itogi vyborov i sostav deputatov mestnykh sovetov narodnykh deputatov. Moscow: 1977.

322   POLITICS

Kanet, Roger E. 'The Rise and Fall of the All-People's State', *Soviet Studies*, vol. 20, no. 1, July 1968.

Karatnycky, A. et al. (eds). *Workers' Rights, East and West*. Transaction Books, New Brunswick, 1980.

Kelley, D.R. 'Environmental Policy-Making in the USSR: The Role of Industrial and Environmental Interests Groups', *Soviet Studies*, vol. 28, no. 4, 1976.

Kosolapov, R. 'The "Wholeness" of Developed Socialism', translated in *The Current Digest of the Soviet Press*, vol. 35, no. 10, 6 April 1983, pp. 4–6.

Kowalewski, D. 'Trends in Human Rights Movement', in Donald R. Kelley (ed.), *Soviet Politics in the Brezhnev Era*. New York: Prague, 1980

Kowalewski, D. 'Human Rights Protest in the USSR: Statistical Trends for 1965–78', *Universal Human Rights*, vol. 2, no. 1, Jan–March 1980.

'KPSS v tsifrakh', *Partiynaya zhizn*', no. 14, 1981.

Kudryavtsev, V. 'The New Constitution and the Development of Socialist Law', in *The Development of Soviet Law and Jurisprudence*. Moscow: Academy of Sciences, 1978.

Lane, Christel. 'Power and Legitimacy in the Soviet Union Through Socialist Ritual', *British Journal of Political Science*, vol. 14, 1984, pp. 207–17.

Lazreg, Marnia. 'Human Rights, State and Ideology: An Historical Perspective', in A. Pollis and P. Schwab, *Human Rights: Cultural and Ideological Perspectives*. New York: Praeger, 1979.

Lenski, Gerhard E. *Power and Privilege: A Theory of Social Stratification*. New York: McGraw Hill, 1966.

Leonhard, Wolfgang. *The Kremlin Since Stalin*, translated by Elizabeth Wiskemann and M. Jackson. London: Oxford University Press, 1962.

Linden, C.A. *Khrushchev and the Soviet Leadership 1957–1964*. Baltimore, Maryland: Johns Hopkins University Press, 1966.

Mandel, Ernest. *Marxist Economic Theory*. London: Merlin, 1968.

Matthews, M. *Class and Society in Soviet Russia*. London: Allen Lane, 1972.

Medvedev, Zhores and Roy. *A Question of Madness: How a Russian Scientist was put in a Soviet Mental Hospital and how he got out*. London: Macmillan, 1971.

Medvedev, Roy. 'USSR After Brezhnev', *Marxism Today*, September 1982.

Medvedev, Roy. *On Socialist Democracy*. New York: Alfred A. Knopf, 1975.

Michael, John C. 'The Independent Trade-Union Movement in the Soviet Union', *Radio Liberty*, RL 304/79, 1979 p. 1.

Michael, John C. 'Independent Worker Movements in the USSR: A Primer', *Workers Under Communism*, Winter, 1983.

Mickiewicz, E.P. *Soviet Political Schools: The Communist Party Adult Instruction System*. New Haven, Conn.: Yale University Press, 1967.

Mickiewicz, E.P. 'Feedback, Surveys and Soviet Communication Theory', *Journal of Communication*, Spring, 1983.

Miller, R.F. and Rigby, T.H. *26th Congress of the CPSU in Current Political Perspective*. Canberra: ANU. Occasional Paper, no. 16, 1982.

Moses, Joel C. 'The Impact of *Nomenklatura* in Soviet Elite Recruitment,' *Soviet Union*, vol. 8, 1981.

Nelson, Daniel N. *Communism and the Politics of Inequalities*, Lexington, Mass.: D.C. Heath, 1983.

Nove, Alec. *Was Stalin Really Necessary?: Some Problems of Soviet Political Economy*. London: Allen and Unwin, 1964.

Odom, W.E. *The Soviet Volunteers: Modernisation and Bureaucracy in a Public Mass Organisation*. Princeton, Princeton University Press, 1973.

Panitch, L. 'The Development of Corporatism in Liberal Democracies', in P.C. Schmitter and G. Lehmbruch, *Trends Towards Corporatist Intermediation*. London: Sage, 1979.

Parsons, Talcott. 'Characteristics of Industrial Societies', in C.E. Black (ed.), *The Transformation of Russian Society*. Cambridge, Mass.: Harvard University Press, 1960, pp. 13–41.

Partiya i rabochi klass v usloviyakh stroitel'stva kommunizma. Moscow: 1973.

Pinter, W.M. and Rowney, D.K. *Russian Officialdom: The Bureaucratization of Russian Society from the Seventeenth to the Twentieth Century*. London: Macmillan, 1980.

Purdy, David. *The Soviet Union: State Capitalist or Socialist?* London: Communist Party of Great Britain, n.d.

Reddaway, Peter. *Uncensored Russia: the Human Rights Movements in the Soviet Union*. London: Cape, 1972.

Rigby, T.H. *Communist Party Membership in the USSR, 1917–1967*. Princeton: Princeton University Press, 1968.

Rigby, T.H. 'The Soviet Politbureau: A Comparative Profile 1951–71', *Soviet Studies*, vol. 24, no. 1, July 1972.

Rigby, T.H. 'The Soviet Government Since Khrushchev', *Politics*, vol. 12, no. 1, May 1977, pp. 5–22.

Rigby, T.H. 'The Soviet Regional Leadership: The Brezhnev Generation', *Slavic Review*, March 1978.

Rigby, T.H. 'A Conceptual Approach to Authority, Power and Policy in the Soviet Union', in Rigby, T.H. et al. (eds), *Authority, Power and Policy in the USSR*. London: Macmillan, 1980.

Rigby, T.H. 'Introduction, Political Legitimacy, Weber and Communist Mono-organisational Systems' in T.H. Rigby and Ferenc Fehér, *Political Legitimation in Communist States*. London: Macmillan, 1982.

Rules of the Communist Party of the Soviet Union. London: Soviet Books, 1977, English edn.

Rush, Myron. *Political Succession in the USSR*. New York: Columbia University Press, 1968, 2nd edn.

Schulz, D.E. and J.S. Adams, (eds.) *Political Participation in Communist Systems*. New York: Pergamon, 1981.

Semenov, V.S. *Dialektika razvitiya sotsial'noy struktury sovetskogo obshchestva*. Moscow: 1977.

Shatz, M.S. *Soviet Dissent in Historical Perspective*. Cambridge: Cambridge University Press, 1981.

Simis, K.M. *USSR: Secrets of a Corrupt Society* London: Dent, 1982.

Smith, Gordon B. 'Bureaucratic Politics and Public Policy in the Soviet Union', in G.B. Smith, *Public Policy and Administration in the Soviet Union*. New York: Praeger, 1980.

Solomon, P.H. Jr., *Soviet Criminologists and Criminal Policy: Specialists in Policy-Making*. London: Macmillan, 1978.

Stalin, J.V. *Problems of Leninism*. Moscow, 1941.

Taubman, William. *Governing Soviet Cities. Bureaucratic Politics and Urban Development in the USSR*. London: Pall Mall Press, 1973.

Teague, L. 'The Central Committee and the Central Auditing Committee Elected at the Twenty-Sixth Congress of the CPSU', *Radio Liberty Research*, RL 171/81, Munich, 1981.

Ticktin, Hillel H. 'The Contradictions of Soviet Society and Professor Bettelheim', *Critique*, no. 6, Spring 1976, pp. 17–44.

Tökés, Rudolf. *Dissent in the USSR*. Baltimore: Johns Hopkins University Press, 1975.

Verkhovny Sovet SSSR (1979), p. 41, Moscow: 1979.

Vladmirov, L. 'Glavlit: How the Soviet Censor Works', *Index*, 1973.

White, Stephen. 'Contradiction and Change in State Socialism', *Soviet Studies*, vol. 26, no. 1, January 1974.

White, Stephen. 'The USSR: Patterns of Autocracy and Industrialism', in A. Brown and J. Gray, *Political Culture and Political Change in Communist States*, London: Macmillan 1977.

White, Stephen. 'The Supreme Soviet and Budgetary Politics in the USSR', *British Journal of Political Science*, vol. 13, January 1982.

White, Stephen. 'Political Communications in the USSR: Letters to Party, State and Press', *Political Studies*, vol. 31, 1983.

Wittfogel, Karl. *Oriental Despotism: A Comparative Study of Total Power*. New Haven, Conn.: Yale University Press, 1963.

'Workers' Opposition in the USSR', *Labour Focus on Eastern Europe*, vol. 2, no. 1, 1978.

Zaslavsky, V. and Brym, R.J. 'The Functions of Elections in the USSR', *Soviet Studies*, vol. 30, July 1978.

APPENDIX A

Membership of the CPSU

January 1	Members	Candidates	Total
1905	8,400	—	8,400
1907	46,000	—	46,000
1917 (March)	24,000	—	24,000
1917 (October)	350,000	—	350,000
1918 (March)	390,000	—	390,000
1919 (March)	350,000	—	350,000
1920 (March)	611,978	—	611,978
1921 (March)	732,521	—	732,521
1922	410,430	117,924	528,354
1923	381,400	117,700	499,100
1924	350,000	122,000	472,000
1925	440,365	361,439	801,804
1926	639,652	440,162	1,079,814
1927	786,288	426,217	1,212,505
1928	914,307	391,547	1,305,854
1929	1,090,508	444,854	1,535,362
1930	1,184,651	493,259	1,677,910
1931	1,369,406	842,819	2,212,225
1932	1,769,773	1,347,477	3,117,250
1933	2,203,951	1,351,387	3,555,338
1934	1,826,756	874,252	2,701,008
1935	1,659,104	699,610	2,358,714
1936	1,489,907	586,935	2,076,842
1937	1,453,828	527,869	1,981,697
1938	1,405,879	514,123	1,920,002
1939	1,514,181	792,792	2,306,973
1940	1,982,743	1,417,232	3,399,975
1941	2,490,479	1,381,986	3,872,465
1942	2,155,336	908,540	3,063,876
1943	2,451,511	1,403,190	3,854,701
1944	3,126,627	1,791,934	4,918,561

APPENDIX A (CON'T)

January 1	Members	Candidates	Total
1945	3,965,530	1,794,839	5,760,369
1946	4,127,689	1,383,173	5,510,862
1947	4,774,886	1,277,015	6,051,901
1948	5,181,199	1,209,082	6,390,281
1949	5,334,811	1,017,761	6,352,572
1950	5,510,787	829,396	6,340,183
1951	5,658,577	804,398	6,462,975
1952	5,853,200	854,339	6,707,539
1953	6,067,027	830,197	6,897,224
1954	6,402,284	462,579	6,864,863
1955	6,610,238	346,867	6,957,105
1956	6,767,644	405,877	7,173,521
1957	7,001,114	493,459	7,494,573
1958	7,296,559	546,637	7,843,196
1959	7,622,356	616,775	8,239,131
1960	8,017,249	691,418	8,708,667
1961	8,472,396	803,430	9,275,826
1962	9,051,934	839,134	9,891,068
1963	9,581,149	806,047	10,387,196
1964	10,182,916	839,453	11,022,369
1965	10,811,443	946,726	11,758,169
1966	11,548,287	809,021	12,357,308
1967	12,135,103	549,030	12,684,133
1968	12,484,836	695,389	13,180,225
1969	12,958,303	681,588	13,639,891
1970	13,395,253	616,531	14,011,784
1971	13,745,980	626,583	14,372,563
1972	14,109,432	521,857	14,631,289
1973	14,330,525	490,506	14,821,031
1974	14,493,524	532,391	15,025,915
1975	14,719,062	575,741	15,294,803
1976	15,029,562	609,329	15,638,891
1977	15,365,600	628,876	15,994,476
1978	15,701,658	658,212	16,359,870
1979	16,042,710	678,612	16,721,322
1980	16,398,340	683,949	17,082,289
1981	16,732,408	698,005	17,430,413
1982	17,076,530	693,138	17,769,668
1983	17,405,293	712,610	18,117,903

Source: Partiynaya zhizn': no. 15, 1983. pp. 14–15.

APPENDIX B

Dates of Party Conferences and Congresses 1898–1981

First Congress of the RSDLP	Minsk, March 1898.
Second Congress	Brussels–London, July–August 1903.
Third Congress	London, April 1905.
First Conference	Tammerfors, December 1905
Fourth (Unification) Congress	Stockholm, April 1906
Second Conference (First All-Russian)	Tammerfors, November 1906
Fifth (London) Congress	London, April–May 1907
Third Conference (Second All-Russian)	Kotka (Finland), July 1907.
Fourth Conference (Third All-Russian)	Helsingfors, November 1907
Fifth Conference	Paris, December 1908
Sixth (Prague) Conference	Prague, January 1912
Seventh (April) All-Russian Conference of the RSDLP(B)	Petrograd, April 1917.
Sixth Congress	Petrograd, July–August 1917.
Seventh Congress of the RCP(B)	Petrograd, March 1918.
Eighth Congress	Moscow, March 1919
Eighth All-Russian Conference	December 1919.
Ninth Congress	March–April 1920.
Ninth All-Russian Conference	September 1920.
Tenth Congress	March 1921.
Tenth All-Russian Conference	May 1921.
Eleventh All-Russian Conference	December 1921.
Eleventh Congress	March–April 1922.
Twelfth All-Russian Conference	August 1922.
Twelfth Congress	April 1923.
Thirteenth Conference	January 1924.
Thirteenth Congress	May 1924.
Fourteenth Conference	April 1925.
Fourteenth Congress of the AUCP (B)	December 1925.
Fifteenth Conference	October–November 1926.

Fifteenth Congress	December 1927.
Sixteenth Conference	April 1929.
Sixteenth Congress	June–July 1930.
Seventeenth Conference	January–February 1932.
Seventeenth Congress	January–February 1934.
Eighteenth Congress	March 1939.
Eighteenth Conference	February 1941.
Nineteenth Congress of the CPSU	October 1952.
Twentieth Congress	February 1956.
Twenty-First Congress	January–February 1959.
Twenty-Second Congress	October 1961.
Twenty-Third Congress	March–April 1966.
Twenty-Fourth Congress	March 1971.
Twenty-Fifth Congress	February 1976.
Twenty-Sixth Congress	February 1981.

The official title of the Party was as follows:

1898– Russian Social-Democratic Labour Party (sometimes rendered as Russian Social-Democratic Workers' Party) – RSDLP

1917– All-Russian Social-Democratic Labour Party (Bolsheviks) – RSDLP(B)

1918– All-Russian Communist Party (Bolsheviks) – RCP(B)

1925– All-Union Communist Party – AUCP(B)

1952– Communist Party of the Soviet Union – CPSU

APPENDIX C

Rules of the CPSU[1]

The Communist Party of the Soviet Union is the tried and tested militant vanguard of the Soviet people, which unites, on a voluntary basis, the more advanced, politically more conscious section of the working class, collective-farm peasantry and intelligentsia of the USSR.

Founded by V.I. Lenin as the vanguard of the working class, the Communist Party has travelled a glorious road of struggle, and brought the working class and the working peasantry to the victory of the Great October Socialist Revolution and to the establishment of the dictatorship of the proletariat in the USSR. Under the leadership of the Communist Party, the exploiting classes were abolished in the Soviet Union, and the moral and political unity of Soviet society has taken shape and grown in strength. Socialism has triumphed completely and finally. The Communist Party, the party of the working class, has today become the party of the Soviet people as a whole.

The Party exists for, and serves, the people. It is the highest form of social and political organization, and is the leading and guiding force of Soviet society. It directs the great activity of the Soviet people, and imparts an organized, planned, and scientifically-based character to their struggle to achieve the ultimate goal, the victory of communism.

The CPSU bases its work on unswerving adherence to the Leninist standards of Party life—the principle of collective leadership, the promotion, in every possible way, of inner-Party democracy, the activity and initiative of the Communists, criticism and self-criticism.

Ideological and organizational unity, monolithic cohesion of its ranks, and a high degree of conscious discipline on the part of all Communists are an inviolable law of the CPSU. All manifestations of factionalism and group activity are incompatible with Marxist-Leninist Party principles, and with Party membership. The Party rids itself of the individuals who violate the programme and the Rules of the CPSU and who compromise by their behaviour the lofty name of communist.

In all its activities, the CPSU takes guidance from Marxist-Leninist theory and

[1]English edition Moscow: Progress Publishers 1977. Adopted at the *22nd Congress of the CPSU*, 31 Oct. 1961, and as amended at the 23rd and 24th Congresses.

the Programme based on it, which defines the fundamental tasks of the Party for the period of the construction of communist society.

In creatively developing Marxism-Leninism, the CPSU vigorously combats all manifestations of revisionism and dogmatism, which are utterly alien to revolutionary theory.

The Communist Party of the Soviet Union is an integral part of the international Communist and working class movement. It firmly adheres to the tried and tested Marxist-Leninist principles of proletarian internationalism; it actively promotes the unity of the international Communist and working-class movement as a whole, and fraternal ties with the great army of the Communists of all countries.

I. PARTY MEMBERS, THEIR DUTIES AND RIGHTS

1. Membership of the CPSU is open to any citizen of the Soviet Union who accepts the Programme and the Rules of the Party, takes an active part in communist construction, works in one of Party organizations, carries out all Party decisions, and pays membership dues.

2. It is duty of a Party member:

(a) to work for the creation of the material and technical basis of communism; to serve as an example of the communist attitude towards labour: to raise labour productivity; to display the initiative in all that is new and progressive; to support and propagate advanced methods, to master techniques, to improve his skill; to protect and increase public socialist property, the mainstay of the might and prosperity of the Soviet country;

(b) to put Party decisions firmly and steadfastly into effect; to explain the policy of the Party to the masses; to help strengthen and multiply the Party's bonds with the people; to be considerate and attentive to people; to respond promptly to the needs and requirements of the working people;

(c) to take an active part in the political life of the country, in the administration of state affairs, and in economic and cultural development; to set an example in the fulfilment of his public duty to assist in developing and strengthening communist social relations;

(d) to master Marxist-Leninist theory, to improve his ideological knowledge, and to contribute to the moulding and education of the man of communist society. To combat vigorously all manifestations of bourgeois ideology, remnants of a private-property psychology, religious prejudices, and other survivals of the past; to observe the principles of communist morality, and place public interests above his own;

(e) to be an active proponent of the ideas of socialist internationalism and Soviet patriotism among the masses of the working people; to combat survivals of nationalism and chauvinism; to contribute by word and by deed to the consolidation of the friendship of the peoples of the USSR and the fraternal bonds linking the Soviet people with the peoples of the countries of the socialist camp, with the proletarians and other working people in all countries;

(f) to strengthen to the utmost the ideological and organizational unity of the Party; to safeguard the Party against the infiltration of people unworthy of the lofty name of Communist; to be truthful and honest with the Party and the people; to display vigilance, to guard Party and state secrets;

(g) to develop criticism and self-criticism, boldly lay bare shortcomings and strive for their removal; to combat ostentation, conceit, complacency, and parochial tendencies; to rebuff firmly all attempts at suppressing criticism; to resist all actions injurious to the Party and the state, and to give information of them to Party bodies, up to and including the Central Committee of the CPSU;

(h) to implement undeviatingly the Party's policy with regard to the proper selection of personnel according to their political qualifications and professional qualities. To be uncompromising whenever the Leninist principles of the selection and education of personnel are infringed;

(i) to observe Party and state discipline, which is equally binding on all Party members. The Party has one discipline, one law, for all Communists, irrespective of their past services or the positions they occupy;

(j) to help, in every possible way, to strengthen the defence potential of the USSR; to wage an unflagging struggle for peace and friendship among nations.

3. A Party member has the right:

(a) to elect and be elected to Party bodies;

(b) to discuss freely questions of the Party's policies and practical activities at Party meetings, conferences and congresses, at the meetings of Party committees and in the Party press; to table motions; openly to express and uphold his opinion as long as the Party organization concerned has not adopted a decision;

(c) to criticize any Communist, irrespective of the position he holds, at Party meetings, conferences and congresses, and at the full meetings of Party committees. Those commit the offence of suppressing criticism or victimizing anyone for criticism are responsible to and will be penalised by the Party, to the point of expulsion from the CPSU;

(d) to attend in person all Party meetings and all bureau and committee meetings that discuss his activities or conduct;

(e) to address any question, statement or proposal to any Party body, up to and including the Central Committee of the CPSU, and to demand an answer on the substance of his address.

4. Applicants are admitted to Party membership only individually. Membership of the Party is open to politically conscious and active workers, peasants and representatives of the intelligentsia, devoted to the communist cause. New members are admitted from among the candidate members who have passed through the established probationary period.

Persons may join the Party on attaining the age of eighteen. Young people up to and including the age of twenty-three may join the Party only through the Leninist Young Communist League of the Soviet Union (YCL).

The procedure for the admission of candidate members to full Party membership is as follows:

(a) Applicants for Party membership must submit recommendations from three members of the CPSU who have a Party standing of not less than five years and who know the applicants from having worked with them, professionally and socially, for not less than one year.

Note 1. – In the case of members of the YCL applying for membership of the Party, the recommendation of a district or city committee of the YCL is equivalent to the recommendation of one Party member.

Note 2. – Members and alternate members of the Central Committee of the CPSU shall refrain from giving recommendations.

(b) Applications for Party membership are discussed and a decision is taken by the general meeting of the basic Party organization; the decision of the latter is valid if not less than two-thirds of the Party members attending the meeting have voted for it, and comes into effect after endorsement by the district Party committee, or by the city Party committee in cities with no district divisions.

The presence of those who have recommended an applicant for Party membership at the discussion of the application concerned is optional;

(c) citizens of the USSR who formerly belonged to the Communist or Workers' Party of another country are admitted to membership of the Communist Party of the Soviet Union in conformity with the rules established by the Central Committee of the CPSU.

Former members of other parties are admitted to membership of the CPSU in conformity with the regular procedure, except that their admission must be endorsed by a regional or territorial committee or the Central Committee of the Communist Party of a Union Republic.

5. Communists recommending applicants for Party membership are responsible to Party organizations for the impartiality of their description of the moral qualities and professional and political qualifications of those they recommend.

6. The Party standing of those admitted to membership dates from the day when the general meeting of the basic Party organization decides to accept them as full members.

7. The procedure of registering members and candidate members of the Party, and their transfer from one organization to another is determined by the appropriate instructions of the Central Committee of the CPSU.

8. If a Party member or candidate member fails to pay membership dues for three months in succession without sufficient reason, the matter shall be discussed by the basic Party organization. If it is revealed as a result that the Party member or candidate member in question has virtually lost contact with the party organization, he shall be regarded as having ceased to be a member of the Party; the basic Party organization shall pass a decision theorem and submit it to the district or city committee of the Party for endorsement.

9. A Party member or candidate member who fails to fulfil his duties as laid down in the Rules, or commits other offences, shall be called to account, and may be subjected to the penalty of admonition, reprimand (severe reprimand), or reprimand (severe reprimand) with entry in the registration card. The highest Party penalty is expulsion from the Party.

In the case of insignificant offences, measures of Party education and influence should be applied – in the form of comradely criticism, Party censure, warning, or reproof. When the question of expelling a member from the Party is discussed, the maximum attention must be shown, and the grounds for the charges preferred against him must be thoroughly investigated.

10. The decision to expel a Communist from the Party is made by the general meeting of a basic Party organization. The decision of the basic Party organization expelling a member is regarded as adopted if not less than two-thirds of the Party members attending the meeting have voted for it, and enters into force following endorsement by the district or city Party committee.

Until such time as the decision to expel him is endorsed by a regional or territorial Party committee or the Central Committee of the Communist Party a Union Republic, the Party member or candidate member retains his membership card and is entitled to attend closed Party meetings.

An expelled Party member retains the right to appeal, within the period of two months, to the higher Party bodies, up to and including the Central Committee of the CPSU.

11. The question of calling a member or alternate member of the Central Committee of the Communist Party of a Union Republic, of a territorial, regional, area, city or district Party committee, as well as a member or an auditing commission, to account before the Party is discussed by basic Party organization.

Party organizations pass decisions imposing penalties on member or alternate members of the said Party committees, or on members of auditing commissions, in conformity with the regular procedure.

A Party organization which proposes expelling a Communist from the CPSU communicates its proposal to the Party committee of which he is a member. A decision expelling from the Party a member or alternate member of the Central Committee of the Communist Party of a Union Republic or a territorial, regional, area, city or district Party committee, or a member of an auditing commission, is taken at the full meeting of the committee concerned by a majority of two-thirds of the membership.

The decision to expel from the Party a member or alternate member of the Central Committee of the CPSU, or a member of the Central Auditing Commission, is made by the Party congress, and in the interval between two congresses, by a full meeting of the Central Committee, by a majority of two-thirds of its members.

12. Should a Party member commit an indictable offence, he shall be expelled from the Party and prosecuted in conformity with the law.

13. Appeals against expulsion from the Party or against the imposition of a penalty, as well as the decisions of Party organizations on explusion from the Party shall be examined by the appropriate Party bodies within not more than one month from the date of their receipt.

II. CANDIDATE MEMBERS

14. All persons joining the Party must pass through a probationary period as candidate members in order to familiarize themselves more thoroughly with the Programme and the Rules of the CPSU and prepare for admission to full

membership of the Party. Party organizations must assist candidates to prepare for admission to full membership of the Party, and test their personal qualities. The period of probationary membership shall be one year.

15. The procedure for the admission of candidate members (individual admission, submission of recommendations, decision of the primary organization as to admission, and its endorsement) is identical with the procedure for the admission of Party members.

16. On the expiration of a candidate member's probationary period the basic Party organization discusses and passes a decision on his admission to full membership. Should a candidate member fail, in the course of his probationary period, to prove his worthiness, and should his personal traits make it evident that he cannot be admitted to membership of the CPSU, the Party organization shall pass a decision rejecting his admission to membership of the Party; after endorsement of that decision by the district or city Party committee, he shall cease to be considered a candidate member of the CPSU.

17. Candidate members of the Party participate in all the activities of their Party organisations; they shall have a consultative voice at Party meetings. They may not be elected to any leading Party body, nor may they be elected delegates to a Party conference or congress.

18. Candidate members of the CPSU pay membership dues at the same rate as full members.

III. ORGANIZATIONAL STRUCTURE OF THE PARTY. INNER-PARTY DEMOCRACY

19. The guiding principle of the organizational structure of the Party is democratic centralism, which signifies:

(a) election of all leading Party bodies, from the lowest to the highest;

(b) periodical reports of Party bodies to their organizations and to higher bodies;

(c) strict Party discipline and subordination of the minority to the majority;

(d) the decisions of higher bodies are obligatory for lower bodies.

20. The Party is built on the territorial-and-production principle: basic organizations are established wherever Communists are employed, and are associated territorially in district, city, organizations. As organization serving a given area is higher than any Party organization serving part of that area.

21. All Party organizations are autonomous in the decision of local questions, unless their decisions conflict with Party policy.

22. The highest leading body of a Party organization is the general meeting (in the case of basic organizations), conference (in the case of district, city, area, regional or territorial organizations), or congress (in the case of the communist Parties of the Union Republics and the Communist Party of the Soviet Union).

23. The general meeting, conference or congress, elects a bureau or committee which acts as its executive body and directs all the current work of the Party organization.

24. The election of Party bodies shall be effected by secret ballot. In an election, all Party members have the unlimited right to challenge candidates and to criticize them. Each candidate shall be voted upon separately. A candidate is considered elected if more than one-half of those attending the meeting, conference or congress have voted for him.

The principle of a systematic renewal of the composition of Party bodies and of continuity of leadership shall be observed in the election of those bodies from primary organizations to the Cental Committee of the CPSU.

25. The entire activity of a member or alternate member of the CC CPSU must justify the Party's great trust. Members or alternate members of the CC CPSU who degrade their honour and dignity may not remain on the Central Committee. The question of the removal of a member or alternate member of the CC CPSU from that body shall be decided by a plenary meeting of the Central Committee by secret ballot. The decision is regarded as adopted if not less than two-thirds of the membership of the CC CPSU vote for it.

The question of the removal of a member or alternate member of the Central Committee of the Communist Party of a Union Republic, or of a territorial, regional, area, city or district Party committee from the Party body concerned is decided by a full meeting of that body. The decision is regarded as adopted if not less than two-thirds of the membership of the committee in question vote for it by secret ballot.

A member of the Central Auditing Commission who does not justify the great trust placed in him by the Party shall be removed from that body. This question shall be decided by a meeting of the Central Auditing Commission. The decision is regarded as adopted if not less than two-thirds of the membership of the Central Auditing Commission vote by secret ballot for the removal of the member concerned from that body.

The question of the removal of a member from the auditing commission of a republican, territorial, regional, area, city or district Party organizations shall be decided by a meeting of the appropriate commission according to the procedure established for members and alternate members of Party committees.

26. The free and business-like discussion of questions of Party policy in individual Party organizations or in the Party as a whole is the inalienable right of every Party member and an important principle of inner-Party democracy. Only on the basis of inner-party democracy is it possible to develop criticism and self-criticism and to strengthen Party discipline, which must be conscious and not mechanical.

Discussion of controversial or insufficiently clear issues may be held within the framework of individual organizations or the Party as a whole.

Party-wide discussion is necessary:

(a) If the necessity is recognized by several Party organizations at regional or republican level;

(b) if there is not a sufficiently solid majority in the Central Committee on major questions of Party policy;

(c) if the Central Committee of the CPSU considers it necessary to consult the Party as a whole on any particular question of policy.

Wide discussion, especially discussion on a country-wide scale, of questions of Party policy must be so held as to ensure for Party members the free expression of their views and preclude attempts to form factional groupings destroying Party unity, attempts to split the Party.

27. The supreme principle of Party leadership is collective leadership, which is an absolute requisite for the normal functioning of Party organizations, the proper education of cadres, and the promotion of the activity and initiative of Communists. The cult of the individual and the violations of inner-Party democracy resulting from it must not be tolerated in the Party; they are incompatible with the Leninist principles of Party life.

Collective leadership does not exempt individuals in office from personal responsibility for the job entrusted to them.

28. The Central Committees of the Communist Parties of the Union Republics, and territorial, regional, area, city and district Party committees shall systematically inform Party organizations of their work in the interim between congresses and conferences.

29. Meetings of the *aktiv* of district, city, area, regional, and territorial Party organizations and of the Communist Parties of the Union Republics shall be held to discuss major decisions of the Party and to work out measures for their execution, as well as to examine questions of local significance.

IV. HIGHER PARTY ORGANS

30. The supreme organ of the Communist Party of the Soviet Union is the Party Congress. Congresses are convened by the Central Committee not less than every five years. The convocation of a Party Congress and its agenda shall be announced at least six weeks before the Congress. Extraordinary congresses are convened by the Central Committee of the Party on its own initiative or on the demand of not less than one-third of the total membership represented at the preceding Party congress. Extraordinary congresses shall be convened within two months. A congress is considered properly constituted if not less than one-half of the total Party membership is represented at it.

The scale of representation at a Party Congress is determined by the Central Committee.

31. Should the Central Committee of the Party fail to convene an extraordinary congress within the period specified in Article 31, the organizations which demanded it have the right to form an Organizing Committee which shall enjoy the powers of the Central Committee of the Party in respect of the convocation of the extraordinary congress.

32. The Congress:

(a) hears and approves the reports of the Central Committee, of the Central

Auditing Commission, and of the other central organizations;

(b) reviews, amends and endorses the Programme and the Rules of the Party;

(c) determines the line of the Party in matters of home and foreign policy, and examines and decides the most important questions of communist construction;

(d) elects the Central Committee and the Central Auditing Commission.

33. The number of members to be elected to the Central Committee and to the Central Auditing Commission is determined by the Congress. In the event of vacancies occurring in the Central Committee, they are filled from among the alternate members of the Central Committee of the CPSU elected by the Congress.

34. Between congresses, the Central Committee of the Communist Party of the Soviet Union directs the activities of the Party, the local Party bodies, selects and appoints leading officials, directs the work of central government bodies and public organizations of working people through the Party groups in them, sets up various Party organs, institutions and enterprises and directs their activities, appoints the editors of the central newspapers and journals operating under its control, and distributes the funds of the Party budget and controls its execution.

The Central Committee represents the CPSU in its relations with other parties.

35. The Central Committee of the CPSU shall keep the Party organizations regularly informed of its work.

36. The Central Auditing Commission of the CPSU supervises the expeditious and proper handling of affairs by the central bodies of the Party, and audits the accounts of the treasury and the enterprises of the Central Committee of the CPSU.

37. The Central Committee of the CPSU shall hold not less than one full meeting every six months. Alternate members of the Central Committee shall attend its full meetings with consultative voice.

38. The Central Committee of the Communist Party of the Soviet Union elects a Political Bureau to direct the work of the Central Committee between full meetings and a Secretariat to direct current work, chiefly the selection of cadres and the verification of the fulfilment of Party decisions. The Central Committee elects the General Secretary of the CPSU.

39. The Central Committee of the Communist Party of the Soviet Union sets up the Party Control Committee of the Central Committee.

The Party Control Committee of the Central Committee of the CPSU:

(a) verifies the observance of Party discipline by members and candidate members of the CPSU, and takes action against Communists who violate the Programme and the Rules of the Party or state discipline, and against violators of Party ethics;

(b) considers appeals against decisions of Central Committees of the Communist Parties of the Union Republics or of territorial and regional Party committees to expel members from the Party or impose Party penalties upon them.

40. Between Party congresses the Central Committee of the CPSU may if necessary convene a country-wide Party Conference to discuss pressing matters of Party policy. The procedure of holding the Party conference is determined by the CC CPSU.

V. REPUBLICAN, TERRITORIAL, REGIONAL, AREA, CITY AND DISTRICT ORGANIZATIONS OF THE PARTY

41. The republican, territorial, regional, area, city and district Party organizations and their committees take guidance in their activities from the Programme and the Rules of the CPSU, conduct all work for the implementation of Party policy and organize the fulfilment of the directives of the Central Committee of the CPSU within the republics, territories, regions, areas, cities and districts concerned.

42. The basic duties of republican, territorial, regional, area, city and district Party organizations, and of their leading bodies, are:

(a) political and organizational work among the masses, mobilization of the masses for the fulfilment of the tasks of communist construction, for the maximum development of industrial and agricultural production, for the fulfilment and over-fulfilment of state plans; solicitude for the steady improvement of the material and cultural standards of the working people;

(b) organization of ideological work, propaganda of Marxism-Leninism, promotion of the communist awareness of the working people, guidance of the local press, radio and television, and supervision over the activities of cultural and educational institutions;

(c) guidance of Soviets, trade unions, the YCL, the co-operatives and other public organizations through the Party groups in them, and increasingly broader enlistment of working people in the activities of these organizations, development of the initiative and activity of the masses as an essential condition for the gradual transition from socialist statehood to public self-government under communism.

Party organizations must not act in place of government, trade union, co-operative or other public organizations of the working people; they must not allow either the merging of the functions of Party and other bodies or undue parallelism in work;

(d) selection and appointment of leading personnel, their education in the spirit of communist ideas, honesty and truthfulness, and high sense of responsibility to the Party and the people for the work entrusted to them;

(e) large-scale enlistment of Communists in the conduct of Party activities as voluntary workers, as a form of social work;

(f) organisation of various institutions and enterprises of the Party within the bounds of their republic, territory, region, area, city or district and guidance of their activities; distribution of Party funds within the given organization; the provision of systematic information to the higher Party body and accountability to it for their work.

Leading Bodies of Republican, Territorial and Regional Party Organizations

43. The highest body of regional, territorial and republican Party organizations is the respective regional or territorial Party conference or the congress of the

Communist Party of the Union Republic, and in the interim between them the regional committee, territorial committee or the Central Committee of the Communist Party of the Union Republic.

44. Regular regional and territorial Party conferences are convened by the respective regional or territorial committees once every two-three years.

A regular congress of the Communist Party of a Union Republic shall be convened by the Central Committee of the Communist Party of the Union Republic not less than every five years. Extraordinary conferences and congresses are convened by decision of regional or territorial committees, or the Central Committees of the Communist Parties of the Union Republics, or on the demand of one-third of the total membership of the organizations belonging to the regional, territorial or republican Party organization.

The rates of representation at regional and territorial conferences and at congresses of the Communist Parties of the Union Republics are determined by the respective Party committees.

Regional and territorial conferences and congresses of the Communist Parties of the Union Republics, hear the reports of the respective regional or territorial committees, or the Central Committee of the Communist Party of the Union Republic, and of the auditing commission; discuss at their own discretion other matters of Party, economic and cultural development, and elect the regional or territorial committee, the Central Committee of the Union Republic, the auditing commission and the delegates to the Congress of the CPSU.

Between congresses of the Communist Parties of the Union Republics, their Central Committees may if necessary convene republican Party conferences to discuss urgent questions of the activity of Party organizations. The procedure of holding republican Party conferences is determined by the Central Committees of the Communist Parties of the Union Republics.

45. The regional and territorial committees and the Central Committees of the Communist Parties of the Union Republics elect bureaus, which also include secretaries of the committees. The secretaries must have a Party standing of not less than five years. The full meetings of the committees also confirm the chairmen of Party commissions, heads of departments of these committees, editors of Party newspapers and journals.

Regional and territorial committees and the Central Committees of the Communist Parties of the Union Republics may set up secretariats to examine current business and verify the execution of decisions.

46. The full meetings of regional and territorial committees and the Central Committees of the Communist Parties of the Union Republics shall be convened at least once every four months.

47. The regional and territorial committees and the Central Committees of the Communist Parties of the Union Republics direct the area, city and district Party organizations, inspect their work and regularly hear reports of area, city and district Party committees.

Party organizations in Autonomous Republics and other regions forming part of a territory or a Union Republic, function under the guidance of the respective territorial committees or Central Committees of the Communist Parties of the Union Republics.

Leading Bodies of Area, City and District (Urban and Rural) Party Organizations

48. The highest body of an area, city or district Party organization is the area, city and district Party conference or the general meeting of Communists convened by the area, city or district committee at least once in two years, and the extraordinary conference convened by decision of the respective committee or on the demand of one-third of the total membership of the Party organization concerned.

The area, city or district conference (general meeting) hears reports of the committee and auditing commission, discusses at its own discretion other questions of Party, economic and cultural development, and elects the area, city and district committee, the auditing commission and delegates to the regional and territorial conference or the congress of the Communist Party of the Union Republic.

The quota of representation to the area, city or district conference is established by the respective Party committee.

49. The area, city or district committee elects a bureau, including the committee secretaries, and confirms the appointment of heads of committee departments and newspaper editors. The secretaries of the area, city and district committees must have a Party standing of at least three years. The committee secretaries are confirmed by the respective regional or territorial committee, or the Central Committee of the Communist Party of the Union Republic.

50. The area, city and district committee organizes and confirms the basic Party organizations, directs and work, regularly hears reports concerning the work of Party organizations, and keeps a register of Communists.

51. The full meeting of the area, city and district committee is convened at least once in three months.

52. The area city and district committee has voluntary officials, sets up standing or *ad hoc* commissions on various aspects of Party work and uses other ways to draw Communists into the activities of the Party committee on a voluntary basis.

VI. BASIC (OR PRIMARY) PARTY ORGANIZATIONS

53. The basic Party organizations are the basis of the Party.

Basic Party organizations are formed at the places of work of Party members – in factories, state farms and other enterprises, collective farms, units of the Soviet Army, offices, educational establishments, etc., wherever there are not less than three Party members. Basic Party organizations may also be organized on the residential principle in villages and in blocks of flats.

In individual cases, given the permission of the regional or territorial committee, or the Central Committee of the Communist Party of the Union Republic, primary

Party organizations may be formed in the framework of several enterprises forming an industrial association and located, as a rule, in the territory of one district or several districts of one city.

54. At enterprises, collective farms and institutions with over fifty Party members and candidate members, shop, sectional, farm, team, departmental, etc., Party organizations may be formed as units of the general basic Party organization with the sanction of the district, city or area committee.

Within shop, sectional, etc., organizations, and also within basic Party organizations having less than fifty members and candidate members, Party groups may be formed in the teams and other production units.

55. The highest organ of the basic Party organization is the Party meeting, which is convened at least once a month. In Party organizations encompassing shop or departmental organizations general Party meetings are held at least once in every two months.

In large Party organizations with a membership of more than 300 Communists, a general Party meeting is convened when necessary at times fixed by the Party committee or on the demand of a number of shop or departmental Party organizations.

56. For the conduct of current business the branch, shop or departmental Party organization elects a bureau for the term of one year. The number of its members is fixed by the Party meeting. Branch, shop and departmental Party organizations with less than fifteen Party members do not elect a bureau. Instead, they elect a secretary and deputy secretary of the Party organization.

Secretaries of branch, shop and departmental Party organizations must have a Party standing of at least one year.

Basic Party organizations with less than 150 Party members shall have, as a rule, no salaried officials released from their regular work.

57. In large factories and offices with more than 300 members and candidate members of the Party, and in exceptional cases in factories and offices with over 100 Communists by virtue of special production conditions and territorial dispersion, subject to the approval of the regional committee, territorial committee or Central Committee of the Communist Party of the Union Republic, Party committees may be formed, the shop and departmental Party organizations at these factories and offices being granted the status of basic Party organizations.

The Party organizations of collective and state farms may set up Party committees if they have a minimum of fifty Communists.

In individual cases, given the permission of the regional or territorial Party committee or the Central Committee of the Communist Party of the Union Republic, Party organizations numbering more than 500 Communists may form Party committees in the larger shops or department, and the Party organizations.

Party committees are elected for a term of two-three years, and the number of their members is determined by a general Party meeting or conference.

58. Given the permission of the Central Committee of the Communist Party of a Union Republic, Party committees of primary organizations numbering more than 1,000 Communists may be granted the status of a district Party committee in the

matter of admission to the CPSU, the keeping of the records of Party members and candidate members, and in examining cases of misconduct by Communists.

59. In its activities the basic Party organization takes guidance from the Programme and the Rules of the CPSU. It conducts its work directly among the working people, rallies them round the Communist Party of the Soviet Union, organises the masses to carry out the Party policy and to work for the building of communism.

The basic Party organization:

(a) admits new members to the CPSU;

(b) educates Communists in a spirit of loyalty to the Party cause, ideological staunchness and communist ethics;

(c) organises the study by Communists of Marxist-Leninist theory in close connection with the practice of communist construction and opposes all attempts to introduce revisionist distortions of Marxism-Leninism or a dogmatic interpretation of Marxism-Leninism;

(d) ensures the vanguard role of Communists in the sphere of labour and in the social and political and economic activities of enterprises, collective farms, institutions, educational establishments, etc.;

(e) acts as the organiser of the working people for the performance of the current tasks of communist construction, heads the socialist emulation movement for the fulfilment of state plans and undertakings of the working people, rallies the masses to disclose and make the best use of untapped resources at enterprises and collective farms, and to apply in production on a broad scale the achievements of science, engineering and the experience of front-rankers; works for the strengthening of labour discipline, the steady increase of labour productivity and improvement of the quality of production, and shows concern for the protection and increase of social wealth at enterprises, state farms and collective farms;

(f) conducts agitational and propaganda work among the masses, educates them in the communist spirit, helps the working people to acquire proficiency in administering state and social affairs;

(g) on the basis of extensive criticism and self-criticism, combats cases of bureaucracy, parochialism, and violations of state discipline, thwarts attempts to deceive the state, acts against negligence, waste and extravagance at enterprises, collective farms and offices;

(h) assists the area, city and district committees in their activities and is accountable to them for its work.

The Party organization must see to it that every Communist should observe in his own life and cultivate among working people the moral principles set forth in the Programme of the CPSU, in the moral code of the builder of communism and cultivate them among the working people:

loyalty to the communist cause, love of his own socialist country, and of other socialist countries;

conscientious labour for the benefit of society, for he who does not work, neither shall he eat;

concern on everyone's part for the protection and increase of social wealth;

lofty sense of public duty, intolerance of violations of public interests;
collectivism and comradely mutual assistance: one for all, and all for one;
humane relations and mutual respect among people: man is to man a friend,
   comrade and brother;
honesty and truthfulness, moral purity, unpretentiousness and modesty in public
   and personal life;
mutual respect in the family circle and concern for the upbringing of children;
intolerance of injustice, parasitism, dishonesty, careerism and money-grubbing;
friendship and fraternity among all peoples of the USSR, intolerance of national
   and racial hostility;
intolerance of the enemies of communism, the enemies of peace and those who
   oppose the freedom of the peoples;
fraternal solidarity with the working peoples of all countries, with all peoples.

60. Basic Party organizations of industrial enterprises and trading establishments,
state farms, collective farms and designing organizations, drafting offices
and research institutes directly related to production, enjoy the right to control
the work of the administration.

The Party organizations at Ministries, State Committees, and other central and
local government or economic agencies and departments exercise control over the
work of the administration in fulfilling Party and government directives and in
observing Soviet law. They must actively promote improvement of the apparatus,
cultivate among the personnel a high sense of responsibility for work entrusted to
them, promote state discipline and the better servicing of the population, firmly
combat bureaucracy and red tape, inform the appropriate Party bodies in good
time of shortcomings in the work of the respective offices and individuals,
regardless of what posts the latter may occupy.

VII. THE PARTY AND THE YCL

61. The Leninist Young Communist League of the Soviet Union is an
independently acting social organization of young people, an active helper and
reserve of the Party. The YCL helps the Party educate the youth in a communist
spirit, to draw it into the work of building a new society, to train a rising generation
of harmoniously developed people who will live and work and administer public
affairs under communism.

62. The YCL organizations enjoy the right of broad initiative in discussing and
submitting to the appropriate Party organizations questions relating to the work of
enterprises, collective farms and offices. They must be active levers in the
implementation of Party directives in all spheres of communist construction,
especially where there are no basic Party organizations.

63. The YCL conducts its activities under the guidance of the Communist Party
of the Soviet Union. The work of the local YCL organizations is directed and
controlled by the appropriate republican, territorial, regional, area, city and district
Party organizations.

In their communist educational work among the youth, local Party bodies and primary Party organizations rely on the support of the YCL organizations, and uphold and promote their useful undertakings.

64. Members of the YCL who have been admitted into the CPSU cease to belong to the YCL the moment they join the Party, provided they do not hold leading posts in YCL organizations.

VIII. PARTY ORGANIZATIONS IN THE SOVIET ARMY

65. Party organizations in the Soviet Army are guided in their work by the Programme and the Rules of the CPSU and operate on the basis of instructions issued by the Central Committee.

The Party organizations of the Soviet Army carry out the policy of the Party in the Armed Forces, rally servicemen round the Communist Party, educate them in the spirit of Marxism-Leninism and boundless loyalty to the socialist homeland, actively further the unity of the army and the people, work for the strengthening of military discipline, rally servicemen to carry out the tasks of military and political training and acquire skill in the use of new techniques and weapons, and to carry out irreproachably their military duty and the orders and instructions of the command.

66. The guidance of Party work in the Armed Forces is exercised by the Central Committee of the CPSU through the Chief Political Administration of the Soviet Army and Navy, which functions as a department of the Central Committee of the CPSU.

The heads of the political administrations of military areas and fleets and heads of the political administrations of armies must be Party members of five years' standing, and the heads of political departments of military formations must be Party members of three years' standing.

67. The Party organizations and political bodies of the Soviet Army maintain close contract with local Party committees, and keep them informed about political work in the military units. The secretaries of military Party organizations and heads of political bodies participate in the work of local Party committees.

IX. PARTY GROUPS IN NON-PARTY ORGANIZATIONS

68. At congresses, conferences and meetings and in the elective bodies of Soviets, trade unions, co-operatives and other mass organizations of the working people, having at least three Party members, Party groups are formed for the purpose of strengthening the influence of the Party in every way and carrying out Party policy among non-Party people, strengthening Party and state discipline, combating bureaucracy, and verifying the fulfilment of Party and government directives.

69. The Party groups are subordinate to the appropriate Party bodies: the Central Committee of the Communist Party of the Soviet Union, the Central Committees of the Communist Parties of the Union Republics, territorial, regional, area, city or district Party committees.

In all matters the groups must strictly and unswervingly abide by decisions of the leading Party bodies.

X. PARTY FUNDS

70. The funds of Party and its organizations are derived from membership dues, incomes from Party enterprises and other revenue.

71. The monthly membership dues for Party members and candidate members are as follows:

Monthly earnings	Dues	
up to 50 roubles	10 kopeks	
from 51 to 100 roubles	0.5 per cent	
from 101 to 150 roubles	1.0 per cent	
from 151 to 200 roubles	1.5 per cent	of monthly
from 201 to 250 roubles	2.0 per cent	earnings
from 251 to 300 roubles	2.5 per cent	
over 300 roubles	3.0 per cent	

72. An entrance fee of 2 per cent of monthly earnings is paid on admission to the Party as a candidate member.

APPENDIX D

The Constitution (Fundamental Law) of the USSR, 1977

The Great October Socialist Revolution, made by the workers and peasants of Russia under the leadership of the Communist Party headed by Lenin, overthrew capitalist and landowner rule, broke the fetters of oppression, established the dictatorship of the proletariat, and created the Soviet state, a new type of state, the basic instrument for defending the gains of the revolution and for building socialism and communism. Humanity thereby began the epoch-making turn from capitalism to socialism.

After achieving victory in the Civil War and repulsing imperialist intervention, the Soviet government carried through far-reaching social and economic transformations, and put an end once and for all to exploitation of man by man, antagonisms between classes, and strife between nationalities. The unification of the Soviet Republics in the Union of Soviet Socialist Republics multiplied the forces and opportunities of the peoples of the country in the building of socialism. Social ownership of the means of production and genuine democracy for the working masses were established. For the first time in the history of mankind a socialist society was created.

The strength of socialism was vividly demonstrated by the immortal feat of the Soviet people and their Armed Forces in achieving their historic victory in the Great Patriotic War.* This victory consolidated the influence and international standing of the Soviet Union and created new opportunities for growth of the forces of socialism, national liberation, democracy and peace throughout the world.

Continuing their creative endeavours, the working people of the Soviet Union have ensured rapid, all-round development of the country and steady improvement of the socialist system. They have consolidated the alliance of the working class, collective-farm peasantry, and people's intelligentsia, and friendship of the nations and nationalities of the USSR. Socio-political and ideological unity of Soviet society, in which the working class is the leading force, has been achieved. The aims of the dictatorship of the proletariat having been fulfilled, the Soviet state has

---

* i.e. Second World War.

become a state of the whole people. The leading role of the Communist Party, the vanguard of all the people, has grown.

In the USSR a developed socialist society has been built. At this stage, when socialism is developing on its own foundations, the creative forces of the new system and the advantages of the socialist way of life are becoming increasingly evident, and the working people are more and more widely enjoying the fruits of their great revolutionary gains.

It is a society in which powerful productive forces and progressive science and culture have been created, in which the well-being of the people is constantly rising, and more and more favourable conditions are being provided for the all-round development of the individual.

It is a society of mature socialist social relations, in which, on the basis of the drawing together of all classes and social strata and of the juridical and factual equality of all its nations and nationalities and their fraternal co-operation, a new historical community of people has been formed – the Soviet people.

It is a society of high organizational capacity, ideological commitment, and consciousness of the working people, who are patriots and internationalists.

It is a society in which the law of life is concern of all for the good of each and concern of each for the good of all.

It is a society of true democracy, the political system of which ensures effective management of all public affairs, ever more active participation of the working people in running the state, and the combining of citizens' real rights and freedoms with their obligations and responsibility to society.

Developed socialist society is a natural, logical stage on the road to communism.

The supreme goal of the Soviet state is the building of a classless communist society in which there will be public, communist self-government. The main aims of the people's socialist state are: to lay the material and technical foundation of communism, to perfect socialist social relations and transform them into communist relations, to mould the citizen of communist society, to raise the people's living and cultural standards, to safeguard the country's security, and to further the consolidation of peace and development of international co-operation.

The Soviet people, guided by the ideas of scientific communism and true to their revolutionary traditions, relying on the great social, economic, and political gains of socialism, striving for the further development of socialist democracy, taking into account the international position of the USSR as part of the world system of socialism, and conscious of their internationalist responsibility, preserving continuity of the ideas and principles of the first Soviet Constitution of 1918, the 1924 Constitution of the USSR and the 1936 Constitution of the USSR, hereby affirm the principles of the social structure and policy of USSR, and define the rights, freedoms and obligations of citizens, and the principles of the organization of the socialist state of the whole people, and its aims, and proclaim these in this Constitution.

I. PRINCIPLES OF THE SOCIAL STRUCTURE AND POLICY OF THE USSR

Chapter 1

The Political System

Article 1. The Union of Soviet Socialist Republics is a socialist state of the whole people, expressing the will and interests of the workers, peasants, and intelligentsia, the working people of all the nations and nationalities of the country.

Article 2. All power in the USSR belongs to the people.

The people exercise state power through Soviets of People's Deputies, which constitute the political foundation of the USSR.

All other state bodies are under the control of, and accountable to, the Soviets of People's Deputies.

Article 3. The Soviet state is organized and functions on the principle of democratic centralism, namely the electiveness of all bodies of state authority from the lowest to the highest, their accountability to the people, and the obligation of lower bodies to observe the decisions of higher ones. Democratic centralism combines central leadership with local initiative and creative activity and with the responsibility of each state body and official for the work entrusted to them.

Article 4. The Soviet state and all its bodies function on the basis of socialist law, ensure the maintenance of law and order, and safeguard the interests of society and the rights and freedoms of citizens.

State organizations, public organizations and officials shall observe the Constitution of the USSR and Soviet laws.

Article 5. Major matters of state shall be submitted to nationwide discussion and put to a popular vote (referendum).

Article 6. The leading and guiding force of Soviet society and the nucleus of its political system, of all state organizations and public organizations, is the Communist Party of the Soviet Union. The CPSU exists for the people and serves the people.

The Communist Party, armed with Marxism-Leninism, determines the general perspectives of the development of society and the course of the home and foreign policy of the USSR, directs the great constructive work of the Soviet people, and imparts a planned, systematic and theoretically substantiated character to their struggle for the victory of communism.

All Party organizations shall function within the framework of the Constitution of the USSR.

Article 7. Trade unions, the All-Union Leninist Young Communist League, co-operatives, and other public organizations, participate, in accordance with the aims laid down in their rules, in managing state and public affairs, and in deciding political, economic, and social and cultural matters.

Article 8. Work collectives take part in discussing and deciding state and public affairs, in planning production and social development, in training and placing personnel, and in discussing and deciding matters pertaining to the management of enterprises and institutions, the improvement of working and living conditions, and the use of funds allocated both for developing production and for social and cultural purposes and financial incentives.

Work collectives promote socialist emulation, the spread of progressive methods of work, and the strengthening of production discipline, educate their members in the spirit of communist morality, and strive to enhance their political consciousness and raise their cultural level and skills and qualifications.

Article 9. The principal direction in the development of the political system of Soviet society is the extension of socialist democracy, namely ever broader participation of citizens in managing the affairs of society and the state, continuous improvement of the machinery of state, heightening of the activity of public organizations, strengthening of the system of people's control, consolidation of the legal foundations of the functioning of the state and of public life, greater openness and publicity, and constant responsiveness to public opinion.

Chapter 2

The Economic System

Article 10. The foundation of the economic system of the USSR is socialist ownership of the means of production in the form of state property (belonging to all the people), and collective farm-and-co-operative property.

Socialist ownership also embraces the property of trade unions and other public organizations which they require to carry out their purposes under their rules.

The state protects socialist property and provides conditions for its growth.

No one has the right to use socialist property for personal gain or other selfish ends.

Article 11. State property, i.e. the common property of the Soviet people, is the principal form of socialist property.

The land, its minerals, waters, and forests are the exclusive property of the state. The state owns the basic means of production in industry, construction, and agriculture; means of transport and communication; the bank; the property of state-run trade organizations and public utilities, and other state-run undertakings; most urban housing; and other property necessary for state purposes.

Article 12. The property of collective farms and other co-operative organizations, and of their joint undertakings, comprises the means of production and other assets which they require for the purposes laid down in their rules.

The land held by collective farms is secured to them for their free use in perpetuity.

The state promotes development of collective farm and co-operative property and its approximation to state property.

Collective farms, like other land users, are obliged to make effective and thrifty use of the land and to increase its fertility.

Article 13. Earned income forms the basis of the personal property of Soviet citizens. The personal property of citizens of the USSR may include articles of everyday use, personal consumption and convenience, the implements and other objects of a small-holding, a house, and earned savings. The personal property of citizens and the right to inherit it are protected by the state.

Citizens may be granted the use of plots of land, in the manner prescribed by law, for a subsidiary small-holding (including the keeping of livestock and poultry), for fruit and vegetable growing or for building an individual dwelling. Citizens are required to make rational use of the land allotted to them. The state, and collective farms provide assistance to citizens in working their small-holdings.

Property owned or used by citizens shall not serve as a means of deriving unearned income or be employed to the detriment of the interests of society.

Article 14. The source of the growth of social wealth and of the well-being of the people, and of each individual, is the labour, free from exploitation, of Soviet people.

The state exercises control over the measure of labour and of consumption in accordance with the principle of socialism: "From each according to his ability, to each according to his work". It fixes the rate of taxation on taxable income.

Socially useful work and its results determine a person's status in society. By combining material and moral incentives and encouraging innovation and a creative attitude to work, the state helps transform labour into the prime vital need of every Soviet citizen.

Article 15. The supreme goal of social production under socialism is the fullest possible satisfaction of the people's growing material, and cultural and intellectual requirements.

Relying on the creative initiative of the working people, socialist emulation, and scientific and technological progress, and by improving the forms and methods of economic management, the state ensures growth of the productivity of labour, raising of the efficiency of production and of the quality of work, and dynamic, planned, proportionate development of the economy.

Article 16. The economy of the USSR is an integral economic complex comprising all the elements of social production, distribution, and exchange on its territory.

The economy is managed on the basis of state plans for economic and social development, with due account of the sectoral and territorial principles, and by combing centralized direction with the managerial independence and initiative of individual and amalgamated enterprises and other organizations, for which active use is made of management accounting, profit, cost, and other economic levers and incentives.

Article 17. In the USSR, the law permits individual labour in handicrafts, farming, the provision of services for the public, and other forms of activity based exclusively on the personal work of individual citizens and members of their families. The state makes regulations for such work to ensure that it serves the interests of society.

Article 18. In the interests of the present and future generations, the necessary steps are taken in the USSR to protect and make scientific, rational use of the land and its mineral and water resources, and the plant and animal kingdoms, to preserve the purity of air and water, ensure reproduction of natural wealth, and improve the human environment.

Chapter 3

Social Development and Culture

Article 19. The social basis of the USSR is the unbreakable alliance of the workers, peasants, and intelligentsia.

The state helps enhance the social homogeneity of society, namely the elimination of class differences and of the essential distinctions between town and country and between mental and physical labour, and the all-round development and drawing together of all the nations and nationalities of the USSR.

Article 20. In accordance with the communist ideal – 'The free development of each is the condition of the free development of all' – the state pursues the aim of giving citizens more and more real opportunities to apply their creative energies, abilities, and talents, and to develop their personalities in every way.

Article 21. The state concerns itself with improving working conditions, safety and labour protection and the scientific organization of work, and with reducing and ultimately eliminating all arduous physical labour through comprehensive mechanization and automation of production processes in all branches of the economy.

Article 22. A programme is being consistently implemented in the USSR to convert agricultural work into a variety of industrial work, to extend the network of educational, cultural and medical institutions, and of trade, public catering, service and public utility facilities in rural localities, and transform hamlets and villages into well-planned and well-appointed settlements.

Article 23. The state pursues a steady policy of raising people's pay levels and real incomes through increase in productivity.

In order to satisfy the needs of Soviet people more fully social consumption funds are created. The state, with the broad participation of public organizations and work collectives, ensures the growth and just distribution of these funds.

Article 24. In the USSR, state systems of health protection, social security, trade and public catering, communal services and amenities, and public utilities, operate and are being extended.

The state encourages co-operatives and other public organizations to provide all types of services for the population. It encourages the development of mass physical culture and sport.

Article 25. In the USSR there is a uniform system of public education, which is being constantly improved, that provides general education and vocational training for citizens, serves the communist education and intellectual and physical development of the youth, and trains them for work and social activity.

Article 26. In accordance with society's needs the state provides for planned development of science and the training of scientific personnel and organizes introduction of the results of research in the economy and other spheres of life.

Article 27. The state concerns itself with protecting, augmenting and making extensive use of society's cultural wealth for the moral and aesthetic education of the Soviet people, for raising their cultural level.

In the USSR development of the professional, amateur and folk arts is encouraged in every way.

Chapter 4

Foreign Policy

Article 28. The USSR steadfastly pursues a Leninist policy of peace and stands for strengthening of the security of nations and broad international co-operation.

The foreign policy of the USSR is aimed at ensuring international conditions favourable for building communism in the USSR, safeguarding the state interests of the Soviet Union, consolidating the positions of world socialism, supporting the struggle of peoples for national liberation and social progress, preventing wars of aggression, achieving universal and complete disarmament, and consistently implementing the principle of the peaceful coexistence of states with different social systems.

In the USSR war propaganda is banned.

Article 29. The USSR's relations with other states are based on observance of the following principles: sovereign equality; mutual renunciation of the use or threat of force; inviolability of frontiers; territorial integrity of states; peaceful settlement of disputes; non-intervention in internal affairs; respect for human rights and fundamental freedoms; the equal rights of peoples and their right to decide their own destiny; co-operation among states; and fulfilment in good faith of obligations arising from the generally recognized principles and rules of international law, and from the international treaties signed by the USSR.

Article 30. The USSR, as part of the world system of socialism and of the socialist community, promotes and strengthens friendship, co-operation, and comradely mutual assistance with other socialist countries on the basis of the principle of socialist internationalism, and takes an active part in socialist economic integration and the socialist international division of labour.

Chapter 5

Defence of the Socialist Motherland

Article 31. Defence of the Socialist Motherland is one of the most important functions of the state, and is the concern of the whole people.

In order to defend the gains of socialism, the peaceful labour of the Soviet people, and the sovereignty and territorial integrity of the state, the USSR maintains Armed Forces and has instituted universal military service.

The duty of the Armed Forces of the USSR to the people is to provide reliable defence of the Socialist Motherland and to be in constant combat readiness, guaranteeing that any aggressor is instantly repulsed.

Article 32. The state ensures the security and defence capability of the country, and supplies the Armed Forces of the USSR with everything necessary for that purpose.

The duties of state bodies, public organizations, officials, and citizens in regard to safeguarding the country's security and strengthening its defence capacity are defined by the legislation of the USSR.

II. THE STATE AND THE INDIVIDUAL

Chapter 6

Citizenship of the USSR. Equality of Citizens' Rights

Article 33. Uniform federal citizenship is established for the USSR. Every citizen of a Union Republic is a citizen of the USSR.

The grounds and procedure for acquiring or forfeiting Soviet citizenship are defined by the Law on Citizenship of the USSR.

When abroad, citizens of the USSR enjoy the protection and assistance of the Soviet state.

Article 34. Citizens of the USSR are equal before the law, without distinction of origin, social or property status, race or nationality, sex, education, language, attitude to religion, type and nature of occupation, domicile, or other status.

The equal rights of citizens of the USSR are guaranteed in all fields of economic, political, social, and cultural life.

Article 35. Women and men have equal rights in the USSR.

Exercise of these rights in ensured by according women equal access with men to education and vocational and professional training, equal opportunities in employment, remuneration, and promotion, and in social and political, and cultural activity, and by special labour and health protection measures for women; by providing conditions enabling mothers to work; by legal protection, and material and moral support for mothers and children, including paid leaves and other benefits for expectant mothers and mothers, and gradual reduction of working time for mothers with small children.

Article 36. Citizens of the USSR of different races and nationalities have equal rights.

Exercise of these rights is ensured by a policy of all-round development and drawing together of all the nations and nationalities of the USSR, by educating citizens in the spirit of Soviet patriotism and socialist internationalism, and by the possibility to use their native language and the languages of other peoples of the USSR.

Any direct or indirect limitation of the rights of citizens or establishment of direct or indirect privileges on grounds of race or nationality, and any advocacy of racial or national exclusiveness, hostility or contempt, are punishable by law.

Article 37. Citizens of other countries and stateless persons in the USSR are guaranteed the rights and freedoms provided by law, including the right to apply to a court and other state bodies for the protection of their personal, property, family and other rights.

Citizens of other countries and stateless persons, when in the USSR, are obliged to respect the Constitution of the USSR and observe Soviet laws.

Article 38. The USSR grants the right of asylum to foreigners persecuted for defending the interests of the working people and the cause of peace, or for participation in the revolutionary and national-liberation movement, or for progressive social and political, scientific or other creative activity.

Chapter 7

The Basic Rights, Freedoms, and Duties of Citizens of the USSR

Article 39. Citizens of the USSR enjoy in full the social, economic, political and personal rights and freedoms proclaimed and guaranteed by the Constitution of the USSR and by Soviet laws. The socialist system ensures enlargement of the rights and freedoms of citizens and continuous improvement of their living standards as social, economic, and cultural development programmes are fulfilled.

Enjoyment by citizens of their rights and freedoms must not be to the detriment of the interests of society or the state, or infringe the rights of other citizens.

Article 40. Citizens of the USSR have the right to work (that is, to guaranteed employment and pay in accordance with the quantity and quality of their work, and not below the state-established minimum), including the right to choose their trade or profession, type of job and work in accordance with their inclinations, abilities, training and education, with due account of the needs of society.

This right is ensured by the socialist economic system, steady growth of the productive forces, free vocational and professional training, improvement of skills, training in new trades or professions, and development of the systems of vocational guidance and job placement.

Article 41. Citizens of the USSR have the right to rest and leisure.

This right is ensured by the establishment of a working week not exceeding 41 hours, for workers and other employees, a shorter working day in a number of trades and industries, and shorter hours for night work; by the provision of paid annual holidays, weekly days of rest, extension of the network of cultural, educational and health-building institutions, and the development on a mass scale of sport, physical cultural, and camping and tourism; by the provision of neighbourhood recreational facilities, and of other opportunity for rational use of free time.

The length of collective farmers' working and leisure time is established by their collective farms.

Article 42. Citizens of the USSR have the right to health protection.

This right is ensured by free, qualified medical care provided by state health institutions; by extension of the network of therapeutic and health-building institutions; by the development and improvement of safety and hygiene in industry; by carrying out broad prophylactic measures; by measures to improve the environment; by special care for the health of the rising generation, including prohibition of child labour, excluding the work done by children as part of the school curriculum; and by developing research to prevent and reduce the incidence of disease and ensure citizens a long and active life.

Article 43. Citizens of the USSR have the right to maintenance in old age, in sickness, and in the event of complete or partial disability or loss of the breadwinner.

This right is guaranteed by social insurance of workers and other employees and collective farmers; by allowances for temporary disability; by the provision by the state or by collective farms of retirement pensions, disability pensions, and pensions for loss of the breadwinner; by providing employment for the partially disabled; by care for the elderly and the disabled; and by other forms of social security.

Article 44. Citizens of the USSR have the right to housing.

This right is ensured by the development and upkeep of state and socially-owned housing; by assistance for co-operative and individual house building; by fair distribution, under public control, of the housing that becomes available through fulfilment of the programme of building well-appointed dwellings, and by low rents and low charges for utility services. Citizens of the USSR shall take good care of the housing allocated to them.

Article 45. Citizens of the USSR have the right to education.

This right is ensured by free provision of all forms of education, by the institution of universal, compulsory secondary education, and broad development of vocational, specialized secondary, and higher education, in which instruction is oriented toward practical activity and production; by the development of extramural, correspondence and evening courses; by the provision of state scholarships and grants and privileges for students; by the free issue of school text-books; by the opportunity to attend a school where teaching is in the native language; and by the provision of facilities for self-education.

Article 46. Citizens of the USSR have the right to enjoy cultural benefits.

This right is ensured by broad access to the cultural treasures of their own land and of the world that are preserved in state and other public collections; by the development and fair distribution of cultural and educational institutions throughout the country; by developing television and radio broadcasting and the publishing of books, newspapers and periodicals, and by extending the free library service; and by expanding cultural exchanges with other countries.

Article 47. Citizens of the USSR, in accordance with the aims of building communism, are guaranteed freedom of scientific, technical, and artistic work. This freedom is ensured by broadening scientific research, encouraging invention and innovation, and developing literature and the arts. The state provides the necessary material conditions for this and support for voluntary societies and unions of workers in the arts, organizes introduction of inventions and innovations in production and other spheres of activity.

The rights of authors, inventors and innovators are protected by the state.

Article 48. Citizens of the USSR have the right to take part in the management and administration of state and public affairs and in the discussion and adoption of laws and measures of All-Union and local significance.

This right is ensured by the opportunity to vote and to be elected to Soviets of People's Deputies and other elective state bodies, to take part in nationwide discussions and referendums, in people's control, in the work of state bodies, public organizations, and local community groups, and in meetings at places of work or residence.

Article 49. Every citizen of the USSR has the right to submit proposals to state bodies and public organizations for improving their activity, and to criticize shortcomings in their work.

Officials are obliged, within established time-limits, to examine citizens' proposals and requests, to reply to them, and to take appropriate action.

Persecution for criticism is prohibited. Persons guilty of such persecution shall be called to account.

Article 50. In accordance with the interests of the people and in order to strengthen and develop the socialist system, citizens of the USSR are guaranteed freedom of speech, of the press, and of assembly, meetings, street processions and demonstrations.

Exercise of these political freedoms is ensured by putting public buildings, streets and squares at the disposal of the working people and their organizations, by broad dissemination of information, and by the opportunity to use the press, television, and radio.

Article 51. In accordance with the aims of building communism, citizens of the USSR have the right to associate in public organizations that promote their political activity and initiative and satisfaction of their various interests.

Public organisations are guaranteed conditions for successfully performing the functions defined in their rules.

Article 52. Citizens of the USSR are guaranteed freedom of conscience, that is, the right to profess or not to profess any religion, and to conduct religious worship or atheistic propaganda. Incitement of hostility or hatred on religious grounds is prohibited.

In the USSR, the church is separated from the state, and the school from the church.

Article 53. The family enjoys the protection of the state.

Marriage is based on the free consent of the woman and the man; the spouses are completely equal in their family relations.

The state helps the family by providing and developing a broad system of childcare institutions, by organizing and improving communal services and public catering, by paying grants on the birth of a child, by providing children's allowances and benefits for large families, and other forms of family allowances and assistance.

Article 54. Citizens of the USSR are guaranteed inviolability of the person. No one may be arrested except by a court decision or on the warrant of a procurator.

Article 55. Citizens of the USSR are guaranteed inviolability of the home. No one may, without lawful grounds, enter a home against the will of those residing in it.

Article 56. The privacy of citizens, and of their correspondence, telephone conversations, and telegraphic communications is protected by law.

Article 57. Respect for the individual and protection of the rights and freedoms of citizens are the duty of all state bodies, public organizations, and officials.

Citizens of the USSR have the right to protection by the courts against encroachments on their honour and reputation, life and health, and personal freedom and property.

Article 58. Citizens of the USSR have the right to lodge a complaint against the actions of officials, state bodies and public bodies. Complaints shall be examined according to the procedure and within the time-limit established by law. Actions by officials that contravene the law or exceed their powers, and infringe the rights of citizens, may be appealed against in a court in the manner prescribed by law.

Citizens of the USSR have the right to compensation for damage resulting from unlawful actions by state organizations and public organizations, or by officials in the performance of their duties.

Article 59. Citizens' exercise of their rights and freedoms is inseparable from the performance of their duties and obligations.

Citizens of the USSR are obliged to observe the Constitution of the USSR and Soviet laws, comply with the standards of socialist conduct, and uphold the honour and dignity of Soviet citizenship.

Article 60. It is the duty of, and a matter of honour for, every able-bodied citizen of the USSR to work conscientiously in his chosen, socially useful occupation, and strictly to observe labour discipline. Evasion of socially useful work is incompatible with the principles of socialist society.

Article 61. Citizens of the USSR are obliged to preserve and protect socialist property. It is the duty of a citizen of the USSR to combat misappropriation and squandering of state and socially-owned property and to make thrifty use of the people's wealth.

Persons encroaching in any way on socialist property shall be punished according to the law.

Article 62. Citizens of the USSR are obliged to safeguard the interests of the Soviet state, and to enhance its power and prestige.

Defence of the Socialist Motherland is the sacred duty of every citizen of the USSR.

Betrayal of the Motherland is the gravest of crimes against the people.

Article 63. Military service in the ranks of the Armed Forces of the USSR is an honourable duty of Soviet citizens.

Article 64. It is the duty of every citizen of the USSR to respect the national dignity of other citizens, and to strengthen friendship of the nations and nationalities of the multinational Soviet state.

Article 65. A citizen of the USSR is obliged to respect the rights and lawful interests of other persons, to be uncompromising toward anti-social behaviour, and to help maintain public order.

Article 66. Citizens of the USSR are obliged to concern themselves with the upbringing of children, to train them for socially useful work, and to raise them as worthy members of socialist society. Children are obliged to care for their parents and help them.

Article 67. Citizens of the USSR are obliged to protect nature and conserve its riches.

Article 68. Concern for the preservation of historical monuments and other cultural values is a duty and obligation of citizens of the USSR.

Article 69. It is the internationalist duty of citizens of the USSR to promote friendship and co-operation with peoples of other lands and help maintain and strengthen world peace.

III. THE NATIONAL – STATE STRUCTURE OF THE USSR

Chapter 8

The USSR – a Federal State

Article 70. The Union of Soviet Socialist Republics is an integral, federal, multinational state formed on the principle of socialist federalism as a result of the free self-determination of nations and the voluntary association of equal Soviet Socialist Republics.

The USSR embodies the state unity of the Soviet people and draws all its nations and nationalities together for the purpose of jointly building communism.

Article 71. The Union of Soviet Socialist Republics unites:
the Russian Soviet Federative Socialist Republic,
the Ukrainian Soviet Socialist Republic,
the Byelorussian Soviet Socialist Republic,
the Uzbek Soviet Socialist Republic,
the Kazakh Soviet Socialist Republic,
the Georgian Soviet Socialist Republic,
the Azerbaijan Soviet Socialist Republic,
the Lithuanian Soviet Socialist Republic,
the Moldavian Soviet Socialist Republic,
the Latvian Soviet Socialist Republic,
the Kirghiz Soviet Socialist Republic,
the Tajik Soviet Socialist Republic,

the Armenian Soviet Socialist Republic,
the Turkmen Soviet Socialist Republic,
the Estonian Soviet Socialist Republic.

Article 72. Each Union Republic shall retain the right freely to secede from the USSR.

Article 73. The jurisdiction of the Union of Soviet Socialist Republics, as represented by its highest bodies of state authority and administration, shall cover:

1) the admission of new republics to the USSR; endorsement of the formation of new autonomous republics and autonomous regions within Union Republics;

2) determination of the state boundaries of the USSR and approval of changes in the boundaries between Union Republics;

3) establishment of the general principles for the organization and functioning of republican and local bodies of state authority and administration;

4) the ensurance of uniformity of legislative norms throughout the USSR and establishment of the fundamentals of the legislation of the Union of Soviet Socialist Republics and Union Republics;

5) pursuance of a uniform social and economic policy; direction of the country's economy; determination of the main lines of scientific and technological progress and the general measures for rational exploitation and conservation of natural resources; the drafting and approval of state plans for the economic and social development of the USSR, and endorsement of reports on their fulfilment;

6) the drafting and approval of the consolidated Budget of the USSR, and endorsement of the report on its execution; management of a single monetary and credit system; determination of the taxes and revenues forming the Budget of the USSR; and the formulation of prices and wages policy;

7) direction of the sectors of the economy, and of enterprises and amalgamations under Union jurisdiction, and general direction of industries under Union-Republican jurisdiction;

8) issues of war and peace, defence of the sovereignty of the USSR and safeguarding of its frontiers and territory, and organization of defence; direction of the Armed Forces of the USSR;

9) state security;

10) representation of the USSR in international relations; the USSR's relations with other states and with international organizations; establishment of the general procedure for, and co-ordination of, the relations of Union Republics with other states and with international organizations; foreign trade and other forms of external economic activity on the basis of state monopoly;

11) control over observance of the Constitution of the USSR, and ensurance of conformity of the Constitutions of Union Republics to the Constitution of the USSR;

12) and settlement of other matters of All-Union importance.

Article 74. The laws of the USSR shall have the same force in all Union

Republics. In the event of a discrepancy between a Union Republic law and an All-Union law, the law of the USSR shall prevail.

Article 75. The territory of the Union of Soviet Socialist Republics is a single entity and comprises the territories of the Union Republics.

The sovereignty of the USSR extends throughout its territory.

Chapter 9

The Union Soviet Socialist Republics

Article 76. A Union Republic is a sovereign Soviet socialist state that has united with other Soviet Republics in the Union of Soviet Socialist Republics.

Outside the spheres listed in Article 73 of the Constitution of the USSR, a Union Republic exercises independent authority on its territory.

A Union Republic shall have its own Constitution conforming to the Constitution of the USSR with the specific features of the Republic being taken into account.

Article 77. Union Republics take part in decision-making in the Supreme Soviet of the USSR, the Presidium of the Supreme Soviet of the USSR, the Government of the USSR, and other bodies of the Union of Soviet Socialist Republics in matters that come within the jurisdiction of the Union of Soviet Socialist Republics.

A Union Republic shall ensure comprehensive economic and social development on its territory, facilitate exercise of the powers of the USSR on its territory, and implement the decisions of the highest bodies of state authority and administration of the USSR.

In matters that come within its jurisdiction, a Union Republic shall co-ordinate and control the activity of enterprises, institutions, and organizations subordinate to the Union.

Article 78. The territory of a Union Republic may not be altered without its consent. The boundaries between Union Republics may be altered by mutual agreement of the Republics concerned, subject to ratification by the Union of Soviet Socialist Republics.

Article 79. A Union Republic shall determine its division into territories, regions, areas, and districts, and decide other matters relating to its administrative and territorial structure.

Article 80. A Union Republic has the right to enter into relations with other states, conclude treaties with them, exchange diplomatic and consular representatives, and take part in the work of international organizations.

Article 81. The sovereign rights of Union Republics shall be safeguarded by the USSR.

Chapter 10

The Autonomous Soviet Socialist Republic

Article 82. An Autonomous Republic is a constituent part of a Union Republic. In spheres not within the jurisdiction of the Union of Soviet Socialist Republics and the Union Republic, an Autonomous Republic shall deal independently with matters within its jurisdiction.

An Autonomous Republic shall have its own Constitution conforming to the Constitutions of the USSR and the Union Republic with the specific features of the Autonomous Republic being taken into account.

Article 83. An Autonomous Republic takes part in decision-making through the highest bodies of state authority and administration of the USSR and of the Union Republic respectively, in matters that come within the jurisdiction of the USSR and the Union Republic.

An Autonomous Republic shall ensure comprehensive economic and social development on its territory, facilitate exercise of the powers of the USSR and the Union Republic on its territory, and implement decisions of the highest bodies of state authority and administration of the USSR and the Union Republic.

In matters within its jurisdiction, an Autonomous Republic shall co-ordinate and control the activity of enterprises, institutions, and organizations subordinate to the Union or the Union Republic.

Article 84. The territory of an Autonomous Republic may not be altered without its consent.

Article 85. The Russian Soviet Federative Socialist Republic includes the Bashkir, Buryat, Daghestan, Kabardin-Balkar, Kalmyk, Karelian, Komi, Mari, Mordovian, North Ossetian, Tatar, Tuva, Udmurt, Chechen-Ingush, Chuvash, and Yakut Autonomous Soviet Socialist Republics.

The Uzbek Soviet Socialist Republic includes the Kara-Kalpak Autonomous Soviet Socialist Republic.

The Georgian Soviet Socialist Republic includes the Abkhasian and Adzhar Autonomous Soviet Socialist Republics.

The Azerbaijan Soviet Socialist Republic includes the Nakhichevan Autonomous Soviet Socialist Republic.

Chapter 11

The Autonomous Region and Autonomous Area

Article 86. An Autonomous Region is a constituent part of a Union Republic or Territory. The Law on an Autonomous Region, upon submission by the Soviet of People's Deputies of the Autonomous Region concerned, shall be adopted by the Supreme Soviet of the Union Republic.

Article 87. The Russian Soviet Federative Socialist Republic includes the Adygei, Gorno-Altai, Jewish, Karachai-Circassian, and Khakass Autonomous Regions.

The Georgian Soviet Socialist Republic includes the South Ossetian Autonomous Region.

The Azerbaijan Soviet Socialist Republic includes the Nagorno-Karabakh Autonomous Region.

The Tajik Soviet Socialist Republic includes the Gorno-Badakhshan Autonomous Region.

Article 88. An Autonomous Area is a constituent part of a Territory or Region. The Law on an Autonomous Area shall be adopted by the Supreme Soviet of the Union Republic concerned.

IV. SOVIETS OF PEOPLE'S DEPUTIES AND ELECTORAL PROCEDURE

Chapter 12

The System of Soviets of People's Deputies and the Principles of their Work

Article 89. The Soviets of People's Deputies, i.e. the Supreme Soviet of the USSR, the Supreme Soviets of Union Republics, the Supreme Soviets of Autonomous Republics, the Soviets of People's Deputies of Territories and Regions, the Soviets of People's Deputies of Autonomous Regions and Autonomous Areas, and the Soviets of People's Deputies of districts, cities, city districts, settlements and villages shall constitute a single system of bodies of state authority.

Article 90. The term of the Supreme Soviet of the USSR, the Supreme Soviets of Union Republics, and the Supreme Soviets of Autonomous Republics shall be five years.

The term of local Soviets of People's Deputies shall be two and a half years.

Elections to Soviets of People's Deputies shall be called not later than two months before expiry of the term of the Soviet concerned.

Article 91. The most important matters within the jurisdiction of the respective Soviets of People's Deputies shall be considered and settled at their sessions.

Soviets of People's Deputies shall elect standing commissions and form executive-administrative, and other bodies accountable to them.

Article 92. Soviets of People's Deputies shall form people's control bodies combining state control with control by the working people at enterprises, collective farms, institutions, and organizations.

People's control bodies shall check on the fulfilment of state plans and assignments, combat breaches of state discipline, localistic tendencies, narrow departmental attitudes, mismanagement, extravagance and waste, red tape and bureaucracy, and help improve the working of the state machinery.

Article 93. Soviets of People's Deputies shall direct all sectors of state, economic and social and cultural development, either directly or through bodies instituted by them, take decisions and ensure their execution, and verify their implementation.

Article 94. Soviets of People's Deputies shall function publicly on the basis of collective, free, constructive discussion and decision-making, of systematic reporting back to them and the people by their executive-administrative and other bodies, and of involving citizens on a broad scale in their work.

Soviets of People's Deputies and the bodies set up by them shall systematically inform the public about their work and the decisions taken by them.

Chapter 13

The Electoral System

Article 95. Deputies to all Soviets shall be elected on the basis of universal, equal, and direct suffrage by secret ballot.

Article 96. Elections shall be universal: all citizens of the USSR who have reached the age of 18 shall have the right to vote and to be elected, with the exception of persons who have been legally certified insane.

To be eligible for election to the Supreme Soviet of the USSR a citizen of the USSR must have reached the age of 21.

Article 97. Elections shall be equal: each citizen shall have one vote; all voters shall exercise the franchise on an equal footing.

Article 98. Elections shall be direct: Deputies to all Soviets of People's Deputies shall be elected by citizens by direct vote.

Article 99. Voting at elections shall be secret: control over voters' exercise of the franchise is inadmissible.

Article 100. The following shall have the right to nominate candidates: branches and organizations of the Communist Party of the Soviet Union, trade unions, and the All-Union Leninist Young Communist League; co-operatives and other public organisations; work collectives, and meetings of servicemen in their military units.

Citizens of the USSR and public organizations are guaranteed the right to free and all-round discussion of the political and personal qualities and competence of candidates, and the right to campaign for them at meetings, in the press, and on television and radio.

The expenses involved in holding elections to Soviets of People's Deputies shall be met by the state.

Article 101. Deputies to Soviets of People's Deputies shall be elected by constituencies.

A citizen of the USSR may not, as a rule, be elected to more than two Soviets of People's Deputies.

Elections to the Soviets shall be conducted by electoral commissions consisting of representatives of public organizations and work collectives, and of meetings of servicemen in military units.

The procedure for holding elections to Soviets of People's Deputies shall be defined by the laws of the USSR, and of Union and Autonomous Republics.

Article 102. Electors give mandates to their Deputies.

The appropriate Soviets of People's Deputies shall examine electors' mandates, take them into account in drafting economic and social development plans and in drawing up the budget, organize implementation of the mandates, and inform citizens about it.

Chapter 14

People's Deputies

Article 103. Deputies are the plenipotentiary representatives of the people in the Soviets of People's Deputies.

In the Soviets, Deputies deal with matters relating to state, economic and social and cultural development, organize implementation of the decisions of the Soviets, and exercise control over the work of state bodies, enterprises, institutions and organizations.

Deputies shall be guided in their activities by the interests of the state, and shall take the needs of their constituents into account and work to implement their electors' mandates.

Article 104. Deputies shall exercise their powers without discontinuing their regular employment or duties.

During sessions of the Soviet, and so as to exercise their Deputy's powers in other cases stipulated by law, Deputies shall be released from their regular employment or duties, with retention of their average earnings at their permanent place of work.

Article 105. A Deputy has the right to address inquiries to the appropriate state bodies and officials, who are obliged to reply to them at a session of the Soviet.

Deputies have the right to approach any state or public body, enterprise, institution, or organization on matters arising from their work as Deputies and to take part in considering the questions raised by them. The heads of the state or public bodies, enterprises, institutions or organizations concerned are obliged to receive Deputies without delay and to consider their proposals within the time-limit established by law.

Article 106. Deputies shall be ensured conditions for the unhampered and effective exercise of their rights and duties.

The immunity of Deputies, and other guarantees of their activity as Deputies, are defined in the Law on the Status of Deputies and other legislative acts of the USSR and of Union and Autonomous Republics.

Article 107. Deputies shall report on their work and on that of the Soviet to their constituents, and to the work collectives and public organizations that nominated them.

Deputies who have not justified the confidence of their constituents may be recalled at any time by decision of a majority of the electors in accordance with the procedure established by law.

V. HIGHER BODIES OF STATE AUTHORITY AND ADMINISTRATION OF THE USSR

Chapter 15

The Supreme Soviet of the USSR

Article 108. The highest body of state authority of the USSR shall be the Supreme Soviet of the USSR.

The Supreme Soviet of the USSR is empowered to deal with all matters within the jurisdiction of the Union of Soviet Socialist Republics, as defined by this Constitution.

The adoption and amendment of the Constitution of the USSR; admission of new Republics to the USSR; endorsement of the formation of new Autonomous Republics and Autonomous Regions; approval of the state plans for economic and social development, of the Budget of the USSR, and of reports on their execution; and the institution of bodies of the USSR accountable to it, are the exclusive prerogative of the Supreme Soviet of the USSR.

Laws of the USSR shall be enacted by the Supreme Soviet of the USSR or by a nationwide vote (referendum) held by decision of the Supreme Soviet of the USSR.

Article 109. The Supreme Soviet of the USSR shall consist of two chambers: the Soviet of the Union and the Soviet of Nationalities.

The two chambers of the Supreme Soviet of the USSR shall have equal rights.

Article 110. The Soviet of the Union and the Soviet of Nationalities shall have equal numbers of deputies.

The Soviet of the Union shall be elected by constituencies with equal populations.

The Soviet of Nationalities shall be elected on the basis of the following representation: 32 Deputies from each Union Republic, 11 Deputies from each Autonomous Republic, five Deputies from each Autonomous Region, and one Deputy from each Autonomous Area.

The Soviet of the Union and the Soviet of Nationalities, upon submission by the credentials commissions elected by them, shall decide on the validity of Deputies' credentials, and, in cases in which the election law has been violated, shall declare the election of the Deputies concerned null and void.

Article 111. Each chamber of the Supreme Soviet of the USSR shall elect a Chairman and four Vice-Chairmen.

The Chairmen of the Soviet of the Union and of the Soviet of Nationalities shall preside over the sittings of the respective chambers and conduct their affairs.

Joint sittings of the chambers of the Supreme Soviet of the USSR shall be presided over alternately by the Chairman of the Soviet of the Union and the Chairman of the Soviet of Nationalities.

Article 112. Sessions of the Supreme Soviet of the USSR shall be convened twice a year.

Special sessions shall be convened by the Presidium of the Supreme Soviet of the USSR at its discretion or on the proposal of a Union Republic, or of not less than one-third of the Deputies of one of the chambers.

A session of the Supreme Soviet of the USSR shall consist of separate and joint sittings of the chambers, and of meetings of the standing commissions of the chambers or commissions of the Supreme Soviet of the USSR held between the sittings of the chambers. A session may be opened and closed at either separate or joint sitting of the chambers.

Article 113. The right to initiate legislation in the Supreme Soviet of the USSR is vested in the Soviet of the Union and the Soviet of Nationalities, the Presidium of the Supreme Soviet of the USSR, the Council of Ministers of the USSR, Union Republics through their higher bodies of state authority, commissions of the Supreme Soviet of the USSR and standing commissions of its chambers, Deputies of the Supreme Soviet of the USSR, the Supreme Court of the USSR, and the Procurator-General of the USSR.

The right to initiate legislation is also vested in public organizations through their All-Union bodies.

Article 114. Bills and other matters submitted to the Supreme Soviet of the USSR shall be debated by its chambers at separate or joint sittings. Where necessary, a bill or other matter may be referred to one or more commissions for preliminary or additional consideration.

A law of the USSR shall be deemed adopted when it has been passed in each chamber of the Supreme Soviet of the USSR by a majority of the total number of its Deputies. Decisions and other acts of the Supreme Soviet of the USSR are adopted by a majority of the total number of Deputies of the Supreme Soviet of the USSR.

Bills and other very important matters of state may be submitted for nationwide discussion by a decision of the Supreme Soviet of the USSR or its Presidium taken on their own initiative or on the proposal of a Union Republic.

Article 115. In the event of disagreement between the Soviet of the Union and the Soviet of Nationalities, the matter at issue shall be referred for settlement to a conciliation commission formed by the chambers on a parity basis, after which it shall be considered for a second time by the Soviet of the Union and the Soviet of Nationalities at a joint sitting. If agreement is again not reached, the matter shall be postponed for debate at the next session of the Supreme Soviet of the USSR or submitted by the Supreme Soviet to a nationwide vote (referendum).

Article 116. Laws of the USSR and decisions and other acts of the Supreme Soviet of the USSR shall be published in the languages of the Union Republics over the signatures of the Chairman and Secretary of the Presidium of the Supreme Soviet of the USSR.

Article 117. A Deputy of the Supreme Soviet of the USSR has the right to address inquiries to the Council of Ministers of the USSR, and to Ministers and the heads of other bodies formed by the Supreme Soviet of the USSR. The Council of Ministers of the USSR, or the official to whom the inquiry is addressed, is obliged to give a verbal or written reply within three days at the given session of the Supreme Soviet of the USSR.

Article 118. A Deputy of the Supreme Soviet of the USSR may not be prosecuted, or arrested, or incur a court-imposed penalty, without the sanction of the Supreme Soviet of the USSR or, between its sessions, of the Presidium of the Supreme Soviet of the USSR.

Article 119. The Supreme Soviet of the USSR, at a joint sitting of its chambers, shall elect a Presidium of the Supreme Soviet of the USSR, which shall be a standing body of the Supreme Soviet of the USSR, accountable to it for all its work and exercising the functions of the highest body of state authority of the USSR between sessions of the Supreme Soviet, within the limits prescribed by the Constitution.

Article 120. The Presidium of the Supreme Soviet of the USSR shall be elected from among the Deputies and shall consist of a Chairman, First Vice-Chairman, 15 Vice-Chairman (one from each Union Republic), a Secretary, and 21 members.

Article 121. The Presidium of the Supreme Soviet of the USSR shall:
1) name the date of elections to the Supreme Soviet of the USSR;
2) convene sessions of the Supreme Soviet of the USSR;
3) co-ordinate the work of the standing commissions of the chambers of the Supreme Soviet of the USSR;

4) ensure observance of the Constitution of the USSR and conformity of the Constitutions and laws of Union Republics to the Constitution and laws of the USSR;

5) interpret the laws of the USSR;

6) ratify and denounce international treaties of the USSR;

7) revoke decisions and ordinances of the Council of Ministers of the USSR and of the Councils of Ministers of Union Republics should they fail to conform to the law;

8) institute military and diplomatic ranks and other special titles; and confer the highest military and diplomatic ranks and other special titles;

9) institute orders and medals of the USSR, and honorific titles of the USSR; award orders and medals of the USSR; and confer honorific titles of the USSR;

10) grant citizenship of the USSR, and rule on matters of the renunciation or deprivation of citizenship of the USSR and of granting asylum;

11) issue All-Union acts of amnesty and exercise the right of pardon;

12) appoint and recall diplomatic representatives of the USSR to other countries and to international organizations;

13) receive the letters of credence and recall of the diplomatic representatives of foreign states accredited to it;

14) form the Council of Defence of the USSR and confirm its composition; appoint and dismiss the high command of the Armed Forces of the USSR;

15) proclaim martial law in particular localities or throughout the country in the interests of defence of the USSR;

16) order general or partial mobilization;

17) between sessions of the Supreme Soviet of the USSR, proclaim a state of war in the event of an armed attack on the USSR, or when it is necessary to meet international treaty obligations relating to mutual defence against aggression;

18) and exercise other powers vested in it by the Constitution and laws of the USSR.

Article 122. The Presidium of the Supreme Soviet of the USSR, between sessions of the Supreme Soviet of the USSR and subject to submission for its confirmation at the next sessions, shall:

1) amend existing legislative acts of the USSR when necessary;

2) approve changes in the boundaries between Union Republics;

3) form and abolish Ministries and State Committees of the USSR on the recommendation of the Council of Ministers of the USSR;

4) relieve individual members of the Council of Ministers of the USSR of their responsibilities and appoint persons to the Council of Ministers on the recommendation of the Chairman of the Council of Ministers of the USSR.

Article 123. The Presidium of the Supreme Soviet of the USSR promulgates decrees and adopts decisions.

Article 124. On expiry of the term of the Supreme Soviet of the USSR, the

Presidium of the Supreme Soviet of the USSR shall retain its powers until the newly elected Supreme Soviet of the USSR has elected a new Presidium.

The newly elected Supreme Soviet of the USSR shall be convened by the outgoing Presidium of the Supreme Soviet of the USSR within two months of the elections.

Article 125. The Soviet of the Union and the Soviet of Nationalities shall elect standing commissions from among the Deputies to make a preliminary review of matters coming within the jurisdiction of the Supreme Soviet of the USSR, to promote execution of the laws of the USSR and other acts of the Supreme Soviet of the USSR and its Presidium, and to check on the work of state bodies and organisations. The chambers of the Supreme Soviet of the USSR may also set up joint commissions on a parity basis.

When it deems it necessary, the Supreme Soviet of the USSR sets up commissions of inquiry and audit, and commissions on any other matter.

All state and public bodies, organizations and officials are obliged to meet the requests of the commissions of the Supreme Soviet of the USSR and of its chambers, and submit the requisite materials and documents to them.

The commissions' recommendations shall be subject to consideration by state and public bodies, institutions and organizations. The commissions shall be informed, within the prescribed time-limit, of the results of such consideration or of the action taken.

Article 126. The Supreme Soviet of the USSR shall supervise the work of all state bodies accountable to it.

The Supreme Soviet of the USSR shall form a Committee of People's Control of the USSR to head the system of people's control.

The organisation and procedure of people's control bodies are defined by the Law on People's Control in the USSR.

Article 127. The procedure of the Supreme Soviet of the USSR and of its bodies shall be defined in the Rules and Regulations of the Supreme Soviet of the USSR and other laws of the USSR enacted on the basis of the Constitution of the USSR.

Chapter 16

The Council of Ministers of the USSR

Article 128. The Council of Ministers of the USSR, i.e. the Government of the USSR, is the highest executive and administrative body of state authority of the USSR.

Article 129. The Council of Ministers of the USSR shall be formed by the Supreme Soviet of the USSR at a joint sitting of the Soviet of the Union and the Soviet of Nationalities, and shall consist of the Chairman of the Council of Ministers of the USSR, First Vice-Chairmen and Vice-Chairman, Ministers of the USSR, and Chairmen of State Committees of the USSR.

The Chairmen of the Councils of Ministers of Union Republics shall be ex officio members of the Council of Ministers of the USSR.

The Supreme Soviet of the USSR, on the recommendation of the Chairman of the Council of Ministers of the USSR, may include in the Government of the USSR the heads of other bodies and organizations of the USSR.

The Council of Ministers of the USSR shall tender its resignation to a newly-elected Supreme Soviet of the USSR at its first session.

Article 130. The Council of Ministers of the USSR shall be responsible and accountable to the Supreme Soviet of the USSR and, between sessions of the Supreme Soviet of the USSR, to the Presidium of the Supreme Soviet of the USSR.

The Council of Ministers of the USSR shall report regularly on its work to the Supreme Soviet of the USSR.

Article 131. The Council of Ministers of the USSR is empowered to deal with all matters of state administration within the jurisdiction of the Union of Soviet Socialist Republics insofar as, under the Constitution, they do not come within the competence of the Supreme Soviet of the USSR or the Presidium of the Supreme Soviet of the USSR.

Within its powers the Council of Ministers of the USSR shall:

1) ensure direction of economic, social and cultural development; draft and implement measures to promote the well-being and cultural development of the people, to develop science and engineering, to ensure rational exploitation and conservation of natural resources, to consolidate the monetary and credit system, to pursue a uniform prices, wages, and social security policy, and to organize state insurance and a uniform system of accounting and statistics; and to organize the management of industrial, constructional, and agricultural enterprises and amalgamations, transport and communications undertakings, banks, and other organizations and institutions of Union subordination;

2) draft current and long-term state plans for the economic and social development of the USSR and the Budget of the USSR, and submit them to the Supreme Soviet of the USSR; take measures to execute the state plans and Budget; and report to the Supreme Soviet of the USSR on the implementation of the plans and Budget;

3) implement measures to defend the interests of the state, protect socialist property and maintain public order, and guarantee and protect citizens' rights and freedoms;

4) take measures to ensure state security;

5) exercise general direction of the development of the Armed Forces of the USSR, and determine the annual contingent of citizens to be called up for active military service;

6) provide general direction in regard to relations with other states, foreign trade and economic, scientific, technical, and cultural co-operation of the USSR with other countries; take measures to ensure fulfilment of the USSR's international treaties; and ratify and denounce intergovernmental international agreements;

7) and when necessary, form committees, central boards and other departments under the Council of Ministers of the USSR to deal with matters of economic, social and cultural development, and defence.

Article 132. A Presidium of the Council of Ministers of the USSR, consisting of the Chairman, the First Vice-Chairmen, and Vice-Chairmen of the Council of Ministers of the USSR, shall function as a standing body of the Council of Ministers of the USSR to deal with questions relating to guidance of the economy, and with other matters of state administration.

Article 133. The Council of Ministers of the USSR, on the basis of, and in pursuance of, the laws of the USSR and other decisions of the Supreme Soviet of the USSR and its Presidium, shall issue decisions and ordinances and verify their execution. The decisions and ordinances of the Council of Ministers of the USSR shall be binding throughout the USSR.

Article 134. The Council of Ministers of the USSR has the right, in matters within the jurisdiction of the Union of Soviet Socialist Republics, to suspend execution of decisions and ordinances of the Councils of Ministers of Union Republics, and to rescind acts of ministries and state committees of the USSR, and of other bodies subordinate to it.

Article 135. The Council of Ministers of the USSR shall co-ordinate and direct the work of All-Union and Union-Republican ministries, state committees of the USSR, and other bodies subordinate to it.

All-Union ministries and state committees of the USSR shall direct the work of the branches of administration entrusted to them, or exercise inter-branch administration, throughout the territory of the USSR directly or through bodies set up by them.

Union-Republican ministries and state committees of the USSR direct the work of the branches of administration entrusted to them, or exercise inter-branch administration, as a rule, through the corresponding ministries and state committees, and other bodies of Union Republics, and directly administer individual enterprises and amalgamations of Union subordination. The procedure for transferring enterprises and amalgamations from Republic or local subordination to Union subordination shall be defined by the Presidium of the Supreme Soviet of the USSR.

Ministries and state committees of the USSR shall be responsible for the condition and development of the spheres of administration entrusted to them; within their competence, they issue orders and other acts on the basis of, and in execution of, the laws of the USSR and other decisions of the Supreme Soviet of the USSR and its Presidium, and of decisions and ordinances of the Council of Ministers of the USSR, and organise and verify their implementation.

Article 136. The competence of the Council of Ministers of the USSR and its Presidium, the procedure for their work, relationships between the Council of Ministers and other state bodies, and the list of All-Union and Union-Republican ministries and state committees of the USSR are defined, on the basis of the Constitution, in the Law on the Council of Ministers of the USSR.

VI. BASIC PRINCIPLES OF THE STRUCTURE OF THE BODIES OF STATE AUTHORITY AND ADMINISTRATION IN UNION REPUBLICS

Chapter 17

Higher Bodies of State Authority and Administration of a Union Republic

Article 137. The highest body of state authority of a Union Republic shall be the Supreme Soviet of that Republic.

The Supreme Soviet of a Union Republic is empowered to deal with all matters within the jurisdiction of the Republic under the Constitutions of the USSR and the Republic.

Adoption and amendment of the Constitution of a Union Republic; endorsement of state plans for economic and social development, of the Republic's Budget, and of reports on their fulfilment; and the formation of bodies accountable to the Supreme Soviet of the Union Republic are the exclusive prerogative of that Supreme Soviet.

Laws of a Union Republic shall be enacted by the Supreme Soviet of the Union Republic or by a popular vote (referendum) held by decision of the Republic's Supreme Soviet.

Article 138. The Supreme Soviet of a Union Republic shall elect a Presidium, which is a standing body of that Supreme Soviet and accountable to it for all its work. The composition and powers of the Presidium of the Supreme Soviet of a Union Republic shall be defined in the Constitution of the Union Republic.

Article 139. The Supreme Soviet of a Union Republic shall form a Council of Ministers of the Union Republic, i.e. the Government of that Republic, which shall be the highest executive and administrative body of state authority in the Republic.

The Council of Ministers of a Union Republic shall be responsible and accountable to the Supreme Soviet of that Republic or, between sessions of the Supreme Soviet, to its Presidium.

Article 140. The Council of Ministers of a Union Republic issues decisions and ordinances on the basis of, and in pursuance of, the legislative acts of the USSR and of the Union Republic, and of decisions and ordinances of the Council of Ministers of the USSR, and shall organize and verify their execution.

Article 141. The Council of Ministers of a Union Republic has the right to suspend the execution of decisions and ordinances of the Councils of Ministers of Autonomous Republics, to rescind the decisions and orders of the Executive Committees of Soviets of People's Deputies of Territories, Regions, and cities (i.e. cities under Republic jurisdiction) and of Autonomous Regions, and in Union

Republics not divided into regions, of the Executive Committees of district and corresponding city Soviets of People's Deputies.

Article 142. The Council of Ministers of a Union Republic shall co-ordinate and direct the work of the Union-Republican and Republican ministries and of state committees of the Union Republic, and other bodies under its jurisdiction.

The Union-Republican ministries and state committees of a Union Republic shall direct the branches of administration entrusted to them, or exercise inter-branch control, and shall be subordinate to both the Council of Ministers of the Union Republic and the corresponding Union-Republican ministry or state committee of the USSR.

Republican ministries and state committees shall direct the branches of administration entrusted to them, or exercise inter-branch control, and shall be subordinate to the Council of Ministers of the Union Republic.

Chapter 18

Higher Bodies of State Authority and Administration of an Autonomous Republic

Article 143. The highest body of state authority of an Autonomous Republic shall be the Supreme Soviet of that Republic.

Adoption and amendment of the Constitution of an Autonomous Republic; endorsement of state plans for economic and social development, and of the Republic's Budget; and the formation of bodies accountable to the Supreme Soviet of the Autonomous Republic are the exclusive prerogative of that Supreme Soviet.

Laws of an Autonomous Republic shall be enacted by the Supreme Soviet of the Autonomous Republic.

Article 144. The Supreme Soviet of an Autonomous Republic shall elect a Presidium of the Supreme Soviet of the Autonomous Republic and shall form a Council of Ministers of the Autonomous Republic, i.e. the Government of that Republic.

Chapter 19

Local Bodies of State Authority and Administration

Article 145. The bodies of state authority in Territories, Regions, Autonomous Regions, Autonomous Areas, districts, cities, city districts, settlements, and rural communities shall be the corresponding Soviets of People's Deputies.

Article 146. Local Soviets of People's Deputies shall deal with all matters of local significance in accordance with the interests of the whole state and of the citizens residing in the area under their jurisdiction, implement decisions of higher bodies of state authority, guide the work of lower Soviets of People's Deputies, take part in the discussion of matters of Republican and All-Union signifiance, and submit their proposals concerning them.

Local Soviets of People's Deputies shall direct state, economic, social and cultural development within their territory; endorse plans of economic and social development and the local budget; exercise general guidance over state bodies, enterprises, institutions and organizations subordinates to them; ensure observance of the laws, maintenance of law and order, and protection of citizens' rights, and help strengthen the country's defence capacity.

Article 147. Within their powers, local Soviets of People's Deputies shall ensure the comprehensive, all-round economic and social development of their area; exercise control over the observance of legislation by enterprises, institutions and organizations subordinate to higher authorities and located in this area; and co-ordinate and supervise their activity as regards land use, nature conservation, building, employment of manpower, production of consumer goods, and social, cultural, communal and other services and amenities for the public.

Article 148. Local Soviets of People's Deputies shall decide matters within the powers accorded them by the legislation of the USSR and of the appropriate Union Republic and Autonomous Republic. Their decisions shall be binding on all enterprises, institutions, and organizations located in their area and on officials and citizens.

Article 149. The executive-administrative bodies of local Soviets shall be the Executive Committees elected by them from among their Deputies.

Executive Committees shall report on their work at least once a year to the Soviets that elected them and to meetings of citizens at their places of work or residence.

Article 150. Executive Committees of local Soviets of People's Deputies shall be directly accountable both to the Soviet that elected them and to the higher executive-administrative body.

VII. JUSTICE, ARBITRATION, AND PROCURATOR'S SUPERVISION

Chapter 20

Courts and Arbitration

Article 151. In the USSR justice is administered only by the courts.

In the USSR there are the following courts: the Supreme Court of the USSR, the Supreme Courts of Union Republics, the Supreme Courts of Autonomous Republics, Territorial, Regional, and city courts, courts of Autonomous Regions, courts of Autonomous Areas, district (city) people's courts, and military tribunals in the Armed Forces.

Article 152. All courts in the USSR shall be formed on the principle of the electiveness of judges and people's assessors.

People's judges of district (city) people's courts shall be elected for a term of five years by the citizens of the district (city) on the basis of universal, equal and direct suffrage by secret ballot. People's assessors of district (city) people's courts shall be elected for a term of two and a half years at meetings of citizens at their places of work or residence by a show of hands.

Higher courts shall be elected for a term of five years by the corresponding Soviet of People's Deputies.

The judges of military tribunals shall be elected for a term of five years by the Presidium of the Supreme Soviet of the USSR and people's assessors for a term of two and a half years by meetings of servicemen.

Judges and people's assessors are responsible and accountable to their electors or the bodies that elected them, shall report to them, and may be recalled by them in the manner prescribed by law.

Article 153. The Supreme Court of the USSR is the highest judicial body in the USSR and supervises the administration of justice by the courts of the USSR and Union Republics within the limits established by law.

The Supreme Court of the USSR shall be elected by the Supreme Soviet of the USSR and shall consist of a Chairman, Vice-Chairmen, members, and people's assessors. The Chairmen of the Supreme Courts of Union Republics are ex officio members of the Supreme Court of the USSR.

The organisation and procedure of the Supreme Court of the USSR are defined in the Law on the Supreme Court of the USSR.

Article 154. The hearing of civil and criminal cases in all courts is collegial; in courts of first instance cases are heard with the participation of people's assessors. In the administration of justice people's assessors have all the rights of a judge.

Article 155. Judges and people's assessors are independent and subject only to the law.

Article 156. Justice is administered in the USSR on the principle of the equality of citizens before the law and the court.

Article 157. Proceedings in all courts shall be open to the public. Hearings in camera are only allowed in cases provided for by law, with observance of all the rules of judicial procedure.

Article 158. A defendant in a criminal action is guaranteed the right to legal assistance.

Article 159. Judicial proceedings shall be conducted in the language of the Union Republic, Autonomous Republic, Autonomous Region, or Autonomous Area, or in the language spoken by the majority of the people in the locality. Persons participating in court proceedings, who do not know the language in which they are being conducted, shall be ensured the right to become fully acquainted with the materials in the case; the services of an interpreter during the proceedings; and the right to address the court in their own language.

Article 160. No one may be adjudged guilty of a crime and subjected to punishment as a criminal except by the sentence of a court and in conformity with the law.

Article 161. Colleges of advocates are available to give legal assistance to citizens and organisations. In cases provided for by legislation citizens shall be given legal assistance free of charge.

The organization and procedure of the bar are determined by legislation of the USSR and Union Republics.

Article 162. Representatives of public organisations and of work collectives may take part in civil and criminal proceedings.

Article 163. Economic disputes between enterprises, institutions, and organizations are settled by state arbitration bodies within the limits of their jurisdiction.

The organization and manner of functioning of state arbitration bodies are defined in the Law on State Arbitration in the USSR.

Chapter 21

The Procurator's Office

Article 164. Supreme power of supervision over the strict and uniform observance of laws by all ministers, state committees and departments, enterprises, institutions and organizations, executive-administrative bodies of local Soviets of People's Deputies, collective farms, co-operatives and other public organizations, officials and citizens is vested in the Procurator-General of the USSR and procurators subordinate to him.

Article 165. The Procurator-General of the USSR is appointed by the Supreme Soviet of the USSR and is responsible and accountable to it and, between sessions of the Supreme Soviet, to the Presidium of the Supreme Soviet of the USSR.

Article 166. The procurators of Union Republics, Autonomous Republics, Territories, Regions and Autonomous Regions are appointed by the Procurator-General of the USSR. The procurators of Autonomous Areas and district and city procurators are appointed by the procurators of Union Republics, subject to confirmation by the Procurator-General of the USSR.

Article 167. The term of office of the Procurator-General of the USSR and all lower-ranking procurators shall be five years.

Article 168. The agencies of the Procurator's Office exercise their powers independently of any local bodies whatsoever, and are subordinate solely to the Procurator-General of the USSR.

The organization and procedure of the agencies of the Procurator's Office are defined in the Law on the Procurator's Office of the USSR.

VIII. THE EMBLEM, FLAG, ANTHEM, AND CAPITAL OF THE USSR

Article 169. The State Emblem of the Union of Soviet Socialist Republics is a hammer and sickle on a globe depicted in the rays of the sun and framed by ears of wheat, with the inscription 'Workers of All Countries, Unite!' in the languages of the Union Republics. At the top of the Emblem is a five-pointed star.

Article 170. The State Flag of the Union of Soviet Socialist Republics is a rectangle of red cloth with a hammer and sickle depicted in gold in the upper corner next to the staff and with a five-pointed red star edged in gold above them. The ratio of the width of the flag to its length is 1:2.

Article 171: The State Anthem of the Union of Soviet Socialist Republics is confirmed by the Presidium of the Supreme Soviet of the USSR.

Article 172. The Capital of the Union of Soviet Socialist Republics is the city of Moscow.

IX. THE LEGAL FORCE OF THE CONSTITUTION OF THE USSR AND PROCEDURE FOR AMENDING THE CONSTITUTION

Article 173. The Constitution of the USSR shall have supreme legal force. All laws and other acts of state bodies shall be promulgated on the basis of and in confirmity with it.

Article 174. The Constitution of the USSR may be amended by a decision of the Supreme Soviet of the USSR adopted by a majority of not less than two-thirds of the total number of Deputies of each of its chambers.

APPENDIX E

The Soviet Government: USSR Council of Ministers

PRESIDIUM OF THE USSR COUNCIL OF MINISTERS

CHAIRMAN OF THE USSR COUNCIL OF MINISTERS (1)
FIRST DEPUTY CHAIRMEN (2)
DEPUTY CHAIRMEN (11)
Including: Chairman, USSR State Planning Committee (Gosplan)
USSR Representative, Council for Mutual Economic Assistance (Comecon)
Chairman, USSR State Committee for Science and Technology
Chairman, USSR State Committee for Material and Technical Supply
Chairman, USSR State Committee for Construction Affairs
Chairman, Commission of Presidium of USSR Council of Ministers for Foreign Economic Questions
Chairman, Military-industrial Commission of Presidium of USSR Council of Ministers

OTHER MEMBERS OF THE COUNCIL OF MINISTERS
(U) = Union Republic Organizations* (A) = All-Union Organizations*

Minister of Agriculture (U)
Minister of Automotive Industry (A)
Minister of the Aviation Industry (A)
Minister of the Chemical Industry (A)
Minister of the Chemical and Petroleum Machine Building (A)
Minister of Civil Aviation (A)

---

* The All-Union Ministries govern the branch of state administration entrusted to them throughout the territory of the USSR either directly or through bodies appointed by them. According to Article 76 of the USSR Constitution, the Union Republic Ministries, as a rule, direct the branches of state administration entrusted to them through the relevant Ministries of the Union Republics; they administer directly only a certain limited number of enterprises according to a list approved by the Presidium of the Supreme Soviet of the USSR.

Minister of the Coal Industry (U)
Minister of Communications (U)
Minister of the Communications Equipment Industry (A)
Minister of Construction (U)
Minister of Construction of Heavy Industry Enterprises (U)
Minister of the Construction Materials Industry (U)
Minister of Construction of Petroleum and Gas Industry Enterprises (A)
Minister of Construction, Road, and Municipal Machine Building (A)
Minister of Culture (U)
Minister of Defence (U)
Minister of the Defence Industry (A)
Minister of Education (U)
Minister of the Electrical Equipment Industry (A)
Minister of the Electronics Industry (A)
Minister of Ferrous Metallurgy (U)
Minister of Finance (U)
Minister of the Fish Industry (U)
Minister of the Food Industry (U)
Minister of Foreign Affairs (U)
Minister of Foreign Trade (A)
Minister of the Gas Industry (A)
Minister of General Machine Building (A)
Minister of Geology (U)
Minister of Health (U)
Minister of Heavy and Transport Machine Building (A)
Minister of Higher and Secondary Specialized Education (U)
Minister of Industrial Construction (U)
Minister of Installation and Special Construction Work (U)
Minister of Instrument-making, Automation Equipment, and Control Systems (A)
Minister of Internal Affairs (U)
Minister of Justice (U)
Minister of Land Reclamation and Water Resources (U)
Minister of Light Industry (U)
Minister of Machine Building (A)
Minister of Machine Building for Cattle Raising and Fodder Production (A)
Minister of Machine Building for Light and Food Industry and Household
  Appliances (A)
Minister of the Machine Tool and Tool Building Industry (A)
Minister of the Maritime Fleet (A)
Minister of the Meat and Dairy Industry (U)
Minister of the Medical Industry (A)
Minister of Medium Machine Building (A)
Minister of Nonferrous Metallurgy (U)
Minister of the Petroleum Industry (A)
Minister of the Petroleum Refining and Petrochemical Industry (U)
Minister of Power and Electrification (U)

Minister of Power Machine Building (A)
Minister of Procurement (U)
Minister of the Pulp and Paper Industry (A)
Minister of the Radio Industry (A)
Minister of Railways (A)
Minister of Rural Construction (U)
Minister of the Shipbuilding Industry (A)
Minister of the Timber and Wood Processing Industry (U)
Minister of Tractor and Agricultural Machine Building (A)
Minister of Trade (U)
Minister of Transport Construction (A)
Chairman, State Committee for Cinematography (Goskino USSR) (U)
Chairman, State Committee for Construction Affairs (Gosstroi USSR) (U)
Chairman, State Committee for Foreign Economic Relations (GKES) (A)
Chairman, State Committee for Forestry (Gosleskhoz USSR) (U)
Chairman, State Committee for Inventions and Discoveries (A)
Chairman, State Committee for Labour and Social Questions (Goskomtrud USSR)
    (U)
Chairman, State Committee for Material and Technical Supply (Gossnab USSR)
    (U)
Chairman, State Planning Committee (Gosplan USSR) (U)
Chairman, State Committee for Prices (Goskomtsen USSR) (U)
Chairman, State Committee for Publishing Houses, Printing Plants, and the Book
    Trade (Goskomizdat USSR) (U)
Chairman, State Committee for Science and Technology (GKNT) (A)
Chairman, State Committee for Standards (Gosstandart USSR) (A)
Chairman, State Committee for Television and Radio Broadcasting (Gosteleradio
    USSR) (U)
Chairman, State Committee for Vocational and Technical Education (U)
Chairman, Committee for People's Control (U)
Chairman, Committee for State Security (KGB) (U)
Chief, Central Statistical Administration (TsSU USSR) (U)
Chairman, *Soyuzsel'khoztekhnika* (U) (Association for the Sale of Agricultural
    Equipment and the Organization of Machinery Repairs and Utilization)
Chairman of Board, USSR State Bank (Gosbank USSR)
Chairman, Armenian SSR Council of Ministers*
Chairman, Azerbaijan SSR Council of Ministers
Chairman, Byelorussian SSR Council of Ministers
Chairman, Estonian SSR Council of Ministers
Chairman, Georgian SSR Council of Ministers
Chairman, Kazak SSR Council of Ministers
Chairman, Kirghiz SSR Council of Ministers

---

* According to Article 128 of the 1977 USSR Constitution the Council of Ministers of the USSR includes
the Chairman of the Councils of Ministers of the Union Republics ex officio.

Chairman, Latvian SSR Council of Ministers
Chairman, Lithuanian SSR Council of Ministers
Chairman, Moldavian SSR Council of Ministers
Chairman, RSFSR Council of Ministers
Chairman, Tajik SSR Council of Ministers
Chairman, Turkmen SSR Council of Ministers
Chairman, Ukrainian SSR Council of Ministers
Chairman, Uzbek SSR Council of Ministers

HEADS OF ORGANS OF THE USSR COUNCIL OF MINISTERS NOT HAVING MINISTERIAL STATUS

Administrator, Administration of Affairs of the Council of Ministers
Chief Arbiter, State Board of Arbitration (Gosarbitrazh) (U)
Chief, Main Archives Administration (GAU)
Chairman, State Committee for Utilization of Atomic Energy
Board Chairman, All-Union Bank for Financing Capital Investments (Stroibank)
Chairman, Higher Certification Commission (VAK) (A)
Chief, Main Administration of Geodesy and Cartography (GUGK)
Chief, Main Administration of Hydrometeorological Service (Glavgidrometsluzhba USSR)
Chief, Main Administration of the Microbiological Industry
Chairman, Commission for the Establishment of Personal Pensions
Chairman, Committee for Physical Culture and Sports (U)
Chairman, Committee for Lenin Prizes and State Prizes in Literature, Art, and Architecture.
Chairman, Committee for Lenin Prizes and State Prizes in Science and Technology
Chairman, Council for Religious Affairs
Chief, Main Administration of State Material Reserves (GUGMR)
Chief, Main Administration for Safeguarding State Secrets in the Press (Glavlit) (U)
Chairman, State Commission for Stockpiling Useful Minerals (GKZ) (A)
Chairman, State Committee for Supervision of Safe Working Practices in Industry and for Mine Supervision (Gosgortekhnadzor) (U)
Director General, Telegraph Agency of the Soviet Union (TASS) (U)
Chief, Main Administration for Foreign Tourism (Glavinturist USSR) (U)

HEADS OF OTHER ORGANS

Chairman, Main Committee for Exhibition of Achievements of the National Economy (VDNKh) (headed by a Deputy Chairman of the USSR Council of Ministers)
Chairman, State Committee for Civil Construction and Architecture (Gosgrazhdanstroi) (A) (subordinate to State Committee for Construction Affairs above)

Source: Based on *Radio Liberty* research. RL 95/77.
For a list of those elected in April 1984, see *Soviet News* (London) 18 April 1984

APPENDIX F
Statute on Party Control of Administration

'On the Commission of the Primary Party Organization in Exercising Control over the Activity of the Administration and the Work of the Apparat'

The Central Committee of the CPSU notes that Comrade Brezhnev's instructions requiring the primary party organizations to make fuller and better use of their right to control the administration are to a significant degree being carried out through the commissions of control created by the primary organizations. As experience has shown, the party organizations with the help of these commissions can establish control over the activity of the administration or over the work of the *apparat* in carrying out party and government directives and observing Soviet laws more precisely and purposefully. The commissions help the party committees and the party offices practically to expose weaknesses and then to remove them; they also help to develop initiative and principledness among communists, to encourage criticism and self-criticism and to educate cadres in the correct way.

The following statute on the commissions of the primary party organizations for the establishment of control over the activity of the administration and over the work of the *apparat* has been approved with the aim of clarifying the tasks, rights and duties of the commissions and of improving the work of the leadership.

In accordance with the Statute, the Central Committes of the Communist Parties of the union republics, and the krai, oblast, city and rayon committees of the party, will all be able to activate the work of the primary party organization commissions in establishing control over the activity of the administration or over the work of the *apparat*. Especial attention is to be paid to the establishment of commissions dealing with questions relating to the improvement of production and management—such commissions are to be created in enterprises, on collective state farms, in institutions, organizations and departments. The commissions should enable party work to draw still closer to practical matters of economic and social developments; they should also encourage leading cadres and rank and file workers to take serious responsibility for matters in their own collectives and to observe general state interests.

Source: Paritiynaya zhizn', no. 6, 1982.

383

It must be ensured that those elected onto the commissions are conscientious, principled communists who basically come from the ranks of ordinary workers, collective farmers and specialists; it must be possible to rely on those elected, knowing that, in the words of Lenin, they will take nothing on trust, that they will say nothing against their consciences and that they will fear no struggle to achieve their important goal. The practice of keeping quiet about the work of commissions in certain party organizations at reporting and electoral meetings must be considered incorrect. The work of the commissions must be reported back on and evaluated regularly in the party organizations. The party organizations must provide help in the work of the commissions and their members must be trained, checked and guided in their commission work.

The editorial boards of the party newspapers and journals must systematically publicize the work of the commissions. The Academy of Social Sciences attached to the Central Committee of the CPSU must disseminate the experience gained by the commissions of the party organizations in different branches of the economy and, together with Politizdat, must publish their findings.

STATUTE

On the Commissions of the Primary Party Organizations in Exercising Control over the Activity of the Administration and the Work of the Apparat.

Commissions may be formed from the ranks of the membership and candidate membership of the CPSU with the aim of raising the role and responsibility of the primary party organizations for putting party policies and decisions into practice. The commissions allow primary organizations to exercise more fully the right of control given to them by the constitution of the CPSU; they should improve party leadership in the development of the economy, science and culture; they should educate people and also broaden still further the base of inner-party democracy and should develop habits of criticism and self-criticism, initiative and self-directed activity.

Commissions may be formed to control the activity of the administration in the party organizations of industry, transport, communications, construction, material-technical equipment, trade, public catering, communal services, collective and state farms and other agricultural enterprises, planning organizations, construction offices, scientific-research institutes, schools and colleges, cultural and health institutions; in the party organizations of ministries, state committees and other central and local Soviet economic institutions and departments, commissions may be formed to control the work of the *apparat* in fulfilling party and government directives and in enforcing Soviet laws.

Tasks of the party organization, commissions, their rights and duties:

1. With the help of the commissions, the primary party organizations will carry out systematic control over the fulfilling of the decisions of the Communist Party

and the Soviet government and of the plans for economic and social development. The commissions together with all the communists in the given primary party organization are called on to do all they can to facilitate the putting into practice of the important programme of the Party for raising efficiency and intensifying the economy. Their task is to achieve maximum use of reserves and opportunities for speeding up scientific-technical progress, for increasing productivity, for improving the quantity and quality of production, for facilitating the economic use of material, financial and labour resources, for perfecting the planning and directing of the economy and for improving the style and methods of economic management.

The activity of the commissions is directed at the fulfilling of the tasks which the labour collectives have to carry out. They should in good time take note of and support all that is new and progressive; they should go deeply into questions of distribution and education of cadres and into matters relating to labour conditions and the daily life of the people; they should check on the exact observation of state, planning and technological discipline; they should raise workers' responsibility for jobs entrusted to them; they should develop the initiative and principledness of communists; they should act decisively against slackness, bad management, squandering, self-seeking and profiteering at the state's expense; they should carry out an uncompromising struggle against any evidence of an unconscientious attitude towards the fulfilling of service duties, against bureaucratism and red tape, humbug, parochialism and a narrow departmental approach.

The commissions work under the leadership of the party committees, the party offices, the secretaries of the primary party organisations.

2. The primary party organizations can create permanent and temporary commissions to control the activity of the administration or the work of the *apparat*. Depending on the specific concrete conditions, the character and importance of the tasks being carried out by the given enterprise, production combine (*kombinat*), state farm, collective farm, institution, organization, or department, the primary party organizations independently decide on which aspect of work it is appropriate to set up commissions.

3. The commissions should systematically and deeply study the state of affairs and the reasons for weaknesses; they should make regular reports on this to the party committee, the party office, the management of the enterprise, production combine, state farm, collective farm, organization, institution or department and together they should take measures to improve matters. Relying on the support of the social organizations and a broad *aktiv* the members of the commissions should in a principled and sharp way raise questions about how to get rid of discovered weaknesses and they should not go along with the administration when it is acting incorrectly; through their own personal involvement they should see matters through to a successful end.

The party committees and party officers when it is necessary must bring questions raised by the commissions to discussion at party meetings and meetings of workers, collective farmers or office-workers.

With regard to those managers who fail to get rid of weaknesses discovered by the commissions sufficiently quickly, the party organizations should take active measures. In necessary circumstances the primary party organizations may turn to rayon, city, okrug, oblast', kray and republican party, Soviet and economic organs for concerned action. If the local primary party organization indicates that the necessary steps are not being carried out, a direct approach may be made in the final resort, to the Central Committee of CPSU or to the Soviet of Ministers of the USSR.

4. The managers of enterprises, production combines, organizations, collective farms, state farms, schools and colleges, institutions and departments should do all they can to help the commissions in their work, providing them with all the necessary materials and data relating to questions under investigation and they should give objective information on the state of affairs; they should actively look at the commissions' proposals and quickly take measures to get rid of any weaknesses discovered.

The commissions cannot interfere in the operative activity of the administration or change or cancel any administrative edicts. In their work they should encourage a raising of the authority and influence of the leadership, a better carrying out of their orders and edicts, a strengthening of labour and production discipline.

5. In those circumstances when the weaknesses exposed by the commissions are the consequences of the bad work of other collectives, the party organizations can inform the party organizations of the other collectives about this and the latter party organizations are obliged to take the necessary measures and to take practical responsibility for the state of affairs.

Order of formation and accountability of the Commissions:

6. The Commissions are formed, as a rule, by party meetings or conferences for the period of office of the party committee or party bureau. In necessary circumstances the party meeting can create new commissions or reconsider the membership of the existing ones within its period of office.

In large primary party organizations at enterprises, production combines, collective farms, state farms and other organizations, institutions and departments, commissions can also be formed in party organizations on production, in work-shops or work-groups or bridges, on farms, in sub-departments or divisions, in laboratories or faculties and so on, where there are concrete and extremely important questions for examination.

The size and composition of the commissions are determined by the volume and character of the work to be carried out. Elections for the commissions take place by open ballot. Included in the composition of the commissions are members and candidate-members of the CPSU–basically workers, collective-farmers and specialists. It is not appropriate that communists who have responsibility for the work carried out in the area being investigated by the commission should be recommended for that commission.

The commissions report back on their activity to reporting and electoral party meetings or conferences and, in addition no less than once a year to a general meeting of communists, the party committee or party bureau. In all these cases the work of the commissions is evaluated and the direction of future activity is defined.

7. Commissions at defence and other secret enterprises and production

combines, organizations, institutions and departments are formed on the same basis. Their activity must fully conform to the requirement of secrecy and must exclude any possibility of state secrets being disclosed.

8. In small primary party organizations control of the activity of the administration or over the work of the *apparat* is, as a rule, carried out by all the communists of the party organizations under the leadership of the secretary. In labour collectives where there are no party organizations, the functions of control and information for the party organs about offences against the state, discipline and other weaknesses are carried out through the trade union and Komsomol organizations, and by those in positions and groups of people's control. This is done in accordance with the existing statutes on the work of the trade union organizations, the organs of people's control and also the Constitution of the CPSU with regard to the Komsomol.

9. Party committees and party bureaus should facilitate coordination of the work of the commissions and other forms of party control with the organs of social control existing in trade unions, the Komsomol, groups and positions of people's control; they should achieve participation of the masses of workers in control and they should pay constant attention to the expression and effectiveness of control. Party control should be constructed in such a way that checks are not needlessly duplicated, that departmental control is not undermined and that the administration of production collectives, organizations, institutions and departments is not diverted from the fulfilling of its direct service functions.

10. District and city committees of the party and their corresponding departments, when giving their daily leadership to the primary party committees, should hold at the centre of their attention the work of the commissions on the control of the administration and over the work of the *apparat*. Giving especial importance to raising the level of responsibility and principledness of communists and of the elected members of the commission, and to training them in the skills of control work, the local party committees should check on the correct formation of the commissions, and on the direction of their activity; they should systematically make known the result of their work; they should organize training for the members of the commission, they should support their initiative and in necessary cases should protect them from persecution; they should raise the authority of those communists who by their work enable the primary party organizations to establish their right of control over the activity of the administration or the work of the *apparat*.

GLOSSARY

Anti-Party Group	Applied to those who, in 1957, tried to unseat Khrushchev. Molotov, Kaganovich, Malenkov, and Shepilov are among the best known individuals identified with it.
Apparat	Apparatus, staff. The top officials of the CPSU or of the goverment.
Apparatchik	A member of the apparatus: a Party functionary.
ASSR	Autonomous Soviet Socialist Republic.
AUCCTU	All-Union Central Committee of Trade Unions.
AUCECB	All-Union Council of the Evangelical Christians and Baptists.
Bolsheviks	Faction of Russian Social-Democratic Labour Party led by Lenin. In 1918 formed into Communist Party (Bolsheviks).
CCTU	Central Council of Trade Unions.
CDSP	Current Digest of the Soviet Press, published weekly.
COMECON	Council of Economic Mutual Assistance. Formed in 1949 with the purpose of improving socialist economic co-operation. Membership includes the USSR, the socialist states of East Europe and Mongolia.
Cominform	Communist Information Bureau. Established September 1947, abolished April 1956.
Comintern	Communist International, 1919–43.
CPSU	Communist Party of the Soviet Union (in Russian, KPSS).
Desyatina	Measure of area: one desyatina equals 2.7 acres.
Duma	Name of advisory assembly in Tsarist Russia. There were Town Dumas and the State Duma.
Edinonachalie	One-man management.
Gorispolkom	Executive Committee of a City (Town) Soviet.
Gorkom	City Party Committee.
Gosbank	State Bank.
Gosplan	State Planning Committee (Commission).

388

Hectare	Area equal to 10,000 square metres or 2.471 acres.
Ispolkom	Executive Committee.
KGB	Committee of State Security: Security Police.
Kolkhoz	Collective Farm. Co-operative form of agricultural production.
Komsomol	YCL. Young Communist League. (Full title – All-Union Communist League of Youth).
Kray	Territory. A large sparsely populated, administrative region.
Kraykom	Territorial Party Committee.
Kremlinology	A process of forecasting based on indexes of Soviet protocol (e.g. order of appearance of names).
Kulak	Rich peasant.
Mensheviks	Non-Leninist faction of Russian Social Democratic Labour Party. Favoured trade-union type and decentralized form of party.
Mestnichestvo	Localism, regionalism. Pursuit of local interests at the expense of national interests.
Mir	See Obshchina
MTS	Machine-tractor station. Until 1958 the government owned and operated MTSs which supplied the collectives with agricultural equipment.
MVD	Ministry of Internal Affairs.
Narkhoz SSSR	*Narodnoe khozyastvo SSSR,* The Statistical Handbook of the USSR, published annually.
Narodniki	Populists. Nineteenth–century revolutionaries.
NEP	New Economic Policy. Practised by Bolsheviks between 1921 and 1928. Allowed limited private enterprise and trade.
NKGB	People's Commissariat of State Security.
NKVD	People's Commissariat of Internal Affairs.
Nomenklatura	Appointment list controlled directly or indirectly by the Party.
Oblast	Province, region.
Oblispolkom	Executive Committee of Province Soviet.
Obkom	Region or Province Party Committee.
Obshchenarodnoe gosudarstvo	State of the whole people. (Official description of the Soviet State since 1961).
Obshchina	A village community, a commune (in Tsarist Russia).
Okrug	Area, district.
Politbureau	Supreme body of CPSU. Called Presidium between 1952 and 1966.
Partiynost'	Party allegiance; party spirit.
Plenum	Full assembly of all members (e.g. of the Central Committee of the Communist Party).

Provisional Government	Established after abdication of Nicholas II in February 1917. Overthrown by Bolsheviks in October 1917.
Rayon	District; an administrative division of a region, territory, republic, or of a large city.
Rayispolkom	Executive Committee of District Soviet.
Raykom	District Party Committee.
RSFSR	Russian Soviet Federative Socialist Republic.
RTS	Tractor repair station.
Samizdat	Illegal 'do it yourself' publications.
Sovkhoz	State Farm. Organized on same principles as industrial enterprise.
Sovnarkom	Council of People's Commissars.
Sovnarkhoz	Council of National Economy. Established on a regional basis in May 1957.
USSR	Union of Soviet Socialist Republics.
USSR Council of Ministers	Highest executive and administrative branch in the Soviet Union. Has power to issue decrees and is subject to ratification by the Supreme Soviet.
USSR Presidium of the Supreme Soviet	Elected by the Supreme Soviet, the Presidium of the Supreme Soviet is in full power while the Supreme Soviet is not in session.
USSR Supreme Soviet	The highest legislative body in the USSR. It consists of two Houses, the Council (or Soviet) of the Union and the Council (or Soviet) of Nationalities.
VSNKH (Vesenkha)	Supreme Economic Council.

INDEX